ECCLE[barcode]SIOLOGY
AND EXCLUSION

BOUNDARIES OF BEING AND BELONGING
IN POSTMODERN TIMES

Editors:

Dennis M. Doyle
Timothy J. Furry
Pascal D. Bazzell

ORBIS BOOKS
Maryknoll, New York 10545

Founded in 1970, Orbis Books endeavors to publish works that enlighten the mind, nourish the spirit, and challenge the conscience. The publishing arm of the Maryknoll Fathers and Brothers, Orbis seeks to explore the global dimensions of the Christian faith and mission, to invite dialogue with diverse cultures and religious traditions, and to serve the cause of reconciliation and peace. The books published reflect the views of their authors and do not represent the official position of the Maryknoll Society. To learn more about Maryknoll and Orbis Books, please visit our website at http://www.maryknollsociety.org.

Library of Congress Cataloging-in-Publication Data

Ecclesiology and exclusion : boundaries of being and belonging in
  postmodern times / editors, Dennis M. Doyle, Timothy J. Furry,
  Pascal D. Bazzell.
      p.   cm.
  ISBN 978-1-57075-982-6 (pbk.)
  1. Church and minorities.   2. Social integration—Religious
  aspects—Christianity.   3. Marginality, Social—Religious
  aspects—Christianity.   4. Reconciliation—Religious aspects—
  Christianity.   5. Church membership.   6. Postmodernism—
  Religious aspects—Christianity.   I. Doyle, Dennis M. (Dennis
  Michael), 1952–   II. Furry, Timothy J.   III. Bazzell, Pascal D.
  BV639.M56E23 2012
  262—dc23
                                                    2012009279

Contents

Foreword vii
    Richard R. Gaillardetz

Introduction 1

Part I. Ecclesiology and Exclusion in a Postmodern Context

Gerard Mannion's *Ecclesiology and Postmodernity* 7
    "Exclusivism" and "Neo-Exclusivism" 7
    Dennis M. Doyle

    Reflections on the "Grace of Self-Doubt" 13
    Paul Lakeland

    Ecclesiology and Postmodernity: An Anglican Perspective. 18
    Mark D. Chapman

    Response: Ecclesiology and the Humility of God:
    Embracing the Risk of Loving the World 24
    Gerard Mannion

The Church: A Place of Exclusion or an Intercultural
    Community? 43
    Giovanni Pernigotto

Ecclesiology and Exclusions in the Public Space:
    A Political Perspective 51
    Debora Spini

Part II. Exclusion and Marginal People

The Catholic Church and the Immigration Crisis
    in the Americas 65
    Mark Ensalaco

"But I See That Somebody Is Missing": Ecclesiology and
Exclusion in the Context of Immigration 71
    Gioacchino Campese

Being an Otherwise-Documented Church: An Ecclesiology for
All Us Immigrants. 93
    David L. Johns

Ecclesial Identity and the Excluded Homeless Population:
A Funnel Ecclesiology as a Framework of Inclusion 105
    Pascal Daniel Bazzell

Part III. Exclusion and Racial Justice

Bryan N. Massingale's *Racial Justice and the Catholic Church*. 119

    Race and Social Context: Language, "Colorblindness,"
    and Intergroup Contact. 119
        Leslie H. Picca

    The Struggle against Racism and the Global Horizon of
    Christian Hope 125
        Agbonkhianmeghe E. Orobator

    Response: The Challenge of Idolatry and Ecclesial Identity 130
        Bryan N. Massingale

Transcending the Exclusionary Ecclesial Practices of Racial
Hierarchies of Authority: An Early Pentecostal Trajectory 137
    David D. Daniels III

Part IV. Exclusion and Gender

Phyllis Zagano's *Women & Catholicism: Gender, Communion,
and Authority* 155

    An Introduction 155
        Miriam Haar

    Implementing Vatican II's Ecclesiology 161
        Sandra Mazzolini

    The Viewpoint of an Orthodox Theologian 168
        Vladimir Latinovic

    Response: Toward a Nonexclusionary View of Women. 175
        Phyllis Zagano

Church and Homosexuality: Beyond Exclusion 183
    Stefanie Knauss

Part V. Exclusion and the Church

Inclusion and Exclusion in the Ecclesiology of the New Catholic
  Movements... 199
    Massimo Faggioli

Ecclesiology and Exclusion: Setting Boundaries for the Church 215
    Neil Ormerod

The Prophetic Mission of the Local Church: Community
  Organizing as a School for the Social Imaginary............. 221
    Bradford Hinze

Part VI. Exclusion and Sacramental Practices

Ecclesiology, Exclusion, and Sacraments....................... 239
    Mary McClintock Fulkerson

Whose Exclusion? Which Inclusion? 247
    Barry Harvey

A Case of Ecclesial Exclusion: Eucharistic Sharing............... 255
    Susan K. Wood

Eucharist at a Divided Table............................... 265
    C. Pierson Shaw Jr.

Rethinking the Sacrament of Reconciliation/Healing in the
  Light of Postmodern Thought........................... 279
    Stephen Annan

Part VII. Exclusion and Ecumenical Reality

Inclusion and Exclusion in the Anglican Communion:
  The Case of the Anglican Covenant 295
    Mark D. Chapman

The Arduous Journey from Exclusion to Communion:
  Overcoming Relationships of Distrust between
  Orthodox and Catholics............................... 307
    Peter De Mey

Toward a New Dayton Momentum? Exclusion, Sociocultural
  Identities, and the Ecumenical Movement.................. 317
    E. A. J. G. Van der Borght

Retrospective 325
    Vincent J. Miller

List of Contributors 329

Foreword

Richard R. Gaillardetz

It was in late April of 2011, a few weeks before the Dayton "Ecclesiology and Exclusion" conference, that I had to contact my good friend and esteemed colleague, Dennis Doyle, to inform him that I would not be able to participate in the conference as I had planned. Our family was then engaged in a grace-filled deathwatch for my father-in-law, Weyman Horadam. My regret at missing the conference was well founded. As the essays in this volume demonstrate, the Dayton conference proved to be a theological event of extraordinary value on at least two counts. First, it constituted a unique gathering in North America of some of the most prestigious scholars in ecclesiology from throughout the world (with such distinguished participants as Mark Chapman, Agbonkhianmeghe E. Orobator, Mary McClintock Fulkerson, Paul Lakeland, Neil Ormerod, Dennis Doyle, Gerard Mannion, Bryan N. Massingale, Sandra Mazzolini, Peter De Mey, Susan Wood, and Bradford E. Hinze) and belonging to diverse Christian faith traditions. Second, the conference was addressing a topic, the question of exclusion, which has emerged as one of the most pressing issues for the churches today. It is an issue of particular significance for my own Roman Catholic tradition.

Over the past few decades, a growing number of Catholic bishops have adopted a particular form of sacramental exclusion by withholding communion from Catholic politicians who were deemed to not have sufficiently promoted Roman Catholic teaching on abortion in their legislative voting records. In the spring of 2009, a number of prominent Catholic bishops objected to the decision of the University of Notre Dame to invite President Barack Obama to give a commencement address, again largely because of the president's position on abortion. On December 21, 2010, Catholic Bishop Thomas Olmsted of the Diocese of Phoenix decreed that St. Joseph's Hospital and Medical Center in Phoenix could no longer be considered Catholic as a consequence, in part, for the hospital's continued insistence that it had acted ethically in terminating a pregnancy in order to save the mother in the tragic situation in which, without any medical intervention, it was likely that both mother and child would die. On March 30, 2011, little more than a month before the Dayton conference, the United States Conference of Catholic Bishops' Committee on Doctrine issued a statement regarding what it saw as serious doctrinal deficiencies in a recent theological work of a noted Catholic theologian, Professor Elizabeth Johnson. Add to these recent events Catholicism's long-standing positions excluding women from priestly ordination, the divorced and remarried from Eucharistic communion, and gays from sacramental or even civil marriage and you get a religious tradition that, rightly or wrongly, now appears inextricably linked with an ethos of exclusion.

Of course, many of these policies and practices of exclusion are not unique to Roman Catholicism, as is made clear in several essays in this volume. One of the great strengths of this collection of essays lies in the willingness of the authors to tackle the thorny ecclesiological problem of exclusion from multiple perspectives, often shedding fresh light on a long-standing ecclesial issue. Here we find thoughtful pieces examining the role of race, gender, immigration, sexual orientation, and creedal commitments in the discernment of ecclesial practices and policies of hospitality and exclusion.

An honest engagement with the issue of ecclesial exclusion is complicated by the tendency of many today to view exclusionary practices and policies in an almost entirely negative light. Yet doing so fails to do justice to the complex place of exclusionary practices in the Christian tradition. These practices and policies often presuppose long-standing traditions and theological rationales that cannot be facilely dismissed. As Neil Ormerod and others have noted in these pages, the question of establishing and maintaining boundaries, often to the point of acts of formal exclusion, have strong biblical precedents. The Christian tradition can be read as an ongoing negotiation between two biblical trajectories. The first is manifested in Jesus' radical practice of open table fellowship (eating with sinners, prostitutes, and tax collectors), a practice that constituted a subversion of the "table etiquette" of both first-century Judaism and the Greco-Roman symposium.[1] The second trajectory, rooted in such passages as Matthew 18:15–17 and 1 Corinthians 5:1–13, grants the practice of excommunication in certain pastoral contexts both as a way of preserving ecclesial unity and as a medicinal pastoral practice. Christianity has often struggled to hold together the enduring theological and pastoral insights embedded in each trajectory.

The challenge for the churches today is to find fruitful ways to renew this negotiation in a postmodern context. The question of ecclesial inclusion/exclusion is inevitably bound up with postmodern preoccupations regarding the politics of identity and the nature of communal belonging. How can we as a church be characterized by both a strong center and open doors?[2] How can we continue to preach the good news of Jesus Christ in and out of season (thereby sustaining a strong center), while maintaining permeable boundaries? There are no easy answers to these questions, but the contributors to this volume do us a tremendous service by forcing us to set aside lazy assumptions and premature judgments in favor of rigorous historical, theological, and sociological reflection. We are in their debt.

Notes

[1] Patrick McCormick, *A Banqueter's Guide to the All-Night Soup Kitchen of the Kingdom of God* (Collegeville, MN: Liturgical Press, 2004), 41–42. For the Greco-Roman symposium as a framework for understanding the development of the Christian Eucharist, see Dennis E. Smith, *From Symposium to Eucharist: The Banquet in the Early Christian World* (Minneapolis: Fortress, Press, 2003).

[2] For this way of framing the issue, see Gordon Lathrop, *Holy Things: A Liturgical Theology* (Minneapolis: Fortress Press, 1993).

Introduction

The theme addressed at the academic conference from which the essays in this volume stemmed, "Ecclesiology and Exclusion," hit people in the guts. The initial ideas for the conference were connected both with ecumenical concerns and with relations between church and society. Once the title of the conference was announced, the immediate reactions to the phrase "ecclesiology and exclusion" broadened the theme far beyond the initial ecumenical and church-society questions to include more explicitly the relationship of churches with a diverse range of marginalized and excluded peoples.

The event was the fifth international conference of the Ecclesiological Investigations Research Network (EI), held at the University of Dayton, the first in the United States. The very first EI international conference gathered at the St. Deiniol's Library in Wales in 2007. It addressed the nature and role of the church and helped to identify key priorities for future work. The 2008 EI conference in Kerala, India, addressed the theme, "Church in Pluralist Contexts." A linked conference on "Inculturation and Church" was also held that year in Trichur at the University of Calicut. The third international conference met in association with an event entirely planned and implemented by the Durham University Centre for Catholic Studies at Ushaw College in 2009 on the theme of "Receptive Ecumenism."

Then in 2010, at K.U. Leuven in Belgium, EI collaborated with the university's Center for Ecumenical Research as well as the International Academy for Marian Spirituality (INTAMS) to give a conference exploring the theme "The Household of God and Local Households: Revisiting the Domestic Church." Also in 2010, EI teamed up with the Congregational Studies Network and the Ecclesiology and Ethnography Network to hold a conference at the headquarters of the Protestant Church in Utrecht of the Netherlands addressing the topic "Being Surprised by God: Embodied Ecclesiology in Local Settings." The 2011 conference in Dayton has since been followed by the April 2012 conference in Assisi: "Where We Dwell in Common: Pathways for Dialogue in the 21st Century." EI is also well known for the multiple sessions it has been sponsoring at the American Academy of Religion annual meetings since 2006.

The spirit of hospitality, dialogue, and hope that characterized the Dayton conference was remarkable. Participants had come from the Americas, from Europe, from Africa, from Asia, and from Australia. There was a refreshing mixture of established authors and bright, young scholars and many in between. Respectful, substantive conversations took place in formal sessions, in the hallways, at meals, at socials, and in vehicles from and to the airport. Community prayer was an important element of the mix.

Some of the spirit of the conference can be attributed to the tradition of hospitality of the Society of Mary, the religious order that founded the University of Dayton. The sense of community and family present among the Marianists can be felt in palpable ways. Another large part of the conference's spirit came from the EI and the energy and vision of the people who make it work. EI has burst onto the theological scene in recent years as a progressive force in ecclesiological and ecumenical concerns.

A significant range of diverse voices was heard at the conference and is represented in this volume. Throughout the planning of the conference, we strove to model the inclusivity called for by our theme. "Coming from different places" was not limited to ethnography or geography. The respectful conversations we have referred to were often taking place among people who seriously disagreed with each other. The essays in this volume not only discuss but also embody various forms of human diversity.

Still, there were notable limits to our own ability to be "inclusive." The majority of the participants were from the United States and Europe. Although EI strives to be and is a radically ecumenical group, about half of those who presented on panels or in parallel sessions at this particular gathering were Roman Catholic, which was due, in part, to the conference being planned mainly by a Catholic theologian and being held at a Catholic university. Not all possible related topics were covered. Not all points of view were represented. Not all proposals to the conference were accepted. Not all papers submitted were selected for the volume. None of these things should be surprising, but, given the conference theme, otherwise routine decisions took on an added weight.

Our attempt to be inclusive influenced the structure and form of this volume. The conference's mixture of experience and youthfulness has carried over. There were two types of conference presentations: plenary panel sessions and parallel paper sessions. In order to include as wide a range of voices on as many topics as possible, we asked everyone to keep their contributions short to medium in length. Some of the essays are recognizably based on oral presentations and contain few to no endnotes.

Other essays are trimmed from what could have been developed as longer, scholarly articles. In all cases, the authors of this volume were asked to hold back in some ways and get to the point.

The volume begins with a book panel focused on Gerard Mannion's *Ecclesiology and Postmodernity*, for this book served as an opening focal point for the entire conference. Mannion was not alone in starting and shaping the EI, but he is widely recognized as its founding figure as well as its current mover and shaker. At an EI business meeting held during the second Receptive Ecumenism conference in Durham, England, in January 2009, Dennis Doyle suggested that a future EI conference might be shaped around Mannion's book. All at once, about twenty-five chairs and the bodies they held twisted toward Doyle, as one person asked, "Would you be willing to host such a conference in Dayton?" The rest is history.

The preliminary theme of the conference was "Ecclesiology and Post-modernity" and was expected to be interdisciplinary, including especially not only theological but also philosophical and social scientific perspectives. Back in Dayton, Doyle's colleague Vincent Miller suggested "Ecclesiology and Exclusion" as a more attractive title, though the interdisciplinary element remained. The book's subtitle, "Boundaries of Being and Belonging in Postmodern Times," refers to these initial and still remaining concerns. Mannion's book became the subject of the first daytime panel at which he responded to Doyle, Paul Lakeland, and Mark D. Chapman. The essays by Giovanni Pernigotto and Debora Spini fill out this opening section on postmodern thought.

There were three evening panels free and open to the public and aimed at larger audiences. The next three segments of this volume, on marginal peoples, racial justice, and gender, address the topics of these evening sessions. Speakers for these sessions, in particular, were asked to put their subjects "on the ground," that is, to connect with real contexts and with issues to which audiences could relate. The contributions by Mark Ensalaco and Gioacchino Campese represent the opening evening panel on migration.

Two of the evening sessions were also book panels. We were fortunate both to get Bryan Massingale to respond to a panel on *Racial Justice and the Catholic Church* and then to have Phyllis Zagano kick off the public release of *Women & Catholicism* with her own panel response. Both of these books represent recent, significant texts in areas key to our overall theme. Along with Mannion's text, they served as centerpieces for the conference discussions. The panelists, Leslie Picca, Cecilia Moore (whose contribution was promised for publication elsewhere), Agbonkhianmeghe E. Orobator, Miriam Haar, Sandra Mazzolini, and Vladimir Latinovic, provided the authors with much thoughtful material to which to respond. The essays by David L. Johns, Pascal Daniel Bazzell, David D. Daniels III, and Stefanie Knauss help to deepen these sections of the volume.

The final three sections of the book reflect an ordering familiar to any theologian: church, sacraments, and ecumenism. Contributions from panelists such as Mary McClintock Fulkerson, Barry Harvey, Susan K. Wood, Peter De Mey, and Eddy van der Borght are complemented with essays by Massimo Faggioli, Neil Ormerod, Bradford Hinze, C. Pierson Shaw, Stephen Annan, and Mark D. Chapman. Chapman is the only author with two essays in the volume; he graciously filled in on a panel when another scholar had to back out.

Richard R. Gaillardetz kindly agreed to provide a foreword. The retrospective by Vincent Miller is culled from his reflections on the conference given at the closing banquet.

We live in an everyday world chock full of "exclusion," much of it necessary and justified, much of it unneeded, painful, and sinful. "Ecclesiology and Exclusion" functioned as a topic that brought us together to exchange ideas and experiences about those things that are keeping people apart and how to overcome them. For all of the warmth and hospitality of the event from which this volume has emerged, there is a seriousness to this subject that has held our attention and that is reflected throughout the essays. It is the hope of the editors that at least a good part of the conversation that was the Dayton conference is expressed here and that this volume will serve as a starting point for many further conversations.

Acknowledgments

The editors wish to thank those who sponsored and supported the fifth annual international conference of the EI held at the University of Dayton in May 2011: The University of Dayton's Office of the Provost; the Office of the Dean of the College of Arts and Sciences, the Religious Studies Department, and the Philosophy Department; Charles R. Carroll of St. Brigid Parish in Xenia, Ohio; and Payne Theological Seminary, Wilberforce, Ohio. Thanks are also due to our Editorial Advisory Board members, Gerard Mannion and Timothy Lim Teck Ngern. In addition, we thank the people who helped to plan the conference and its plenary sessions, Danielle Poe, Vincent Miller, David O'Brien, Anthony Godzieba, Paul Collins, William Johnston, Donna Cox, Jeffrey Gros, and Sandra Yocum. We thank as well as those whom we consulted in various capacities: Jack Ling, Cyril Orji, John McGrath, William Roberts, Michael Barnes, Kelly Johnson, Ramón Luzarraga, Ed Hahnenberg, Cheryl Peterson, Rob Slocum, David Hammond, Silviu Bunta, and Jana Bennett. We are grateful to University of Dayton graduate assistants Katherine Schmidt, Nick Mayrand, John Allen, Regina Ingiosi, Jacob Hayden, and Maria Crookston as well as many who go unnamed here. Finally, we wish to thank Susan Perry of Orbis Books for her advice and encouragement all along the way.

PART I

ECCLESIOLOGY AND EXCLUSION
IN A POSTMODERN CONTEXT

Gerard Mannion's *Ecclesiology and Postmodernity*

"Exclusivism" and "Neo-Exclusivism"

Dennis M. Doyle

I will begin with a brief description of Gerard Mannion's 2007 book, *Ecclesiology and Postmodernity: Questions for the Church in Our Time.*[1] Then, I will focus on his use of the categories of "exclusivism" and "neo-exclusivism." Finally, I will raise some critical questions.

Mannion's *Ecclesiology and Postmodernity*

Mannion aims at constructing an ecclesiology designed to address the postmodern world in which we live. He presents his approach in contrast with what he perceives as a reactionary response to postmodernism that cuts across denominational lines. The Roman Catholic example of this reactionary response was the Congregation for the Doctrine of the Faith (CDF) and its head who had, by that time, become Pope Benedict XVI. Mannion labels this overall approach "neo-exclusivism." Along with the CDF, Mannion acknowledges the need to reject "relativism," but he thinks that the opposite extreme of "dogmatism" needs to be equally rejected. He proposes an ecclesiology based upon a virtue ethic as the best way to accomplish this.

Mannion then examines the ecclesiological virtue ethic of Stanley Hauerwas but finds it wanting, especially in its depiction of Christians as "Resident Aliens." He finds in Hauerwas's overall approach another form of "neo-exclusivism."

In constructing his own ecclesiology based upon a virtue ethic, Mannion turns to a range of authors writing about trinitarian theology. He does this in order to counter what he sees as ecclesiologies that are too narrowly christological. He then draws upon the work of Roger Haight to carve out an approach that is transdenominational. The main thrust of Mannion's ecclesiology is to reject claims to superiority in favor of striving to live out the faith to which the community bears witness. As a result, Christians are called simultaneously to do three things: (1) remain faithful to their tradition, (2) become radically open to other traditions, and (3) practice a universal justice that includes all of humankind.

Mannion's Use of the Term "Exclusivism"

I want to be clear that Mannion does not just whip out from nowhere the term "neo-exclusivism" and then start sticking labels on people. In the background are the well-established academic categories of "exclusivism," "inclusivism," and "pluralism." These categories, of course, along with others and with some variation, have been used to describe the spectrum of positions taken by theologians in regard to the relationship between Christianity and other world religions. Briefly, "exclusivists" take their own religion to be superior and reject other religions. "Inclusivists" also take their own religion to be superior but find a way to "include" other religions in a positive manner. "Pluralists" reject any claim to the necessary superiority of any one religion over another, as they tend to stress the limitedness of all religions in relation to the ultimate.

When Mannion does apply the label "neo-exclusivist" to the CDF and to Hauerwas, he is very clear that he is using the term in an analogous sense and that, in some ways, his own use is quite different from the original use. He thinks, however, that a similar mentality underlies both forms of an exclusivist position. In the post-Vatican II era, exclusivism labeled the old tendency to be closed toward other Christians, other religions, and the world. The postconciliar shift, as experienced not only by Catholics but by many other Christians as well, was directed toward a new openness and affirmation toward other Christians, religions, and the world. Mannion finds in the CDF of the last quarter century and in Hauerwas the reverse tendency to be overly suspicious of the world and to withdraw inside one's own community. It is in this reverse tendency that Mannion senses a type of exclusion that is at root another version of the same old problem. In particular, he finds the CDF, especially in *Dominus Iesus* (2000), to be exclusive toward other Christians and toward other religions. He finds Hauerwas, with his concept of Christians as resident aliens, to be exclusive toward the world in which we all live.

Mannion thinks that a similar mentality underlies both forms of exclusivism:

1. top-down methodology, "from above,"
2. presumption of one's own superiority,
3. negative judgment of the other,

4. one-sidedness,
5. lack of humility,
6. being out of touch with present-day realities,
7. defensiveness,
8. lack of appreciation of what is good in the modern world.

Some Critical Questions

It is important to understand that from the point of view of pluralists, both exclusivists and inclusivists appear to be relatively exclusivist in their view of other religions. Let me say that again: from the perspective of the pluralists, exclusivists practice exclusivism, as one would expect; but it is also true that, from the perspective of the pluralists, the so-called inclusivist position is relatively exclusive in its retention of the idea that its own religion is superior to others.

Before raising my critical questions, I would also like to say that I think Mannion's book has made a significant contribution to contemporary ecclesiological discussions. I have many sympathies with the positions that he takes, and some—though not all—of the critical questions I will raise for him are questions that I could ask of myself as well.

1. Following Roger Haight, Mannion emphasizes the unity that Christians share and minimizes the importance of current differences. He wants Christians to feel at home in their own traditions as they affirm other Christians in other traditions. Is not achieving that balance, however, much more difficult than what Mannion seems to acknowledge?

The experience of conversion evokes recognition that, most often through no merit of one's own, one has become radically better than one would have been if one were not experiencing such conversion. On the one hand, one wants to avoid simply projecting one's own experience on to others, either implying that the other is unconverted or that conversion is impossible apart from one's own community's path. On the other hand, however, one usually has convictions that neither can nor should be completely divorced from the particularities of one's own experience and one's own community's path. I am trying to say by this that the complexities of faith and religion present legitimate tensions regarding the first two of Mannion's goals: affirming one's own tradition and feeling easy in affirming the tradition of the other. These tensions increase when we consider that conversion is linked with ultimate meaning and the absolute. Mannion stresses the one side of how standing in the face of the ultimate should make us humble. Is there not necessarily and legitimately another side to this? Is it not impossible and even undesirable to do away completely with the belief that belonging to and participating in one's own community is superior to not doing so? Does this not present complications when it comes to affirming other Christians in other traditions? Can one acknowledge these complications and still remain self-critical and relatively open? Can there be humility in accepting patiently the slow pace of ecumenical progress as Christians of all traditions try to sort the wheat from the chaff?

2. Mannion discusses a transdenominational reality in which the fault lines of the things that unite and divide us religiously fall across the swath of Christian traditions more so than uniting traditions within themselves and dividing traditions from each other. And surely anyone who would assume that all Roman Catholics think one way, all Methodists another, and all Anglicans another should find this point and the supporting evidence to be quite illuminating. The point is a necessary and helpful corrective to naïve views of the way in which particular beliefs and practices unite and divide Christians from each other today. But how far should one take this point?

I see this point as a corrective to a view that remains fundamentally true even when naïve understandings are peeled away. Mannion seems to present the point more as a replacement for what he takes to be the false view that there is anything substantial and legitimately church-dividing in the things about which groups of Christians currently still disagree. As I see it, Mannion is attempting to use this point to subvert any notion that belonging to a particular church tradition can rest upon convictions concerning important matters of faith that unite those church members with each other in a way that distinguishes them from other Christians and that transcends the personal and the subjective.

I am particularly sensitive to this point, because, as a Roman Catholic, I believe that one of the strengths of my tradition is that we share among ourselves a unity of faith in a manner and degree that many other Christians do not share with each other in their own traditions. We have clearly designated teachers and official teachings, and for all of our diversity and problems, we do not experience the same type or degree of divisions leading even to schisms that many other Christians experience.

This is not to say that differences and divisions do not exist among Roman Catholics, or that we appreciate our own diversity sufficiently or deny that even in this matter of unity we need to listen to and learn from other Christians. It is, moreover, not to deny that a number of Roman Catholics have left the Roman Catholic Church. Neither is it to deny that those currently experiencing schism are exhibiting on both sides the courage to fight for what in conscience they believe to be of the Lord. The point Mannion makes about transdenominational realities offers important qualifications about the reality of Roman Catholic unity as well as overall Christian unity. In my judgment, though, it is precisely that, a qualification when applied to the real strength and distinctiveness of Roman Catholic unity. Should it become a point used to subvert or deny that unity or the importance of that unity?

Are the ones being labeled "neo-exclusivist" simply those who hold a different position than Mannion concerning the relationship between the "church" and the "world"? The actual position of many of the people labeled "exclusivist" is often the "inclusivist" position of the Vatican II period. Even Joseph Ratzinger's (the present Pope Benedict XVI) own position on other religions, as expressed in *Truth and Tolerance,* though conservative, is itself more sophisticated than a simple inclusivism. He explicitly recognizes the need to respect other faiths.

I think it worth noting, furthermore, that for most Christians, the question about the possibility of salvation for others, which was most crucial in regard to the categories under discussion, no longer appears to be on the table in a serious way; that is, even those whom Mannion labels "exclusivist" lean in a somewhat universalist direction on this key matter. This difference is large enough to call into question even a highly analogous use of the "exclusivist" label. It also calls into question the practice of taking present-day conservatives and lumping them together with the traditionalists. I grant that *Dominus Iesus* is truly problematic. Is it either accurate or fair, however, to depict conservative theologians and church leaders in an overall sense as trying to reverse the gains associated with Vatican II? For the most part, are not we really talking more about competing interpretations among those who affirm the Council?

Moreover, are present-day conservatives not engaging in legitimate discourse when they depict the "world" as a dark and sinful place? Does Mannion agree with David Tracy that, whereas the dialectical will reject the analogical, the analogical must include the dialectical?

An even bigger problem with using "exclusivism" to describe people, such as Ratzinger and Hauerwas, lies in the fact that in today's world the term "exclusivism" is associated with systematic forms of oppression. The word "exclusivist" is used to label the oppressors when it comes to matters of social, economic, gender, and racial discrimination. Whether Mannion intends it or not, and aside from any genealogy of his personal use of the term, the use of that label insinuates deep and dreadful things about those to whom you apply it. Does Mannion's use of the label "neo-exclusivist" meet his own stated criterion of fostering a critical engagement that transcends mere polemics?

Mannion and I agree on many big points and many little points. We are both interested in developing positions that balance concerns about relativism with concerns about dogmatism. In my own work, I have raised my own critical questions about certain documents of the CDF. I think that where Mannion and I differ is in our overall approach to those whom he labels "neo-exclusivists." I read them, often disagree with them, but then emphasize that they represent legitimate positions and that their voices need to be part of a larger conversation. I have learned too many valuable things from such authors to be able to simply dismiss them. Many of the concerns that they raise are serious ones, and those of us who find ourselves on the other side of the present-day culture wars neglect those concerns at our peril.

Notes

[1] Gerard Mannion, *Ecclesiology and Postmodernity: Questions for the Church in Our Time* (Collegeville, MN: Liturgical Press, 2007).

Reflections on the "Grace of Self-Doubt"

Paul Lakeland

Among the many illuminating reflections in Gerard Mannion's thoughtful book is the attention he gives to the need for ecclesial humility.[1] He first addresses this question in his discussion of *Dominus Iesus* and returns to it in "Preliminaries for an Ecclesiological Methodology for Postmodern Times," where he considers its importance in developing a method for dialogue. "The postmodern *aggiornamento* of ecclesiology, of mission and practice," writes Mannion, "cannot be effectively achieved without ecclesial humility" (134). Mannion's point, indeed, is crucial; any *aggiornamento* encounters a world open, at its best, to dialogue and completely uninterested in dogmatic proclamation. In Rowan Williams's felicitous distinction, we must, as Christians, want to enter into dialogue with a world that evinces *procedural* and not *programmatic* secularism; that is, its *modus operandi* is one in which "religious convictions are granted a public hearing in debate," though not necessarily any privilege.[2] If ecclesial humility is possible, it will accept these conditions and require that others do the same.

While the virtue of humility is by no means prominent in Mannion's book, measured by the number of pages on which it is even mentioned, it is nevertheless central to his project. Because Mannion's overriding concern is to develop an ecclesiology that is workable in the postmodern world, he is bound to the exigencies of dialogue, witness, and comfort with the church at work and play in a pluralistic encounter with people of all religions and none. Though conviction, strength of purpose, and prophetic speech are certainly valuable characteristics of the church in this postmodern world, the world looks suspiciously upon dogmatism, close-mindedness, and the insistence of any culture or society, religious or not, that claims for itself the fullness of truth. Unfortunately, the paranoia of the nineteenth-century church in the face of what it saw as the modernist threat has been exchanged in the early twenty-first century for a similarly immoderate suspicion of the postmodern world and for much the same reason. From Pius IX to Pius XII, and now once again in the current papacy, fear of the secular is the driving force. Liberalism, *laïcisme*, modernism, and socialism (though not fascism) formed the background to the continued ahistorical absolutism of what John O'Malley has called "the long nineteenth century," while secularism, feminism, and relativism are the apparent bugaboos of today's Vatican. Humility, as Mannion has told us, is required for the *aggiornamento* that was central to the vision of Vatican II. Without it, a century from now people might look back to the Council and the papacies of John XXIII and Paul VI as a brief historical hiccup, a tragically missed opportunity to proclaim the gospel in a world beyond absolutism.

In the remainder of this short presentation I will raise a series of questions about the ecclesial virtue of humility with the intention of encouraging Mannion to develop his ideas in three further directions. The need for humility in dialogue between church and world is indisputable, at least in the obvious sense that without it, true dialogue is quite impossible. All genuine dialogue entails a willingness to change if it is not simply *perlocutionary* in Habermas's sense: a strategic subterfuge aimed at achieving ends other than those that would be arrived at by a commitment to open discourse.

So my first question to Mannion is, can any institution committed to the defense of a metanarrative allow itself to employ anything more than the appearance of humility, if true humility means a readiness to admit that we are open to correction? My second question will shift attention from a humble ecclesial posture toward the world and to the question of "internal humility." Is humility still a virtue to be desired in the proclamation of magisterial teaching, and if so, what would it look like? Third and finally, I am asking Mannion to reflect on the *theological* virtue of humility. Is humility vis-à-vis the world and vis-à-vis the community of faith theologically warranted and, if so, how? This question format is, of course, a rhetorical conceit, because I will now go on to offer at least some provisional responses to my own questions. My purpose is not to preempt Mannion's responses so much as to give him something into which to get his teeth, if not indeed to set them on edge.

There are so many examples available of the missteps occasioned by the failure to tap into what Margaret Farley has so aptly called "the grace of self-doubt." The principal example Mannion offers us is the 2000 Declaration of the CDF "On the Unicity and Salvific Universality of Jesus Christ and the Church," usually referred to simply as *Dominus Iesus*. Whether or not it is true that this document was primarily addressed to Catholic theologians toying with the question of the universal salvific significance of Jesus Christ, the ecumenical fallout was considerable and tempered only by the good sense of our non-Catholic brothers and sisters who have heard this kind of thing so many times before. The document affirms that non-Catholic Christian communities "suffer from defects" (17). Non-Christian religions receive similar treatment: "If it is true that the followers of other religions can receive divine grace, it is also certain that *objectively speaking* they are in a gravely deficient situation in comparison with those who, in the Church, have the fullness of the means of salvation" (22). Buddhists and Baptists alike were afforded a glimpse into the way that Rome understood the limits of dialogue and could be forgiven for wondering what, in the end, the Catholic Church has to dialogue *about*. Surely, totalizing claims can leave little room for movement. How can the one true church meet defective "ecclesial communities" on a level playing field, and how, indeed, can monotheism be anything other than intolerant of the truth claims of other religions?

The answer, of course, is "only humbly." Humility in dialogue is not achieved with an assumption of the moral or spiritual superiority of the dialogue partner any more than it is in the assumption of our own fast track to the truth. It is, rather, a matter of recognizing the holy mystery within which we all stand and which relativizes every perspective. It was this attitude, I think, which led Karl Rahner beyond the encouraging wording of *Lumen Gentium* that saw *all* human beings as "somehow incorporated in or related to" the People of God, to his stated opinion that these words imply "the possibility of a properly salvific revelation-faith even beyond the Christian revelatory word."[3] So does the answer to my first question about how to be humble when protecting a metanarrative lie perhaps in undermining the "meta" by relating to a mystery that goes beyond all narratives?

Moving forward to today and narrowing our gaze to the U.S. church over the last couple of years, we can see many examples of the damage that comes from failing to recognize the limitations to which even episcopal teaching is subject. In a longer paper we could examine in detail the overwrought address of the U.S. bishops to discerning a properly moral vote in the last presidential election, to their opposition to the Obama health care legislation, to movements in various states toward the recognition of same-sex civil marriage, and to the propriety of the University of Notre Dame's granting of an honorary degree to the sitting president of the United States. We could also look at the apparent abandon with which certain individual bishops choose to fling around the threat of excommunication and to act on it at times. Furthermore, we could see all this alongside the continuing unwillingness to confront the true extent of episcopal culpability in the ongoing disclosures of sex abuse of which Philadelphia is only the latest and probably not the last.

When we start to look around for an explanation of the flaccidity of church leadership in our times, we are drawn back to Mannion's identification of the vital importance of dialogue for a future ecclesiology, though this does not entirely answer the question of what, then, is to be done. My own belief is that in church leadership, as in other walks of life, the more you know the more complex becomes the answer; the most dangerous kind of church leader is the one who does not know what he does not know and consequently does not know when to speak and when to be silent. I am also sure that teachers in the church, like teachers anywhere else, should recognize that if teaching is not effective, the probability is that it is not due to the obtuseness of the student but rather to the opacity of the pedagogy. If students fail to get it, then consider the possibility that one is teaching the wrong thing or perhaps the right thing in an ineffective way. Repeating oneself or, still worse, raising one's voice is not the answer, because respect for your audience requires humility.

There is, however, a more disquieting concern that was hinted at in an editorial in *Horizons* last year, when Anthony Godzieba wrote that he detected "a whiff of Donatism" in the attitudes of some U.S. bishops to their responsibilities as teachers and leaders. Donatism in the looser sense being the demand for purity that can so easily become confidence in the purity of oneself and one's own kind, is certainly "in the air" whenever—as in the present moment—not a few bishops seem to look with equanimity on the possibility of a smaller and more obedient American Catholic Church shorn of its impure dissenters. This kind of impulse, the misplaced "enthusiasm" that Ronald Knox saw to be the root of all heresy, begins in a worthy impulse towards spiritual perfection and ends—if there is no humility—in the "us versus them" of schism. In Donatism it was bishops themselves who went into schism. How close are we to that in our church today?

In the end, these journalistic observations have to give way to theological convictions, and Ronald Knox is again helpful in this regard. Reflecting on the implicit separatism of the enthusiasm, Knox saw its roots in a different theology of grace. Whereas our tradition sees grace perfecting nature, for the enthusiast "grace has destroyed nature, and replaced it." In particular, "he decries the use of human reason as a guide to any sort of religious truth" and accepts secular authority only on sufferance: "Always the enthusiast hankers after a theocracy, in which the anomalies of the present situation will be done away, and the righteous bear rule openly."[4] I invite you to reflect on whether or not our present situation may not come close to this condition. Knox's picture, by the way, is very similar to Rahner's depiction of "the heresy of integrism," where church teaching is understood as a kind of template for secular society.[5]

And this thought brings me to my conclusion and back to humility. The fundamental theological issue in fostering the grace of self-doubt, even among the official teachers in the church, is the recognition that the grace of God is spread throughout the world; that it is not coextensive with the church; and, indeed, that there is worldly grace that the church does not control or even know. When grace is seen as the work of the Spirit and not as the preserve of the church, there is absolutely no option but that of humility, both before the world and in face of the worldly experience of the Catholic laity whose vocation Vatican II assured us is essentially secular.[6]

Notes

[1] Gerard Mannion, *Ecclesiology and Postmodernity: Questions for the Church in Our Time* (Collegeville, MN: Liturgical Press, 2007).

[2] In an address to the Pontifical Academy of Social Sciences, "Secularism, Faith and Freedom." The full text can be found at the Archbishop of Canterbury's own website, http://www.archbishopofcanterbury.org/654.

[3] Karl Rahner, S.J., "Towards a Fundamental Theological Interpretation of Vatican II," in *Vatican II: The Unfinished Agenda*, ed. Lucien Richard, with Daniel Harrington and John W. O'Malley (New York: Paulist Press, 1987), 14.

[4] R. A. Knox, *Enthusiasm: A Chapter in the History of Religion* (London: Oxford University Press, 1950), 3.

[5] Karl Rahner, S.J., ed., *Encyclopedia of Theology: A Concise Sacramentum Mundi* (London: Burns & Oates, 1975), 242–42.

[6] Cf. *Lumen Gentium*, 31; *Apostolicam Actuositatem*, 2.

Ecclesiology and Postmodernity:
An Anglican Perspective

Mark D. Chapman

These reflections on *Ecclesiology and Postmodernity* from outside the Roman Catholic tradition focus on one key theme, that of an ecclesiology of dialogue. This is the counterpart of those ecclesiologies that seek to cut themselves off from dialogue to maintain what one might call an imaginary "storm-free arena." Some observations from my own tradition should help illustrate some of the problems inherent in a dialogical method. It is worth starting, though, with a note of optimism: however bad things might be these days, and however different the ecumenical situation might be from the excitement of Vatican II, things have moved a long way from the situation before the Council. For those interested in history, it is worth pointing out that in November 1864, shortly before his appointment as Archbishop of Westminster, Henry Manning (1808–92) wrote an open letter to the great Oxford theologian, Edward Bouverie Pusey where he stated that the "Anglican Church," the church of his own baptism,

> is not only no part of the Church, but no church of divine foundation. It is a human institution, sustained as it was founded by a human authority, without priesthood, without sacraments, without absolution, without the real presence of Jesus upon its altars. I know these truths are hard. It seems heartless, cruel, unfilial, unbrotherly, ungrateful so to speak of all the beautiful fragments of Christianity which mark the face of England, from its thousand towns to its green villages, so dear even to us who believe it to be both in heresy and in schism.[1]

Such was the tone of ecumenism in the 1860s. This makes the "defects" language of *Dominus Iesus* look extremely positive.[2]

In Vatican II, of course, ecumenism was transformed. In a new spirit of receptivity, openness, and even humility, "all the Catholic faithful were to recognize the signs of the times and to participate skillfully in the work of ecumenism" (*Unitatis Redintegratio* §4).[3] Even through what Mannion calls the ecumenical winter of the late twentieth century, the underlying ecumenical climate has been subject to significant warming when looked at in a longer perspective. Despite recent setbacks, ecumenism has come a very long way, at the very least in its rhetoric and hospitality. Thus, as *Ecclesiology and Postmodernity* details, even though things are far less rosy between the churches, there are still signs of promise.[4]

In many ways the concentration of the book on dialogue and the need for conversation without the presupposition of exclusive truth—a key aspect of the focus on comparative theology—is as much internally directed toward different strands within the churches (or ecclesial bodies) as externally between them. Indeed this is the backdrop for the whole of the book, which points towards the concept of an open future implied by the concept of a pilgrim church. In many ways, the book is concerned with promoting what is regarded as the unfinished business of Vatican II. While Mannion is principally concerned with the internal tensions within his own church, he recognizes that neo-exclusivism is a problem for all churches. Indeed, those who wrote the ecumenically insensitive *Dominus Iesus*, to which Mannion devotes a great deal of space in an often hard-hitting critique, will find many allies in other denominations, including my own. While it will be of little consolation for those struggling for a voice within the Catholic Church to learn that the divisions are every bit as strong outside, Roman Catholicism cannot be discussed in isolation from the broader religious context. The battles may be framed differently in different confessions, but they are equally bitter. The neo-exclusivist barricades are going up at precisely the same time as others seek to promote dialogue, conversation, and openness.

That said, the Catholic context is significantly different from other churches. As Mannion discusses in detail, the distinctive conception of the local or particular, and the universal, shapes ecclesiological discourse in any church: in Roman Catholicism the polarity between collegiality and primacy, especially creeping infallibility, shapes much of the debate. And this tension raises serious questions about the relationships between the interconnected but often competing authorities of the papacy, the curia, the local church, and what might be called the gospel. The last term can be a cipher for an ecclesiological method that forces on the church a constant critical reflection on its teaching, life, and practice. This, I think, is at the heart of Mannion's method of a "postmodern critical consciousness," which will lead to the dawn of a dialogical spring after the ecumenical winter (101). The careful delineation of an authority in dialogue, which is differentiated from relativism, will lead to a form of church that has little to fear from the outsider and "other" as it sets about the historical task of connecting past, present, and future (206).

All this means that resistance to an overrealized and absolutist eschatology is paramount in the ecclesiological task, which is as much about getting Christology right as anything else. This leads to a genuine catholicity that is not afraid of the outsider but leads to what might be called a humble catholic pluralism rather than relativism (147). The fragmented postmodern world requires the ecclesiologist to discern the very different signs of the times in which a metaphysics of unity may be considered an abuse by one context of another. In a church with an obvious center that Mannion suggests is "too structured by Latinism," this becomes a pressing problem (168). For Mannion, in contrast, there is a more experimental flavor to the sort of authority that is shaped by the encounters with the other both inside and outside the church (177). This leads to a virtue ecclesiology that sees the church not as a countercultural community witnessing against a hostile world but a community that seeks to live out the love of the Trinity as best it can. Although he does not develop the idea at length, Mannion speaks of the church as a school of virtue that might teach its members—in words reminiscent of the Book of Common Prayer—to listen for the voice of God in love and charity with their neighbors (199). This does not imply a woolly pluralism where anything goes—and there will be some boundaries—but it does imply that the boundaries are set only at the end of a process rather than being presupposed from the beginning.

My own Anglican Communion can be used to illustrate some of the problems of a dialogical ecclesiology. These emerge from the very real conflict between those whom Mannion would label "neo-exclusivist" and those who are humbly prepared to engage in dialogue and to recognize the possibility of disagreement. The starting point is quite the opposite from that of the Roman Catholic Church: the Anglican Communion exists only by bonds of affection; there is no Anglican Communion Canon Law; and there is little effective central authority. Even the gathering of bishops from across the Anglican Communion, the Lambeth Conference, which takes place every ten years, has nothing more than a moral and persuasive authority. There are thirty-eight independent churches that have chosen to remain in communion with one another. Context is thus fundamental to Christian identity in such a situation. In turn, there is no presupposition of a metaphysics of unity except that given through mutual recognition of a bare minimum of dogmatic teaching together with an acceptance of episcopacy.

Without a central authority, however, conflict cannot be resolved through central decision making; there is no center to make any decisions, even though the Archbishop of Canterbury reserves the limited right of not inviting bishops to the Lambeth Conference or the other inter-Anglican institutions. In a situation of unprecedented conflict, this has created an unsustainable situation among the churches. After the resolution of the Lambeth Conference of 1998, which ruled that homosexual practice was incompatible with scripture, and the resultant consecration of a partnered gay man as bishop of New Hampshire, the loose bonds of communion have been stretched to the breaking point. Some churches are abstaining from meetings; some are setting up parallel jurisdictions; there have been excommunications and defections. In this context, the Archbishop of Canterbury, who has virtually no authority outside England, has been forced to work out a system for maintaining communion among churches that frequently wish to exclude others and that regard others as having strayed from the gospel truth. But, there is no arbiter or referee in these intercommunion squabbles.

I do not wish to say anything here about the proposed Anglican Communion Covenant, but instead I will briefly point to the method attempted at the Lambeth Conference in 2008. Virtually no decisions were made, but the bishops who came were broken down into small groups to discuss issues of mutual interest in facilitated conversations. This may have been the largest experiment in ecclesial dialogue in the history of the church. The idea was to "enable the bishops to meet in real encounter in a way which would not be dominated by political positioning or parliamentary process."[5] This was to be achieved by the *indaba* process, which was based on a Zulu method of conflict resolution. Rowan Williams guided the conference on the basis of a theology of what he called "interactive pluralism," a dialogical process based upon a minimum set of agreed rules for debate and dialogue and with the outcome that people learn to live with one another even when they do not agree. What emerged was a conference where bishops (and their wives) got to know one another and learned about the difficulties of living the Christian life in different contexts. Many changed their minds.

Many Anglican bishops, however, chose not to take part in the conference, and they could not be compelled to attend. A few hundred, mainly from Africa and parts of southeast Asia, as well as some conservatives from North America, consequently abstained from the dialogical process. Many met in Jerusalem shortly beforehand at the Global Anglican Futures Conference (GAFCON) to draw up a different version of Anglicanism based not on dialogue but on a metaphysics of unity rooted in the exclusive dogmas of the reformation and a fixed interpretation of scripture. Ironically, their goal seems to be far closer to a tightly controlled curial model reminiscent of neo-exclusive Roman Catholicism. Their words resemble those of Cardinal

Ratzinger's response to the ARCIC Report: "For if one were to agree completely on regarding all the different confessions simply as traditions, then one would have cut oneself completely loose from the question of truth."[6] The rhetoric of GAFCON is strongly focused throughout on oneness: plurality is regarded as little more than a weakness associated with the loss of security and certainty. Consequently, for GAFCON, as for Ratzinger, a dialogue that fails to retain this unitive understanding of truth threatens to be little more than liberal relativism that could hardly serve the cause of unity. A similar emphasis on unity emerges from *Dominus Iesus*: "in connection with the unicity and universality of the salvific mediation of Jesus Christ, the unicity of the Church founded by him must be firmly believed as a truth of Catholic faith (§16)." The one Jesus Christ requires the one church expressed in the Catholic faith, which is upheld by the visible teaching office or a dogmatic confession.

Dialogue, then, is an inherently risky business, both ecumenically and within churches; it requires a desire to participate, which is something that is unlikely to be popular among those who fear the outsider or who seek to separate from the world. When truth and unity are contained solely within the church rather than regarded as visible within the world created by a loving God, there will be a resistance to dialogue. A hermeneutics of unity does not bode well for the immediate future of Anglicanism, ecumenism, or an open church. However, the advantage of Roman Catholicism is the possibility that things could be very different depending on who succeeds the present pope. What sort of authority is needed to ensure dialogue happens is something that my own church is slowly and cautiously struggling to discern, although what may eventually emerge is a fragmentation and a dismemberment of the Anglican Communion and a regrouping of neo-exclusivists and those prepared to engage in critical dialogue. The notion of primacy and authority is extremely problematic. Anglicans are all too aware that pluralism carries with it the danger of anarchy and schism. With Gerard Mannion, I hope that dialogue in love might offer a way forward, but it requires a commitment and a desire to make it work as well as the recognition that we might be wrong. This, I think, is what he means by his "virtuous community." His communion, like my own, "does not need a rigid paradigm for all peoples of all times and in all places, but a way, a dispositional existential orientation: the way of Jesus Christ" (228). After all, we are all fellow pilgrims on the same journey.

Notes

[1] Henry Edward Manning, *The Workings of the Holy Spirit in the Church of England: A Letter to the Rev. E. B. Pusey, D.D.* (London: Longmans, 1864), 42.

[2] *Dominus Iesus* (October 2000), http://www.vatican.va/roman_curia/congregations/cfaith/documents/rc_con_cfaith_doc_20000806_dominus-iesus_en.html.

[3] Walter M. Abbott, S.J., ed., *The Documents of Vatican II* (London: Chapman, 1966), 347.

[4] See Gerard Mannion, *Ecclesiology and Postmodernity: Questions for the Church in Our Time* (Collegeville, MN: Liturgical Press, 2007), 92. There are inconsistencies and mixed messages, however: the gift of priestly stoles and episcopal rings to a church whose orders are utterly null and void, for instance, is a prime example of ecumenical double-speak.

[5] Lambeth Conference 2008 Design group, http://www.aco.org/vault/Reflections%20document.pdf.

[6] "Postscript," in Christopher Hill and Edward Yarnold SJ (eds.), *Anglicans and Roman Catholics: The Search for Unity* (London: SPCK/CTS, 1994), 281.

Response: Ecclesiology and the Humility of God: Embracing the Risk of Loving the World

Gerard Mannion

This essay comes in the form of a response to those preceding it. It is an attempt to try to address some of the themes, issues, and questions that have been raised in the foregoing contributions and, indeed, to relate in a more indirect fashion, to those raised in a number of the chapters that will follow. In particular, I will seek to discern whether some of the key theses set down in my book, *Ecclesiology and Postmodernity*, have stood the test of the time since passed, to survey the scene of "where we are" today, and finally to reiterate the ever-more pressing need for more open, constructive, and dialogical ecclesiologies and practices in the church today and into the future.[1] The essays to which I am responding incline me to focus mainly here upon intra-Roman Catholic debates and developments in recent times. As in the original book itself, however, it is my firm belief that there are parallel and analogous developments and debates throughout many of the other churches, representing the ecclesiological phenomenon I have sought to describe as a "trans-denominational reformation."

Ecclesiology and Postmodernity: Its Method, Nature, and Purpose

It is always important for anyone who teaches at a university to provide students with a hermeneutical key to the issues, texts, and scholars with whom they are being asked to engage. In relation to this book, something of a hermeneutical key is offered inside the front cover in two quotations—one from Pope Paul's VI's first encyclical and the other attributed to an eighteenth-century Quaker Book of Sayings. I cite them here for those who may not have seen the book or who habitually skip past some of the front matter that is often deemed to be less significant than the main body of the text in the numbered chapters. First, Pope Paul VI: "Charity is the key to everything. It sets all to rights. There is nothing which charity cannot achieve and renew. Charity "beareth all things, believeth all things, hopeth all things, endureth all things" (1 Cor 13:7). Who is there among us who does not realize this? *And since we realize it, is not this the time to put it into practice?*"[2] The second citation is simply this: "Speak Truth to Power." Between these two citations the focus, method, and approach of the book are pretty well summed up.

It has been very humbling and yet so rewarding, both before and during the conference proceedings, to have three great minds whose work I enormously respect engage so thoroughly with the book. In my opinion, these people are among some of the very finest contemporary ecclesiologists around. But I also wish to say that they are people I have come to know and respect in many more ways than simply for their work—I admire them equally for the *way* in which they work and the way in which they continue to engage in a constructive fashion with the most pressing challenges facing the church in our times.

This also provides something of a clue to the general thrust of this response and, indeed, a further clue to the interpretation of the book itself. In a sense, *Ecclesiology and Postmodernity* was, to a great extent, about the *way* in which people in the church in key positions and in which ecclesiologists and indeed theologians in general go about their work and about what questions and issues they choose to focus upon. The book suggested that some in the church, particularly but not exclusively the Roman Catholic Church, had adopted methods, perspectives, and ways of going about their business that have not been so helpful for the church in these times in relation to the challenges it faces. Some of these approaches were overbearing, arrogant, and proud rather than in keeping with the more tentative and literally more humble (grounded) approaches of so much of the church's tradition. Such approaches accentuated divisions between the church and the "wider world" in which all Christians, bar none, must live out their faith and also divisions between Christians and between theologians themselves. These ecclesiological dispositions appeared to allow only a unidirectional understanding of how the church and world might interact in terms of positive influence. Above all else, in such a world-renouncing stance and in the attitude toward other Christians, faiths, and those of no particular faith that it helped to encourage and give rise to, I sensed that we were witnessing the advent of a novel form of those ecclesiologies and understandings of the faith, doctrine, and ecclesial life that aggressively accentuate the superiority of certain understandings of the Christian faith to all other human pathways for meaning, purpose, and fulfillment.

In *Ecclesiology and Postmodernity,* I termed such approaches "neo-exclusivistic"—and characterized them as holding in common an approach that was driven by an idealizing and absolutizing of both the church and aspects of Christian theology as well as a drive to turn inward and away from the wider world. For many others in the church of our times, such an approach seemed only to spell trouble and decline and is the last thing today's world actually needs.

I labeled this development "neo-exclusivism" through reflecting upon and borrowing from the ideal types employed successfully as heuristic devices in much discourse in theology and religious studies in preceding decades.[3] In the book, I acknowledged the limitations of such devices but also their value.[4] So, a crucial part of the work was necessarily engaged in analysis and critique.[5]

But the book, primarily, was about helping bring the focus in the church back onto what can help the church thrive and flourish today as it seeks to live out the gospel in challenging times. It was also concerned with trying to encourage the church to retrieve the dynamism and spirit of dialogue through *aggiornamento* that was Vatican II's great legacy. But the task of identifying the "questions for the church in our time" entailed some necessarily open, honest, and, at times, frank critique.

Discerning the Signs of *Our* Times: On Ecclesial Risk Takers

For those who decide to speak to the contemporary situation precisely as they find it, there is always an element of risk involved. And we have some dedicated risk takers among those who have contributed the preceding chapters and other notable ecclesiological risk takers among those who have contributed the chapters that follow. We can literally say thank God for the risk takers: without such, the church at crucial junctures of its history would have taken disastrous turns. Dissent from the prevailing perspectives and powerful voices of the day has always been an ecclesial virtue—indeed one finds such in the sayings and actions of Jesus, in Paul's letters, and throughout the long story of the church. Ecclesial dissent, then, has literally proved a saving grace at various points of church history. But often it comes at a price, and we know the many ways in which such a price can be exacted from such voices. Seen in this light, Vatican II was the endorsement of ecclesial risk takers. Pope John XXIII took an enormous risk in simply calling the Council in the first place, as did the core of theologians who relentlessly and in a dedicated fashion kept pushing the agenda forward behind the scenes in order, as Karl Rahner later said, to take the risk of allowing the church to be truly open and global.[6]

But to address one of the issues lying beneath the questions raised in the chapter by Dennis Doyle, one cannot criticize polemical voices without being necessarily open and frank in one's descriptive and, eventually, evaluative language. One realizes all too well when conducting the research for books, which tackle difficult and challenging issues, that it may turn out not to be to everyone's liking. But if the constructive aims behind *Ecclesiology and Postmodernity* were to be served, there seemed little to be gained in beating around the bush and trying to dress up alarming developments in church life and theology as something other than what they were. Trends could be identified in the church across decades, and these were not, by and large, positive trends. There was no fence to sit on here. The questions need to be tackled openly and honestly. I am touched that many have since shared their agreement with and understanding of this necessity. In terms of reception, I am very grateful to anyone who has taken the time to pick the book up and engage it. It is for others to judge how successful the project may or may not have been in its attempt to discern the questions and challenges for the church in our time. But its intentions were and remain sincere, dialogical, and constructive.

In one sense, this book was about a snapshot of what had been happening in the church, why some of these developments were problematic, and what alternatives might be possible. For the mind-set of the "Ratzinger Fan Club" in one church, we had the devotees of the approach taken by those such as Stanley Hauerwas in other churches, the seduction of the bombastic rhetoric of Radical Orthodoxy elsewhere, and a worrying convergence of perspectives across such schools of ecclesial thought. We have seen that polarizing forces have spread their influence in many churches and in many schools of theology.

In the years since the book was being written and since its publication, we have seen the influence and spread of neo-exclusivism grow in many places. Many are taking refuge from postmodernity in certitude and forms of absolutism. Lines *have* since been drawn ever more definitively by Christians in relation to many issues, and there has been an ongoing and increasing tendency to seek to *exclude*: to exclude other viewpoints, even to exclude individuals and groups from the conversations—even from the church itself. And yet we have also seen how so many other people are abandoning the church in droves. Increasingly people feel that the church, or rather its leaders, ministers, and sadly, sometimes even its liturgy,[7] no longer connects with them or addresses where they are. In a world of turmoil, they seek refuge elsewhere. They perceive a church that is hopelessly out of touch. In the United States, for example, we hear again and again that ex-Catholics are the second largest religious grouping in this enormous nation. And yet we see that the neo-exclusivists appear not to be concerned about quantity as such, but rather they murmur the rhetorical mantra, "a smaller but purer church," without seeing the contradictory irony that is displayed by such a mentality.

As still more alienating liturgical reform is being introduced, railroaded through in anything but a pure fashion, the darkness of what can often lie at the heart of administration and leadership is increasingly revealed by the daily revelations of the abuse crisis and with how it has been dealt. A Pontifical Council for the New Evangelization has recently been set up that appears to be charged with seeing through to completion the intentions and objectives of the Communio project formed by a group of prominent theologians in the late 1960s and that has slowly but surely taken over increasing areas of ecclesial life and influence so as to become the dominant force in the church for some time now.[8] It is a particular and context-bound and context-influenced ecclesiological perspective—and yet it has become normative in the official teachings, pronouncements, and activities of ecclesial leaders around the globe. Again, this all seems at odds with many of the intentions of the voices that held sway at Vatican II.

But such a strategy, that is, to focus upon the "New Evangelization" and in doing so privilege certain groups and practices within the church that are considered by many to be divisive at best and sectarian at worst, again demonstrates a failure to appreciate what the real, genuine, and most pressing problems facing the church in *our* times really are and what the most forward-looking and gospel-oriented solutions might be. Vatican II had a much more pertinent approach—literally seeking to discern the signs of the times in a *dialogical* fashion. This was ecclesial humility in *action*: listening and learning, allowing viewpoints to interact and some form of consensus to emerge, but without pretending genuine differences did not or could not remain. *Gaudium et Spes* clearly illustrated and proclaimed for all to hear that the Council did not see the church-world relationship, especially in terms of positive influence, in a unidirectional fashion—quite the opposite.

Vatican II embraced risk taking and innovation in the name of tradition for the sake of the church and world alike. Today such risk taking and innovation is sternly opposed, punished, and stifled. Ecclesial risk taking and risk takers have become the perceived foes of a so-called authentic and normative ecclesiology for postmodern times that infuses so much of its activities with the rhetoric of *semper idem*, while simultaneously changing so much and clearly not, in the opinion of many, for the ecclesial and gospel better. It is not simply an attempt to return to some imaginary golden age. It is a very postmodern reaction to the perceived challenges of postmodernity itself, one by which truth itself is redefined through the spoken and active expressions that emerge from a neo-exclusivistic ecclesial mind-set. Where, then, might the church go from here? Where does ecclesiology go from here?

The Virtue of Ecclesial Humility:
Some Further Thoughts on Method and Responses
to Particular Questions

Ecclesiology and Postmodernity sought to utilize a comparative method in ecclesiology—comparing and contrasting differing ecclesiologies, as well as drawing upon lessons from wider philosophical and social scientific perspectives, and, importantly, seeking to give due attention to historical consciousness throughout. The value of that method, thanks to the great pioneering work of Roger Haight, S.J., and also stellar contributions from some of those who have contributed to this Dayton collection, has since been demonstrated clearly, and great future promise looks to follow from this approach, which does indeed commend an ecclesiology "from below."[9]

So heavy has the overhead artillery been fired across many churches that at times in recent years many ecclesiologists have literally felt as if they have been doing ecclesiology "from the trenches." An ecclesiological approach "from below"[10] helps to encourage both epistemological and existential humility—it is literally grounded (*humus*). Anglicans (with parallels in other churches) still continue to have their wonderful "Prayer of Humble Access" in their liturgy. The theological equivalent of humble discernment—of God, of reality, of the church and its mission—is an ecclesiology from below. The theological and ecclesiological preferential option for humility is well versed—"God resists the proud but gives grace to the humble" as the Epistles of James (4:6) and 1 Peter (5:5) make clear. Augustine clearly agrees when in the *City of God*, from book 1 onward, he counsels that love of power and domination should find no place among Christians. Aquinas saw humility as a master virtue that could aid the practice of all others.[11]

In the space remaining, I will seek to address a selection of the points raised by my thoughtful dialogue partners who have preceded me in this volume. The importance of ecclesiological humility features in each of their responses and is indeed underlined in each of their own contributions as well as their wider work.

Dennis Doyle, as always, has offered such balanced, friendly yet so insightfully critical comments, communicating how the book's intentions must transcend divisions within the church. And Dennis is owed an especial debt of gratitude for proposing that the book should be collectively explored in such a way in the first place. He was, I think, one of the first people to seriously engage it the year it appeared. And I seek to address many of the significant questions he raises at various points in what follows.

But first of all I turn to Mark Chapman's contribution, which made important observations concerning how the book's assessment of the current ecclesial situation, despite focusing in the main upon intra-Roman

Catholic divisions in recent times, mirrors developments in other churches, especially his own Anglican Church. He is also astute in highlighting that further key intentions behind the volume were to emphasize that the present ecumenical winter needs to give way to a church of dialogue, particularly the development of a dialogical form of authority that would be grounded in postmodern critical consciousness as a bulwark against both neo-exclusivism and any slide toward overt relativism. He observed how the virtue of humility was commended as a vital resource in shaping a Roman Catholic pluralism for our times. The church seen as a virtuous community and, indeed, as a school of virtue, the focus of the later chapters of the book, was suggested to be a better response to the challenges of postmodern times than retreating from the world and even our Christian neighbors.

Mark's insightful parallels with the Anglican Church help illustrate what positive outcomes might come from a collaborative engagement in more positive ecclesiological modes of being church. One of the churches I especially had in mind when speaking about the "trans-denominational" reformation was indeed the Anglican family, which I know so well from the many great Anglican theologians who taught me throughout my own university years and with whom I have shared so much friendship and collaboration with in the years since. Christian (and so much wider) fellowship has many faces, and it is an imperative that calls us to ecumenical dialogue anew—a dialogue that today must be as attentive to *intra-* as to *inter*-ecclesial issues. There are more forms analogous to the *indaba* process that the wise Zulus developed and that Rowan Williams experimented with as "interactive pluralism" at Lambeth in 2008 than might at first appear.[12]

This brings us to some of the concerns expressed by Dennis Doyle and indeed more stringent reactions from others concerning whether it is appropriate for us to speak frankly about the divisions within our churches. In relation to all this, Mark Chapman reflected upon the sad episode when many Anglicans self-excluded themselves from Lambeth in 2008 and indeed set about trying to counter and negate what was being attempted there. Mark's illustration shows that some simply and sadly do not care for or wish for dialogue—they only seek monologue and acceptance of their own position. We can see, in various differing contexts, how being honest and, when necessary, frank in ecclesiological assessments is something that some shy away from—whether out of fear, expediency, or inherent subordination to authorities elsewhere. This leads some therefore to feel naturally inclined toward criticism of those who are critical, despite the irony that those identified as the intransigent and reactionary forces, the neo-exclusivists of today's churches, are so hostile as well as vehemently and aggressively critical of all their opponents.

In many ways, the experience of migrant communities offers much food for ecclesiological thought today. The process of being able to engage wholeheartedly in dialogue, debate, and being part of the wider "world," while remaining committed to the traditions and values of one's own community and place of origin, is a good example of how and why it is not too difficult to achieve the dialogue outlined in *Ecclesiology and Postmodernity*. Migrants are necessarily drawn toward existing in "multiple" ways of belonging. In this sense, when Dennis is concerned that "affirming one's own tradition and feeling easy in affirming the tradition of the other" might prove too much for Catholics and other Christians and those of other faiths today, I would seek to reassure him and others that there is so much to prove the converse. The experiences of Christians in places such as India, Pakistan, and Sri Lanka, while also demonstrating the harshest lessons of when dialogue is refused and pluralist coexistence proves so difficult, are equally places that actually demonstrate across centuries how pluralism and coexistence are the only effective ways of being in such societies, which are themselves microcosms of the world itself in their rich and varied diversity.

For those contextualized Christians who do not reach out to such diversity and who perceive their own cultural background and experiences as somehow being normative for the whole church, all of this will, of course, prove challenging and difficult at first. Such was a similar experience for some of the earliest Christians. But they overcame it and resolutely accepted the pluralist reality of God's grandeur in bringing into and maintaining in being such a rich tapestry of the world in which we and our communities each form a small part in terms of both space and time.

So I think Dennis Doyle need worry less about those developments—the challenges to us all today are difficult and do call for humility in the face of the pace at which ecumenism can presently progress. But progress it must. And not in a fashion that effectively negates genuine openness and change. So in reply to this particular point from Dennis, I wish nobody to give up what they cherish and treasure insofar as those things are virtuous, wholesome, and affirming of the gospel. The comparative method in theology, and so therefore also in ecclesiology, demands as much by default. Plurality lies at the heart of the very being of God's own self: the analogy of distinctive yet complementary modes of being all grounded in making love actual. Such is the most illuminating and distinctive aspect of the Christian doctrine of God. The "trans-denominational" vicious circle has a virtuous counterpart.

In such a spirit, we can amicably agree to disagree on certain other matters—it would not be the first time, and I am sure it will not be the last! For example, I do not find the theology of Joseph Ratzinger ultimately inclusivist if one explores his corpus across his entire career. Consistently, the implications of his theological pronouncements are exclusivist both in ecumenical and interfaith terms alike, with the qualified exception of the Eastern Orthodox Churches, although even then it appears such are still perceived in inferior terms to the Roman Catholic Church.

Dennis next mentions "competing claims among those who affirm the Council," but one cannot perceive roadblocks placed in the path of such a monumental moment of grace in the church's history as affirmative in any fashion. And those historians of Vatican II, much more steeped in the conciliar processes and minutiae than I, are even more emphatic than *Ecclesiology and Postmodernity* in unmasking what is, in effect, something of a magisterial coup d'état in relation to the teachings of an Ecumenical Council of the Roman Catholic Church. Dennis also recalls David Tracy's dictum that the dialectical should be included but never at the expense of the analogical. Amen—which returns us to our earlier reflections. I tried especially hard in the book to stress clearly that "mere polemics" will get us nowhere. But nor, also, will sweeping genuine issues of concern under the carpet of feigning all is well, and all manner of things shall be well in the church if people do not speak out. The history of the church demonstrates clearly that open and honest expression of doubts and concerns serves the church far better than pretending that serious issues, wrongs, and divisions can be ignored.

The book makes clear that dialogue often, by necessity, here following Gregory Baum's wise path, will entail conflict and uncomfortable exchanges.[13] Anyone who recalls family disagreements, however, will know that a loving family often has disagreements by necessity and sometimes by fault on the part of one or more or all of the conversations partners. Such is life. They remain a family nonetheless. Returning to Mark Chapman's response, I believe he really hits the nail on the head when he reminds us that, "Dialogue, then, is an inherently risky business, both ecumenically and within churches: it requires a desire to participate, which is something that is unlikely to be popular among those who fear the outsider or who seek to separate from the world outside."

Mark, also, with the wisdom that is his trademark, picked up on how the arguments of the book might lend themselves to an expanded discussion in relation to the doctrine of creation—a theme and task on which I have, indeed, been working for some time now. This focus on creation will connect well with the comments of Paul Lakeland, who, as always, was so very astute in focusing in upon the virtue of humility, itself, as something of a key to the line of ecclesial interpretation running throughout the entire book. Without wishing to blur distinctions between his questions on differing notions of humility, I think if we start with the theological notion of humility and work from there, it will take us in the right direction and also allow us to help address further aspects of the dialogue raised by both Professors Chapman and Doyle as well, who both also focused upon the notion and nature of humility in a number of different ways, even, in some parts of their responses, perhaps unconsciously.

I hope that Paul's questions will be addressed in what follows—humility can be an ecclesial disposition that reaches far and wide, and I think Paul would agree that in the processes and outcomes of the Second Vatican Council, as well as in numerous interchurch and interfaith encounters and those between members of faith communities and the "wider world," we have seen such illustrated often in exemplary fashion. Not only Rahner, but Aquinas and so many before him, helped remind Christians that they need both existential and epistemological humility and therefore ecclesial humility when faced with the absolute mystery of the loving being of God that has brought us into being and charges our being with so much grandeur in each and every moment of its continuation. And, of course, "beyond": eschatology makes us all humble. Few Christians would seek to suggest that we can control and offer definitive and descriptive certainties about that.[14] What Paul's essay makes possible here is a further opening up of the conversation.

A Contemporary "Forgetting" of the Doctrine of Creation

So here I wish to turn not only to draw together some of the issues raised above, as well as to combine the retrospective and prospective reflections on the ecclesiological issues raised and addressed in the book, but also to address some of the issues raised by the foregoing chapters and to try and address them together.[15]

The Doctrine of Creation-Providence entails that God brought the world into being and sustains the world in that being in every moment of its existence. The world exists as a result of God's love and the nature of God's being. Given this, it is therefore surprising the extent to which numerous theologies (and indeed ecclesiologies) have become world renouncing in recent decades. This returns us to our remarks at the outset in unpacking the notion of "neo-exclusivism."

In many such theologies, the "world" is frequently perceived to be evil, something exterior to and even alien to the church. The solution to the vagaries and flux and change of a postmodern age are to assert loudly "the" Christian and theological truth and then wait for the rest of the world to accept this truth and to turn inward and away from the world in the meantime. As indicated, these theologies spread across the denominational divide, and they are manifested particularly in the ecclesiological musings of various prominent contemporary theologians even, with no little irony, to various degrees in a number of scholars who describe their work today as "public theology." It is found in doctrinal, ethical, and methodological discourse alike. In particular, one sees it manifested in the aversion to other forms of intellectual enquiry, particularly those of the social sciences and philosophy. This flies in the face of the direction in which many churches necessarily moved in the decades of the middle to the second half of the twentieth century. It is also manifest in the pejorative understanding of culture beyond the church. This development has particularly serious implications for the existence of the church in pluralistic environments, for church mission, and obviously for theologies of religious dialogue and inculturation.

And yet these world-renouncing theologies appear, in a fundamental sense, to have "forgotten" the doctrine of creation. Logically speaking, it would appear that they are denouncing this doctrine in what they say about the world, the world that God not only brought into being but sustains in its being.

It is not enough to argue that when such theologians use the term "world," they employ it as shorthand for the wayward or sinful errors of the "ways of the world" for the substance of their writings, and the entailments of their argumentation constitute something deeper than this—they really do appear to reject the world and perceive it in a pejorative fashion. In such approaches the doctrines of grace and pneumatology are likewise "forgotten" in favor of rigid and limited Christological conceptions of church, mission, and existence in general. Genuine historical consciousness is often shunned. All this further compounds the "forgetting" of creation and, indeed, amounts to the denigration of creation itself. It is not enough to try to hearken back to the very different eschatological expectations of the early church in attempting to justify such a "forgetting" of creation.[16]

The church is not and cannot be separated from the world itself. It is called, however, to be a sign and instrument of God's gracious self-communication in and, very importantly, *through* the world. If it is to fulfill this gospel mission today, then world-renouncing theologies must become a thing of the past, as also must alienated ecclesiologies and, therefore, the mind-sets and ecclesial ways of thinking and acting that have been collectively termed neo-exclusivism. The sacramental (or if one prefers, analogical) nature and purpose of the church must not be neglected in favor of partisan and rhetorical theological approaches. There is no half-way house—although to state such is not to assert a zero-sum option—such are rather offered by such approaches as neo-exclusivism. Rather, it is to suggest that if we take the key beliefs and teachings of Christianity seriously, then we cannot denounce, renounce, and abandon the world.

Ultimately, the key question that draws all this together is this: *Do we really believe that the God to which Christianity has borne witness for over two thousand years is the sort of being who would approve of such partisan and exclusivistic attitudes and practices as those we have seen on the increase across our churches today?*

This side of whatever lies beyond death, human beings can experience God nowhere other than the world—thus the world is the scene of God's self-communication and enduring presence. Salvation history unfolds *in* the world, not in enclaves cut off from the world and not in some realm beyond the world. It is not simply transcendental philosophy but also the rich tradition of much older approaches in theology, perhaps epitomized in the works of giant figures such as Aquinas, who make it clear that our language and conceptualizing remain rooted within the world, however much we grasp after what we often believe to be somehow "beyond" it. Our theological enquiry, because of where we dwell, necessitates epistemic and therefore existential humility.

Thus, if the doctrine of creation is to be taken fully seriously then—particularly for those ecclesial traditions that place great emphasis upon the sacramental dimension to reality, it is clear that across many Christian communities and in much ecclesiological thinking in recent years the church can be said to be suffering from "alienation"—another way of understanding how a world-renouncing mentality is prevailing and how a marked turn "inward" has developed in many ecclesial quarters. But such ecclesiological alienation means that the church, which is supposed to be that sign and mediator of the loving and gracious self-communication of God in the world, which is, after all, a fundamental aspect of God's creative self-disclosure in itself, has become estranged and "cut off" from its very essence. In their efforts to counter the perceived threats of a postmodern world, such ecclesial outlooks have led to the exacerbation of an "unhappy ecclesial consciousness" whereby the yearning for a mythical sense of certitude vis-à-vis the church's self-identity and an absolutist, exclusivist, and superior mind-set have meant that the church is neither existing nor functioning authentically, for such a mind-set refuses to allow the possibility that truth is indeed grounded in authentic subjectivity.

As noted, in the book I spoke about all this in terms of the advent of a "trans-denominational" reformation. It has played a significant role in the emergence of an ecumenical and interfaith winter, the decline in dialogical and open theological enquiry, and the emergence of new schools of thought, particularly "reactionary" forms of postmodern theology. What brings such theological shifts about relates to the operative understanding of relations between the church and world as well as upon nature and grace and the ecclesiological implications of both.

All of this has profound moral and social implications. It leads to a judgmental mind-set against other ways of seeing the world, interpreting it, and, indeed, of being in the world. This, in turn, leads to further exclusion and exclusivism. Throughout the remainder of this present collection, we see charted some of the many ways in which exclusivism in the church, as well as wider society, have had dreadful consequences for so many communities and individuals. The time has come to learn from the lessons of history particularly pertinent to such exclusion and exclusivism and, indeed, the lessons of *our* particular period of history. The faith we profess, we live out, is not a faith of exclusion: it is a faith of universal salvation. It proclaims the God of love who is all embracing, reaching out to draw together all that God has called into existence to share in the blissful unity of God's own loving self. How, then, can such faith be borne witness to by proclaiming a view of the world that is diametrically opposed to it?

The Humility of God and Reminding Ourselves of Sacramental Being as a Call to Risk Taking

John Macquarrie, whom I consider to be one of the greatest theologians of the entire Christian church in the twentieth century, published a wonderful short book that emerged out of some meditations delivered at Christ Church Cathedral, Oxford, in 1978. Its title was *The Humility of God*.[17] The title, of course, refers to God's bringing the world into being, God's loving self-communication, incarnation, and coming to dwell among humanity, in Macquarrie's own words: God's "down to earthiness, [God's] involvement in the life of [God's] creatures."[18]

And it is important to stress that God's incarnation in Jesus does not exhaust God's overall expression of humility in God's self-communication. For, in fact, the doctrine of creation itself captures that communication also. To return to Macquarrie, God's own self has been poured into creation: "The relation is, we could say, one of caring." God's "act of creation is not an arbitrary exercise of sovereign power, nor was the world which . . . [God] created something entirely external to . . . [Godself] and left to go its own way. Rather, we must say, as in the case of the human artist, this was a caring act. God gave a measure of independent reality to that which had hitherto existed only in [God's] thought. This means that to some extent [God] was already putting [Godself] into [God's] creation; or, to put the matter another way, [God's] creation was also a self-emptying." God takes on the self-limitation that bestowing humans with freedom involves. Macquarrie reminds us of how Herder called humanity "God's risk." He continues, "So when we begin to analyse the idea of creation, we find that it is not so much an exercise of power as rather an exercise of love and generosity, an act of self-limitation and even of self-humiliation on the part of God."[19] Macquarrie further elucidates how this means that God "puts himself into the creation," taking responsibility for it but also giving creation a share of that responsibility, not only limiting God's power, but also making God vulnerable—for such sharing risks suffering.

Those who respond to God's loving and astounding gesture of self-communication in this way are called to imitate that risk, albeit, quite obviously, on a significantly different scale. Those who self-identify as the followers, in particular, of Jesus of Nazareth, the Christ, are called to be risk takers by his teachings in so many ways. One of the most profound and existentially transformative ways is in the manner of which they relate to and coexist with one another and with others in the society around them—Christ called his followers to such a risk-oriented way of being and loving from the very outset. Christians, then, have no option but to be ecclesial risk takers if they are to follow the gospel. God's risk, a risk magnified further still in the humble kenosis of the incarnation itself, becomes the ground for, the call to, *our* risk, and magisterium is nothing other than the technical process by which we are assured that in taking such risks, collectively and individually, we will not be abandoned by God.

That God so loved the world as to do all this brings us back to the sacramental focus once again. Paul Lakeland speaks above about erroneous theological dispositions, whereby grace crushes nature, and here we see rather that the nature-grace divide is a category mistake in many ways. But if we do take the doctrine of creation and of God's own self-humbling in all God's creation, most definitely in the incarnation of God's own self, and if the mission of the church is to be sacramental—a sign and mediation of that loving and gracious self-communication of God in the world that will help effect the reign of righteousness and justice that our imperfect theological musings interpret to be the logical implication of God's own self-giving—then our ecclesial "ways of understanding" and "ways of doing business" need to be more truly sacramental in and of themselves.

In *Ecclesiology and Postmodernity* I spoke about the need for the church to be the *analogia ecclesiae,* an analogous if imperfect image of the loving, coequal, codivine and coeternal blissful threefold community that is the being of the triune God itself.[20] Today we can develop this analogy further still. The humility of God witnessed in an act not of power but of letting be, of self-limitation and of glorious loving, in creation itself, the humility of

God that is the antithesis of domineering power—can this also still inform and shape our ways and means of ecclesial being today?

Or do we continue with the pretense that humanity knows better, and what it knows best is the expediency of raw power, however literally counterevangelical (i.e., working against the gospel) this expediency becomes?

The intention in those constructive sections of *Ecclesiology and Postmodernity* was to promote and encourage dialogue, seeing such as the true legacy of Vatican II but also as the most positive way to negotiate the challenges of a postmodern age. One of the key aims was to underline once more how the church is called to bear witness to and live out the gospel not in an enclave, but in the midst of the world—again, the world that is God's creation. If the church is to do this effectively, then it needs to engage in dialogue with all in that world. Proclamation and evangelization *can* be achieved through and as dialogue. Look at the manner and style in which Jesus first proclaimed his good news. Witness how the early church grew and developed and took that news further afield. Delve deeply into the stories of those moments of grace-filled encounter as that good news has been spread and touched countless numbers of communities across the globe since. Proclaiming the gospel is not simply and crudely doxology, as if the latter could ever be merely formal worship; it is also mission and enhancement of community. God's call to unity with God's very self is timeless and creedless. Confessing and commending the faith today, as in each age, requires an opening out to the wider human family. The gospels frequently point to this latter insight concerning salvation.

The message is clear: the mystery of God's being, the love of the triune God that is the very community of the Trinity itself and that results in not simply the being and existence of the church but also of the world itself is something that we cannot forcibly compress into one authoritative means of explanation or indeed proclamation.

Where are we now, then? What is required is a greater attentiveness to the hermeneutical task of ecclesiology. A key purpose of my 2007 book is to try to encourage Christians to appreciate that, instead of retreating "to the bunker," the task for the churches today is really to embrace the diversity of the world in which we live; to affirm it; and, in response to postmodernity, to find positive ways in which to move beyond both dogmatic foundationalism *and* moral and religious relativism in both ecclesiology and ethics.

It would appear that none of us can ultimately ignore the fact that our communities are very much, in the main, indicative of the pluralistic world in which we now live. *Therefore*, an inward-looking ecclesial and moral vision appears, to many, to be a most unhelpful approach to take in discerning the relations between Christians and the majority of the world's peoples who reside beyond Christianity's "borders."

Concluding Remarks

So what alternative principles might be offered in relation to constructing that more open and dialogical outlook that we perceived might best serve the church and world alike at the outset? None of what has been said above is to deny that there is all too much in the world that is lamentable and contrary to the love that Christians believe constitutes the very being of God. That is not enough ground, however, for a world-renouncing theology, for there is equally all too much in the church that is so terribly lamentable and contrary to the love of God. One cannot have an ecclesiology that is sacramental—both a sign and instrument of God's love to the world, if it is bent on running away from that world. Such would constitute a sacramental dereliction of duty. Discerning the signs of the times *is* an act of ecclesial humility and the practice of an ecclesial virtue—learning to listen, helping to inform the debates and discussions.

Notes

[1] I wish to express my deep gratitude to Danielle Poe for chairing the conference session from which this discussion emerged and also both her and Dennis Doyle for somehow thinking that this book of mine might not only form the focus of a plenary discussion but also lend itself to having a conference shaped around some of the themes and wider implications of what was covered in that book.

[2] Pope Paul VI, *Ecclesiam Suam* §56.

[3] Namely, exclusivism, inclusivism and pluralism. Cf. Gerard Mannion, *Ecclesiology and Postmodernity: Questions for the Church in Our Time* (Collegeville, MN: Liturgical Press, 2007), chaps. 1–4, esp. chap. 3, 43–74.

[4] That typology has been criticized variously by those whose viewpoints would be placed at each end of the spectrum of ecclesial positions such might represent, but I was convinced they retain a heuristic value nonetheless, and, in any case, I was seeking to expand and build upon the earlier typology—hence the neologism.

[5] But the book also—and necessarily—explored many voices and perspectives that were going about their business in a much more positive fashion and in ways that could help the church today. It is important to emphasize that five of the nine chapters and well over half of the book were concerned with constructive proposals and suggestions; some 66 percent of the volume in total, then, was focused on constructive matters; and the first two chapters were concerned with sketching the historical backdrop to the issues about to be discussed. So the vast majority of the book (around 86 percent) was positively oriented. But in order to get there, the problems facing the church today had to be first identified and engaged with.

[6] Cf. Karl Rahner, *The Shape of the Church to Come*, trans. and introduced by Edward Quinn (London: SPCK, 1974), 93. See also Richard Lennan, *Risking the Church: The Challenges of Catholic Faith* (Oxford: Oxford University Press,

2004), and Richard R. Gaillardetz, *Ecclesiology for a Global Church* (Maryknoll, NY, Orbis Books, 2008).

[7] A trend that, for Catholics, is about to increase rapidly given the recent "revisions" of the liturgy (revision*ism* might be a more appropriate and revealing description here).

[8] Cf. Joseph Ratzinger, "Communio: A Program," *Communio: International Review* 19, no. 3 (1992): 436–49 (English trans. by Peter Casarella of "Communio—Ein Programm," *Internationale Katholische Zeitschrift* 21 (1992): 454–63.

[9] Cf. Roger Haight, *Christian Community in History* (New York: Continuum, 3 vols: vol 1, *Historical Ecclesiology*, 2004, vol. 2, *Comparative Ecclesiology*, 2005, vol. 3, *Ecclesial Existence*, 2008). See also Roger Haight, "Comparative Ecclesiology," in *The Routledge Companion to the Christian Church*, ed. Gerard Mannion and Lewis Seymour Mudge (New York: Routledge, 2008), 387–401, and the exploration of Haight's work and broader considerations of comparative ecclesiology in Gerard Mannion, ed., *Comparative Ecclesiology: Critical Investigations*, Ecclesiological Investigations Series, vol. 3 (New York: T & T Clark/Continuum, 2008), especially, "What Is Comparative Ecclesiology and Why Is It Important? Roger Haight's Pioneering Methodological Insights," chap. 1, 13–40, and Gerard Mannion, "Constructive Comparative Ecclesiology: The Pioneering Work of Roger Haight" in *Ecclesiology*, vol. 5, no. 2 (2009): 161–91.

[10] This is an approach sternly dismissed as somehow being solely an attempt at sociological and democratic reductionism in Ratzinger, "Communio—A Program."

[11] Cf. *Summa Theologiae*, II–II, Question 161.

[12] In many ways, the Ecclesiological Investigations Research Network emerged out of and was founded in order to promote such interactive pluralism, and the "Ecclesiological Dayton Accord" that emerged during the conference in May 2011 was a wonderful epitome of what such dialogue might help achieve.

[13] See Mannion, *Ecclesiology and Postmodernity*, 142–46.

[14] Here see Pope Benedict XVI's encyclical from 2007, *Spes Salvi*.

[15] Thankfully, their wise and careful interpretations have brought together a range of areas of development of the core theses and conclusions of the book that have been ongoing areas of interest and attention for myself since its completion.

[16] These neo-exclusivist theologies forget the words of Karl Rahner from the mid-1960s: "[I]f the Church of today is to conduct a dialogue with the world, then it must not be overlooked that this 'world' is not simply 'outside', but is rather present in the Church herself. This means that the first, and perhaps the decisive dialogue with the world is that which takes place precisely within the Church" (Rahner, "Dialogue in the Church" [1967], *Theological Investigations*, X, trans. David Bourke [London: Darton, Longman & Todd, 1973], 103–21 [106]).

[17] John Macquarrie, *The Humility of God: Christian Meditations* (London: SCM, 1978), the title being a play on Karl Barth's own short book, *The Humanity of God*.

[18] Macquarrie, *The Humility of God*, Preface.

[19] Macquarrie, *The Humility of God*, 4. Macquarrie further elucidates how this means God "puts himself into the creation," taking responsibility for it but also giving creation a share of that responsibility, not only limiting God's power, but also making God vulnerable—for such sharing risks suffering.

[20] Mannion, *Ecclesiology and Postmodernity*, 175–91.

The Church:
A Place of Exclusion or an Intercultural Community?

Giovanni Pernigotto

Is it possible to imagine the church as an intercultural community that is radically oriented toward choosing love over exclusion? This present paper draws upon the work of Roberto Mancini, an Italian philosopher, to tackle this question. For Mancini, the center of an authentic experience of a true community lies in an attitude of radical listening and recognition of the "other." In Mancini's work, I find hope concerning the possibility of valuing human dignity in both its particular and universal dimensions without losing either the preciousness of different cultures and traditions or the unity between the local and the global. My intention is in an initial way to apply Mancini's thought to ecclesial practices and structures in a manner that both addresses and takes us beyond the theme of "exclusion." I will draw upon passages and specific images from scripture to frame my discussion. Before examining possible causes of exclusion, I will try to describe the origin of human and Christian attitudes to sociality, that is, to living together.

Three Births

Do multicultural societies represent a new Babel?

Now the whole earth used the same language and the same words. . . . the LORD confused the language of the whole earth; and from there the LORD scattered them abroad over the face of the whole earth. (Gen 11: 1, 9)

Roberto Mancini's focus on a reflection and a practice of "radical listening" helps us in searching for a philosophical bridge between church and intercultural community.[1] Listening is the essential dynamism that, in Mancini's thought, defines the birth of the individual and the aggregation of every human group as well, although in different ways. Listening plays an integral role in giving birth to three different subjects: the human being, the human community, and the ecclesial community.

The Birth of a Human Being: Listening to a Divine and Performative Word

> Then God said: "Let us make man in our image." . . . God created man in his image; in the divine image he created him; male and female he created them. (Gen 1: 26–27)

A human being is first of all someone who has been generated. Mancini calls this fundamental reality the "gift of origins." The gift of origins consists of a fact: before we could think anything, we were already "thought of" and "chosen."[2] Mancini writes, "Our existence, since its beginning and in its beauty, depends on being formed by the mind of someone, either a God or one who called us to birth, or one who lives close to us."[3] He adds, "We can understand how essential it is to come back to this fact: we were chosen, we are chosen."[4] Being a human being is not simply "put on" in this world somewhere randomly.[5]

Birth as a Community: Listening to the "Other" as a Way of Building a Community of Proximity

> Now the word of the LORD came to Jonah the second time, saying, "Arise, go to Nineveh the great city and proclaim to it the proclamation which I am going to tell you." So Jonah arose and went to Nineveh according to the word of the LORD. Now Nineveh was an exceedingly great city, a three days' walk. Then Jonah began to go through the city one day's walk; and he cried out and said, "Yet forty days and Nineveh will be overthrown." Then the people of Nineveh believed in God; and they called a fast and put on sackcloth from the greatest to the least of them. When the word reached the king of Nineveh, he arose from his throne, laid aside his robe from him, covered *himself* with sackcloth and sat on the ashes. (Jon 3:1–6)

At first, Jonah does everything he can to run away from the Lord's call to preach to the Assyrians in Nineveh. He does not even think that God should care about these people. When they hear God's word through Jonah and repent, they become transformed human beings and are thereby saved from God's wrath. Mancini, following some of the most important Jewish philosophers (Arendt, Weil, Buber, Levinas), grounds the value of human interrelation upon human dignity and the event of the "other," which becomes a word of responsibility that brings about the possibility of a new humanity. From this viewpoint, he criticizes ethical approaches derived too directly and immediately from the globalization phenomenon, and instead he suggests an intercultural ethics grounded on the value of humankind considered for itself. There is an unconditional obligation linked to the human being that stands simply "because he or she is a human being." In this sense, one can talk about intercultural ethics when one is ready to listen to other people as a brother or a sister. This attitude to listening becomes action and issues in a form of proximity: from a philosophical point of view, but at the same time drawing upon fundamental elements of the Christian experience, Mancini calls these interpersonal and social relationships "brotherhood" and "sisterhood."[6]

Birth as an Ecclesial Community

So faith *comes* from hearing, and hearing by the word of Christ. (Rom 10:17)

Of the various birth moments of the Church expressed in scripture, perhaps the most significant is the event of Pentecost: the word of the Lord this time does not cause dispersion (as after the Babel diaspora), but instead causes unity that saves the differences and the cultures:

When the day of Pentecost had come, they were all together in one place. . . . And they were all filled with the Holy Spirit and began to speak with other tongues, as the Spirit was giving them utterance. Now there were Jews living in Jerusalem, devout men from every nation under heaven. And when this sound occurred, the crowd came together and were bewildered because each one of them was hearing them speak in his own language. ". . . we hear them in our *own* tongues speaking of the mighty deeds of God." And they all continued in amazement and great perplexity, saying to one another, "What does this mean?" (Acts 2:1–12)

Pope John XXIII expressed his hope that Vatican II would lead to a new Pentecost. Mancini's work can help Christians to realize that in our postmodern world, a new Pentecost will require that everyone become open to hearing the "other" as if they were speaking in one's own tongue.

Identifying the Cause of Exclusion: A Question of Distance

Obviously, we are talking about exclusion in a negative way. Let us ignore, for now, the possibility of a positive meaning of exclusion linked with the topic of identity (but an open identity, where one needs to exclude evil and a bad practice of socialization but not at all to exclude differences). In Mancini's perspective, exclusion begins as a kind of crisis in relation, which itself begins by a quite specific and identifiable process. It does not begin with a choice (that always has a positive background because you can really choose just the good, never the evil), but with a decision (already in an etymological sense, the Latin *de-cido* means to cut off something, to cut with a sword, deciding in a definitive way). So, we see that we can decide on evil, and so we can look for a short way to solve a problem or to face a conflict; it is enough to cut off the question itself or even the person that in our mind has caused our trouble. Mancini describes the process that leads to the decision to exclude as being caused by a kind of anguish with no love, an anguish that considers the other just as a threat, because in this way one is looking to the other with no confidence, just as if he or she was an enemy.[7]

But prior to this anguish with no love can be found a situation that can be analyzed as representing "right distance." In every relation there is a proper distance to be maintained. This is a structural fact, which is part of every human relationship. This distance has to be chosen, not to be decided (with the meaning of decision stipulated earlier). A distance in a relation is not an evil in itself, and in fact it could be very positive depending on the way one considers it. It happens, though, that one can feel distance as a barrier; or one can think that it would be too small (where the other is thought of as a threat); or still, because of the distance, one cannot even see the other's face, as in a grey fog or in a dark night. Thus, we can locate the beginning of evil, in this case what we are labeling "exclusion," in an emotional and/or cognitive misunderstanding of the relation with the other or with ourselves. Yet the decision to exclude is made at a point that offers other possibilities that could be "chosen." As Mancini writes, "Here the crisis of living together could become real and effective."[8]

The reflection of Mancini on the roots of social conflict is, of course, more precise and complex than what I can briefly present here. He offers this summary of the process in the following scheme:

1. structural existence (not negative) of distance in relations;
2. its misunderstanding, which can be active or passive, with a judgment or an action;
3. beginning of a crisis in the relation;

4. settlement of anguish with no love (and with no care for the other);
5. the crisis becomes acute; and
6. decision to adopt negative attitudes and behaviors, to offend, exclude, destroy.[9]

We can see that usually the beginning of evil that quite often could lead to exclusion can be described as a kind of kidnapping: the person neither recognizes oneself nor recognizes the other in his or her difference (allowed by a right distance), so the other becomes a "bad" person. In Latin a bad person is called *captivus*, that is, captured, prisoner. By excluding other people, however, one not only jails them (in a real or in a metaphorical way) but also jails oneself. By excluding, one shuts oneself up in deadly isolation.[10]

How is it possible to avoid the risk of exclusion? More specifically, how is it possible that the Christian community would be a place of mutual exchange, where the right distance (between different traditions and cultures, between different roles in the community, even between God and creatures) and the richness of diversity could be maintained and respected?

Mancini's proposal is clear: this will be not just a dream but an effective reality, if, instead of a process of exclusion, the community will continue to live an open, autocritical process of interculturality. Mancini, the philosopher, recognizes in the gospel an important source of this interculturality. A Christian theological approach can find in the gospel interculturality's most radical source: one that offers a narrative, a symbolic language, and a range of images that express and support a performative process of openness; one that is not against but in favor of an authentic Christian tradition.

Church as an Intercultural Community: Church as a Tent of Interculturality

Inspired by Mancini, and as an initial step in the quest for a real intercultural ecclesiology, I wish to adopt an image: the church no longer just as a house or a building with fixed walls but instead as a tent located in the desert of postmodernity.

Tent as a Place of Narrative World

There is a story that precedes us and that gives us birth: the church-tent offers the witness (in a narrative form) of the dead and risen Lord. The community of the first witnesses offers the good news, a good narration, full of meaning that could give the individual and groups living signs of resurrection and revival. But will this church, thought of as a tent, be able to listen to the narrations of other individuals and other communities, to let itself be changed by this listening? As expressed in *Gaudium et Spes*:

> With the help of the Holy Spirit, it is the task of the entire People of God, especially pastors and theologians, to hear, distinguish and interpret the many voices of our age, and to judge them in the light of the divine word, so that revealed truth can always be more deeply penetrated, better understood and set forth to greater advantage. (44; see also *GS* 58)

A true dialogue does not leave anybody in their former condition.

Tent as Hospitality

Christians do not have to interpret "right distance" as a threat. Is it finally possible to go beyond the *extra ecclesiam nulla salus*? Not only is a neo-exclusivism inappropriate for our postmodern world, but so also is a form of ecclesial inclusivism that seeks a globalized Christianity bent solely on incorporating rather than respecting all others.

The witnesses of the first Christian community went out from the closed rooms of the Upper Hall—from the shadow of their fear—and became ready to give the announcement. They turned their fear into confidence, a confidence that became hospitality. The community can give hospitality, and in turn it can also be hosted. There are other tents in the desert of postmodernity, which can be places of hospitality for each other, oases of truth and redemption.

As Mancini writes, "Intercultural encounter is the hermeneutical practice of correlating differences."[11] It is a never-ending operation as it is for every good hermeneutical process. Therefore, a real community is not just a physical place. We should overcome at last the old "them and us" mentality that based identity on exclusion (against someone) or on inclusion (that often means homologation and negation of the other's identity). First of all, community is relation; it is built on a communion principle.[12]

Tent as a Sign of a Non-definitive Place: Sign of the Kingdom

We can address our relational crises and choose to work out our anguish with love. We do not have to decide that the other is the enemy. Ecclesial community becomes the sign, temporary and necessary as well, of another tent, that of the divine: "And the Word became flesh, and dwelt among us" (literally in Greek: pitched a tent with us; John 1:14).

This human-divine tent, a sign of communion of God with humankind and among different human cultures and groups in every place and in every time, will become a place of listening, just as in the beginning it was a place of silence. There are too many words nowadays, but the promised humankind, as Mancini tells us, calls for a true silence. This silence is like a womb. It allows a distance, the right distance that we have seen earlier, where thought finds place, and where listening finds a deep sense, at last, among many questions and attempts to answer.

In this silent way, the church becomes a moving tent as it was for Israel during the exodus. It becomes a nomadic church living with nomadic people. So now the church finds itself out again in the meantime in the "not-yet" waiting for the definitive time. It looks to the somewhere else; it recognizes itself as a foreigner in a foreign land. So, the tradition, the good news, the truth that the church has on its shoulders, becomes really light and not too heavy to carry.

In this freedom and in this recovered lightness, the church lives again the first joyful day. Christians themselves will proclaim, "We hear them (the intercultural world!) in our *own* tongues speaking of the mighty deeds of God" (Acts 2:11). Christians can listen again to the hidden announcement of salvation this time from pagans of every place and every time.

In an intercultural way, the church can become a believing community again as it was in the beginning: a tent of listening and thus of silence and respect, a tent of mutual hospitality where no one loses one's own identity; instead one shares one's stories and one's life on the basis of a common human-divine dignity. Mancini himself appeals to Jesus on this point:

> We need to exit from the "propriety order.". . . Maybe we cannot avoid that religions were born as a form of appropriation of divine reality . . . but if they represent a specific embodiment of the loving relation between God and humankind, if believers listen to and know this movement of incarnation and they follow it, they are driven beyond the limits of a possessive order. Then, more than an exclusive belonging, what is important will be a new birth as children, as brothers and sisters; more than a representative dogmatic conscience, what will count is a more radical memory, the memory of the divine origin of all. . . . We don't have to abandon our own tradition. Instead, in this tent each of us could preserve our identity and culture, respecting those of other people. It is a question of letting the content of faith live, its representations and narratives, religious cultures and ethics inside the universal context of all being children of God. It is a question of doing and loving not as believers of a religion that has itself as its end, but as Jesus did.[13]

The main question underlying "exclusion" is about a new birth of Christian community itself, a church that once again puts in the center the listening to the divine word and different human words. At the end of this process and as an effect of this gestation, there will be a community ready to become mother not just of members of a congregation but of full human individuals signed by Christ's humanity, he that *pitched a tent with us*.

Notes

[1] Roberto Mancini, *L'ascolto come radice: Teoria dialogica della verità* (Naples: Edizioni Scientifiche Italiane, 1995). [All translations from the Italian were done by the author.]

[2] Roberto Mancini, *Il silenzio, via verso la vita* (Magnano, Italy: Qiqajon, 2002), 130.

[3] Mancini, *L'ascolto come radice*, 131.

[4] Ibid., 168.

[5] Cf. Mancini, *L'ascolto come radice*, 212.

[6] Ibid., 139–53.

[7] Robert Mancini, *L'uomo e la comunità* (Magnano, Italy: Qiqajon, 2004), 209.

[8] Ibid., 210.

[9] Ibid., 218.

[10] Ibid., 219. Here Mancini quotes Dietrich Bonhoeffer: "He who is alone with his sin is utterly alone" (see *Life Together*, trans. John W. Doberstein [New York: Harper and Row, 1954; German 1938], 110).

[11] Roberto Mancini, *Senso e futuro della política* (Assisi, Italy: Cittadella Editrice, 2002), 170.

[12] Cf. Roberto Mancini, *L'uomo e la comunità*, 10–11.

[13] Roberto Mancini, *L'umanità promessa: Vivere il cristianesimo nell'età della globalizzazione* (Magnano, Italy: Qiqajon, 2009), 60–63.

Ecclesiology and Exclusions in the Public Space:
A Political Perspective

Debora Spini

This essay does not originate in the field of theology, and it will not concentrate specifically on the topic of inclusion and exclusion within the Christian church community. Rather, it will reflect upon the specific condition of Christian religious groups in the public space. Its focus is the dynamics of exclusion and inclusion in public democratic spaces and whether these dynamics have a specific relationship with Christian religious groups.

I will articulate three main points. First of all, I will reflect about different forms of inclusion within the public space and what they mean for religious groups in modernity. I will then proceed to analyze how religious groups or, more precisely, Christian groups and churches situate themselves in the public space. I will close with a mildly provocative argument against the project of a "public theology," and in favor of a "theology in public."

Inclusion in the Public Space

In Western modernity the relationship between citizenship and religious identities has appeared under many different forms, but before this variety of forms might be taken into consideration, the origin of political modernity should be recalled. In fact, the very essence of modernity is connected to the quest for a space of human action independent from religion—the process commonly referred to as "secularization."[1]

Thomas Hobbes, a milestone in the modern conception of politics, articulates the relationship between "religion" and "politics" (both terms used in a broad, somehow rough sense) in such a manner that is not inappropriate to define as tragic. What we would call "religion" or, more precisely, beliefs in truths that go beyond the power of human reason, is presented by Hobbes as extremely dangerous for politics in that it constitutes a source of endless conflict. The ultimate goal of political action is, in fact, the achievement of peace, and religious strivings are the most dangerous of all, as the least reconcilable. In other words, religious conflicts are all the more harmful as they are grounded in a reference to a truth that transcends human understanding. Religious beliefs often promise punishments or rewards in the afterlife, thereby neutralizing the fear of death, which is the only possible barrier against war. Modern sovereignty— the power of an earthly, human authority—must be that "mortal god" capable of imposing peace. For this reason, in the Hobbesian model it is up to political authority to legislate in matters of religious belief. Political authorities need to exercise a firm control over religious groups if peace is to be maintained.

However, the mode of relationship between religion and politics that we may call "liberal," and whose origin is commonly associated with the name of John Locke, is no doubt the most long lived. It provides interesting insights for the concept of exclusion-inclusion, and, to a certain extent, we are still coming to terms with it today in our contemporary democratic societies. In the Lockean perspective—I am here taking as a reference *A Letter Concerning Toleration* (1689)—religion is expelled from the political sphere and firmly pushed back into the private sphere. The separation between the confessional and political dimensions of identity thus defuses their conflict-generating potential. Throughout history, the Lockean model developed into classic liberalism (from John Stuart Mill onward), which affirmed the need both for a separation between the dimensions of religion and politics and for the affirmation of the neutrality of the state vis-à-vis religious differences. Religious identities had to be pushed away from the public space, surely, so that no one should be excluded from the condition of citizenship because of one's beliefs. In light of this specific historical experience, neutrality was therefore perceived as inclusive. In their public life, individuals should consider themselves citizens first; all other determinations of identity are to be considered as "private" and therefore irrelevant for their political sphere of agency. The separation between a private and a public identity is still advocated today by some important voices: John Rawls's "political liberalism" is but one example.[2]

This model today is evidently challenged for a number of reasons that may be recalled only briefly here. It was born in a strictly European, intra-Christian context that surely does not resonate with other confessional or religious traditions. The separation between a "private" and a "public" sphere of life may come relatively easy to those who are part of a certain Christian theological lineage but is not so easy to operate with for those men and women who come, for example, from the Muslim tradition. In our contemporary democratic societies, the challenge is to come up with a redefinition of citizenship that does not require citizens to self-amputate themselves of their identity. In fact, today the simple claim of the neutrality by the state is no longer a guarantee for inclusion.

Modern politics has also provided other forms of inclusion besides liberal neutrality: this is the case with national identity. The "nation," as we all know, has been conceptualized differently in the European and in the American experience; however, as far as the construction of the modern European state is concerned, the reference to a nation has succeeded in replacing all prepolitical identities—such as local and confessional—with one "blanket" identity. A good example is provided by the "emancipation" and "assimilation" of Jews in nineteenth-century *Mitteleuropa*; for our present consideration, however, the best example is the French *républicanisme* that found in the *fraternité* provided by the possibility to identify in the nation a powerful social and political bond, coming first even before religious identities.

However, inclusion through assimilation is now challenged by all those processes that we currently define as globalization and that have transformed our societies. In Europe as well as in America, we are now confronted with democratic societies that are marked by profound cultural, linguistic, and religious differences, and we are all aware that no melting pot solution is readily at hand. This situation calls for the priority of the quest for a richer paradigm for citizenship, one that may permit a harmonizing of democracy and difference and that may go beyond an overly simple "multiculturalism." On this point, our democratic societies owe a major debt to the tradition of second-wave, difference-sensitive feminism that taught Western democracy that liberty is not about being equal, as it was for John Stuart Mill, when claiming that women just needed to be given a chance so that they could show they are "as good as men." Political thought and practices focusing on difference have indicated that equality is not about "being alike."[3]

Authentic democratic equality means equal possibilities to affirm differences in the public space as a richness not as a hindrance. The assumption behind these considerations is that being in the public space means to be confronted with alterity. We could, in quasi-Arendtian terms, call this condition the challenge of plurality; at any rate, the context of a democratic public space places the question of identity in a completely different light. A minimalist view sees democracy simply as a way to select leadership. In a very different light, democracy is that political system grounded upon the aspiration to preserve personal autonomy while at the same time living in society, as in the *Social Contract* of Rousseau. With the due differences, this aspiration is still at the heart of the Habermasian conception of politics.[4] Maintaining autonomy while living in society requires that political power be legitimated by consensus. "Majority wins."

We all know that this is the recipe for legitimate power; however, things are not so simple, as the crux of democratic life rests on how the will of the majority is to be formed. In other words, everything depends upon whether such a will consists simply of a sum of individual choices—a possibility that goes hand in hand with the minimalist view outlined above—or if it can be conceptualized as some sort of "public will." Such a public will will necessarily be very different from a strictly Rousseauian *volonté générale*. The latter, in fact, resulted from the interaction among individuals who entered the public arena unencumbered by any previous allegiance or membership so as to be completely devoted to the common *moi* constituted by the political community.[5] Today, this model is not only unrealistic but also undesirable. Citizens all come into the public spaces carrying with them a variety of preexisting definitions of identity. Democratic political communities therefore are faced with the challenge of providing the necessary conditions for the emergence of a public will. Among such preconditions, the existence of free, accessible, and genuinely "inclusive" public spaces is of paramount importance.

Public Spaces in a Changing Context

Public spaces today are different from those of early modernity, and surely politics are not confronted with the same set of issues that were around before Hobbes, Locke, and Rousseau. Today identity conflicts seem to be a typical feature of so-called postmodern societies; according to this perspective, the life of public spaces should be primarily dominated by identity-related issues rather than by redistribution conflicts—hence, there has appeared a new and stronger role for religious groups in general, with no exception for Christian churches and movements.[6] This affirmation, now quite common in scholarly works, should be questioned for at least one compelling reason. We must not forget, in the first place, that justice issues still exist at the heart of our so-called developed societies. Furthermore, justice issues now repropose themselves on a global scale, in the widening gap between what Bauman has called the "winners" and the "losers" of globalization.[7] This affirmation deserves to be further articulated, but for this essay I will concentrate on the issue of identity conflicts within democratic societies.

Our contemporary democracies are faced with the challenge of including citizens who do not necessarily share the same image of the world; the same conception of what is a "good" life; in a word, the same identity. Although not the sole cause of conflict in our contemporary world, "identity" definitely seems to be a crucial dimension in contemporary politics.[8] In this case, "identity" means the nucleus of values and images of the world that allow us to say "we," thus determining inclusion or exclusion from a particular community or group. Given this definition, it is clear why religious beliefs may be relevant for the determination of collective identities and consequently why religious beliefs could play a role in identity conflicts. Moreover, identity and citizenship interact in contemporary democracies in terms that are extremely different from those typical of the onset of modernity and that motivated the neutralist paradigm. As brilliantly indicated by Gauchet,[9] today individuals feel part of the public space not *despite* their identities but *because* they participate in a shared identity that is, to a certain extent, independent from that provided by citizenship. In fact, in a fully developed modernity, individuals do not inherit (from birth, or tradition) their identities; rather, identity is the result of a conscious choice, of an affirmation of subjectivity, which is, in turn, at the root of democratic politics. Therefore, in a democratic polity identity determinations cannot be separated from the condition of citizenship.

On the other hand, the reference to a shared national identity, which was typical of the French *républicanisme*, does not itself provide a viable option. The key actor of modernity—the national territorial state—finds it hard to fulfill its traditional functions, such as providing security, which were identified by Hobbes as the key to legitimacy. This difficulty should not be restricted to military issues or to the "war against terror" but should be analyzed in a wider perspective. States are incapable of facing a new generation of risks or challenges that deserve to be called "global," as they could, potentially, question the very existence of the planet.[10] States also find it increasingly hard to enforce those redistribution mechanisms that permitted them to provide the social rights that constituted, especially in Europe, a key dimension of citizenship. Last but not least, in our global political scenario unprecedented forms of political integration, such as the European Union, exist side by side with extreme trends toward political fragmentation, in a condition that has been defined as "fragmegrated," that is, marked by a combination of fragmentation and integration.[11] Correspondingly, new and fertile forms of hybrid identities coexist with unexpected phenomena of identity reentrenchment that deserved the definition of "new tribalism," as in Michel Maffesoli,[12] and that have often escalated into ethnic or religious violence. Given these premises, it is not hard to see why that "blanket identity" represented by a reference to the nation has lost its appeal.

But if the liberal and the nation-based republican models are under strain, still it is not clear what alternatives might be available. Taking a distance from false neutrality or republican nostalgia, of course, does not obliterate the need either to find a *modus vivendi* among different identities or to provide a context where individuals may perceive themselves as members of a political community. Some extreme version of multiculturalism—those that have been described with the metaphor of a "tossed salad"—do not hope for anything more than a peaceful coexistence among different "identities" and have little or no expectation about the capacity, or the inclination, of different groups to engage with each other in the quest for some kind of shared ground. The paradigm of recognition, as articulated by Axel Honneth in his original reelaboration of Hegel, has provided a fertile way out of this dilemma.[13] Recognition as a social grammar goes well beyond neutrality and allows for the formation of individual identity as well as social relationships. In this perspective, different identities engage in dynamics of recognition among themselves as well as receiving recognition by the state.

Applying the paradigm of recognition to our contemporary public spaces does foster genuine inclusion, but it does not come without a price. Seen from the side of the state's attitude toward different groups, recognition implies overcoming the ideal of neutrality to move forward toward a public appreciation of identity. Recognition can, in fact, be conceptualized in terms of redistribution, though it is redistribution of a very special category of "social goods" such as, for example, respect and esteem.[14] Seen from the side of the relationships between different groups within the public space of a democratic state, the paradigm of recognition requires paying an even higher price. Every group that wishes to participate in the "game" of recognition has to be prepared to be somehow transformed in the process, "losing" and "gaining" at the same time. At the heart of recognition is, in fact, a dialectical relationship that is necessarily transformative. This makes it necessary to differentiate between aspects of identity that can be forsaken and those that cannot.

The question "What should we hang on to?" becomes, of course, particularly relevant in view of the conception of democracy briefly outlined at the end of the previous section as it may have a major influence in determining what kind of public "conversations" can help men and women to define their political orientation and, consequently, to elaborate a "public will." Mainstream liberalism provides a clear and effective answer. In the public space citizens engage in deliberations being guided by their reason; their self-interest; and, in the case of Rawls, by their basic sense of justice. Ultimately, this perspective contemplates the possibility of reaching a consensus such as that which can be expected among rational beings.[15] This conception implies that public spaces should be occupied only by issues that can be solved on an immanent plane, resorting to arguments that can be ascertained on the basis of human reason, and that discussions on conceptions of "Good" with the capital G should be kept off the table. A separate mention should be made of the Habermasian perspective, which opens a different line of reflection, presenting a view of democratic societies as the seat not only of deliberation but also of an incessant activity of "mutual explanation" in the light of a wider framework of a discursive conception of ethics.

It is almost redundant to point out how important this model is, and yet this essay will not embrace it but will rather look at other perspectives that follow a very different pattern and that emerge from a distinct array of contrasting anthropological assumptions.[16] In this light, politics has to do with much more, and much else, than rational choices: political choices, beliefs, and behaviors originate and develop in a more complex and elusive sphere. The nonrational fabric of politics is composed by passions, deep-set fears, "habits of the heart." Adopting this richer view of political agency makes it, of course, harder to imagine public spaces where citizens can actually reach consensus. In this perspective, the life of democratic society has a much wider range of tasks to accomplish besides the redistribution of resources, and therefore citizens of democratic polities need a much wider and more complex set of motivational resources than the quest for justice and the appeal to reason and fairness.

From this point of view, the paradigm of recognition can be fruitfully integrated by another perspective, that of the narrative conception of identity as elaborated by Paul Ricoeur.[17] In Ricoeur's view, identity is a narrative, a process that needs a narrator and a listener. It has thus an irretrievably intersubjective relationship. The presence of the listener makes it necessary for the narrator to "explain," to "make sense" of the narrative. A narrative dialogue requires a level of attention and participation that goes beyond the request for rational consensus, a level in which both parties are engaged on a deeper level. Narrator and listener do not simply agree "rationally" but meet on the level of existential experience. In this perspective, democratic public spaces perform the crucial task of providing the adequate framework for this kind of narrative dialogue, which could bring new flesh and blood to the life of our polities. Still, the question of whether it is possible to tame and groom identity so completely that it no longer represents a nonexploded bomb in the public space remains open. Amartya Sen's solution, to disentangle culture and identity, is important, but does not solve every dilemma.[18] Collective identities often are based on a core that is intrinsically resistant to every form of reduction to discourse. Public spaces therefore do not exhaust their sphere of agency in the quest for consensus but remain confronted with the task of dealing with conflict.

Why "Theology in Public" Is Better Than "Public Theology"

Do religious groups—or even better, Christian confessions—have a specific way of being in the public space? Is anything the matter with them that makes their presence in the public space in any way more problematic than that of most other groups? Indeed, something is the matter with religious groups, even with Christian churches. Augustine reminds us that Christians live in this world holding a sort of "double citizenship." Using Hobbes's language (though taken out of his context), Christians do come from the kingdom of darkness—the realm of attempted interpretations of what cannot be explained. The previous paragraph has discussed the relationship between identity and politics. Religious groups—and Christian churches are not an exception—constitute a very special source of collective identities. Today, some interpreters of modernity, Sloterdijk to take but the most illustrious example, pose the question of whether monotheism does not represent a specific form of identity that, by its very nature, is prone to exclusion and violence because of its specific relationship with an exclusivist view of "truth."[19] There is no need to embrace such an extreme view to recognize that, in fact, religious groups—or at least revelation-based religious groups (again, Christians are no exception)—may not appear as the best candidates to engage in public conversations precisely because of their reference to a "somewhere else." In recent years, many interpreters—the reference is obviously to Habermas's reflection on faith and science—have tried to construct a bridge between theology and "rational" thought. In this perspective, nonreligious citizens are required to accept the value of religious beliefs as based on a different validity claim than rational affirmation, while religious citizens are required to submit their ethical beliefs to the discursive practices of democratic polities. These efforts have indeed performed an important function, as they have contributed in clearing from the atmosphere the last shades of positivist attitudes. However, this essay takes the liberty of assuming a different point of view.

After this long excursus on democratic public spaces, it is now high time to go back to the topic of this conference, "Ecclesiology and Exclusion." In light of what has been briefly mentioned above, inclusion takes on a meaning wider than what had originally been suggested by the term. Inclusion does not mean to "belong" to a community because of a shared common identity. In a democratic public space, "inclusion" means for individuals and groups to have the possibility of participating in the creation of a public will. This understanding of inclusion does not seek to eliminate differences but rests on a vision of public spaces as marked by plurality.

We have been discussing inclusion and exclusion both within the church and in the relationship between the church and "the world." Here,

I would like to provocatively propose to think in terms of the paradox of inclusiveness: a too broad inclusion risks leaning toward the opposite direction, that is, toward the marginalization of differences. More practically, I would simply like to introduce a few distinctions between the ecclesiological and the political level.

How much of their identity are churches required to negotiate in the public sphere? This problem applies to all religious groups, or at least this is valid for the Abrahamic religions, as they all share a reference to a transcendental sphere. Nonetheless, concentrating solely on Christian churches, their situation in the public space could be summed up provocatively in the affirmation that the less inclusive they are the better. Churches should relinquish a lot and, at the same time, negotiate very little. Of course, this provocation needs to be explained. Churches or religious groups have sometimes cultivated the aspiration—that in some cases could be named even as intellectual arrogance—to accommodate and reconcile their message to the level of some kind of public ethic or civic ethos. This is what I meant when I said I was going to make a case against public theology, if this definition indicates a theological approach aiming at interacting on an even basis with public ethics and political values. This kind of public theology contains a hidden risk: that of Christian communities giving in to a temptation of seeing themselves as the only possible source of ethical orientation for our political communities.

The churches' role is not to provide a "minimum common denominator" on ethical and social matters that could be "spent" in the public space and that could nourish the claim to consensus. Christian churches are not the "ethics departments" in our advanced democracies. Of course, churches can and must advocate for the freedom to express themselves on issues of· common concern, and they cannot do so insofar as churches see themselves as components of civil society, which is indeed the realm of free thoughts and speech. They should not be tempted to act as "providers of values" for a democratic politics that is is—supposedly—incapable of finding its own foundation. One might recall here the well-known debate between Habermas and Böckenförde.[20] However inviting it might be, the role of churches is not to provide "reasonable comprehensive doctrines," to use a Rawlsian term.

The Christian message cannot be completely domesticated within the realm of human reason, nor should it be reduced to a basis for moral decency. The kerygma that is at the very core of Christian identity only loses, and does not gain, in freedom and meaning when it tries to accommodate itself with human reason. The gospel is a folly, Erasmus said with the words of Paul the Apostle. In other terms, Christian churches are living in witness of a word that cannot be reduced to political categories: agape is not a political concept; agape is more than justice, even more than solidarity. The challenge for Christians is to live up to the vision and promise of an agapic community being at the same time fully aware that this witness has to take place in the city of man.

Affirming that Christian witness has to keep its basic *otherness* is not tantamount to some kind of postmodern integralism; on the contrary, Christian churches should not think in terms of "including" all reasons and points of view. The point is not to be all embracing—which would be yet another way of saying *extra ecclesia nulla salus*. Rather, churches should be aware of their partiality—of representing a "confessing" identity in the spirit of those who say "Here I stand, I can do no more." Churches should not see themselves as providers of a public ethic meant as a viewpoint that could claim consensus but as proclaimers of the word of God in the full awareness that no human discourse alone can ever enshrine, comprehend, or exhaust the living force of the gospel. In this perspective, it is clear that the basic point of a truly inclusive action of churches in the public space is to respect alterity without attempting to annihilate it and to overcome difference. Finding common ground for citizens' deliberations and for public conversation is the task of politics, not of the churches.

This is why this paper closes with a mild provocation against "public theology." The need to reflect theologically on issues of public concern is not here in question, and from this point of view, engaging with "public theology" is more of a duty than an option for Christian churches. However, theology cannot be public, because it is based on assumptions that are completely dis-homogenous from those arguments that may be used in the public sphere. "Doing theology" is a work that is constantly reminded of the radical alterity of the gospel vis-à-vis all other human discourses and has given up, once and for all, any claim to a reconciliation between "faith and reason." A "theology in public," on the contrary, could be a way of doing theology that is, on the one hand, "in the world" engaged with the issues and the tragedies of our time, engaged with the men and women who live in it, and at the same time profoundly aware of the presence of a "mystery" whose content can never be rationalized or explained. Christian theological reflection, and more importantly practice, suggests a view of inclusion that does not coincide with homogenization; it does not rest on the comforting thought that "after all, we are all more or less alike." Inclusion is about honoring the mystery of difference.

Notes

[1] The various understandings of secularization, ranging from Weber to Blumenberg to end with Gauchet and Taylor cannot be here discussed in detail, although, of course, this debate constitutes a sort of background for this paper.

[2] John Rawls, *Political Liberalism* (Cambridge: Cambridge University Press, 1993).

[3] Here I refer to the school of feminist thought that moves from the acceptance of "sexual difference," primarily Luce Irigaray and Adriana Cavarero. For a reflection about democracy and difference, the work of Iris M. Young remains a milestone.

[4] Jürgen Habermas, *Between Facts and Norms: Contributions to a Discourse Theory of Law and Democracy* (Cambridge, MA: MIT Press, 1998).

[5] The reference is to chapter III in book II of the *Social Contract*.

[6] Personally I do not consider the expression "postmodernity" as the best possible term to capture the transformations of modernity that are currently taking place. Following Ulrich Beck I would rather suggest the term "second modernity."

[7] Zygmunt Bauman, *In Search of Politics* (Cambridge: Polity, 1999).

[8] It is important to differentiate between personal and collective identities and also between cultural identity and a specifically political identity. Politics refers to the political principles and values that an individual or collectivity stand for; cultural identity is different in that is connected to our *lebenswelt*, to our maternal language expressed in our traditions.

[9] Marcel Gauchet, *La Religion dans la démocratie : parcours de la laïcité* (Paris: Gallimard, 1998).

[10] Furio Cerutti, *Global Challenges for Leviathan: A Political Philosophy of Nuclear Weapons and Global Warming* (Lanham, MD: Rowman & Littlefield, 2007).

[11] James N. Rosenau, *Distant Proximities: Dynamics beyond Globalization* (Princeton, NJ: Princeton University Press, 2003).

[12] Michel Maffesoli, *The Time of the Tribes: The Decline of Individualism in Mass Society* (London: Sage, 1996).

[13] Axel Honneth, *The Struggle for Recognition: The Moral Grammar of Social Conflicts* (Cambridge, MA: MIT Press, 1996).

[14] Nancy Fraser and Alex Honneth, *Umverteilung oder Annerkennung? Eine politisch-philosophische Kontroverse* (Frankfurt/Main, Germany: Suhrkamp, 2003).

[15] John Rawls, *A Theory of Justice* (Cambridge, MA: The Belknap Press of Harvard University, 1971); also T. M. Scanlon, "Rawls on Justification," in *The Cambridge Companion to Rawls*, ed. S. Freeman (Cambridge: Cambridge University Press, 2002), 139–67.

[16] Gauchet, *La Religion dans la démocratie*.

[17] Paul Ricoeur, *Time and Narrative* (*Temps et Récit*), 3 vols., trans. Kathleen McLaughlin and David Pellauer (Chicago: University of Chicago Press, 1984, 1985, 1988 [1983, 1984, 1985]).

[18] Amartya Sen, *Identity and Violence: The Illusion of Destiny* (New York: W. W. Norton, 2006).

[19] Peter Sloterdijk, *God's Zeal: The Battle of the Three Monotheisms* (Cambridge: Polity Press, 2009).

[20] Jürgen Habermas and Joseph Ratzinger, *The Dialectics of Secularization: On Reason and Religion* (San Francisco: Ignatius Press, 2006); Ernst-Wolfgang Böckenförde originally proposed the paradox of a modern world that needs to rely on internal controls that it cannot provide without renouncing its own liberalism in "Die Entstehung des Staates als Vorgang der Säkularisation," in *Säkularisation und Utopie. Ebracher Studien. Ernst Forsthoff zum 65. Geburtstag* (Stuttgart, Germany: K. Doering & W. G. Greve Hrsg, 1967).

PART II

EXCLUSION AND MARGINAL PEOPLE

The Catholic Church and
the Immigration Crisis in the Americas

Mark Ensalaco

The Catholic Church in the United States began calling for comprehensive immigration reform well before Congress took up the controversial issue at the end of President Bush's second term in office. In 2003 the Catholic bishops of the United States and Mexico published a pastoral letter, "Strangers No Longer: Together on a Journey of Hope," that called on Catholics to stand in solidarity with migrants and framed a set of moral principles and policy guidelines aimed at creating a "more just and generous immigration system."[1] The following year the United States Conference of Catholic Bishops (USCCB) launched its Justice for Migrants campaign to advocate for enactment of legislation that would, among other things, create a path to citizenship for the more than ten million undocumented migrants living in the United States. It appeared that Congress was disposed to act when President Bush appealed to Congress to resolve the status of the more than ten million illegal immigrants living in the United States: "We need to resolve the status of the illegal immigrants who are already in our country, without animosity and without amnesty. Let us have a serious, civil, and conclusive debate so that you can pass—and I can sign—comprehensive immigration reform into law."[2] Six months later, however, after a national debate that was far from civil, the Senate defeated comprehensive immigration reform by a fourteen-vote margin. The question of amnesty figured prominently in the debate.

The defeat left the professional staff of the USCCB pondering what more they could have done. The bishops' Committee on Migration and the Migration and Refugee Services had framed a set of reasonable and humane policy guidelines concerned with enforcement policies, a guest workers program, and creating a path to legalization and family reunification. But the opponents of the bipartisan legislation in Congress cleverly portrayed the legislation as a sweeping amnesty that rewarded illegal aliens for breaking the law. The consensus among the bishops' professional staff was that, although they themselves had gotten the policy right, the opposition had won the debate by framing the political message. In fact, the opposition had come close to the truth by claiming the bishops favored amnesty. "Strangers No Longer" categorically asserts the right of illegal migrants to seek work in the United States, an assertion that does not resonate with most Americans.

As the USCCB renews its Justice for Migrants campaign, it is worthwhile to reexamine "Strangers No Longer." The letter is important not only as a statement of the church's position on immigration policy but also as an expression of the church's vision of justice and as a proclamation of the church's identity and mission. "Strangers No Longer," in addition to being a statement about justice for migrants, is also an exposition on ecclesiology. Catholics should take it seriously.

Immigration and the Social Doctrine of the Church

The Catholic Church, as an important institution in the United States, played a preeminent role in the advocacy campaign to promote comprehensive immigration reform. But the church is not an advocacy organization. It is the people of God who share the joys and hopes, the griefs and anxieties of the poor and afflicted (*Gaudium et Spes* 1). It is a community of faith entrusted with the prophetic mission to proclaim the gospel and promote justice and denounce injustice. Its advocacy for the fundamental human rights of migrants, informed by its evolving social doctrine, is integral to its mission to evangelize. Through its advocacy the church bears authentic witness to the gospel. This is the Catholic Church's understanding of its social advocacy and the inspiration that instructs the development of the church's social doctrine.

Vatican II deepened this understanding through its call for dialogue with the world and its commitment to the rights and duties, needs and legitimate aspirations, and indeed "the general welfare of the entire human family" (*Gaudium et Spes* 26). But the church's social doctrine predates Vatican II. The church's pastoral concern for migrants, in particular, can be traced back to Pius XII's "On the Spiritual Care of Migrants." For more than a half century, the church has repeatedly asserted claims with regard to the rights of migrants that no secular human rights organization asserts.[3] Indeed, the church's teaching seems almost radical in comparison with the consensus norms of international human rights law.

The American Bishops' Appeal for Justice for Migrants

The church's social doctrine gives the American bishops' advocacy for comprehensive immigration reform the unique moral cogency reflected in "Strangers No Longer." The bishops, as pastors, were motivated to address the question of illegal migration because they said "migrants and immigrants are in our parishes and in our communities. In both our countries, we see much injustice and violence against them and much suffering and despair among them" (para. 5). They found it impossible to ignore the plight of migrants, saying, "We judge ourselves as a community of faith by the way we treat the most vulnerable among us" (para. 6). As a community of faith, the church had to be active in "promoting justice and in denouncing injustice towards migrants and immigrants, courageously defending their basic human rights" (para. 43).

In the interest of justice "Strangers No Longer" enunciated a set of normative principles drawn from the church's social doctrine that encompasses the right of all persons to find opportunities to live in dignity in their own country and to migrate to support their families when those opportunities are lacking; the conditional right of states to control their territories; the international community's obligation to protect refugees and asylum-seekers; and governments' obligations to protect the dignity and rights of migrants regardless of their immigration status. There is nothing controversial about the assertions that all persons have a right to a life of dignity in their own country, that the international community should protect refugees and asylum-seekers, or that governments should respect the dignity and rights of migrants. International human rights conventions affirm these basic human rights and humanitarian principles.

However, international human rights law simply does not support either the bishops' assertions with regard to the right of migrants to seek work in other countries or the conditions they place on sovereign states' right to control their borders. "Strangers No Longer" categorically asserts that "when persons cannot find employment in their country of origin to support themselves and their families, they have a right to find work elsewhere in order to survive," and that "sovereign nations should provide ways to accommodate this right." Moreover, "more powerful economic nations, which have the ability to protect and feed their residents, have a stronger obligation to accommodate migration flows." Therefore, while "the Church recognizes the right of sovereign nations to control their territories," it "rejects such control when it is exerted merely for the purpose of acquiring additional wealth" (paras. 34–39).

These assertions stand in stark contrast to the provisions of international human rights law, principally the 1951 Convention on the Status of Refugees and more relevantly the 1990 Convention on the Rights of All Migrant Workers and Their Families. The Refugee Convention is hardly relevant at all, because undocumented migrants in the United States generally are neither refugees nor asylum-seekers under the convention's definition. More problematically, the Convention on the Rights of All Migrant Workers and Their Families, which generally concerns only the rights of documented migrant workers, recognizes neither the "right" of undocumented workers to cross national frontiers in search of work without authorization nor the "obligation" of any state to accommodate migration flows. To the contrary, the convention specifically obligates states to take measures to prevent and eliminate the clandestine movement and employment of undocumented migrants and to impose effective sanctions on both smugglers and the employers of undocumented workers with the sole limitation that states cannot resort to collective expulsion (arts. 68 and 22). The only provision of the convention that accommodates the bishops' appeal for justice for migrants is found in Article 69, which implies that states with large numbers of undocumented workers should "consider the possibility of regularizing the situation of [undocumented migrant workers] in accordance with applicable national legislation and bilateral or multilateral agreements."

The very purpose of the bishops' legislative advocacy, of course, was to induce Congress to reform the "applicable national legislation." During the debate, the bishops raised pragmatic concerns, for example, the impracticability of deporting tens of millions of immigrants filling labor-intensive jobs few Americans wanted. But, fundamentally, the bishops ground their claims in Catholic social teaching's categorical claims about migrants' rights rather than in international human rights law. In support of the claim that migrants have the right to seek work in foreign lands, the bishops cite the authority of John XIII: "Every human being has the right to freedom of movement and of residence within the confines of his own country; and, when there are just reasons for it, the right to emigrate to other countries and take up residence there" (*Pacem in Terris* 25). The American bishops openly asserted this position in congressional testimony.[4] The bishops cite Paul VI in defense of the assertion that wealthy states have a special obligation to accommodate migrant flows because "all the goods of the earth belong to all people."[5] Here, the bishops implicitly drew upon Catholic social teaching regarding the universal destination of goods, a doctrine that clashes with most Americans' beliefs about private property rights as well as the consensus norms of the international community with regard to state economic sovereignty. These are not popular positions. But in framing the issues this way, the bishops remained faithful to the church's prophetic mission to proclaim the gospel and its social teaching regarding the radical equality and natural unity of the human family.

The fulfillment of this prophetic mission is seen too in the bishops' denunciation of injustice. "Strangers No Longer" raises a number of serious concerns in the context of their appeals for humane enforcement policies. The bishops express "alarm" at xenophobic and racist attitudes that result in the treatment of migrants as criminals, the "shameful" handling of unaccompanied minors, abuse of migrants by American border patrol agents, and border enforcement policies that contribute to the deaths of migrants in both Mexico and the United States (paras. 80–82 and 86–87). The bishops' most severe criticism is directed at corruption, brutality, and "systematic abuses of basic human rights" of Mexican law enforcement officials as well "bandits" who extort and abuse migrants attempting to reach the United States (para. 83). To be sure, most migrants' rights advocacy groups raise these same concerns. "Strangers No Longer," however, is distinctive in its tone. It is a pastoral letter rather than the report of a human rights organization, and, as such, "Strangers No Longer" draws upon the church's ancient tradition of prophetic denunciation, which appeals to biblical teaching rather than to secular human rights agreements.

Yet "Strangers No Longer" can be criticized for its failure to denounce the Mexican state's systemic failures to provide the economic, political, and social opportunities that would enable Mexican citizens to live in dignity in their own country. The bishops came close to such a criticism only once when they noted, "In the current condition of the world, in which global poverty and persecution are rampant, the presumption is that persons must migrate in order to support and protect themselves" (para. 39). Here the bishops do imply that Mexican migrants are fleeing the poverty and persecution rampant in Mexico, but it is only an implication. The bishops continue the gentle treatment of the Mexican state in their analysis of the root cause of migration. The bishops attribute migration to the economic inequality *between* Mexico and the United States resulting, in part, from the implementation of the North American Free Trade Agreement (NAFTA) (paras. 59 and 60). The bishops are silent, however, concerning the endemic and widening economic inequalities *within* Mexico, inequalities aggravated by the same neo-liberal economic policies that prompted Mexican authorities to ratify NAFTA. The bishops might have called attention to the tragic fact that more than three-quarters of a million persons, the majority of them Mexican citizens, flee their homelands each year to search for opportunities in the United States.[6] Instead of placing some of the moral burden on Mexico, the bishops gently call on Mexico to "create economic opportunities to help reduce poverty and mitigate the incentive for many migrants to look for employment in the United States" (para. 61). The implication of the bishops here is that the United States principally bears the responsibility to resolve the immigration crisis through the enactment of comprehensive immigration reform. This is an implicit position the bishops would do well to reconsider as they renew the Justice for Migrants campaign.

Conclusion

"Strangers No Longer" is an important statement of principle and policy. But it is important also for what it reveals about the church's understanding of its mission in the world, a mission that imposes a duty to "make judgments on human affairs to the extent that they are required by the fundamental rights of the human person."[7] That mission inspires the church's social doctrine. As the USCCB renews its efforts to promote comprehensive immigration reform, it is important to mobilize the support of American Catholics who are generally suspicious about immigration and immigrants, despite the bishops' strong support for migrants' rights.[8] American Catholics, especially those in influential positions in government and business, should be mindful that the church's social doctrine, as it relates to migrants, is an integral aspect of its moral teaching and that, therefore, as the people of God, they have an obligation to adhere to it.[9]

Notes

[1] United States Conference of Catholic Bishops, Inc. and *Conferencia del Episcopado Mexicano*, "Strangers No Longer: Together on a Journey of Hope" (2003), http://usccb.org/issues-and-action/human-life-and-dignity/immigration/strangers-no-longer-together-on-the-journey-of-hope.cfm.

[2] President George W. Bush, "State of the Union Address 2007," January 23, 2007.

[3] See Pius XII, *Exsul Familia*, and his radio address on Christmas 1952; John XIII, *Pacem in Terris*; Paul XI, *Pastoralis Migratorum*; John Paul II, *Ecclesia in America*.

[4] Testimony of Most Reverend Thomas G. Wenski, Bishop of Orlando, Florida, before the House Subcommittee on Immigration, Citizenship, Refugees, Border Security, and International Law on Comprehensive Immigration Reform, May 22, 2007.

[5] New Norms for the Care of Migrants, "*Pastoralis Migratorum*" (1969), no. 7.

[6] Jeffrey Passel, "The Size and Characteristics of the Unauthorized Migrant Population in the United States," *PEW Hispanic Research Center*, March 2005.

[7] Pontifical Council of Justice and Peace, *Compendium of the Social Doctrine of the Church*, no. 71.

[8] Gregory Smith, "Attitudes toward Immigration: In the Pulpit and the Pew," *PEW Research Center Publications*, April 2006.

[9] *Compendium of the Social Doctrine of the Church*, no. 80.

"But I See That Somebody Is Missing": Ecclesiology and Exclusion in the Context of Immigration

Gioacchino Campese

"I see finally that this church is full again, and I am happy to notice that very many of you have returned. But I also see that somebody is missing. You can realize it yourselves. John is not here. Do you remember him? He came to church every Sunday. Missing are also Christian and Laurent. And Didou, the little Didou. His parents are missing. They were like you, with darker skin. They came from Africa. They are not here because they have been kicked out."[1] These are the words of Father Pino Carrà, the Roman Catholic pastor of Rosarno, a small town in Calabria (southern Italy), during his first Sunday homily after the riots that, at the beginning of January 2010, made this place famous, or better infamous, around the world.[2] In this territory controlled by the local mafia, a very powerful criminal organization known as "*ndrangheta*," lived hundreds of African immigrants who worked in the citrus groves in subhuman conditions. They accepted the work that Italians do not want to do anymore with long working hours and a miserable salary, just as has happened in the United States. Like the great majority of immigrants working in Italian agriculture, they experience exploitation and structural violence.

When this violence became unbearable, that is, after two of them were shot at by some local people, these African immigrants rioted. As a response, the Italian government intervened by relocating all of them elsewhere in southern Italy. The Italian government did not launch a serious investigation about the real causes of these riots. It did not ask who and what were really causing this violence. It just kicked out the most vulnerable people involved, the immigrants who were, as a matter of fact, the only people courageous enough to react against the all-pervasive influence and power of the *ndrangheta*. The Italian mass media showed the violence caused by these riots, but most of the reporters did not ask questions about the underlying situation of structural violence and illegality.[3]

From across the ocean, precisely from Postville (Iowa), comes the extremely moving witness of Sr. Mary McCauley concerning a parallel incident in the United States. Sr. McCauley is the Roman Catholic pastoral administrator of St. Bridget's Parish in this little town where, on May 12, 2008, there took place the largest raid of a workplace in U.S. history: 389 people working at the Agriprocessors meat-packing plant were detained by the agents of ICE (Immigration and Customs Enforcement). Sr. McCauley expressed shock and sorrow at the immense pain inflicted on these immigrant workers and their families: many parents were separated from their little children, some were deported, and many were physically and verbally abused during the raid by ICE agents. All of them, immigrant workers who were working hard under appalling conditions, sacrificing their bodies to earn a decent living, were treated as criminals. At the same time, Sr. McCauley underlined the extraordinary resolve, strength, and hope of these people in this time of trial and the great solidarity of a Christian community that has sustained them throughout this hardship. We will return to this event and to Sr. McCauley's words.[4]

I start my reflections on ecclesiology and exclusion in the context of immigration by recalling these two real life stories happening in different parts of the world for four main reasons: first, because I believe that theology, and therefore ecclesiology, must start from reality, the real issues that real people have to deal with every day. It is crucial to underscore this point in an era in which it has become easier to choose "virtual reality," especially thanks to the influence of the mass media.[5] Second, I want to affirm the social location from which my thought is articulated: it is a transnational location, not only because this is how it should be when it comes to migration, but especially because of my personal experience. I have been ministering with immigrants and studying this phenomenon at the border between Mexico and the United States at Tijuana and in Chicago from 1995 to 2005, and I have since returned to Italy, my home country, a nation that has been changing, particularly in the last thirty years, becoming both a country of emigration and a country of immigration. In both cases, the U.S. and the Italian, the issue of memory is fundamental because both countries know only too well what it means to be a migrant. The problem is that we tend to forget or neglect our history of migration. Third, I want to demonstrate that immigrants, especially asylum seekers, refugees, and undocumented people, are really and painfully experiencing exclusion in our societies and, unfortunately, also in our Christian communities. Fourth, there is a need to point out that a significant part of our societies and

Christian communities care and struggle to include newcomers and to keep alive the memories and experiences of migrations.

This essay will be divided into three parts. The first one will provide elements for a portrait of the situation in the United States and Italy in terms of immigration and exclusion. The second part will pose the following question: What does academic ecclesiology say about this situation and the whole issue of migration? The third part will offer some suggestions about the fundamental importance of the issue of immigration for ecclesiology today. It is important for the readers to know that these reflections have been elaborated from a Roman Catholic perspective, the tradition to which I belong, the same tradition that teaches me to develop and maintain at all times an ecumenical and interreligious sensitivity.

The Situation: Italy and the United States

I am fully aware of the great differences existing between the U.S. and Italian contexts and their complexities, but in this analysis I will focus on some of the similarities between these two countries in terms of immigration and exclusion without the pretension that this is an exhaustive reading of these transnational realities. I will direct my attention to some of the most vulnerable immigrants who are the asylum seekers and the undocumented.

There are a number of elements in common between the United States and Italy in terms of the reality of exclusion in the context of migration. First, immigration is one of the main issues that both countries must face from historical, social, cultural, political and religious viewpoints. Immigrants contribute considerably to the life of both countries, but their arrival, presence, and contributions cause a variety of very strong reactions: understanding and confusion, welcoming and rejection, hope and fear.

Second, immigrants arrive in Italy and the United States because there are specific jobs available to them, jobs that natives simply avoid because of low salaries and the image of low social status attached to them. They are the so-called 3D jobs (dangerous, dirty, and demanding) that are found mostly in the fields of agriculture, construction, domestic work and care, cleaning, and other services.[6]

Third, some politicians in Italy and the United States are exploiting immigration for their election campaigns both at the national and local levels, and some of them have been successful. For instance, some of the members of the most anti-immigrant party in Italy, the Lega Nord, belong to the political coalition that currently governs Italy. Instead of responding to the understandable fear and suspicion of natives with rational arguments and initiatives, these politicians nurture that fear by enacting and implementing restrictive and useless laws and by speaking of immigration and immigrants in terms of invasion, plague, rats, clandestine people, illegal aliens, and so on. In the last fifteen to twenty years some of these politicians have, on various occasions, publicly affirmed that we should use cannons and machine guns to stop migrants from entering Italy. Also, in the United States this kind of political attitude and language has been repeatedly used by some politicians. Quite recently Kansas lawmaker Virgil Peck has said that undocumented immigrants should be shot from helicopters like feral hogs.[7]

Fourth, some of the people who govern our countries think and want people to think that immigration can be stopped with the construction of highly sophisticated walls, thousands of border patrol agents, and the so-called attrition strategy, which means to make the life of immigrants unbearable by implementing state and federal laws that, for instance, make their access to the public health system extremely difficult or make it almost impossible for them to rent a house in a particular state, county, or city.[8] A *New York Times* editorial published in 2007 rightly observed that some political leaders think of immigration reform in the U.S. in terms of "pest control."[9]

The increasingly restrictive and, we dare to say, violent character of immigration politics and policies—not limited only to the success of the extreme right parties and politicians in Europe and the United States, but already used by the more moderate parties and politicians who resort to the same anti-immigrant rhetoric to not lose voters—has led some scholars to talk about "institutional racism" or "racism of the state." State and national governments and congresses themselves have become the agents of racial discrimination against immigrants by the laws that they implement and with their public speech.[10]

To be more concrete, in recent years we have seen in the United States the case of the Arizona bill known as SB 1070 signed into law by Governor Jan Brewer in April 2010[11] and the umpteenth repeal by the Congress of the DREAM Act, a bill that would give hope to at least two million young immigrants who have arrived in the United States as minors. In Italy we have witnessed the adoption of the so-called security package proposed by the Berlusconi government and officially made into law by Congress in August 2009, a bill that, as its title clearly implies, deals with immigration as if it were solely a security issue.[12] These are revealing examples of just how ineffective, and we might add irrational, is the approach of governments to the phenomenon of human migration. These approaches do not tackle the real issues at stake such as the integration of immigrants in our societies, the management of the millions of undocumented immigrants who are necessary but often unwanted members of our communities, and the larger questions connected with how labor is related to immigration. The problem is that this approach might be socially ineffective, but it has very painful and at times mortal consequences for the lives of immigrants.

Fifth, precisely because of this irrational approach based solely on security, immigrants are dying by the thousands in the seas, rivers, and deserts at the borders between nations in their journeys toward what they consider the promised land, and while they are working in subhuman conditions in their new countries of residence. Years ago I witnessed the death of hundreds of immigrants at the U.S.-Mexico border, and I am now witnessing the death of hundreds of immigrants in the Mediterranean Sea whose transformation is briefly, but thoroughly, described by a very recent editorial of the well-known Italian review *Famiglia Cristiana*.

This is the Mediterranean Sea that for centuries has been the space of coexistence of civilizations and religions and the crossroads of peoples coming from different continents, the sea that the ancient Romans called *Mare Nostrum*, "our sea"; it has been transformed into a *Mare Monstrum*, a "monster sea" that has already swallowed thousands of immigrants coming from Africa and Asia, a situation that should be a cause of shame for all "civilized" European nations.[13] Lack of just and humane laws means suffering and death for immigrants, but, as we noted earlier, equally fatal is the language that we use to speak of and about immigrants. Words are important; words matter because they can give comfort, and they can offend; they can give life, and they can cause death. It is a shame that, too often, the mass media contributes to the circulation of exclusionary language and therefore to the diffusion of negative imagery about the immigrants.

Sixth, all the factors that we have mentioned and many others show that exclusion is a fact and a daily experience in the lives of immigrants, especially undocumented immigrants and asylum seekers, and their children.[14] This becomes very clear in the contemporary debate on citizenship. The difference between the United States and Italy in this field is evident: while the former has the *ius soli*, which recognizes birthright citizenship, the latter instead has the *ius sanguinis,* by which only the child of an Italian citizen becomes automatically a citizen. However, the contemporary debate shows how certain political movements in these countries are trying their best to put obstacles in the way of the integration of the second generation and the 1.5 generation, that is, the people who have immigrated as minors.

In the United States, for instance, there are some politicians who have talked about repealing birthright citizenship,[15] and there is a Congress that has not been able, until now, to approve the DREAM Act; in Italy any bill has been systematically rejected that goes in the direction of the *ius soli* for the children of immigrants born in the country and to facilitate the path to citizenship for immigrant children.[16]

Proposals, such as the ones we have just mentioned, are dictated by common sense and by a "far-sighted vision" of society and its transformations: it should be common sense for any society to straighten for its youth the path toward full participation so that these people will become responsible citizens. But for reasons that often seem rather irrational, some people think it is more convenient to push its youth, the future of any nation, toward the margins of society.

Seventh, there is a part of our societies, individuals and associations, that shows a more balanced and realistic understanding of the phenomenon of immigration and its complexities and builds on this in its ways of dealing with immigrants. These are the organizations and the people who struggle to create spaces and times in which immigration can be envisioned differently, and immigrants can be treated as human beings.

Eighth, there are also Christian churches that care. These are individuals, faith communities, and institutions within the church that do their best to offer a different vision of the whole issue of immigration and to welcome and embrace the immigrants. One of the limits of their action could be paternalism, that is, to treat the immigrants as poor people who are unable to fend for themselves and have no voice.

Ninth, unfortunately there is a part of Christian churches overcome by fear and prejudice and that consequently reacts negatively toward immigrants and often excludes them. These are people who consider themselves good Christians, but, when it comes to immigration, they go with the flow: immigrants are illegal aliens; they are stealing jobs from U.S. citizens; they are criminals, and so they are a danger to society; they should worship in their own churches; and so on.

A story that has been related to me by a friend of mine, a Catholic priest ministering to immigrants in Florida, epitomizes this situation. During the celebration of the sacrament of first communion in a parish in Florida, the parents of one of the children who was going to receive the sacrament looked back at a Mexican family whose child was there for the same reason and, thinking that these "poor ignorant Mexicans" could not understand any English, made the following comment: "Here we go, look at these people. I think we should call ICE (Immigration and Customs Enforcement)."

The priest who was told this story after the liturgical ceremony was obviously shocked: what is wrong with our Christian people? Because something is clearly wrong if, during the mass that celebrates in a special way the communion of a faith community with Jesus and all its members, somebody thinks that people have no right to belong there because they might be "illegal" or they "look and speak differently." We are not talking here about any idea or reality but about *communion*, one of the central concepts of contemporary ecclesiology, arguably the central ecclesiological concept after the Second Vatican Council.[17] But communion remains just an idea, an ineffective abstraction, if it is not lived out concretely in the faith communities. The episode that we have just related shows that immigration is a very controversial issue causing exclusion within our churches.

Then there are some practicing and nonpracticing Christians who take it upon themselves to defend the "Christian identity" of their nations, who not only criticize, but even insult and offend those Christians who help and support immigrants. It is a fact that among the nastiest letters that some Catholic bishops receive, the topic is what is thought to be a "too benevolent" treatment of "illegal aliens." Sr. McCauley in her talk about the Postville raid spoke of how encouraging it was to receive the support of so many people to the families of the immigrants who were affected by this event. But she also said that criticism was tough to receive, and that some people warned her that she "could be in serious trouble for harboring illegals."[18]

Two of the most outstanding Catholic leaders in the United States and in Italy have taken a courageous and far-sighted stance on the issue of immigration. I am referring to Cardinal Roger Mahony, archbishop emeritus of Los Angeles, who has repeatedly and publicly spoken in favor of immigrants, and especially undocumented immigrants, and in support of a just and humane immigration reform in the United States,[19] as well as to Cardinal Dionigi Tettamanzi, archbishop emeritus of Milan,[20] who, because of his supportive stance toward immigrants, has been openly and publicly insulted, especially by politicians belonging to the Lega Nord, who openly proclaim themselves to be the defenders of the Italian Christian identity and tradition. These politicians have gone from ironically asking if Tettamanzi is a "cardinal or an imam" because of the latter's insistence on dialogue with the Muslim immigrants, to affirming, and these are the words of one of the most prominent members of the Lega, Roberto Calderoli, that "Tettamanzi has nothing to do with his territory. It is like having a mafioso priest in Sicily."[21]

Tenth, the immigrants whose lives are made miserable by the "attrition strategy" are afraid: they are afraid of going to work, to church, to the grocery store, to accompany their children to school, or simply for a trip because they might be detained for no reason and deported, leaving their loved ones, who are often little children, behind.

A story told by Cardinal Mahoney about a young woman from Honduras detained on a highway in Maryland speaks about the horrendous experience of her three little children who were left on the highway for hours waiting for their father but also about the total lack of humanity of the police agents who did such a thing.[22] It is because of this lack of humanity and understanding of their situation that the immigrants ask the following question: Why do they hate us so much?[23] This question should sound an alarm for people in the United States. I was at the border between Mexico and the United States when the tragic events of 9/11 happened, and I remember very well that one of the main questions that people, shocked by this senseless violence, were asking was precisely the same question that immigrants in the United States are asking today: "Why do they hate us so much?" This brings us to another key question: What are we learning from our history and from our suffering?

What is most worrying about this situation that we have tried to portray by highlighting these ten points? I believe that what should really alarm society and Christian churches, both in the United States and in Italy, is the level of barbarism that the public debate about immigration has reached. Very powerful movements and people are doing their best to promote a culture of fear, suspicion, intolerance, discrimination, and hate. The problem is that many of them hide this inhuman and un-Christian culture behind "good" reasons: the defense of national and Christian identity, as well as the well-being of citizens, over the well-being of immigrants that, according to some people and political organizations, receive too many privileges. This anti-immigrant culture is poisoning the wells from which we drink everyday by making acceptable violent behaviors and a public language that is not respectful of human dignity. Individual Christians and Christian communities are caught up in this process, and often there is little or no reaction to what is completely unacceptable both from a human and a Christian viewpoint. We complain about the invasion of foreigners, the "barbarians" in our countries, and by doing that we exclude them from the semantic field of what is human.

Yet the way we treat immigrants suggests that we might be the real barbarians. Tzvetan Todorov warns us about the reactions we have toward strangers because it is precisely this uncontrolled fear of the barbarians that will make us barbarians. The evil that we will provoke will be superior to the one we thought we were going to suffer, or, in other words, the medicine that we are choosing will be worse than the illness we want to treat.[24] Very recently, Roger Cohen, commented on the massacre that occurred in Norway in July 2011, where more than seventy people were killed by Anders Behring Breivik, who from his writings might be described as a Christian and Islamophobic fundamentalist. Cohen observed that the absurd and murderous behavior was brewed in the "poison" that has been injected into the public debate about immigration and Islam by political and religious leaders both in Europe and the United States.[25]

Current Ecclesiology's Lack of Attention to Migration

In a noteworthy article written more than fifteen years ago, Francis Elvey, starting with the transformations that migration was causing around the world, affirmed, "We need to develop ways of responding to mobility, a task that has barely begun. The first step may be to look around and accept that while we do indeed live in a world of mobility, many of our images of the church and our characteristic ministerial responses are based on a more stable world long since past."[26]

This admonition is as relevant today as it was in 1994. Globalization is the catchword used to analyze today's situation: we live in the global village in which diversity of people, cultures, ways of life, religions, and customs is becoming normal. People, ideas, and products move at an incredible speed, and yet it looks like Christian ecclesiology treats reality as if it were static and concerned about territorial, not to say parochial, issues. Most of our ecclesiology has to catch up with the global character of local realities that are no longer as homogenous as they were thought to be. Elvey's affirmation is still relevant precisely because mainstream ecclesiology, aside from a small group of theologians from different continents who are studying and reflecting on the phenomenon of migration from a Christian perspective,[27] has been rather deaf and mute about the human mobility that characterizes our age.

Even the most recent studies in ecclesiology[28] and reflections on the state of the church in Italy and the United States by well-known theologians[29] are basically silent about immigration. They deal with the foundations of Christian ecclesiology and other very important current issues such as the crisis of the relations of the church with civil society and contemporary culture, the challenge of preaching the gospel in a secularized society, the massive exodus from the Roman Catholic Church, the issue of authority within the church, and others. Nothing is being said about immigration; about the way this phenomenon is transforming our societies; about the cultural and religious diversity that it causes; its omnipresence in the political debate; and indeed in the lives of people, both native and immigrant.

The voices of immigrants whose claim for justice and the voices of natives whose claim for some understanding and clarity are not being heard are, so to speak, excluded from ecclesiological reflection. Why? Here are some partial and tentative answers. Ecclesiology is often too inward looking; too interested in internal issues; and, as a consequence, it does not give enough attention and consideration to the real world to which it has been called to announce and witness to the good news. It is sometimes far from or forgetful of the issues that Christians have to deal with daily. It could be said that often it is not faithful to the "duty" mandated by the Pastoral Constitution of the Second Vatican Council, *Gaudium et Spes*, to "scrutinize the signs of the times" (GS 4). In other words, ecclesiology is not often used to reflect on issues that come from the ground, from daily reality such as migration, and how these issues could influence the way the church should be envisioned and lived out. At times, it sounds as a theory disconnected from daily reality.[30]

It is interesting to see in a recent analysis by an Italian Catholic pastor the relevance that he gives to the phenomenon of migration as it is experienced in his own parish and diocese and his conclusion that from these transformations brought about by globalization and human mobility a new church is slowly being born, though not without the pains and travails that accompany any birth.[31] Mainstream ecclesiology seems until now not quite capable of elaborating such a reflection in terms of human mobility.

Another limitation that affects ecclesiology is that it is often too nationalistic, Eurocentric or "Western-centric," that is, it lacks that catholic imagination that is needed to journey toward a truly Catholic church.[32] It is not yet completely ready and willing to listen to voices, experiences, and reflections that come from outside, especially from an outside that we often consider somehow inferior to our Western civilizations. The migrants, because they are strangers, because they have a different way of expressing and celebrating their Christian beliefs, or because they do not belong to the Christian churches, are often excluded from the ecclesiological discourse. This is true for the "implicit" or "working" ecclesiology, that is, the often "parochial" vision of the church that stands behind the opinions, attitudes, and behaviors of many church-going Christians. And it is also true for the experts who analyze the situation of the church today.

For instance, when we deal with the issue of the massive exodus of people from the Roman Catholic Church, which is certainly a central issue today in the United States, immigration is not considered among the important aspects of this phenomenon.[33] Yet, many immigrant Catholics are leaving their church of origin. Why? Because they do not feel welcomed in their original faith communities, because they do not feel the human warmth that is one of the main ingredients of any community, because they do not feel welcomed in the communion of the local faith communities, because they feel intolerance, discrimination, and hate. But they also abandon the church because they are deported, kicked out of the United States because of immigration irregularities, or they decide to leave because it has become impossible for them to stay in the country, the consequence of the already mentioned "attrition strategy." This happens every year to hundreds of thousands of immigrants. How many of them are Catholics or Christians? The priest ministering in Florida whom we have mentioned earlier tells me that in the years 2010 and 2011 some of his communities have been decimated by deportations: community leaders, catechists, and choir members have been detained and expelled from the country, or they have simply left. Moreover, there are immigrants who do not go to church because they are afraid of being detained and separated from their loved ones if they drive. They are afraid to leave home because they do not know if they are going to return.

There is also the suspicion that ecclesiology sometimes follows the not too exemplary lead of some of our church authorities who, with regard to some controversial issues, prefer to be silent or to speak as little as possible, because silence and diplomacy could buy the church some privileges from the political establishment and economic support for Catholic schools and institutions. In this case some eminent scholars in Italy have been speaking about evangelical prophecy that is restrained by diplomacy.[34] This happens also in the United States where I know some pastors do not speak to their communities about immigration because they are afraid their Sunday collection will go down or where youth ministers avoid this issue simply because it is "too controversial." So the suspicion is that ecclesiology is conforming to this kind of domesticated behavior and avoids the issue for fear of being too countercultural in a culture that tends to scapegoat immigrants and at the same time betrays the prophecy that is integral to the proclamation and witnessing of the reign of God.

Finally, our ecclesiology often does not take into consideration the fact that God could be speaking to the churches through the "foreign" and "strange" voices of the immigrants. Here, once again, the challenge and insight comes directly from the pastoral field: Sr. McCauley in her narration of the Postville story affirms, "My firm conviction is that the Spirit spoke and continues to speak through the Postville story, as well as through countless other heartbreaking stories of our immigrant brothers and sisters [around the world, I would add]. The question, the challenge is, *Do we have ears to hear*?" And she continues: "It [the Postville story] is the story of a journey that began in hope and ended in tragedy. My hope is that the journey that appeared to end in tragedy will lead to transformation."[35] Are the churches willing to hear the voice of the Spirit that speaks through the too often broken voices and experiences of immigrants? Are ecclesiologists ready and willing to do that? Are we ready for the transformation that these stories can trigger in our ecclesiologies? Or are we afraid to be transformed by them? If ecclesiology could be written by those who would listen to these stories, what would happen? Let us briefly imagine what these stories of immigration could do to our theologies of the church.

Ecclesiology and Migration: Some Suggestions

In this section of the essay, I would like to illustrate the potential of the experience and reality of migration for ecclesiological reflection today. In 2003 Bryan Hehir gave a talk during the National Migration Conference organized by the Migration and Refugee Services of the United States Conference of Catholic Bishops in Washington, DC, entitled "With No Vision, People Perish."[36] He emphasized that when there is no healthy vision, we have just irrational immigration policies and strategies, selfish laws, and a culture of fear, intolerance, and hate that push the most vulnerable immigrants to the margins and often off the radar of society. In this way, people are made to suffer and die, and together with them the whole of humanity suffers and dies because it is hurting itself; people become less human, indifferent to, or even wishing and causing other people to suffer and die. In other words, with no vision, people, all of us, perish in one way or another.

The vision we need, a vision that motivates us to be respectful of human dignity, a vision that not only does not cause people to perish but allows them to flourish and be who they are supposed to be as human beings and communities made in the image and likeness of God, is the one proclaimed and witnessed to by Jesus. It is the vision of the reign of God, a reign of justice and equality, freedom and compassion, solidarity and harmony, dialogue and *convivencia*, radical openness and inclusivity. And who will provide such a vision today? The church, which the Second Vatican Council defines as "missionary by its very nature" (*Ad Gentes* 2), has been called and sent to fulfill this task. It is its vocation, its mission, the reason for its existence and relevance: to proclaim, witness to and serve the reign of God.[37]

The church, the "community-in-mission," just as God the Trinity is a "communion-in-mission,"[38] must provide what any political entity today cannot provide in terms of migration policies and strategies, because its horizons go only as far as the next electoral campaign. It must provide a far-sighted vision that goes beyond what we normally consider human experience and history, a vision that, by the power of the Spirit, learns from the positive and the negative experiences of the past, inspires the present, and helps us envision a better future, God's future. It is a vision whose horizons we cannot even fathom, a vision in which people can believe and grow into an embracing and inclusive vision. The task of ecclesiology is to reflect on, elaborate, and express this vision that goes beyond the limited horizons of any local church since it recognizes and teaches that the church is not about itself but about the reign of God that Jesus announced and inaugurated. Without this vision, immigrants, asylum seekers, and refugees will continue to perish by the thousands. This is the first task that ecclesiology, an inclusive Christian ecclesiology that embraces those who have been left behind, forgotten, and often trampled on, must fulfill.

Ecclesiology must also welcome the challenge, voiced by Elvey, of finding different and new ways of imagining and describing the church in terms that reflect the dynamism of humanity in this "age of migration."[39] In this sense the images of a pilgrim, migrant, journeying, and itinerant church are very helpful because they identify with and speak to the real experiences of millions of migrants in our world today. The interesting thing is that this dynamic imagery is nothing new but has been for centuries an integral part of the Judaeo-Christian tradition, starting with scripture. The comparison of life to a journey and a road (Dt 5:32–33); the journeys of the God of Israel, the ancestors of and the people of Israel in the wilderness (Ex 13:18, 21); the imagery of the pilgrimage toward the holy city, Jerusalem, tied with the return from the Babylonian exile (Is 35:1, 8, 10);[40] the tent as the dwelling place of God in the Old Testament (2 Sm 7:1–7) and as the metaphorical way in which Jesus comes to dwell among humanity (Jn 1:14);[41] the naming of the first Christian community as the "Way" in Acts 18: 25–26 and other passages of this book. All of these are examples of how widespread the imagery of pilgrimage and journey is in scripture.

More recently, the image of the pilgrim has been applied to the church in some key documents of Vatican II. Chapter VII of the Dogmatic Constitution on the Church, *Lumen Gentium*, is entitled, "The Eschatological Nature of the Pilgrim Church." But, more importantly, one of the fundamental affirmations about the church in the Second Vatican Council appears in the Decree on the Missionary Activity of the Church and reads, "The pilgrim church is missionary by her very nature" (*Ad Gentes* 2).

While the missionary dimension of the church has been abundantly discussed and reflected on, its "pilgrim" dimension has not received the same attention, and, in fact, it remains to be fully elaborated in this age of migration that needs precisely this kind of imagery to convey the message that Christians and the church are none other than pilgrims and migrants walking toward the reign of God with other pilgrims and migrants. These are some of the more dynamic images that ecclesiology should cultivate in an age of human history in which human mobility is central. They are the images of the church that ecclesiology should transmit to the people of God and to a catechesis that is often too static and irrelevant because it is more dogmatically than biblically based. If ecclesiology was more biblically based, it would give more attention to the issue of human mobility since, as we have seen, this is one of the most notable features of the biblical tradition.[42]

Finally, the experiences and stories of immigrants offer us new perspectives from which to interpret the traditional marks of the Christian church: one, holy, catholic, and apostolic. The immigrants are doubtlessly a challenge to the unity of the church. Bryan Hehir, reflecting on the current situation of the Roman Catholic Church in the United States, observes that it is at once a "post-immigrant" church in that it is formed by the descendants of the immigrants who arrived during the nineteenth through the middle of the twentieth century and who are now at the very center of U.S. society and a "newly-immigrant" church because the Catholic immigrants who are arriving now are no longer from Europe but mostly from Latin America, Asia, and Africa. These latest arrivals are at the margins of contemporary U.S. society. So it happens that the church simultaneously is at the center and at the edge of society; it is a "center-edged" church, a fact that, according to Hehir, has potential. But, he adds, "A church that is a 'center-edged' church cannot be two churches."[43] In other words, there must be a unifying vision that brings together the diversities present within the faith community. There will be no unity, that unity that Jesus prayed for and envisioned as he said in John 17:22: "The glory that you have given me I have given them, so that they may be one, as we are one," if we still continue to reason in terms of "us," the citizen members of the church, and "them," the immigrant members of the church.

When we hear this prayer of Jesus about unity, to which reality do we relate it? Do we think about the divisions that run through our Christian communities along the lines of nationality and culture? How do we imagine unity within a church that faces great diversity within and without? We have to learn to become one without becoming the same, or better, without imposing newcomers to become the same. Unity in the church is neither uniformity nor assimilation but rather must be thought in terms of integration in the sense that the church must become able to create spaces where through a process of intercultural exchange a new "we" is created, a faith community where people learn to live in harmony; where there are no longer natives and immigrants; where differences are respected and considered a wealth available to everybody; where people are always open to the "surprising gifts" that newcomers will bring.

To listen to the voices of immigrants poses also the challenge of catholicity, another fundamental quality of the church that we profess during our Sunday celebrations but of which we are often unaware. When we profess that our church is catholic, we are affirming that our church is radically open to differences and that it can be catholic only if we literally think and imagine the church according to the whole and according to all the people who get in touch with our communities. In his message for the World Migration Day of 1999 John Paul II said, "Catholicity is not only expressed in the fraternal communion of the baptized, but also in the hospitality extended to the stranger, whatever his religious belief, in the rejection of all racial exclusion or discrimination, in the recognition of the personal dignity of every man and woman and, consequently, in the commitment to furthering their inalienable rights."[44] It is starting from this conviction that it can be rightly affirmed that immigrants are the "prophets of catholicity"[45] because they are that part of the whole that is too often excluded, that part that reminds the whole church more than anybody else of this crucial quality.

The experiences of immigrants are also a test of the way we understand the holiness of the church. I believe that, in the context of the exclusion of immigrants from the *polis* (city or society), holiness must be seen and practiced mostly as a "political holiness," an expression coined by Jon Sobrino.[46] The church cannot conform to a society that discriminates against the immigrants, that treats them as "nonpersons," that exploits their hard work but cannot accept their presence. Instead, the church must contribute to a different vision of society where justice, equality, welcoming, and dialogue are the pillars of living together.

In this sense, the church has to become the witness of a "political vision" that contests the narrow and petty political visions about immigration that are often promoted and implemented in Western societies. The church must, therefore, become in this too often "anti-immigrant" context a holy faith community, which concretely means a "contrast" community, a "prophetic" community, a "countercultural" community,[47] that is, a community with the reign of God as its vision that offers an alternative view of what a human society should be.

This alternative view, for instance, does not allow the church to call immigrants "aliens" or "illegal" because it believes in the human dignity and rights of all human beings created in the image and likeness of God, regardless of their legal and social status. This alternative view understands "legality" and "security," two of the key catchwords of current politics of immigration that tend to criminalize immigrants, as fundamental needs of the whole population and not just of citizens and natives. To take this alternative stance means for the church to prophetically proclaim and witness to the option for and with the most vulnerable people in our societies such as the undocumented immigrants and the asylum seekers.[48]

Lastly, the experiences and voices of the immigrants will lead us to have a refreshing and more mission-minded understanding of what it means to be an apostolic church. We will not enter here into the usual debate about apostolicity interpreted as "apostolic succession." In this case, we will put aside this dimension of apostolicity to focus on the more literal meaning of the term apostolic, which is "to be sent out." The church has been called by God and empowered by the Spirit to be sent out to continue the proclamation of the good news of the reign inaugurated by Jesus.

The church is, therefore, first and foremost, a "communion-in-mission," a community "sent out" to proclaim, witness to, and serve the vision of the reign of God. So the apostolicity of the church refers, first of all, to this constitutive missionary dimension.

What does it mean to be an apostolic/missionary church in the context of migration? Stephen Bevans offers a few key suggestions as to how the church should go about its apostolicity/mission in the context of migration, but the main and fundamental point that emerges is that mission is not only to the migrants, but it is with the migrants and of the migrants. This means that the migrants must go from being just the "objects" of Christian mission, to be the subjects, the protagonists of mission.[49] They, in other words, are the surprising and unexpected "apostles," the "missionaries," in our apostolic church, that is, the people "sent out" by God to the church itself and to the world to proclaim the good news of the reign of God and to challenge all Christians to be a truly one, holy, catholic, and apostolic church.

Conclusion

The goal of this essay has been to show that the exclusion of the immigrants within society and within the church in Italy and the United States is a reality, though there are parts of society and of the church that struggle actively and courageously against such exclusion. We have also seen that the theologies of the church tend to exclude the "foreign and strange" experiences and voices of the immigrants and how these, when taken seriously, could renew and transform our understanding of the nature and mission of the church. This will be possible only if the church takes a prophetic and countercultural option for and with migrants, remembering that they are neither better nor worse than any other human being or any other Christian. In this spirit, we will conclude this essay with another of the many dramatic but also inspiring true stories of immigrants, a story that is particularly meaningful for the symbolic value that it holds for the church and that at the same time underscores, once again, the fundamental significance that immigrants could have for Christian ecclesiology.

In March 2011 a little baby was born in the Mediterranean Sea, in one of the many run-down and high-risk ships that carry migrants from Africa to the Italian coast. That particular ship carried 280 immigrants. When this baby and his Ethiopian parents arrived in the small island of Lampedusa, just off the coast of Sicily, it was met by the wonderful solidarity of the women of the island who were touched by the incredible and providentially positive journey of this family. This young Ethiopian couple decided to call this baby Yeabsera, which in their language means "gift of God."[50] Certainly the comparison with the baby Jew called Jesus who has changed the course of humanity might even seem preposterous, yet both babies, the Jew and the Ethiopian, have been through the experience of being refugees, as Matthew narrates in Matthew 2:13–18. More importantly, both are gifts from God, vulnerable gifts as vulnerable as a baby could be, and yet so powerful that, if we accept them, they will change the course of our lives, of our Christian churches, and the way we understand and interpret them.

Notes

[1] Daniele Mastrogiacomo, "Rosarno, l'Omelia di Don Pino 'I Cristiani Aiutano Chi Sbaglia,'" http://www.repubblica.it/cronaca/2010/01/10/news/omelia_rosarno-1895623/.

[2] Roberto Saviano, the Italian writer who has become famous with the book *Gomorrah*, which later became a movie, has written an eye-opening op-ed about this event and its significance on the pages of the *New York Times,* January 24, 2010, entitled "Italy's African Heroes," http://www.nytimes.com/2010/01/25/opinion/25saviano. html?scp=2&sq=roberto%20saviano%20on%20Rosarno&st=cse.

[3] See Antonello Mangano, *Gli Africani Salveranno l'Italia* (Milan: Rizzoli, 2010). This book interprets the events of Rosarno following Saviano's interpretation and affirming that by revolting against the mafia, these African immigrants will "save" Italy, which is getting too used to the violent regime imposed by these criminal organizations.

[4] See the text of Sr. Mary McCauley's talk at the Celebration Conference for Effective Liturgy in San Antonio, Texas, January 12–14, 2011, entitled "The Postville Raid: What Mother Church Can Do," http://celebrationpublications. org/sites/default/files/conference_presentations/McCauleyThe%20Postville%20 Raid.pdf.

[5] Here Jon Sobrino would speak about the "docetism of reality," which according to him is one of the things that should concern Christian theology most today. See Jon Sobrino, "Teología desde la realidad," in *Panorama de la Teología Latinoamericana*, ed. Juan-José Tamayo and Juan Bosch (Estella, Spain: Editorial Verbo Divino, 2001), 611–28.

[6] On this and the whole issue of migrants as a labor force, see Stephen Castles and Mark J. Miller, *The Age of Migration: International Population Movements in the Modern World*, 4th rev. ed. (New York: Palgrave Macmillan, 2009), 221–44.

[7] Pat Marrin, "Words Matter," http://ncronline.org/news/immigration-and-church/words-matter (accessed March 23, 2011); Igiaba Scego, "Le Parole Sono Importanti," http://www.unita.it/commenti/igiabascego/le-parole-sono-importanti-1.275948.

[8] See John J. Hoeffner and Michele R. Pistone, "But the Laborers Are . . . Many: Catholic Social Teaching on Business, Labor, and Economic Migration," in *And You Welcomed Me: Migration and Catholic Social Teaching*, ed. Donald Kerwin and Jill Marie Gerschutz (Lanham, MD: Lexington Books, 2009), 69.

[9] "The Misery Strategy," *New York Times*, August 9, 2007, http://www.ny-times.com/2007/08/09/opinion/09thu1.html.

[10] This is the thesis presented by a group of social scientists in Pietro Basso, ed., *Razzismo di Stato: Stati Uniti, Europa, Italia* (Milan: Franco Angeli 2010).

[11] In the wake of Arizona's decision, similar bills have been proposed in other U.S. states, such as Kansas. These state bills show precisely the failure of the federal government to implement an immigration reform that is rational and realistic, that is, based on real facts and the real capabilities of the nation.

[12] For a thorough critique of the "security package" see Stefano Femminis, "Pacchetto Sicurezza, un Anno Dopo," *Popoli* (Agosto-Settembre 2010), 16–21.

[13] "Mediterraneo o Mare Monstrum?," *Famiglia Cristiana* April 13, 2011, http://www.famigliacristiana.it/informazione/news_2/articolo/mediterraneo-non-sia-mare-mostrum_130411115226.aspx. For updates on the deaths of immigrants, see the blog by Gabriele del Grande at http://fortresseurope.blogspot.com/. It reports that from 1988 to this date more than 16,000 people have died along the borders of Fortress Europe.

[14] See the very interesting article by Antonio Izquierdo Escribano, "Times of Losses: A False Awareness of the Integration of Immigrants," *Migraciones Internacionales* 6, no. 1 (2011): 145–84. In this essay the author compares studies on the integration of immigrants in the United States and France. The main U.S. study about integration to which he refers is E. Telles and V. Ortiz, *Generations of Exclusion: Mexican Americans, Assimilation, and Race* (New York: Russell Sage Foundation, 2008). One of the conclusions of Izquierdo Escribano is not only that the exclusion of immigrants exists but that its wounds continue to fester for several generations.

[15] On this issue, see a briefing issued by the Migration and Refugee Services of the United States Conference of Catholic Bishops entitled "Birthright Citizenship: The Real Story," http://www.justiceforimmigrants.org/documents/birthright-citizenship-issue-brief-final.pdf.

[16] In the fall of 2011 in Italy, a campaign began to gather signatures and support for a bill that will give birthright citizenship to children of immigrants born in Italy, facilitate the path to citizenship for immigrant minors and adults, and give the right to vote in local elections to regular immigrant residents. This campaign has been sponsored by many well-known civil associations, church organizations, and labor unions. For further information, see the http://www.litalia-sonoanchio.it/.

[17] See, on this concept, Walter Kasper, *La Chiesa di Gesù Cristo: Scritti di Ecclesiologia* (Brescia: Queriniana, 2011), 7–101; Richard R. Gaillardetz, *Ecclesiology for a Global Church: A People Called and Sent* (Maryknoll, NY: Orbis Books, 2008), 85–131.

[18] McCauley, "The Postville Raid," 6.

[19] Among his most recent talks on this issue, see "Standing with the Eleven Million: Welcoming the Strangers in Our Midst," in http://www.the-tidings.com/2011/012111/cardretire_text.htm; "For Goodness Sake: Why America

Needs Immigration Reform," http://www.the-tidings.com/2011/021111/cardnc. htm.

[20] Dionigi Tettamanzi, *Non c'è Futuro senza Solidarietà: La Crisi Economica e l'Aiuto della Chiesa* (Cinisello Balsamo, Milan: San Paolo, 2009), 101–11. See also Cardinal Tettamanzi's numerous homilies and speeches on the issue of immigration on the website of the Archdiocese of Milan, http://www.chiesadimilano.it/.

[21] Renzo Guolo, *Chi Impugna la Croce: Lega e Chiesa* (Bari, Italy: Laterza, 2011), 47; see also Paolo Bertezzolo, *Padroni a Chiesa Nostra: Vent'Anni di Strategia Religiosa della Lega Nord* (Bologna: EMI, 2011). These two books are very interesting studies on the particular religious stance of the most anti-immigrant political party in Italy, the Lega Nord.

[22] See Cardinal Roger Mahony, "For Goodness Sake: Why America Needs Immigration Reform, an address given at the University of North Carolina, Chapel Hill, on February 2, 2011.

[23] McCauley, "The Postville Raid," 11.

[24] Tzvetan Todorov, *La Paura dei Barbari: Oltre lo Scontro delle Civiltà* (Milan: Garzanti, 2009), 16.

[25] Roger Cohen, "Breivik and His Enablers," *New York Times,* July 25, 2011, http://www.nytimes.com/2011/07/26/opinion/26iht-edcohen26.html (accessed July 29, 2011).

[26] Francis M. Elvey, "Ministry in a World of Mobility," *New Theology Review* 7 (1994): 70.

[27] I will mention here some of the still few writings on the issue that are articles and book chapters. As far as I know, there is not yet a book on the ecclesiology of migration. See Agbonkhianmeghe E. Orobator, *From Crisis to Kairos: The Mission of the Church in the Time of HIV/AIDS: Refugees and Poverty* (Nairobi: Paulines Publications Africa, 2005), 143–79; Michael McCabe, "A Pilgrim People en Route to God's Future: Towards a Vision of the Church for the Twenty-First Century," *Sedos Bulletin* 37, no. 5–6 (2005): 154–58; Gioacchino Campese, "'I Will Make You Live in Tents Again' (Hosea 12:9): The Church in an Age of Mobility," *Traditio Scalabriniana* 7 (2008): 3–13; Emmanuel S. De Guzman, "The Church as 'Imagined Communities' among Differentiated Social Bodies," in *Faith on the Move: Toward a Theology of Migration in Asia,* ed. Fabio Baggio and Agnes Brazal (Manila: Ateneo de Manila University Press, 2008), 118–54; Stephen Bevans, "Mission among the Migrants, Mission of the Migrants, Mission of the Church," in *A Promised Land, a Perilous Journey: Theological Perspectives on Migration,* ed. Daniel G. Groody and Gioacchino Campese (Notre Dame, IN: University of Notre Dame Press, 2008), 89–106; Sandra Mazzolini, "Chiesa Pellegrina," in *Migrazioni: Dizionario Socio-Pastorale,* ed. Graziano Battistella (Cinisello Balsamo, Milan: Edizioni San Paolo, 2010), 145–50; Gemma T. Cruz, *An Intercultural Theology of Migration: Pilgrims in the Wilderness* (Leiden: Brill, 2010), 279–87; Gaetano Parolin, *Chiesa Postconciliare e Migrazioni: Quale Teologia per la Missione con i Migranti* (Rome: Editrice Pontificia Università Gregoriana, 2010), 328–32.

[28] See, for example, the excellent studies by Richard R. Gaillardetz, *Ecclesiology for a Global Church: A People Called and Sent* (Maryknoll, NY: Orbis Books, 2008); Richard P. McBrien, *The Church: The Evolution of Catholicism* (New York: Harper Collins, 2008); Erio Castellucci, *La Famiglia di Dio nel Mondo: Manuale di Ecclesiologia* (Assisi, Italy: Cittadella Editrice, 2008); Gianfranco Calabrese and Philip Goyret and Orazio F. Piazza, eds., *Dizionario di Ecclesiologia* (Rome: Città Nuova, 2010). One of the possible and few exceptions in terms of migration is the ecclesiological reflection by Paul Lakeland, *The Church: Living Communion* (Collegeville, MN: Liturgical Press, 2009), 149–54, who, among the models of the church that emerge from the U.S. experience, highlights the "church as pilgrim" and the "church as immigrant."

[29] See, for example, the interesting essays by Richard R. Gaillardetz, "The State of the Church, 2011: Reflections on the State of American Catholicism Today," http://ncronline.org/news/faith-parish/every-day-church-should-give-birth-church; and Severino Dianich, "Chiesa che Fare?," *Il Regno—Attualità* 20 (2010): 714–22.

[30] There is a very useful debate about an ecclesiology from below in Gerard Mannion, *Ecclesiology and Postmodernity: Questions for the Church of Our Time* (Collegeville, MN: Liturgical Press, 2007), 33; or an inductive ecclesiology in Lakeland, *The Church*, 120–78, or a theology, or an ecclesiology from reality in Jon Sobrino, "La Teología y el Principio Liberación," *Revista Latinoamericana de Teología* 35 (1995): 115–40. From a more pastoral viewpoint in a challenging book on the current situation of the Italian church by Saverio Xeres and Giorgio Campanini, *Manca il Respiro: Un Prete e un Laico Riflettono sulla Chiesa Italiana* (Milan: Ancora, 2011), 43; Xeres affirms that in the field of pastoral ministry and reflection, and I would add ecclesiology, we see that, following the mentality of our age, the "virtual" prevails over what is "real."

[31] Alberto Carrara, "Sulla Chiesa che Sta per Cominciare," *Rivista del Clero Italiano* 91, no. 2 (2010): 99–112.

[32] On Catholic imagination, see Gioacchino Campese, "Beyond Ethnic and National Imagination: Toward a Catholic Theology of U.S. Immigration," in *Religion and Social Justice for Immigrants*, ed. Pierrette Hondagneu-Sotelo (New Brunswick, NJ: Rutgers University Press, 2007), 175–90.

[33] This is the case of Thomas Reese, "The Hidden Exodus: Catholics Becoming Protestants," http://ncronline.org/news/hidden-exodus-catholics-becoming-protestants.

[34] See Bartolomeo Sorge, "Il Silenzio dei Vescovi sull'Italia," *Aggiornamenti Sociali* 3 (2004): 165.

[35] McCauley, "The Postville Raid," 1–2.

[36] J. Bryan Hehir, "With No Vision, People Perish," in *All Come Bearing Gifts*, Proceedings of the National Migration Conference 2003 (Washington, DC: U.S. Conference of Catholic Bishops 2003), 15–22.

[37] On the issue of theology of mission today and the tasks of a missionary church, see the excellent books by Stephen B. Bevans and Roger P. Schroeder,

Constants in Context: A Theology of Mission for Today (Maryknoll, NY: Orbis Books, 2004); *Prophetic Dialogue: Reflections on Christian Mission Today* (Maryknoll, NY: Orbis Books, 2011).

[38] Peter N. V. Hai, "Models of the Asian Church," *Australian eJournal of Theology* 18 (April 2011): 61–73, affirms that the expression "communion-in-mission" to define the church was coined by the FABC (Federation of Asian Bishops' Conferences). Another theologian who often uses this expression is Stephen Bevans (*Prophetic Dialogue*, 26).

[39] Castles and Miller, *The Age of Migration.*

[40] On these and other related passages, see J. C. L. Gibson, *Language and Imagery in the Old Testament* (Peabody, MA: Hendrickson Publishers, 1998), 151–54.

[41] The literal translation of this passage from the Greek should be "The word became flesh and came to pitch its tent among us."

[42] There are a number of theologians from different contexts and perspectives who rightly lament the lack of a more biblically based formation within the Roman Catholic Church and identify in this lacuna one of the most important reasons why certain issues, such as migration, are not that significant within the Christian communities. On this issue, see Frank Crüsemann, "'You Know the Heart of a Stranger' (Exod 23:9): A Recollection of the Torah in the Face of New Nationalism and Xenophobia," in *Migrants and Refugees*, ed. Dietmar Mieth and Lisa Sowle Cahill (London: SMC Press, 1993), 97; Reese, "The Hidden Exodus"; Brunetto Salvarani, *Vocabolario Minimo del Dialogo Interreligioso: Per un'Educazione all'Incontro tra le Fedi*, rev. ed. (Bologna: EDB, 2008), 63–64.

[43] Hehir, "With No Vision," 21.

[44] http://www.vatican.va/holy_father/john_paul_ii/messages/migration/documents/hf_jp-ii_mes_22021999_world-migration-day-1999_en.html.

[45] Graziano G. Tassello, "Los migrantes: profetas de la catolicidad," *Spiritus* 42, no. 2 (2001): 113–24.

[46] Jon Sobrino, *Spirituality of Liberation: Toward Political Holiness* (Maryknoll, NY: Orbis Books, 1988), 80–86.

[47] Bevans and Schroeder speak about these themes in the context of mission theology in their *Prophetic Dialogue*, 46–47, 60–61. The main reference for the church as a "contrast society" related to the dimension of holiness is Gerhard Lohfink, *Jesus and Community* (Philadelphia: Fortress Press, 1984).

[48] As we have seen earlier, Cardinal Roger Mahony in Los Angeles and Cardinal Dionigi Tettamanzi in Milan have been for years the catalysts of this prophetic and countercultural stance in terms of immigration in their respective contexts.

[49] See Bevans, "Mission among the Migrants," 89–106.

[50] See, on this event, the moving article by the director of the Italian newspaper *L'Unità*, Concita De Gregorio, "Dono di Dio," http://concita.blog.unita.it/dono-di-dio-1.279253.

Being an Otherwise-Documented Church:
An Ecclesiology for All Us Immigrants

David L. Johns

In his many writings on the state of our present age, the Polish sociologist Zygmunt Bauman draws our attention to the phenomenon of human waste. One of the most extensive by-products of globalization is a surplus of humanity that is unwanted, inconvenient, and ultimately displaced. He states, "The volume of humans made redundant by capitalism's global triumph grows unstoppably and comes close now to exceeding the managerial capacity of the planet; there is a plausible prospect of capitalist modernity (or modern capitalism) *choking on its own waste products* which it can neither reassimilate or annihilate, nor detoxify."[1]

Shifting labor demands have decimated some communities, and they have reorganized others. The open markets and trade policies of neo-liberalism have resulted in national borders that are permeable to the flow of capital and consumer products but resistant to the flow of labor. Rather, economic migration, humans moving to pursue work, especially for industrial production, the service sector, and domestic labor, is increasingly criminalized in the United States. But rather than be simply criminalized outright, the situation is complexified by the actual economic need for cheap, mobile, and ultimately expendable labor. Thus, an entire shadow economy has arisen that is necessary to cost-efficient production and service, and yet at the same time, demonized and, in the case of Mexico, walled off from the mainstream. The entire issue is so politically charged that it is difficult for some churches to know if and how they can enter into the conversation.

Bauman argues that with the geographical expansion of the "modern mode of life," that is to say, globalizing capitalist consumption, the outlying regions wherein discarded humanity has been dumped previously through the years are becoming fewer, and, consequently, the discarded are not so easily ignored.[2] Not only does this mean that the discarded are more and more evident, but there is also growing recognition that "assignment to waste" is now a potential prospect for widening swaths of the population.

This (dis)ease of recognizing one's own vulnerable state (*en potencia*), rather than inspiring solidarity, often leads to the well-rehearsed practice of scapegoating the minority other. As Bauman puts it, "Newcomers are born and sworn enemies of tranquility and self-congratulation."[3] Since so much of this tension is related to economic uncertainty, a logical scapegoat is the outsider who comes looking for work. "Blaming the immigrant," writes Bauman, "is fast becoming a global habit." He observes that this attitude raises particular problems for the United States: "The U.S. is an admittedly immigrant country: immigration has gone down in American history as a noble pastime, a mission, a heroic exploit of the daring, valiant and brave."[4] Thus, a tension exists in the ordinary patterns of *outsider blaming* in the United States because it cuts to the foundations of American self-identity, the history of Ellis Island, and the rhetoric of the American Dream.

A Mobile People of No Place

There are any number of social challenges we could introduce when considering ecclesiology and exclusion: the church's inconsistent response to the issue of HIV/AIDS, the constant state of war and its attendant suspension of privacy and other human rights, the frequent complicity of the churches to this "state of exception,"[5] as well as the church's silencing of women either through outright doctrinal exclusion or through the enshrinement of the *ideal* of women. We could note the obscene exclusion of the nonhuman creation and earth care from many systematic treatments of theology.[6] However, an issue that has been present to the churches nearly since the beginning, and one that continues to grow considerably, is that of human movement: (re)placement, (dis)placement, and relative absence of such persons from many churches, Catholic, Orthodox, and Protestant. Those who are affected because of their movement suffer exclusion not only from the structures and necessary resources of society but, in many cases, from the church itself.

Human movement results from many factors, some unavoidable and others more self-determinative: from war to environmental devastation caused by natural disasters such as earthquakes and flooding, from political instability or threat, from resource depletion or the need for the economic stability of sustainable work.[7] A common reality in these situations is that the once placed are (dis)placed, and in the context of economics, often the once placed are (re)placed either by cheaper labor, reorganized/redistributed workflow, or by advancements in technological efficiency.

Dislocation creates people of no place. In the case of refugees, for instance, the return home is unthinkable, and the (re)settlement into another's land is unlikely. Thus, the (dis)located are (re)located to no places, and the (dis)located are (re)located to spaces of *extraterritoriality* (Bauman's term). These people are, quite literally, neither here nor there.

A United Methodist pastor and urban missions director reported to me, "I experienced this in Dakar, Senegal, in 2005, where I worked at a refugee center. The people had nowhere to go. Home was lost to them. The United Nations wanted the people to return home. But how can one go home who has had his arms cut off and has been told that if he returns home he would be beheaded? The inhumanity was indescribable. Many experienced depression and even death because they had no home."[8] For many, the stakes are very high.

But my concern in this reflection is principally for those (dis)placed, and/or (re)placed for economic reasons. More specifically, my concern is about those who enter the United States without authorizing documentation. During the 1970s this group numbered approximately 200,000 annually. This number has steadily increased to approximately 850,000 per year, more than half of whom arrive in the United States from Mexico and from parts of Central America (notably, Guatemala, El Salvador, and Honduras).[9] I highlight this group in particular because of its special vulnerability. In her book, *God Needs No Passport: Immigrants and the Changing Religious Landscape*, Peggy Levitt notes that visa-granting policies in the United States privilege applicants with high tech and financial skills, thus leaving unskilled laborers (whose work is undeniably needed) to enter a shadow economy.[10] Thus, while race undeniably plays a factor in the exclusion that occurs, the reality is that there continues to be room for hues of brown if the person is "properly skilled." Many who enter the United States without documentation are unskilled laborers. If Mexican migrants were graduates of the Universidad Nacional Autónima de México, this conversation would be quite different. The laborer is needed; the laborer is despised; this requires that we interrogate the matter from the angle of class and privilege.

There is an interesting parallel in the Greek mythological story of Hephaestus (Vulcan in Roman mythology). Among the Olympian gods, Hephaestus is the only one said to be ugly. At birth he is hurled from Mt. Olympus by his mother and, as a consequence, receives an injury rendering him permanently lame. It is curious that he is portrayed in this manner since he is singular among the gods as a laborer, as one who works with his hands. While other gods cause havoc throughout the cosmos, Hephaestus fashions useful products. The value of what he does is recognized and, conveniently for those who benefit from his work, his lameness keeps him close at hand. He is reconciled, after a fashion, with his mother when she sees what marvelous jewelry he can make. But even after he returns to Olympus, he lives underground where he is able to work undisturbed. This is the story of the poor laborer who migrates to the United States.

But, the reality of being on the move, being (dis)placed, (re)settled, and so on, has been part of the church's narration of the story of faith since the beginning. From Exodus, to Exile, to incarnation, to the Holy Family's flight to Egypt, to the diaspora and beyond, faith's story is cast as much in terms of (un)settledness as it is in settledness. It would seem, then, that quite apart from political correctness, the Christian church in all its manifestations has a stake in solidarity with peoples who are on the move and who find themselves in no place; its story is intertwined in the stories of migration and movement, exile, and being *extrañjero*.

Oscar Cardinal Rodriguez of Tegucigalpa, who has seen much movement from his own country, notes in his public addresses the deep connection between the story of migration and the church.[11] This is no more than has been articulated in Catholic social teachings and is nicely summarized in the 2003 document "Strangers No Longer: Together on the Journey of Hope."[12]

- All persons have the right to find in their own countries the economic, political, and social opportunities to live in dignity and achieve a full life through the use of their God-given gifts. In this context, work that provides a just, living wage is a basic human need (§34).
- The church recognizes the right of sovereign nations to control their territories but rejects such control when it is exerted merely for the purpose of acquiring additional wealth. More powerful economic nations, which have the ability to protect and feed their residents, have a stronger obligation to accommodate migration flows (§36).
- The church recognizes that all goods of the earth belong to all people. When persons cannot find employment in their country of origin to support themselves and their families, they have a right to find work elsewhere in order to survive. Sovereign nations should provide ways to accommodate this right (§35).
- Those who flee wars and persecution should be protected by the global community. This requires, at a minimum, that migrants have a right to claim refugee status without incarceration and to have their claims fully considered by a competent authority (§37).
- Regardless of their legal status, migrants, like all persons, possess inherent human dignity which should be respected. Government policies that respect the basic human rights of the undocumented are necessary (§38).

"Strangers No Longer" also outlines moments in the history of God's people when they have been on the move acknowledges human movement in the national stories of both the United States and Mexico. The rationale for solidarity is woven into the history of every one of us.

Ecclesial Identity as Contrast?

How does one think about church in this context? That is, to the degree that such movement forms the context in which the church exists and interacts, how might we consider the question of ecclesial identity? How might we imagine an ecclesiological self-understanding that gives rise to ways of being in solidarity with the other? In other words, I am interested here in the rhetoric by which we name ourselves as the people of God.

One ecclesiological direction we might pursue that has gained traction in recent years is the *church as contrast society*. I'm thinking particularly of the neo-Anabaptists who have attracted much attention. Popularized to a significant degree by Hauerwas, Kinneson, Clapp, the Ekklesia Project, and by Gerhard Lohfink, this vision emphasizes the experience of church as alien.[13]

On some levels this is an attractive vision. It formulates an ecclesiology that acknowledges the essentially alien relation of the community of faith to the dominant culture. The faithful are "resident aliens" who are placed somewhere, but who are nowhere at home, except, perhaps, in an ideal churchly community. In the words of Lohfink, also echoed repeatedly in Hauerwas's writings, "the most important and most irreplaceable service Christians can render society is quite simply that they truly be church."[14] Clearly, certain elements of such a vision reflect the experience of social displacement of the immigrant, the refugee, the one on the move. This version of neo-Anabaptism could have merit in reflecting ecclesial identity in the face of vulnerable populations that are pressed to the margins through their geographical movement.

However, this ecclesiological vision in its U.S. articulation is more a response to Christianity's cultural disestablishment than it is a response to the situation of displaced peoples. That is to say, the church as "alien community" is developed from within the church's experience of cultural disestablishment, not from the vantage point of social, economic, or geographical displacement of those populating this church. To the degree that the church is, particularly in the West, becoming "disestablished," it is becoming disestablished as a dominant cultural force capable of shaping political life, but it is not necessarily (dis)located from a concrete location in space.[15]

Otherwise Documented

This ecclesiological vision is finally unsatisfying. It may utilize language that expresses some dimensions of the experience of the migrant and refugee; however, it grows not out of solidarity with those *on the move* but rather from its user's own social disestablishment. Even more troubling, it perpetuates the social status of alien and alienation by rooting that alienation in the very life of the church in the world. For all the theological benefit we gain by imagining human community and interrelatedness as grounded in the character and commitment of God's triune self, we lose all the ground gained when we argue for the notion of the church as an alien community separate from and over against the world. It makes aliens those who are "at home" and renders *extraterritorial* those who are trying to find a place to be. It detracts from imagining ways of placing the (dis)placed and homing the home(less). Such a vision of church actually perpetuates the injustice of alienation; it legitimizes documenting authorities' practice of declaring illegitimate those *on the move*—the immigrant, the refugee—because it acknowledges that this injustice, a state of alienation, is constitutive of the church itself.[16]

Better is Daniel Groody's suggestion that we reject altogether the use of the term "alien" to describe the (dis)placed one. He writes, "If the term 'alien' is to be used at all, it would be descriptive not of those who lack political documentation but of those who have so disconnected themselves from God and others that they are incapable of seeing in the vulnerable stranger a mirror of themselves, a reflection of Christ, and an invitation to human solidarity."[17] And it is the globalization of solidarity toward which the U.S. and Mexican bishops urge us in "Strangers No Longer."[18] I submit that this solidarity is not possible while utilizing the metaphor of *alien* (or even the language of radical contrast society).

The image of "Pilgrim People," often used in Catholic social teaching, can be helpful, but only to a point. It can easily underwrite an ecclesial vision of homelessness, of permanent displacement, of not belonging where we are. As truthful and theologically articulate as Groody's remark above might be, I take exception to this element of his assertion: "The kingdom calls people into movement, making church members exiles on earth, strangers in this world, and sojourners en route to another place."[19] Such a characterization will never provide a place to the (dis)placed.

However, because this entire question is one of physical movement in the concrete spaces of earth, we cannot avoid asking ourselves about creation. What theology of creation is operative that permits us to name as alien (or, exile) anyone who seeks to live in fellowship with the one who is Creator? That is to say, for those who walk with the Creator, *where on earth can they be alien?*[20] I suggest, alternatively, we consider the image of the *church as otherwise documented*. To be *otherwise documented*, it seems to me, addresses several important matters.

First, it opens us to the possibility of regarding ourselves, our existence as church, as forever belonging *where* we are. This is neither intended to limit movement nor to require that persons "stay in their place(s)," either geographical or social; rather it suggests that *wherever* we are, we are "documented" by the one authorizing agency that has both *de jure* and *de facto* jurisdiction in each potential and actual location.

Leonardo Boff, addressing the question of whether the political falls under the dominion of Christ, offers a way to view the questions we are considering. Where can the follower of the Creator be at home? "La política está incluida en el señorío de Jesucristo, *el cual no es únicamente Señor de pequeños espacios (el corazón, el alma, o la Iglesia), sino que es Señor cósmico, de los grandes espacios*, incluido el de la política."[21]

A church *otherwise documented* is creation centered and, therefore, incarnational.

Secondly, to be *otherwise documented* means that the church understands those documented or not documented by state entities as sisters and brothers, not as "objects" of compassion, nor as those to be pitied. Immigrants, migrants, and refugees, are not objectified as a mission, or a cause, or an issue. As Dan Romero notes, "As much as Latinos are eager to be partners in mission with mainline church folks, they are often still treated as a 'social justice' issue of the church, not true participants."[22]

Such objectifying is perpetuated, I believe, when our ecclesiological vision cannot incorporate into itself a way of walking along side of and identifying with the marginalized other. As expressed in the opening words of *Gaudium et Spes*, "The joys and the hopes, the griefs and the anxieties of [those] of this age, especially those who are poor or in any way afflicted, these too are the joys and hopes, the griefs and anxieties of the followers of Christ." The joys and hopes, and griefs and anxieties, of those who are (dis)placed are not the concern of, or the cause of, or the mission of the followers of Christ. They are their very joys, hopes, griefs, and anxieties. This is a portrait of *solidarity*, not a catalogue of *causes*. Thus, the *entire church* is understood in terms of documentation, not only a segment, and all are marked identically.

Third, by being otherwise documented, the entire church stands side by side, rather than over against or over above. By so doing, the church may have all her many voices, and not solely those that are "legitimately documented," selected, and authorized, to represent the already silenced and marginalized one *on the move*.

Donna Haraway addresses this issue in terms of *articulation* and *representation*. Representation depends upon the distance between representation and the represented as well as between the represented and his or her context. She uses the evocative image of a *ventriloquist* to describe the phenomenon of how representatives speak on behalf of those they identify as "objects of their concern. . . . The assumption that such 'objects' cannot represent themselves renders them forever without their own voices and in need of the services of the ventriloquist."[23] The church can easily exclude the actual voices of the migrant, the refugee, and the one on the move, through a good-hearted benevolence that (re)presents rather than stands along side. These folk are reduced to "the permanent status of the recipient of action never to be a co-actor."[24]

Fourth, to be otherwise documented will inevitably mean challenges with the church and its relationship to the governing and status granting authorities. If the church welcomes the *outsider not validated* by society, the one *on the move*, then its relationship with these status-granting authorities will be affected, compromised even—especially if it dismisses the designation: *alien* or *illegal*—recognizing, instead, their documentation otherwise granted. If, however, the church excludes the *ones made invisible*, it will likely retain its privilege but jeopardize its constitutive mission and vision.[25]

Fortunately, the examples are plentiful of organizations that pulse with the church's energy, that willingly risk standing with those on the move, and that affirm that they are at home *wherever* they are. Nevertheless, there remain too many in churches whose imagination is not shaped by such commitments to solidarity but whose compassion and fellowship are surrounded by a wall, isolating them, making them aliens to those who are otherwise documented.

In short, it is my contention that we theologians and church leaders can contribute to the discussion of human movement by imagining new ways of narrating the story of faith and the identity of the bodies of faithfulness that call and accompany. These "new ways" are not abstracted inventions but organically emerge from the church's own experience in the world. No metaphor is without its limitations, to be sure; however, each metaphor has its moment—a moment when its poignancy is particularly acute and a moment when it speaks truthfulness more clearly than another. My invitation is for us to paint with an expanded pallet of colors and to consider how all of us who walk with the Creator are everywhere at home, documented and legitimate, through the grace of being embraced in the presence of God.

Notes

[1] Zygmunt Bauman, *Liquid Times: Living in an Age of Uncertainty* (Cambridge: Polity Press, 2007), 28–29. Emphasis is in the original.

[2] Ibid., 29–30.

[3] Zygmunt Bauman, *Liquid Love: On the Frailty of Human Bonds* (Cambridge: Polity Press, 2003), 105.

[4] Ibid., 121, 122.

[5] See Michael Hardt and Antonio Negri, *Multitude: War and Democracy in the Age of Empire* (New York: Penguin Press, 2005).

[6] This exclusion results in the church's passive acceptance of travesties as diverse as the summer of 2010's massive oil eruption in the Gulf of Mexico and the enormous amounts of trash produced by church coffee hours.

[7] Some displacement grows out of circumstances afforded by social and economic privilege: the desire for a new neighborhood or a more agreeable climate. Generally, however, these persons have the economic means as well as access to and familiarity with systems of support to move quickly and often seamlessly from dislocation to relocation without becoming disestablished.

[8] Personal conversation with Bruce Hitchcock, UMC pastor and former director of the Urban Mission, Steubenville, Ohio (April 2011).

[9] Jacqueline Maria Hagan, *Migration Miracle: Faith, Hope, and Meaning on the Undocumented Journey* (Cambridge, MA: Harvard University Press, 2008), 9. See also Jeffrey Passel, "Size and Characteristics of the Unauthorized Migrant Population," *Report*, Pew Hispanic Center, Washington, DC, March 2006.

[10] Peggy Levitt, *God Needs No Passport: Immigrants and the Changing Religious Landscape* (New York: New Press, 2007), 196.

[11] "Latin American View on Migrants and Immigration Reform," Address at Xavier University (September 16, 2008).

[12] Jointly issued by the U.S. Conference of Catholic Bishops and la Conferencia del Episcopado Mexicano, 2003. In Spanish: *Carta pastoral de los Obispos Católicos de los Estados Unidos y México sobre la migración*, http://www.usccb.org/mrs/stranger.shtml; http://www.usccb.org/mrs/strangersp.shtml. In English: United States Conference of Catholic Bishops, Inc. and *Conferencia del Episcopado Mexicano*, "Strangers No Longer: Together on a Journey of Hope" (2003), http://usccb.org/issues-and-action/human-life-and-dignity/immigration/strangers-no-longer-together-on-the-journey-of-hope.cfm. See also Pius XII, *Exsul Familia* (1952), John XXIII, *Pacem in Terris* (1963); Paul VI, *De Pastorali Migratorum Cura* (1969); *Church and People on the Move* (1978), http://www.vatican.org; *Refugees: A Challenge to Solidarity* (1992), http://www.vatican.org; *Era Caritas Christi* (2004), http://www.vatican.org.

[13] For example, Stanley Hauerwas, *In Good Company: the Church as Polis* (Notre Dame, IN: University of Notre Dame Press, 1995); Rodney Clapp, *A Peculiar People: The Church as Culture in a Post-Christian Society* (Downer's

Grove, IL: Intervarsity Press, 1996); Phillip Kinneson, *Beyond Sectarianism: Re-Imagining Church and World* (Harrisburg, PA: Trinity Press International, 1999). For a critique of this particular vision of ecclesiology, see Gloria Albrecht, *The Character of Our Communities: Toward an Ethic of Liberation for the Church* (Nashville: Abingdon Press, 1995). While not directly a critique, these provide alternatives to a contrast society vision of ecclesiology: Letty Russell, *Church in the Round: Feminist Interpretation of the Church* (Louisville, KY: Westminster/John Knox, 1993); and Pamela Dickey Young, *Re-Creating the Church: Communities of Eros* (Harrisburg, PA: Trinity Press International, 2000).

[14] Gerhard Lohfink, *Jesus and Community: The Social Dimension of Christian Faith* (Philadelphia: Fortress Press, 1984), 168. See also Gerhard Lohfink, *Does God Need the Church: Toward a Theology of the People of God*, trans. Linda M. Maloney (Collegeville, MN: The Liturgical Press, 1999.

[15] The net effect of this view is a world renouncing ecclesiology. "It [the neo-Anabaptist vision] is overwhelmingly a message of anger, disparagement, and negation" (James Davison Hunter, *To Change the World: The Irony, Tragedy, and Possibility of Christianity in the Late Modern World* [New York: Oxford University Press, 2010], 165).

[16] Additionally, it possesses a highly critical assessment of "the world," broadly defined. "[T]here is little good in the world that deserves praise and no beauty that generates wonder and appreciation. As to the church, there is much to admire about it as a theological abstraction or, say, as it could be or yet will be," but the church is historical, so there is little to admire except the work of a handful of faithful ones. In reality, "the failure of the church is everywhere visible" (Hunter, *To Change the World*, 164).

[17] Daniel G. Groody, "Crossing the Divide: Foundations of a Theology of Migration and Refugees," *Theological Studies* 70 (2009): 667.

[18] "Now is the time for both the United States and Mexico to confront the reality of globalization and to work toward the globalization of solidarity. Both governments have recognized the integration of economic interests through the North American Free Trade Agreement. It is now time to harmonize policies on the movement of people, particularly in a way that respects the human dignity of the migrant and recognizes the social consequences of globalization" ("Strangers No Longer," §57). Mark Ensalaco provided a helpful analysis of "Strangers No Longer" that is both highly appreciative but that also questions the bishops' softness on Mexico. The bishops rightly challenge the U.S. government, he notes, but they do not sufficiently address the Mexican government's inattention to the internal social and economic realities. These realities are resulting in its residents not *migrating to* the U.S., but *fleeing from* Mexico. Presentation at the International Conference on Ecclesiology and Exclusion (May 18, 2011).

[19] Groody, "Crossing the Divide," 661. See also Christine D. Pohl, "Biblical Images in Mission and Migration," *Missiology* 31 (2003): 3–15.

[20] For example, "In becoming neighbor to all in the incarnation, that is, to all who live in the sinful territory of a fallen humanity, God redefines the borders between neighbors and opens up the possibility for a new relationship" (Groody, "Crossing the Divide," 652.)

[21] Leonardo Boff, *Iglesia: Carisma y Poder* (Santander, Spain: Sal Terrae, 1982), 54–55. Emphasis mine. Translation: "The political is part of the lordship of Jesus Christ; he not only Lord of little spaces (like our heart, our soul, or the Church), but he is Lord of the Cosmos, of grand spaces, which includes the political."

[22] Dan Romero, "'Not Like Us': The Mainline's Immigration Problem," *Reflections*, Yale Divinity School 95 (Fall 2008): 20.

[23] Ann Kirkus Wetherilt, *That They May Be Many: Voices of Women, Echoes of God* (New York: Continnum, 1994), 143. See also Donna Haraway, "The Promises of Monsters: A Regenerative Politics for Inappropriate/d Others," in *Cultural Studies*, ed. Lawrence Grossberg, Cary Nelson, and Paula A. Treichler (New York: Routledge, 1992), 295–337.

[24] Haraway, "The Promises of Monsters," 312.

[25] "Since Vatican II, the Catholic Church has largely shifted its role from being an ally of the state to being an advocate for the poor and disenfranchised" (Hagan, *Migration Miracle*, 89). [Ojalá que siguen todas las iglesias, también!]

Ecclesial Identity and the Excluded Homeless Population: A Funnel Ecclesiology as a Framework of Inclusion[1]

Pascal Daniel Bazzell

In the last decades there has been an exciting development of new voices joining the conversation surrounding ecclesial reality, including liberation theology, Dalit theology, black theology, Minjung theology, tribal theology, and so forth. These Western and non-Western theologians have labored with great effort to articulate ecclesial reflections for and from the marginalized in our society. However, as I will point out in this essay, there has been an excluded partner in this conversation: homeless communities.

The theology that will be discussed in this essay is regional; it is specific to the context of a Filipino homeless ecclesial community.[2] I have been serving with and among homeless communities in Davao City, Philippines, since 2003. This context and its individual ecclesial identity shape this essay; the reality of homelessness in other parts of the world may be radically different. The paradigm to be explored here embraces an ecclesial identity among street-living communities and is thus potentially, though not intentionally, controversial. I hope to provide principles and implications that may be useful in other similar contexts as well as in discussions of ecclesiology, urban mission, and intercultural theology.

The reality we often face in street-level ministry is that the ecclesiology or church planting theories we use seldom focus on a people group such as homeless communities.[3] There is extensive dialogue occurring in regard to ecclesiology and the poor, but when it comes to the homeless population, we immediately seem to shift into a paradigm of commodity-based benevolence with a rescue and rehabilitation mentality. Actually, there is often a view found in churches and writings that long-term spiritual and moral growth cannot happen on the streets as it too evil, too enticing, too enslaving.[4] It has even been suggested that those who choose to live on the streets have perhaps rejected life and even God.[5]

There are various groups of people, whether they be homeless communities, the vagabonds in Europe, the Manobo tribes in the Philippines, the nomads, etc., whose lifestyles would be considered by the majority of the world as unsafe, risky, and unstable. Nevertheless, through time they have developed their own cultural identities and social structures relevant to their own contexts and lifestyles. The assumption that unless one has a recognized economic claim to a place, one has no "home" and thus is socially substandard is absurd when one considers the number of wandering societies throughout human history. This categorization includes the biblical notion of "pilgrims" as well as the figures of Abraham, Moses, the entire nation of Israel after the Exodus, including the wandering prophetic voices and the exilic and postexilic theological reevaluators. Some of the most fruitful periods of theologizing in biblical history are recorded as occurring in contexts of displacement, "homelessness," or social marginalization, which should give us cause to listen to them, not only in tolerant and accepting ways, but also as humble and avid learners.

What is more, the realities of overurbanization, overpopulation, and underemployment are daily bringing more people into our streets who have chosen to build intentional communities of their own. As John Bruhn notes,

> Whether housed or homeless, people are inherently social in nature. Through our social encounters we acquire a web of interpersonal social relationships. These relationships form the basis of our personal social networks. It is through social networks that we negotiate our social worlds. Even in dire circumstances, people usually manage to connect with others to maximize their survival.[6]

The notions of the homeless population and community are seldom associated. Spencer E. Cahill and Lyn H. Lofland note that generally, and in most scholarly discourse, the reality of the streets is understood as the antithesis of community. Hence, from this perspective, it is a total oxymoron to use the terminology of a "community of the streets." The authors mention that "the street, as 'everybody' knows, is the site of anonymity, impersonality, isolation, alienation, normlessness, and most particularly, and in consequence, menace. It should be obvious from our deliberate choice of title, then, that we intend this volume as a contribution to the growing body of work in sociology and kindred disciplines which counters this widely accepted view."[7] Although Cahill and Lofland wrote nearly two decades ago, still today our church outreaches, public policies, educational programs, economic projects, and scholarly discourse remain solely focused on the individual or families on the streets and their rescue and rehabilitation. All of these are very important and needed; however, such an exclusive approach further marginalizes awareness of the street-level community, and we miss out on using their social networks to work effectively and relevantly among the homeless population.

It is precisely these social street-level groupings that challenge us in the church. Inevitably our ecclesiology and church planting theories are thrown into question: will we continue to ignore them or are we willing to acknowledge the communal identity of these others among us? Will we allow and equip these street-living communities to wrestle with issues of living as an ecclesial community in their particular contexts and lifestyles? For too long, we have endeavored mightily to seek ways that the "community of the streets" might embrace our ecclesiology or follow our church practices, which has often served to widen the gap between our churches and the homeless population. I would suggest that now is the time to listen to them as we equip them to dialogue with scripture, their own context and pilgrimage, and church traditions in order to articulate their own ecclesiology.[8] This is contrary to the general practice in our churches and writings that seeks ways to integrate the homeless into our churches. Instead of the homeless having to adjust to our churches, the status quo, which is often dictated by values that are contrary to their value systems (and sadly result in more hurt among the homeless population), street-level communities need to be equipped to articulate a biblical vision and ecclesiology that emerge from the context of their own praxis.

Street-level ecclesial communities are simply street-level and not inherently deficient because they take this form. We are in danger of spiritual blindness if we exclude an ecclesial identity due to a group's socioeconomic distinction as indicated by the degree of a group's influence or by its quantity of material possessions. Social and economic criteria have no more to do with ecclesial or theological legitimacy than ethnicity, gender, or political alignment. It seems that we have fallen into a habit of categorizing more under the sway of socioeconomic systems of evaluation than theological insight. If we fall into this trap, we have idolized materialistic worldviews and economic structures. The idea that material possessions or social standing are indicative of spiritual/ecclesial standing, God's inspiration, or his blessing has already been dealt with at length in the Book of Job, the parable of Lazarus and the Rich Man, John 9, and the Sermon on the Mount to name just a few sources. To make a particular ecclesial community unilaterally the object of mission or solely the recipient of theologizing based purely upon socioeconomic classification grants theological and ecclesiological value to status and material wealth in a manner that capitulates to the moral presumptions of this age. Such attitudes run counter to the thrust of Jesus' teaching and life as well as to the overt instruction of the entire New Testament.

One can only wonder how Jesus and the disciples would have responded to prejudicial assumptions about street people, as they themselves were street-level theologians, or in Paul's case, a migrant theologian. A good example of street theologizing is Jesus on the Emmaus Road explaining "the things about himself in all the scriptures" (Lk 24:27). Street theologizing, as I am using the term, is usually narrative theology, with a strong emphasis on journeying together to explore God's truth. As they reflected on the signs of their time (Mt 16:3), their hearts were illuminated by hearing and listening to the word of God. Street theologizing is also sacramental: when they gave thanks to God and broke bread, their eyes were opened (Lk 24:30–35). From my own ministry experience, I can say that street theologizing becomes missional as the homeless go and tell what they have heard, witnessed, and learned to their neighbors living in the streets.

By providing their own ecclesial reflections, the homeless communities can contribute a fresh and unique perspective to our dialogue and practices on ecclesial reality. John O'Brien explains that there are multiplicities of ecclesiological narratives that differ. Rarely heard, they are more likely ignored, silenced, and sidelined (e.g., women's experience of church, the poor, and excluded). He points out concerning the marginalized that "their narrative, precisely as their narrative, was non-existent. Without such narratives, forming as they do a corrective ecclesiology 'from below,' from 'outside the gates,' ecclesiological conversation risks being bland and comfortable, lacking any capacity to articulate how 'the sacred and subversive memory' of Jesus can transform contemporary experience."[9] O'Brien argues that an ecclesiological "narrative can surpass its own hidden rootedness in possible structures of oppression by locating itself in a further triangular hermeneutical space defined by the preferential option for the excluded, a contemplative search for the designs of God and a search for structures of greater inclusiveness. In this way, an adequate ecclesiology may emerge whose temporal distance from classical ecclesiologies can provide a potential productive ground of even deeper understanding."[10] Perhaps there is something about a street-level faith perspective that yields theological truth articulation as a seed of the word that has not been "choked" by "the cares of this world and the deceitfulness of riches" (Mt 13:22).[11]

One defining element of a mature church lies in the congregants' ability to theologize within and for their own context. It is the ability to theologically reflect on the signs of our times (Mt 16:3) and to examine everything to see if what is being said is God's truth (Acts 17:11). Nancey Murphy affirms that theology starts with the amateurs, and not with the professional theologians, because professional theologians are dependent upon the findings of the community. This dependency of the professional theologian is "especially apparent when one thinks of the results of communal discernment as a primary source of data for theology."[12] For Clemens Sedmak, "[d]oing theology means listening to the voices of those without voice, seeing the power of those without power, honoring the life of those without life. We do theology because we see and feel the wounds of our time. We cannot do theology but through wounds. It takes courage and honesty to face the plight of the earth."[13]

As Jesus asked his disciples, he is also asking the homeless population, "But who do you say that I am?" (Mt 16:15). As missionaries, pastors, and theologians, we are in danger of only doing theology *for* the poor without training and equipping them to do their own theology. Engaging in their own theologizing gives voice to the poor's concerns and questions rather than having others' ideas put in their mouths. It affirms their innate, dignifying, and reflective capacity for self-expression that comes from being made in the image of God.[14] Ecclesial reflections stemming from the homeless population can help to equip them with a reflexive mode that affirms who they are in God, a reflexive channel of healing and reconciliation, and builds up their community where they can belong.[15]

Toward a Funnel Ecclesiology

Paul Hiebert provides an insightful analysis of the church that builds on the mathematical concepts of "bounded sets," "fuzzy sets," and "centered sets."[16] Bounded sets function to define and maintain the boundaries with great emphasis on membership: you are either one of us or you are not. In contrast, fuzzy sets have no sharp boundaries and focus on process with no stable point of reference to distinguish, for example, between right and wrong, and with various degrees of inclusion. The characteristic of centered sets is defined by a center and the relationship of things to that center. Something is either moving toward or away from the center. The question raised in this conference is most connected with the concepts of bounded-set and centered-set church. Should we focus more on defining our boundaries (for example, traditions, identity, shared faith and practice, rites of initiation, and the maintenance of standards), which could result in becoming more exclusionary, or should we rather focus on defining a center set church, which could have a tendency leading toward relativism?

As a grassroots minister serving the urban poor, I am torn as I reflect on these issues. My own theological upbringing placed great value on emphasizing boundaries; in no way do I want to neglect those. However, in my missional engagement, I have heard too many stories from the poor of great exclusions, oppression, and injustice from church institutions. From the context in which I live, strong emphasis on these boundaries is often associated with a colonial mind-set. In no way do I wish to condone a standpoint that will further reinforce oppressive structures that will push the poor further into the margins. As a Westerner living in an Asian context, I do wonder if my Western inclination to compartmentalize may be limiting my ability to fully understand this challenge. I would like to believe that there is something beyond such dichotomous extremes, both finding a ground of radical inclusion and providing a place of belonging. Can we do so, while at the same time rightly emphasizing traditions, identity, shared faith and practice, rites of initiation, and the maintenance of standards?

Whatever our preferred emphasis, we cannot escape the reality that an ecclesiological shift has occurred in the last decades. In writing about Fresh Expressions, John Drane observed the following:

> [W]hereas a Christian gathering on a midweek evening in a coffee shop might traditionally have been regarded as a way of engaging people with a hope of getting them to church on Sunday, there is now a recognition that if indeed church is where two or three gather in Christ's name (Matt. 18:20), then the meeting in the coffee shop (or of surfers on a beach, or police officers meeting on their lunch break, or any number of other things) could be as authentic an expression of church as high mass in a cathedral on Sunday morning.[17]

Drane mentions that a major catalyst for this conversation, which is also observable in various other new movements (for example, emerging church, missional church, insiders movements, etc.), is found in the foreword of *Mission-Shaped Church*. In that work, the definition of "church" refers to "what happens when people encounter the Risen Jesus and commit themselves to sustaining and deepening that encounter in their encounter with each other; there is plenty of theological room for diversity of rhythm and style, so long as we have ways of identifying the same living Christ at the heart of every expression of Christian life in common."[18] I have to say that I was taken back by this minimalist definition of church. When I had the opportunity to ask Bishop Cray (chairman of the *Mission-Shaped Church* report) at the Missiology Lecture 2009, Fuller Theological Seminary, about this minimalist definition of church that fails, for example, to mention the sacraments, he responded, that they all—sacraments, scriptures, traditions, the marks of the church, and so on—point toward Christ. How else do you know Christ apart from them?

In one sense then, instead of focusing on setting fences or boundaries in asking the either/or question of what somebody should believe and do, I find it more appropriate to use the term *funnel*. A funnel's boundaries point toward the center. Boundaries or fences are crucial for any mature and healthy church; however, they should not been seen as either/or. Rather, boundaries should provide directions toward the center, Jesus Christ. Instead of moving across lines, an outer circle that distinguishes whether one is in or out often based on a defined list of ideological-cultural boundaries fixed in moral and cultural codes,[19] a community enters into the funnel as they gather together to confess Christ their Lord and Savior. As Miroslav Volf notes, "*Where two or three are gathered in Christ's name, not only is Christ present among them, but a Christian church is there as well,* perhaps a bad church, a church that may well transgress against love and truth, but a church nonetheless."[20] But what boundaries would be ecumenically appropriate? Historically, the majority of Christians have recognized the boundaries as being constituted by embodiment of the one, holy, catholic, and apostolic church that is active and present in every local church.

As two or three gather in Christ's name seeking to follow Christ, they enter a dialectic tension among three elements: the center of the ecclesial identity, *Christ Jesus*; the boundaries, *the marks of the church* (one, holy, catholic, and apostolic) that surround the community; and the context itself, *the community*. This tension corrects its misshapenness, critiques its practices, adjusts its beliefs, and gives guidance and directions to the community as the community members are transformed into the likeness of Christ. However, the marks should not be seen with a fixed definition. Jürgen Moltmann mentions that we need to keep in mind the context of the four marks of the church:

> At that period there was considerable political pressure for the church's unity and universality, so that it might be in a position to administer the unified religion for the Roman Empire. To make this historical observation is not to deny the truth of these statements about the church. But it gives us liberty to move other marks of the true church into the foreground in a changed world situation, and to link these with the traditional ones.[21]

In his own work, Moltmann provides a reinterpretation of the four traditional marks as they relate to the church's "social and political *Sitz im Leben*." LeRon Shults makes a more recent contribution when he argues that interpreting the creedal "marks" of the church in "absolute and exclusive terms . . . may in fact be misleading, [as] these may actually mark forms of religious community that have little to do with Jesus' way of knowing, acting, and being in the world."[22] Instead of upholding a static set of boundaries, the church gathering in the name of Jesus within its own social and political *Sitz im Leben* enters into dialectic tension with the marks of church, which results in shaping their community. Outsiders should not force upon the local church a static interpretation but rather should acknowledge the community's unique cultural context and its pilgrimages and ability to theologize for its own context. Rather than tradition, creeds, and historical or systematic theology setting the boundaries for including or excluding the persons, a funnel ecclesiology allows members to interact with the boundaries on their own terms and time, crucial in many colonial contexts, while at the same time emphasizing the importance of dynamic, living boundaries for any healthy and mature church. It is within this tension and movement that the church is constantly rearticulating the center. As finite persons, even we agree on the center being Jesus Christ, and yet we still need to continue to articulate the content (correct doctrine) of the center. It is this dialectic tension between the boundaries, the context, and its center in Christ that is necessary in order to allow a community to live out and express its identity.

A funnel ecclesiology helps to articulate the function or purpose of the church. Karl Barth observes that the essential components of the church are not only perceived but, in fact, come to be when the church fulfills the purpose for which it exists.[23] Charles Van Engen states that "it is important for us to examine the purpose of the Church's life in the world, as that is derived from the Church's nature as a fellowship of the redeemed."[24] Furthermore, Van Engen argues that "the missionary Church emerges when its members increasingly participate in the Church's being-in-the-world through *koinonia*, *kerygma*, *diakonia*, and *martyria*."[25] To complete Van Engen's list, we add *leitourgia*.

Koininia emphasizes the importance of living and embracing each other while living that love outwardly to neighbors. *Diakonia* means service with an emphasis on service to each other in the church and at the same time to the larger social and political realities of the church's "*Sitz in Leben.*" *Kerygma* is the message of Jesus Christ, the proclamation of the reign of God, and the announcement to the world that the shalom has come. *Martyria* is the commissioning of the church, "You shall be my *witness*" in this world (Acts 1:8). And *Leitourgia* reflects the public ritualistic expression (e.g., Eucharist, baptism, worship) as a Christian community of our faith in God. The church fulfills its purpose or function as it moves in the direction of the ecclesial center, Jesus Christ. A funnel ecclesiology's boundaries and functions move toward the ecclesial center, and, hence, the church becomes more Christ-like while at the same time its influence in the world may increase. In all of this, we do need to acknowledge the pneumatological dimension of the dialectic tension. It is still God's grace and revelation that make the community become the church in context.

A funnel ecclesiology provides us with some conceptual tools for overcoming, at the grassroots level, some of the extreme dichotomies we find in our ecclesial dialogues. It emphasizes that each context must wrestle with these extreme dichotomies and articulates how the community can develop a structure with radical inclusions creating a place of belonging, while at the same time rightly emphasizing traditions. In my own ministry context, the homeless community has intentionally started to reflect on scripture and historical doctrine with focused application in and for its context. Each week the members gather to reflect on what it means to follow Christ on the streets and live this out in their community. Each week they discuss ecclesial issues affecting their faith community, such as how and who should take the Eucharist, initiation into the community, baptism, church discipline, structure of authority, and so on. Ecclesial sacraments, such as the Eucharist and baptism, bring the community together in worship, dedication, healing, and reconciliation to each other. This is not to say that this is a very mature church, like other local churches that have had hundreds of years of ecclesial reflections. However, it is a church that honestly is seeking Christ to be in its midst and reflect Christ's love to its neighbor.

Are we now to deny community members' ecclesial identity because of the context in which they live? Are we to deny the ecclesiality (the essence) of their church because their model of church looks different? Volf offers a powerful argument as he reflects on the Episcopal traditions and whether they should accept the full ecclesiality of the Free Church:

> Today, such exclusivity is no longer credible. I am thinking less of the sociological fact that exclusive positions in modern societies are unpersuasive than of the observation that the dynamic life and the orthodox faith of the many, quickly proliferating Free Churches make it difficult to deny them full ecclesiality. Let me illustrate by referring to a situation that, although doubtless atypical, must nonetheless be the touchstone of any ecclesiology precisely because it is a borderline case. Should, for example, a Catholic or Orthodox diocese whose members are inclined more to superstition than to faith and who identify with the church more for nationalistic reasons—should such a diocese be viewed as a church, while a Baptist congregation that has preserved its faith through the crucible of persecution *not* be considered such? Would not an understanding of ecclesiality that leads to such a conclusion take us to the brink of absurdity? Equally untenable is the early, though still widespread Free Church position that denies ecclesiality to the Episcopal church.[26]

Looking at the ecclesiality from an ecumenical perspective, on what grounds do we deny a homeless community its church identity? A funnel ecclesiology holds that a mature church consists in a group of people gathering to confess Christ. This group of people holds in dialectic tension its own context together with the marks of the church insofar as these give direction toward Christ, the ecclesial center. If a street-level faith community is doing exactly this, then it follows that street-level faith communities are the church as much as any other church may be considered to be the church, and thus they already have the fullness of ecclesial authority and legitimacy whether or not other churches recognize it.

Christians are in danger of committing exclusion and impoverishing the church, especially our experience of church, if we deny the ecclesial identity of street-level faith communities because of the supposedly violent, oppressive, and abusing context in which their members live. Are we inclined to silence their ecclesial voices? If so, we are reinforcing an oppressive structure that pushes the homeless population further toward the margins. The homeless population will not complain; they are accustomed to being voiceless and deemed useless in our societies and churches. But what if we acknowledge, affirm, and even nurture their ecclesial reflections? What if we cherish this dignifying process of theological reflection and recognize their ecclesial identity as a full part of the life of the church? From my own missional engagement, I have seen that if we emphasize the latter, individuals and families, many of whom have rejected the institutional church, come together to be with Christ. A community of violence is transformed into a community of peace; a place of brokenness and abuse becomes a place of healing and reconciliation. If we cultivate these ecclesial street-level communities, they will produce fresh and unique reflections that surely will contribute to the dialogues about our ecclesial reality. As these new reflections interact with our two thousand years of ecclesial reflections, the street-level ecclesial community can learn a lot from these historical ecclesial reflections, while at the same time contributing unique insights that we might have missed all the years.

Notes

¹ I would like to express my deep appreciation to my colleagues, Karen Parchman, Rebecca Giselbrecht, and especially to Adam Ayers, for reading an earlier version of this paper and making several helpful suggestions. Any defects that remain are, of course, my own.

² For an ethnographical analysis of the social structure, social relationship patterns, and cultural themes of the homeless community of my research and ministry focus, see my upcoming Ph.D. dissertation at Fuller Theological Seminary. This community consists of families and individuals who have been living in one particular park for several years (some families for almost twenty years). The community consists of the newborn to the great-grandparents (four generations are present). Also, the community is multiethnic, multilanguage and multireli-

gious (besides dominant Catholic and Protestant groups, there are also other sects as well as Muslims living in the community).

[3] Tobey O. Pitman in his dissertation, "Developing a Strategy for Congregationalizing Homeless People at the Brantley Baptist Center in New Orleans, Louisiana" (New Orleans Baptist Theological Seminary, 2004) and Roddy Keith Youree, in his dissertation, "Developing a Church-Based Model for Relational Ministries among the Homeless" (Southwestern Baptist Theological Seminary, 2007) come to the same conclusion in their doctoral research. However, both authors stay within the paradigm of developing strategies for congregationalizing the homeless people.

[4] Roger S. Greenway and Timothy M. Monsma, *Cities: Missions' New Frontier*, 2nd ed. (Grand Rapids: Baker Books, 2000), 188.

[5] Helen Sheed, "Street Addiction Can Be Broken," in *Street Children: A Guide to Effective Ministry*, ed. P. Kilbourn (Monrovia, CA: MARC, 1997).

[6] John G. Bruhn, *The Sociology of Community Connections* (New York: Springer, 2005), 80.

[7] Spencer E. Cahill and Lyn H. Lofland, *The Community of the Streets*, vol. 1 (Bingley, UK: Emerald Group Publishing, 1994), xi.

[8] See Marlies Gielen, in her article, "Zur Interpretation der paulinishen Formel," in *Zeitschrift für die neutestamentliche Wissenschaft und die Kunde der älteren Kirche*, vol. 77, nos. 1/2 (1986): 109–25; and Leonardo Boff, *Ecclesiogenesis: The Base Communities Reinvent the Church*, trans. Robert R. Barr (Maryknoll, NY: Orbis Books, 1986), 2.

[9] John O'Brien, "Ecclesiology as Narrative," *Ecclesiology* 4 (2008): 160–61.

[10] Ibid., 148.

[11] Cf. the Epistle of James, esp. 2:1–7.

[12] Nancey C. Murphy, *Theology in the Age of Scientific Reasoning* (Ithaca, NY: Cornell University Press, 1993), 196.

[13] Clemens Sedmak, *Doing Local Theology: A Guide for Artisans of a New Humanity* (Maryknoll, NY: Orbis Books, 2002), 9–10.

[14] See also Pascal Bazzell, "Towards A Creational Perspective of Poverty: Genesis 1:26–28, Image of God, and Missiological Implications," in The Book of Genesis and Christian Theology, ed. Nathan MacDonald, Mark Elliot and Grant Macaskill (Grand Rapids, MI: Eerdmans, 2012).

[15] Sedmak notes that "the way Jesus did theology was intended to build up community" (Sedmak, *Doing Local Theology*, 31–33). See also Robert J. Schreiter, *Constructing Local Theologies* (Maryknoll NY: Orbis Books, 2006), 17.

[16] See Paul G Hiebert, *Anthropological Reflections on Missiological Issues* (Grand Rapids, MI: Baker Books, 1994), 110–36.

[17] John Drane, "Resisting McDonaldization," in *Walk Humbly with the Lord: Church and Mission Engaging Plurality*, ed. Viggo Mortensen and Andreas Østerlund Nielsen (Grand Rapids, MI: W. B. Eerdmans, 2011), 157.

[18] Rowan Williams and Graham Cray, *Mission-Shaped Church: Church Planting and Fresh Expressions of Church in a Changing Context* (London: Church House Publishing, 2004), vii. John Drane notes that such a definition of church creates opportunity "for entirely new forms of faith communities to be created and sustained outside traditional parish structures but with full recognition as true manifestation to be one, holy, catholic, and apostolic church" (Drane, *Resisting McDonaldization*, 158).

[19] See Michael Frost and Alan Hirsch, *The Shaping of Things to Come: Innovation and Mission for the 21st-Century Church* (Peabody, MA: Hendrickson Publishers, 2003), 207 (see also pp. 47, 206).

[20] Miroslav Volf, *After Our Likeness: The Church as Image of the Trinity* (Grand Rapids, MI: W. B. Eerdmans, 1998), 136.

[21] Jürgen Moltmann, *The Church in the Power of the Spirit: A Contribution to Messianic Ecclesiology* (Minneapolis: Fortress Press, 1993), 340.

[22] LeRon Shults, "Transforming Ecclesiologies in a Multireligious World," in *Walk Humbly with the Lord: Church and Mission Engaging Plurality*, ed. Viggo Mortensen and Andreas Østerlund Nielsen (Grand Rapids, MI: W. B. Eerdmans, 2011), 149. See also Gioacchino Campese's essay in this volume that provides insights concerning how immigrants produce new perspective on the traditional marks of the church.

[23] Karl Barth, *Church Dogmatics* 4.1 (Edinburgh: T & T Clark, 1958), 650–65.

[24] Charles E. Van Engen, *Mission on the Way: Issues in Mission Theology* (Grand Rapids, MI: Baker Academic, 1996), 89.

[25] Ibid., 89.

[26] Volf, *After Our Likeness*, 133–34.

PART III

EXCLUSION AND RACIAL JUSTICE

Bryan N. Massingale's
Racial Justice and the Catholic Church

Race and Social Context:
Language, "Colorblindness," and Intergroup Contact

Leslie H. Picca

Bryan Massingale's *Racial Justice and the Catholic Church* is a pleasure to read.[1] It is filled not only with rich insight but also with contemporary data (such as predicted U.S. demographic shifts, where whites will no longer be the statistical majority within the next thirty-one years). Yet it remains moving and accessible, especially through Father Massingale's personal reflections and narratives. I am quite taken by one of his main goals: "A key assumption of this . . . project is that Christian faith has a valuable and essential role to play in the effort to bring about a more racially just society" (84).

I am not a religion scholar but rather a sociologist. My own academic focus is on race and ethnicity, especially on how everyday racial interactions maintain the larger racial hierarchy in social structures (like in the legal system, education, media, health care system, religion, the family, and all those "social institutions" that sociologists like to talk about). I was especially pleased with Massingale's ability (1) to move conversations about racial justice away from individual "bad" people and instead examine racism as systemic, institutional, cultural, and foundational to U.S. society; and (2) to focus not just on the oppression of people of color but on white privilege.

My own goal in this brief response to Massingale's book is to address briefly the broader social context of racial relations, addressing (1) language, (2) colorblindness, and (3) intergroup contact.

Let me first say that it can be difficult to talk about race. Most people don't walk away from a conversation about race, especially about racism, and say, "That was great. I feel really good about that!" I talk to a lot of white audiences, and most of them tell me they feel guilty, frustrated, angry, indifferent, and other negative or neutral responses. There are at least two reasons why people (especially whites) feel uncomfortable talking about race: first, we lack sustained and meaningful interactions with people of color; second, we have inadequate language to talk about race.

Language

We don't have very good language to talk about race/ethnicity. Think about the language we have for racial categories such as "black" and "white." No one is exclusively either; we are all variations of brown/beige. Physically, we are more alike than different, yet our language instructs us not to see the similarities but to see the differences. Additionally, we can pose the following questions: What does it mean that we use terms that are polar opposites? What does it mean that such terms are not only opposite but also ranked?

If you get a chance, get out a physical dictionary (as it is not the same with online resources like dictionary.com), and look up the definition for "white." You'll find words like white knight, white flag, and white collar that signify purity, innocence, unblemished, surrender, and nonthreatening. Now look up the definition for "black." You'll find words like black sheep, blackball, and blackmail that signify dirty, threatening, and dangerous. On the whole, the white words are positive, and on the whole, the black words are negative.

Largely, these "color" conceptualizations came first and later were applied to people. There is nothing natural about referring to ourselves by these artificially applied colors that we attribute to our skin. Indeed, before the 1700s, "whites" as a racial category did not exist. Terms like "Christian" and "heathen" were used but were later replaced by "white and black."

"Black" and "white" are not the only racial terms that we use that are problematic. Take a term such as "African American." Many persons who are included in this category identify no ties to Africa but to the Caribbean or Central America. Whoopi Goldberg, for one, insists not to be called African American but rather an American who is a black woman because she claims no ties to Africa.[2] Additionally, there are white people who technically are "African American" who, for the most part, cannot use this label. For example, Teresa Heinz Kerry is a white woman, and wife of 2004 Democratic presidential nominee John Kerry, who happens to be worth $1.2 billion. She claimed to be African American as she is from Africa and an American, and the American public responded with, "Oh, no, rich white woman, you are not African American!"

Obviously terms such as "Asian American," "Latino/Hispanic," and "Native American" are pan-ethnic categories created by the (largely white) United States in order to lump together people of very different backgrounds, histories, religions, economics, and physical appearances. I often hear my students say, "I'm afraid to say anything! Is it black or African American? Latino or Hispanic? Person of color or minority?" All of our words are problematic. Yet if we don't have the language to communicate about race, how are we ever going to get at the root of the substance? This is why we often have conversations about race without ever mentioning race. If I say words like "suburban" or "private schools," what image do you have? Whose face do we see? What about words like "inner city" or "Dayton public schools"—does the image change? Whose face do we see now? Race is never mentioned but it's absolutely implied. In conversations in our communities, we need to keep in mind that even though race may not be explicitly discussed, it is *always* present in our communities.

I often interact with students at the University of Dayton, and I hear students on this campus say, with genuine affection, how much they love the sense of "community" on campus. They talk about the open door policy in student neighborhoods. And yet the largest student neighborhood is known as "the ghetto"—another racially coded word. We need to be more attuned to the implications of the words we use to describe our communities as well as to the gap that can exist between what we believe, often with good intentions, and the reality of who is truly embraced in this "open" community and who is under suspicion.

Colorblindness

I recently was a part of a focus group on Catholic social teaching and racial relations. One participant, a white male at a Catholic high school, shared that at his school, the designation of "Catholic" and "non-Catholic" took on an additional connotation. In some circumstances, it was a polite way to talk about racial differences where, according to this participant, Catholic equals white and non-Catholic equals black. Even though they knew that not all Catholics were white, and that not all whites were Catholic (note the reference group where white and Catholic are at the center), the terms functioned as short-hand to express racialized sentiments in a "colorblind" way.

Colorblindness is most connected in our minds with the famous Dr. Martin Luther King's "I Have a Dream" speech where he envisions a world in which his four children "will not be judged by the color of their skin but by the content of their character." Colorblindness is the notion that it doesn't matter if you are black, white, purple, or polka dotted, we're all members of the human race. For many whites, colorblindness is typically seen as the *solution* to racism. My research challenges this assumption, and indeed most social scientists argue colorblindness is *another* form of racism. There are at least four reasons why colorblindness works against those of us interested in racial justice. First, colorblindness ignores the differences between us. These are differences we should celebrate (food, dance, dress, customs, appearances, and so on). Second, colorblindness promotes an unrealistic goal. Colorblindness can never exist because we have attached racial meanings to other racial markers. We have other ways of assigning race besides how a person looks. Race impacts every aspect of who we are, and we can't ignore that. Our zip code, the clothes we wear, our voice, even our name carries racial meanings. Two economists conducted an experiment in Chicago and Boston using almost five thousand resumés with either a traditionally white name (like Emily and Greg) or traditionally African American name (like LaToya and Jamal). They found a 50 percent gap in callback rate favoring the white names, where a white name yields as many more callbacks as an additional eight years of work experience.[3] Clearly this isn't just about how people look.

Third, colorblindness is typically a code for white. As Father Massingale notes in his book, whiteness is invisible, expected, and the norm. Whites will often say, "I don't see color, I just see people." Yet this is true, as long as you dress like me, talk like me, pray like me, think like me, study my subjects, and so on. Whiteness is also the standard we use to evaluate everyone else. For example, most professors are assessed based on their teaching effectiveness. This is often captured through various measures like student evaluations, a seemingly colorblind standard. ("I didn't mention race.") However, empirical research shows that professors of color regularly receive lower teaching evaluations.[4] Or put another way, white professors regularly receive higher teaching evaluations. When this is the standard used to evaluate contract renewals, tenure, promotion, and merit pay, we can see how whiteness is rewarded yet never called out in a seemingly colorblind measure. The rewards and privileges are invisible to the dominant group.

Fourth, attempts at acting colorblind are often situational and function to disguise the presence of race rather than factor it out. For my research, I have college students keep a journal about their everyday racial interactions. In 2007, I published a book, *Two-Faced Racism: Whites in the Backstage and Frontstage*, with Joe Feagin, where we examined the journals/diaries of approximately six hundred white college students across the United States.[5] What we found was that, for the most part, the interactions of whites, when around people of color ("frontstage"), were entirely different from interactions when whites were by themselves (or when they thought they were by themselves, in the "backstage"). In the frontstage, when whites were with people of color, they usually adopted a colorblind perspective. They avoided anything that could be even tangentially related to race (for example, not saying Mexican restaurant to a Mexican friend) because that might be racist. However, in the backstage, when whites were alone, they could relax these frontstage expectations and could openly violate colorblindness. Racist joking (whites using racist stereotypes and telling racist jokes) was the most common theme reported in the backstage in the tens of thousands of narratives we collected for the book. Most of the jokes were said in white-only social networks, away from people of color. The perception is that it is *not* racist for whites to listen to or tell racist jokes, unless it's said to a person of color. Most whites don't worry about "getting caught" because they are only interacting with whites.

Intergroup Contact

It's easy to tell racist jokes and rely on stereotypes if there isn't meaningful contact with the target of the hostilities. Are there any solutions? One way to decrease reliance on stereotypes and racist jokes is the "contact hypothesis" or "intergroup contact theory." The premise is that if you know more people from that group, then you are less likely to rely on stereotypes and generalizations. In order for the "intergroup contact" to be effective, four criteria must be present:[6] (1) equal status—both groups taken into an equal status relationship; (2) common goals—both groups work on a problem/task and share this as a common goal; (3) acquaintance potential—the opportunity of group members to get to know each other as friends (and not just representatives of their social groups); and (4) the support of authorities that both groups acknowledge, including the definition of norms that support the interactions between the groups.

This intergroup contact is not going to address racial hierarchies in every facet of the culture, but what a wonderful place to start, and what a better body to facilitate this than the church? I want to reiterate Dr. Massingale's claim that "Christian faith has a valuable and essential role to play in the effort to bring about a more racially just society" (84). We have much work to do.

Notes

[1] Bryan N. Massingale, *Racial Justice and the Catholic Church* (Maryknoll, NY: Orbis Books, 2010).

[2] Whoopi Goldberg, *Book* (New York: Avon Books, 1997), 123–33.

[3] Marianne Bertrand and Sendhil Mullainathan, "Are Emily and Greg More Employable Than Lakisha and Jamal? A Field Experiment on Labor Market Discrimination," *American Economic Review* 94 (2004): 991–1013.

[4] Michael A. Messner, "White Guy Habitus in the Classroom: Challenging the Reproduction of Privilege," in *Men and Masculinities* 2 (2000): 457–69.

[5] Leslie Houts Picca and Joe R. Feagin, *Two-Faced Racism: Whites in the Backstage and Frontstage* (New York: Routledge, 2007).

[6] Thomas F. Pettigrew, "New Black-White Patterns: How Best to Conceptualize Them?" *Annual Review of Sociology* 11 (1985): 329–46.

The Struggle against Racism
and the Global Horizon of Christian Hope

Agbonkhianmeghe E. Orobator

In this brief presentation I intend to offer some comments on Bryan Massingale's book *Racial Justice and the Catholic Church* under the overarching theme of ecclesiology and exclusion.[1] His analysis of racism proffers a critical hermeneutical tool for understanding the reality of exclusion as it operates in church and in society. My comments are limited to three broad areas: (1) the global phenomenon of racism, (2) the limitation of Catholic social teaching, and (3) a critique of the means for overcoming racism. I begin with an anecdote.

"The two Africans were simply minding their business." That's how the national press of a European country reported an incident that happened recently that involved a Jesuit colleague and me. My colleague and I were taking a walk to catch a bus to his place of work. As we entered a narrow alley, we noticed a policeman coming from the opposite direction. He looked amiable, even wearing what looked like a friendly, inviting smile. But what came out of him mouth was neither friendly nor inviting. "Africans, go back to Africa! You don't belong in this country. Black people, go back home!"

At the time of the incident I was shocked, dumbfounded, and angry. However, what aggravated these feelings was not the unwillingness of the policeman to apologize, even when I insisted; rather, it was the comments posted on the website of the newspaper that reported on the incident. The comments were sarcastic, vitriolic, and racist. The common thread running through them was a vilification of one race for surreptitiously seeking to benefit from or even jeopardize the hard-earned privileges, advantages, and entitlements of another. Rereading these comments I have no doubt that they confirm Massingale's central thesis that "race matters." When he argues that racism is an archetypal cultural phenomenon and the United States of America's deepest national obsession, I can understand why. Yet, in light of my experience, it is safe to assert that racism is alive not only in America but also elsewhere in the world as well. Simply put, racism is a global phenomenon. It may be socially active, economically prevalent, and historically contextualized in the U.S. society, but it is a reality that is present in the world.

To come back to the anecdote, for this policeman to be disabused of his racist and xenophobic mind-set, it would take more than just an apology— albeit he would later apologize in writing—because such an attitude is undergirded by and firmly rooted in a culture or a set of meanings and symbols that shape the worldview of individuals and their societies and orient their actions. Besides, the continent to which the policemen commanded me and my colleague to return is the object of historical prejudices, media stereotypes, and facile generalizations. To put it bluntly, it is the "heart of darkness." This "dark continent" is routinely associated with all things inferior, hideous, and underdeveloped. This further demonstrates the point that the tendency to equate black with inferior and white with superior is not a national obsession for the United States alone, as Massingale points out. It poses a formidable challenge to peoples of color all over the world.

With regard to the role of the Roman Catholic Church, the arguments in *Racial Justice and the Catholic Church* are compelling in showing that the church is a latecomer in the struggle against racism. More disturbing is Massingale's demonstration of how racism has operated historically within the Catholic Church in myriad subtle and not-so-subtle ways. The scandal of this realization is further compounded when one takes into account several centuries of the tradition of Catholic social teaching. The latter has been described as our best-kept secret; however, in regard to how the church deals with the sin of racism, Massingale is right to argue that it is our best-kept silence. Or, put differently, the church's concern for racism pales in comparison to its passion for abortion/pro-life issues and sexual ethics. Racism does not yet appear as a theological and ethical priority for the church.

One could adduce several reasons for the lack of a more proactive stance by the church vis-à-vis the evil of racism. As mentioned above, the indications are that racism also operates within the structures of the church. If this is true, and there is no reason to doubt Massingale's conviction that it is, one could hardly expect the church to turn voluntarily against itself. Rooting out the evil of racism implies eradicating a culture of unjustly acquired and violently maintained advantages and privileges, dominance, and entitlement. It also implies the transformation of an entire social system that pivots on racism as its dominant and defining culture. Many an institution like the church would find such a radical transformation threatening.

Ironically, there are Catholic resources for racial reconciliation. In light of the foregoing, a prerequisite for applying these resources would be an honest self-critique by the church. This would mean a critical look at some of its practices and teachings that either underestimate or condone the seriousness and urgency of the problem of racism. To combat this evil, it is not enough to issue statements and denouncements. A threefold social, theological, and ethical analysis would allow the church to listen to and hear the voices of victims, while effecting a deep and thorough examination of conscience in regard to its teachings and practices.

The sacramental resources for this task are not lacking. Christianity offers a variety of options that include a radical conversion via a self-emptying (*kenosis*) of sinful attachments, the baptismal incorporation into the body of Christ where all are recognized as equal, and the inclusion of all at the Eucharistic table of fellowship. This offers the possibility of creating an alternative set of meanings and symbols, expressed in confessions of faith or creeds that are nonracist and that prioritize unity, diversity, solidarity, responsibility, a preferential option for the poor, and reconciliation.

Outside of the church, how shall we overcome this evil of racism in society? Massingale makes an impassioned and compelling argument for two practical tools: "lament" and "compassion," which are accessible to both the victim and the privileged. Several illustrations of the former exist in scripture, however a more poignant example can be found in African American spirituals; there can be no denying the strident and haunting quality of lament embodied in spirituals. What poses problems, however, is Massingale's position that as an effective means of confronting the evil of racism, lament transcends logic and reason. If that is true, then it raises the following questions: How can it appeal beyond the borders of emotions? How could emotions alone be compelling? To take a simple example, how do we hear persistent wailing and lamentation? Is it not the case that their shrill tones easily disintegrate into a form of whining, complaining, and nagging in the ears of listeners?

It is easy to become inured to lament and for it to become a negligible irritant. Victims of racism have been lamenting for centuries to rather limited effect—otherwise Massingale would have no need to write a book on it in the twenty-first century! Transposed to the wider context of global historical geopolitical relations, like the biblical Rachel of old, we have lamented unceasingly the exploitation of the global south by the global north, the oppression of the poor by the rich, the subjugation of women by men, and so on. Yet the signs of compassion and solidarity have been few and far between —as elusive as the Parousia! If lament has not changed the status quo in so many centuries, what guarantee is there that it would in our day and age? Or do we simply need to keep increasing the decibels of lament?

Compassion, on the other hand, as Massingale argues, is modeled on the example of Jesus of Nazareth in the gospels. It is capable of transcending artificial and unjust boundaries. Ultimately, compassion places all of us at the level of our shared humanity and begets solidarity. Rather than being a fleeting feeling of pity, it stems from the depth of discontent with socioeconomic, cultural, and political situations that dehumanize a section of the human family in order to safeguard the privileges of another on account of skin color. Yet it remains unclear how human beings begin to cultivate and imbibe the quality of compassion in the construction of socioeconomic relationships, especially when they tend to privilege a particular social or racial group to the detriment of others.

In view of the limitations of this twin methodology of lament and compassion, I believe that the idea of struggle—that fundamental marker of the cultural identity of African Americans—needs to be more radical. It needs to reach to the roots of the problem and extirpate them completely. Struggle, however, involves an antagonist and a protagonist; it involves dispute and contestations, claims and counterclaims. This realization throws up the problem of the inevitability of violence attendant on the desire of one group to maintain its privilege and of another to attain its humanity. In light of this realization, I share Massingale's insightful view that the struggle for racial justice is a vocation for prophets—men and women, black, brown, white—who believe enough in the possibility of a universal table of fellowship and an inclusive beloved community to give up their lives for it.

Furthermore, Massingale is right to argue that creating a race-neutral society falls short of an adequate solution and the ultimate vision of a racially just society. To adopt Dalton's categories, a society of Beigians (where racial difference has been eliminated) or Proportians (where resources are allocated proportionately on the basis of color) remains a racially imbalanced society. What is needed is the radical dismantling of the connection that ties together racial difference, power, privilege, and prestige. Racial reconciliation means eliminating this nexus. It is a task that requires courage and a fair amount of personal sacrifice and suffering.

At this point I would like to sound a note of caution. In the analysis of racism and its manifestations in church and society, Massingale advances what he calls the fundamental norm of African American ethics, namely, freedom and equality of all under God, founded on and animated by a vision of an all-inclusive table of fellowship and beloved community. It is easy to romanticize these values. To illustrate this point from a different but somewhat similar context, oftentimes, in African Christianity, theologians wax eloquent about the values of communion and fullness of life (a/k/a *ubuntu*) as the animating and dynamic principles of African ethics. Yet we must admit the reality that more and more, to many Africans of the postcolonial generation, the talk about *ubuntu* or community for life sounds arcane, passé, and irrelevant to the pressing concerns and quests of Africans for development and survival in a globalized world.

This prompts me to ask the following questions: How relevant is Massingale's 'excavated' vision or fundamental norm of African American ethics to contemporary African Americans? If this vision or norm is transgenerational—passing from one generation to the other—what are the mechanisms of this transmission? Is it written in their DNA? How many of them know about and still celebrate this vision of inclusiveness and love? Or are these not mere vestiges of a dying culture, like recessive genes that are no longer able to respond to the challenges of our day and age? Who really cares about the welcome table or beloved community, *ubuntu*, community, life—apart from academics like Massingale, myself, and the rest?

Nonetheless, the vocation of a Catholic theologian, and in this context, a black scholar, is indispensable. I would argue that we must constantly feel the pulse and heartbeat of the community. And the weaker and more strained this pulse and this heartbeat, the more critical and imperative our lament and our truth telling to those structures in church and society that continue to sanction man's inhumanity to man in defense of racial privilege, status, power, and entitlement.

In this context, I would argue in agreement with Massingale that to be a theologian is to be possessed of a powerful vision of an alternative and possible world, a passion for a liberating truth, and a commitment to the struggle for its realization here and now in communion with and at the service of the community of faith. Therefore, to be possessed of this vision is to live in hope and to permanently resist any attempt to defer the dream of a reconciled community for all—black, brown, white, yellow. While this vocation would need to contend with and overcome several challenges, including bias, inadequate resources, and personal limitations (despair, depression, fear, and cowardice), and answer to the unrelenting demands of serious scholarship, it labors under a horizon of Christian hope that is not a cheap form of optimism. Only this kind of hope can serve as an unfailing guarantee of the pertinence of and joy in the struggle for racial justice and reconciliation in the church and in the world.

Notes

[1] Bryan N. Massingale, *Racial Justice and the Catholic Church* (Maryknoll, NY: Orbis Books, 2010).

Response: The Challenge of Idolatry and Ecclesial Identity

Bryan N. Massingale

I am grateful to the organizers of this conference for including the topic of racial justice at a symposium devoted to ecclesiology. My immense gratitude especially goes to my fellow panelists for both their generous attention to my work and their compelling and thought-provoking insights. I intended *Racial Justice and the Catholic Church* to be not only a work that would be of interest to fellow academics but also an act of love for the church and a contribution to its faith and mission.[1] It is humbling to hear my colleagues' responses to my work and to realize that this hope, at least in their estimation, was not in vain. As their contributions illustrate, though my book advances some searing criticisms of Catholic engagement with the evil of racism, these critiques were advanced out of a deeper love for the authentic faith to which this community is an imperfect witness.

The panelists' contributions to this discussion are rewarding and demanding efforts in their own right. Leslie Picca provides an engaging sociological overview that challenges the shallow and inadequate understandings of racism that dominate our social and theological discourses. Her reading confirms the critiques I make of what I call the "commonsense" understanding of racism. Agbonkhianmeghe Orobator's essay vividly illustrates how "race" and racial justice are global phenomena, that is to say, how racial supremacy and exclusion are not matters of concern solely for the United States. These are realities in the universal church that must be addressed for the sake of the church's credibility in mission and integrity in faith.

Time does not permit a detailed response to the insights of these scholars. Instead, my contribution will detail why the issue of racial supremacy is not only a proper subject for a conference dealing with the nature of the church but indeed a critically important one. In doing so, I will further develop the insights present in my book to address the following question: Why is racial justice and exclusion an ecclesiological concern?

This is not an idle question. When the topic of racial justice is addressed by Christian faith communities in general, and by the Catholic Church in particular, it is most often as a moral issue that poses deep challenges to Christian consciences. That is to say, it is treated solely as an ethical concern and as a summons to moral conversion.[2]

Seldom do we examine racism as a *theological* concern, that is, as a reality that raises profound challenges not only for the church's credibility as a vehicle for the gospel but more so for its very *integrity*. I contend that the complicity of the church in the social evil of racial injustice decisively compromises its very identity as the body of Christ or the people of God, for the church becomes implicated in the sin of idolatry.

Calling racism a form of "idolatry" is neither hyperbole nor overstatement. Official magisterial documents treat racism as a species of idolatry. The following statement from the *Catechism of the Catholic Church* is especially noteworthy:

> Idolatry not only refers to false pagan worship. It remains a constant temptation to faith. Idolatry consists in divinizing what is not God. Man commits idolatry whenever he honors and reveres a creature in the place of God, whether this be gods or demons (for example, satanism), power, pleasure, *race*, ancestors, the state, money, etc. . . . Idolatry rejects the unique Lordship of God; it is therefore incompatible with communion with God.[3]

Thus, the church's complicity in racial injustice and racial supremacy—that is to say, idolatry—raises troubling questions and concerns that for the sake of its credibility and effectiveness can no longer be evaded.

While some doctrinal statements of the Catholic Church understand racism as a form of idolatry, we need to note that this indictment is not a recent development in Christian thought. It had already been lodged very pointedly by the historic black churches and African American theologians and activists. It is as old as Frederick Douglass's nineteenth-century contrast between the "slave-holding religions of this land" and the "pure, peaceable" Christianity of the black churches and abolitionist assemblies.[4] The indictment of idolatry with regard to ecclesial complicity in racial injustice was also raised by Martin Luther King, Jr. In his landmark essay, "Letter from Birmingham City Jail," King developed an extended and eloquent response to moderate white Christian leaders who criticized his crusade for racial justice as "unwise," "untimely," and "extremist." He confessed his deep disappointment "with the white church and its leadership" in a moving and pointed passage:

> I have traveled the length and breadth of Alabama, Mississippi and all the other southern states. On sweltering summer days and crisp autumn mornings I have looked at her beautiful churches with their lofty spires pointing heavenward. . . . Over and over again I have found myself asking: *"What kind of people worship here? Who is their God?* . . . Where were they when Governor Wallace gave his clarion call for defiance and hatred? Where were their voices of support when tired, bruised and weary Negro men and women decided to rise from the dark dungeons of complacency to the bright hills of creative protest?[5]

King refrained from directly stating the obvious conclusion of this line of questions, namely, that the lack of social conscience in the majority of white southern Christians was due to their idolatrous worship of a false god. Yet, while official Catholic teaching and the position statements of several other white Christian bodies now acknowledge racism as a species of idolatry— that is, assigning ultimate significance to and rooting human identity in a human social/cultural construct of skin color—these faith communities typically do not examine either their complicity in this idolatry or how such complicity in the idolatry of whiteness compromises their identity.[6]

Allow me to concretely illustrate how the idolatry of "race"—more specifically, of "whiteness"—functions to determine what is considered "holy" in U.S. and global Catholicism. During Pope Benedict's 2008 pastoral visit to the United States, he presided at a public mass in Washington, DC. The readings for the day celebrated the rich cultural diversity of the U.S. Catholic Church, including the classic account from the Acts of the Apostles describing how the Spirit's descent upon the gathered community empowered the world's peoples to hear the good news in various languages. As the mass continued, after a prayer of the faithful and a presentation of the gifts, marked by diverse languages and spirited gospel and Spanish singing, a noted Catholic commentator on EWTN (the U.S. Catholic cable network that broadcast the mass live) caustically remarked, "We have just been subjected to an over-preening display of multicultural chatter. And now, the Holy Father will begin the sacred part of the Mass." Note the contrast—indeed the opposition—drawn between "multicultural"—that is, nonwhite—and "sacred."

Why is this significant? EWTN is a major "media presence" of the Catholic Church and, for many, the public voice of U.S. Catholicism. That such a statement could be aired on a network celebrated for its orthodoxy— and more significantly, that it was not and still has not been officially repudiated or challenged—does not just illustrate how standing against racism is not a major component of Catholic identity or orthodoxy. It also reveals how influential elites in the church do not consider non-European cultural expressions as really "Catholic"—or even "sacred!" Only "white" or European persons, music, theology, and aesthetics are standard, normative, universal, or "Catholic." Or, as I phrased this in my book, the pervasive conviction is that "Catholic" equals "white." "Black" and "nonwhite" cultural products are, at best, ambiguous, defective, or deficient carriers and mediators of the sacred. To put it bluntly and directly, in U.S. and global Catholicism, God can speak unambiguously only in "white."[7]

I want to underscore that what I am describing is not simply an ethical failure. We are dealing here with something much more troubling than the immoral personal acts of individual sinners. I am pointing, rather, to an operative ecclesial self-understanding, namely, that Catholic equals white/European.[8]

Thus, I contend that U.S. and global Catholicism have been co-opted into an idolatrous belief system that practically maintains that the sacred and the holy can be definitively mediated and unambiguously encountered only through white cultural products. This, I submit, is radically incompatible with Christ's will for the people who would bear his name and continue his universal salvific mission. The belief that God can be mediated or encountered unambiguously only through white or European cultural products is what I mean by ecclesial complicity in racial supremacy and is the essence of a compromised idolatrous identity.

This is why the issue of racial justice is a theological and, more specifically, an ecclesiological concern. Racism and racial justice raise questions that go to the heart of Christian identity and the integrity of Christian belief. Can the church truly be the body of Christ in anything but the most rhetorical and nonincarnational way if it operationally believes that the divine can be revealed, mediated, or encountered unambiguously only in white/European cultural products? What are the ecclesiological implications of a faith community's bondage to an idol of whiteness? Or, in the searing questions posed by James Cone, "Can the Church of Jesus Christ be racist and Christian at the same time? Can the Church of Jesus Christ be politically, socially, and economically identified with the structures of oppression and also be a servant of Christ? Can the Church of Jesus Christ fail to make the liberation of the poor the center of its message and work, and still remain faithful to its Lord?"[9] Or, as I phrase the pressing questions in my book,

What does it mean to "speak the truth" to both church and society, on behalf of all who suffer social oppression, out of a Catholic tradition that is tainted by complicity in and collusion with the social evil of racism? . . . How does the "virulent residue" of slavery, colonialism, and segregation, such as the continuing stigmata of black inferiority, challenge the integrity of the Catholic faith, the mission of the church, and the identity of its theologians?[10]

These are radical and, I must admit, scary questions. Speaking personally, they take me to the limits of my intellectual—and indeed, existential—abilities.[11] And I am not sure that I now can give such questions definitive responses. Yet, I am certain that they cannot be avoided or evaded if the church is to be a proactive agent of racial justice or be true to the identity intended for it by its Lord.

In summary, what makes the Catholic Church complicitous in an idolatrous belief system is not the fact that many of its members engage in acts of race-based malice or bigotry. Idolatry, rather, lies in the pervasive belief that European aesthetics, music, theology, and persons—and only these—are standard, normative, universal, and truly "Catholic." That only these can mediate the divine and carry the holy. That God can only be truly imaged in white. This is, I submit, idolatry, that is "divinizing what is not God." Thus, future Catholic ecclesiological reflection on race and racism must not only name skin color as a major cause of social stratification and injustice. It must also summon the political courage, intellectual honesty, and existential humility to interrogate the church's bondage to an alien identity—its compromised identity—more forthrightly.

Notes

[1] Bryan N. Massingale, *Racial Justice and the Catholic Church* (Maryknoll, NY: Orbis Books, 2010).

[2] However, as I argued in my book, the sad reality is that racial justice is not a major concern of Catholic theology and magisterial teaching.

[3] *The Catechism of the Catholic Church*, #2113; emphasis added. Pope Benedict XVI strongly reiterates the *Catechism*'s teaching. In speaking of the "insane racist ideology" at the heart of anti-Semitism, he declares that such a world view is "born of neo-paganism." Pope Benedict explicitly links false notions of God with racist attacks on human dignity when he states, "The holiness of God was no longer recognized, and consequently, contempt was shown for the sacredness of human life" ("Address of His Holiness Pope Benedict XVI: Visit to the Synagogue of Cologne," [August 19, 2005], http://www.vatican.va/.holy_father/benedict_xiv/speeches/2005/august/documents).

[4] Frederick Douglass, "American Slavery, American Religion, and the Free Church of Scotland: An Address Delivered in London, England, on May 22, 1846," http://www.yale.edu/glc/archive/1077.html. In an earlier text, Douglass expressed similar ideas in a less-developed, slightly more polemical fashion: "be-

tween the Christianity of this land, and the Christianity of Christ, I recognize the widest possible difference–so wide, that to receive the one as good, pure, and holy, is on necessity to reject the other as bad, corrupt, and wicked. To be the friend of one is on necessity to be the enemy of the other. I love the pure, peaceable, and impartial Christianity of Christ: I therefore hate the corrupt, slaveholding, women-whipping, cradle-plundering, partial and hypocritical Christianity of this land. Indeed, I can see no reason, but the most deceitful one, for calling the religion of this land Christianity" (Frederick Douglass, *Narrative of the Life of Frederick Douglass, an American Slave, written by himself* [New York: Fine Creative Media, (1845) 2003], 100).

⁵ James M. Washington, ed., *A Testament of Hope: The Essential Writings of Martin Luther King, Jr.* (San Francisco: Harper and Row, 1986), 299; emphasis added.

⁶ See, for example, the comprehensive examination of racism as an idolatrous faith developed by the Anglican priest-theologian George D. Kelsey, *Racism and the Christian Understanding of Man* (New York: Charles D. Scriber's and Sons, 1965).

⁷ One could offer more examples of this idolatrous complicity in racial supremacy such as the liturgical guidelines of a major U.S. archdiocese that forbid dancing and clapping in Catholic worship unless the majority of those attending are African American—a concession justified because "they [meaning black people] need this"; the papal masses recently offered in Angola and Benin where African worshipers were admonished that, for the sake of "reverence," clapping was prohibited during the service; the practice of another U.S. archdiocese that forbade gospel music during a Catholic mass at its cathedral church because "such music is OK for the central city, but not for the mother church of the archdiocese"; and the decor of cathedrals in major African dioceses that is more Irish than that of St. Patrick's Cathedral in New York City. What one sees, then, is that it is neither an isolated nor unusual situation in Catholicism for God and the sacred to be unambiguously mediated only in European/white cultural products.

⁸ I further develop this point in *Racial Justice and the Catholic Church*, chap. 2.

⁹ James H. Cone, *God of the Oppressed* (Maryknoll, NY: Orbis Books, 1975), 36–37.

¹⁰ Massingale, *Racial Justice and the Catholic Church*, 161.

¹¹ It is my experience that most African American Catholics consistently avoid such questions out of a fear that, if they engage them seriously, they will be compelled to leave the Catholic Church. My consistent response to such fears has been that honoring these questions need not require that one leave the church, but they do demand that one stay in the church in a different way—admittedly, a way that is tenuous, perilous, and largely unmarked.

Transcending the Exclusionary Ecclesial Practices of Racial Hierarchies of Authority: An Early Pentecostal Trajectory

David D. Daniels III

The formation of ecclesial communities that strove to transcend the exclusionary practices of racial hierarchies of authority during the era of racial segregation in the United States merits ecclesiological investigation. They were sites of resistance to the reshaping of American Christianity into the racial configuration of the nation. They offered challenges to the reintroduction of racial segregation into American religious life during the era between the Civil War and World War I. As an historical study, this chapter broaches the topic with a focus on white Christians in the United States who joined denominations led by African American Christians during the early twentieth century. This is in contrast to studies that focus on the hospitality of racial minorities within majority white institutions. These studies keep the focus on power garnered by whites and adjustments they make or fail to make to the introduction of racial minorities into the institutions they control. A concurrent theme of such studies is the plight of minorities among the majority and the degrees of exclusion experienced by minorities. Differing from these studies, this essay spotlights the margins of the racial order where whites recognized black authority. It examines the degrees of inclusion of whites and congregations within black-led denominations and refrains from exploring the motives of the whites who joined the black-led denominations and of the blacks who accepted them.

The African American-led denominations that these Euro-American Christians joined are part of the Pentecostal tradition. Today, during the twenty-first century, on the margins of global Christianity, there are white clergy and congregations in seventeen European countries that belong to the black-led Embassy of God, headed by Rev. Sunday Adelaja, a Nigerian residing in the Ukraine. Among Episcopalians, there is a white Episcopal priest and congregation in the United States under the jurisdiction of Anglican provinces in Nigeria, Kenya, and Rwanda. This essay focuses on the historical context of white Christians accepting black leadership in the early twentieth century. In an era marked by exclusionary practices rooted in legalized racial segregation and white supremacy, early Pentecostal resistance inverted, subverted, and transcended the racial hierarchies of authority that produced in American Christianity exclusionary ecclesial practices based on race.

Constructing Racial Hierarchies of Authority

Racial hierarchies of authority were described by W. E. B. Du Bois, a leading scholar on race, in this manner:

> In every possible way it was impressed and advertised that the white was superior and the Negro an inferior race. This inferiority must be publicly acknowledged and submitted to. Titles of courtesy were denied colored men and women. Certain signs of servility and usages amounting to public and personal insult were insisted upon. The most educated and deserving black man was compelled in many public places to occupy a place beneath the lowest and least deserving of the whites.[1]

Du Bois outlined the hierarchy of race framed by the inequality of races and defined by superior and inferior races with whites as superior. The racial hierarchies of authority were intertwined with hierarchies of respect, status, and credibility. Within the racial hierarchy of authority, African Americans were to recognize and be deferential to whites as the authority in all situations. Within the hierarchy of respectability, African Americans as a race were less respectable than whites and could be treated with disrespect. In biracial settings, respect was reserved for whites, and African Americans were to practice the ethic of servility. Within the hierarchy of status, the accomplishments of African Americans failed to compensate for their inferiority and grant them equal footing with whites, even the most "uncivilized" white. In communication, the hierarchy of credibility meant that knowledge given by whites, even a white opinion, always outranked knowledge given by an African American. The hierarchy of desirability meant that white civilization and people were the ideal embodiment of the good.[2]

The racial hierarchies of authority were fueled by a racial politics of hubris. The "will to power" coupled with military, economic, and political power reinserted white dominance over African Americans during this era of segregation. The right to rule and trespass were combined. The domination of people as the middle and bottom rungs of the racial hierarchy of authority was deemed legally legitimate and, for some sectors, theologically sound, since it was ordained by God. The place of whites as a race was to be at the center of the arena of authority. African Americans were to be dispossessed of their place; they were to be displaced from the arena of authority; as a race, they did not "possess" any authority that whites were required to recognize.

Racial hierarchies of authority are structured by racism. Racism, according to major theorists of race, such William J. Wilson, is the combination of racial privilege, prejudice, plus power. Racism requires that one racial group possesses the power to impose its racial prejudices on another group; it can make the other racial group be treated as inferior. Racial privilege exists in two forms: unearned entitlement and conferred dominance. Privilege is exclusionary by allotting certain opportunities— economic, political, social, religious—to one group and denying these opportunities to another. Racial power, prejudice, and privilege operate according to specific racial regimes that kept whites as a race at the apex of the hierarchy of race and made them as a race the primary beneficiaries of U.S. wealth and geopolitical position.[3]

Racial hierarchies of authority were inscribed in the everyday practice of racial ordering that was structured more in terms of "shades of whiteness" than a white-black binary. "Shades of whiteness" produced a tripartite categorization: colored, white, and in-between. All nationalities were put basically in one of the groups. In the colored category were African Americans, Mexicans, Puerto Ricans, Chinese, Japanese, and Filipinos. In the white category were the English, Scottish, French, Dutch, Danes, Germans, and other northwestern Europeans. The not yet "white" or in-between were the Irish, Italians, Portuguese, Greeks, Hungarians, and other eastern Europeans; additionally, there were the groups of West Asians: Armenians, Lebanese, Assyrians, and Persians.

According to many scholars, it would take as much as sixty years after the advent of the twentieth century for many of these in-betweens to shift into the "white" classification. Racial hierarchies of authority were structured with whites at the apex, followed by the in-betweens, and then African Americans. Within these racial hierarchies of authority, there was a wide legal gap between the rungs occupied by the in-betweens and the ones occupied by African Americans. Latinos, Chinese, and Amerindians would share the lower rungs with African Americans. To read this period solely through the lenses of mid-twentieth-century segregation after the expansion of whiteness fails to capture the complexity of the racial context in which the early resistance to exclusionary practice by the Pentecostals under study took place. In the era before the expansion of whiteness, the racial in-betweens played a pivotal role in challenging the racial hierarchies of authority.[4]

Exposing Racial Hierarchies of Authority

Many denominations have made distinctions between their colored and white members. Some advised electing colored officials to preside over colored assemblies, while others have refused to elevate any colored elder to the episcopacy or any other office corresponding to it having equal power with white bishops. This has led to many misunderstandings and has caused the organizing of many separate colored denominations.[5]

Publishing this statement in 1917, against the backdrop of legalized racial segregation, black and white leaders of the Church of God in Christ exposed the racial hierarchy of authority that was ensconced in American Protestantism during the early twentieth century. It exposed two distinct ecclesial polities of racial subordination: an episcopal or executive leadership system of racial subordination wherein whites supervised blacks and an executive leadership system wherein blacks supervised blacks within a hierarchy controlled by whites. The document identified these racial polities as a primary reason for the collapse of the "interracial" moment within American Protestantism and the formation of "many separate colored denominations." Grounded in racial inequality and exclusionary practices in ecclesial leadership based on race, these ecclesial polities of racial subordination reproduced racial hierarchies of authority.[6]

The existence of interracial worship, congregations, denominations, and ecumenical organizations during the era of racial segregation challenged the exclusionary stance of the dominant racial order and the racial hierarchies of authority. Receiving occasional newspaper coverage, interracial worship in southern states, such as Tennessee, northern states, such as New York, and western states, such as California, publicly exhibited these developments. The existence of black-led "interracial" denominations provided another layer to the challenge; these denominations included the Church of God in Christ, Pentecostal Assemblies of the World, the United Pentecostal Council of the Assemblies of God, the Holy Nazarene Church of the Apostolic Faith, and the All Nations Pentecostal Assembly. Interracial ecumenism was most clearly exhibited by the bilateral agreement between the Church of God in Christ and the Pentecostal Assemblies of the U.S.A.[7]

Recall that outside of these sectors within American Pentecostalism, the few interracial and fewer multiracial congregations that did exist in American religion were predominately white congregations with black members, congregations belonging to the Holiness churches, Christian Science, and Roman Catholicism. The black-led, interracial religious organizations would include the Peace Mission of Father Divine and the Church of God and Saints of Christ.[8]

Key for the Pentecostal challenge to the racial hierarchy of authority was the Azusa Street Revival. Led by William J. Seymour, an African American, the Revival was housed in the Los Angeles, California-based Apostolic Faith Mission, initially an all-black congregation. It became the site for this ecumenical venture that sought in its humble way to witness and embody the unity of the church by countering exclusionary practices. A central figure within the Revival recorded that

> There can be no divisions in a true Pentecost. To formulate a separate body is but to advertise failure, as a people of God. It proves to the world that we cannot get along together, rather than causing them to believe in salvation. . . . We are called to bless and serve the whole "body of Christ," everywhere. Christ is one and His "body" can be but "one." To divide it is but to destroy it.[9]

Marked by "a true Pentecost," the ruptures in the church would be repaired, and exclusionary practices would be replaced, according to this vision. With compelling images of the church, such as "a true Pentecost," the "people of God," and the "body of Christ," the unity of the church is annunciated and assumed. This vision of unity proclaims that the church lives out its life in ways that differ from the world, a world noted for its disunity and racial divisions. The ecumenical unity of the church advances evangelization by "causing" the world, as the above quote noted, "to believe in salvation."[10]

The resistance to exclusionary practices by the black and white Pentecostals being examined here grew out of the ecclesial vision of the Azusa Street Revival of 1906–09, the founding event of North American Pentecostalism. Participants in the Azusa Street Revival described the event as a new Pentecost. Witnesses to the event referred to the Revival as a site on the margins of Christianity where divisions that marred the church were overcome: denominational, doctrinal, racial, classist, and gender-based. While historians, striving to separate myth from reality, debate the validity of these claims, the ecumenical stirrings cast visions of new ways of being and doing church.

It is historically indisputable that a Pentecostal sector did expose the racial hierarchy of authority. Still, the larger segment of early Pentecostalism came to replicate the racial configuration of American Protestants with its denominational racial organization: white-led denominations, black-led denominations,

Latino-led denominations, and white majority denominations with subordinate black groups and subordinate Latino groups.

Resisting Racial Hierarchies of Authority

The Pentecostal sector of black-led, interracial denominations was constituted by a set of reversals related to race as a criterion for congregational membership, membership in judicatories, and denominational leadership. Resisting the dominant pattern of race dictating the criteria for membership in a congregation, some white Christians joined black congregations when the vast majority of whites distanced themselves from African Americans and supported enshrining their exclusionary practices into both denominational polity and the U.S. legal system. Challenging the dominant pattern of race being a criterion for congregations connecting or being assigned to particular denominational associations or judicatories, some white congregations joined black denominations when the vast majority of white congregations belonged to all-white denominations or denominations led by white Christians, both native-born and immigrant. Countering the dominant pattern of race being the criterion for membership within the denominational leadership, some white Christians submitted to the authority of their African American leadership when the vast majority of white Christians refused to recognize any authority exercised by African Americans. These reversals undergirded this particular Pentecostal resistance to exclusionary ecclesial practices based on race.

A statement that gives voice to the resistance to racial hierarchies is the 1917 pronouncement on Christian unity and racial inclusion given by the Church of God in Christ. The pronouncement articulated a robust vision of Christian unity in these terms: "Many denominations have made distinctions between their colored and white members. . . . The Church of God in Christ recognizes the fact that all believers are one in Christ Jesus and all its members have equal rights. Its Overseers, both colored and white, have equal power and authority in the church."[11]

This theological statement invokes equality and rights language to challenge the racial hierarchies of authority. By adopting the vocabulary of the U.S. Constitution, the statement baptizes the language of equality and rights to contextualize the unity in Christ. Racial equality as an ecclesial concept challenges the conflation of the church and its members into a hierarchy of the races as well as the restriction of full participation in the life of the church along the lines of racial hierarchies of authority. The rights language reinforces this theological maneuver by deeming all believers as having equal rights that were given each member by Christ.[12]

Vital to resisting racial hierarchies of authority is the construction of an alternative system of authority. Inclusionary practices of ecclesial governance rooted in the races being "equal in power and authority" served as this alternative. The degrees of participation by African Americans and whites needed to go beyond mere association as an inclusionary accommodation to shared authority. Ecclesial participation raised the unavoidable issue of which race has the predominant authority; this question became as, or perhaps even more central to, the mere fact of the races associating with each other. These Pentecostal resisters of the status quo rejected hierarchies of authority that promoted hypertrophy, where one race, in practice, assumes all the authority and power and does "everything in the church," coupled with atrophy, where one race is functionally denied authority and power and rendered passive. Deeming race as an invalid basis of allocating authority, these Pentecostals imagined ecclesial authority shared by both, if not all, races.[13]

The Church of God in Christ approved and published its 1917 manual that resisted racial hierarchies of authority. The document codified the denomination's policy of inclusionary racial practices. Juxtaposing the denomination's polity of racial inclusion over against the segregationist or exclusionary polity of U.S. denominations, the statement rejected the two regnant ecclesial polities of racial subordination: an episcopal or executive leadership system of racial subordination wherein whites supervised blacks and an executive leadership system wherein blacks supervised blacks within a hierarchy controlled by whites. It affirmed an ecclesial polity that conferred "equal power and authority" to its black and white members and leaders. Such an achievement demonstrated the deliberative and prophetic stance of an inclusive expression of Christianity regarding race and its strivings to transcend exclusionary ecclesial practices of racial hierarchies of authority.[14]

Undergirding the theological vision of racial inclusion are the real efforts at ecclesial inclusion that the Church of God in Christ and the Pentecostal Assemblies of the World engaged in for approximately the first twenty-five years of their history. Between 1909 and 1937, these denominations participated in four experiments to bring black and white Christians together within the same church by structuring an interracial religious body when most denominations were racially homogeneous or segregated.[15]

Inverting Racial Hierarchies of Authority

The Pentecostal Assemblies of the World and Church of God in Christ, along with other black-led, interracial Pentecostal organizations, inverted the racial hierarchies of authority by erecting ecclesial structures where white clergy and congregations were subject to the religious authority of African American clergy. The race that society placed at the lower rungs of the hierarchy of authority exercised authority in this particular interracial setting. Established in 1907 as a predominately black religious organization, the Pentecostal Assemblies of the World became predominately white in 1916 and remained so until 1924. It became majority African American again when most white clergy exited the denomination in 1924; a number of white-led congregations and predominately white congregations did remain. In 1924, the then predominately African American, albeit interracial, denomination elected Garfield T. Haywood, an African American, as presiding bishop. By 1931, the bishopric of the Pentecostal Assemblies of the World was interracial: four African Americans and three white Americans. The denomination sponsored interracial national conventions in northern cities, which included white delegates from the South. The year following Haywood's death in 1931, a group of the African American and white congregations left the Pentecostal Assemblies of the World and merged with a white group of clergy and churches. The Pentecostal Assemblies of the World, as an even smaller religious body, albeit a predominately black denomination, remained interracial and initiated the practice of consecrating a white clergyman as bishop every time an African American clergyman was elevated to the bishopric in order to preserve its ideal of interracial leadership. By creating a more racially mixed denomination through these ecclesial practices, they inverted the racial hierarchies of authorities.[16]

Between 1909 and 1924, the Church of God in Christ consisted of four groups of white clergy and churches that joined the black-led Church of God in Christ. Between 1909 and 1914, the Church of God in Christ functioned as a federation of three clergy networks: the original religious body led by Charles Harrison Mason, a nearly all-white religious body led by Howard Goss and E. N. Bell, and a nearly all-white religious body with a few Latinos led by Leonard P. Adams. In 1914 the Goss-Bell network would leave and join other white groups of clergy and churches to organize the Assemblies of God. The Adams group would be joined by a small white group of clergy who left the newly formed Assemblies of God in 1916; this group was led by William Holt. Holt would be instrumental in the second and third interracial experiments. In the second experiment (1916–24), Holt, Adams, and other whites integrated the leadership of the original religious body led by Mason, with Adams being recognized as a member of the bishopric (called the board of overseers) and Holt becoming the first general secretary; during this second phase, at least four Latino congregations joined the denominations.[17]

From 1924 to 1932, in the third phase, the Church of God in Christ adopted a Protestant model of establishing a minority conference, specifically a white conference, to unite the congregations across the United States that belonged to the predominately black denomination. These leaders and congregations resided in Arkansas, California, Illinois, Indiana, Iowa, Michigan, Massachusetts, and Rhode Island. This development was in response to the argument of the clergy who questioned the anomaly of white congregations in a black denomination as being a racial minority within the larger system but sought to maximize their presence by uniting under a common administrative unit. The conference existed until around 1932 when the predominately black leadership abolished the conference and accused the white leadership of attempting to form a denomination with white members of the Church of God in Christ. For the remainder of the early Pentecostal era, the Church of God in Christ would continue to attract white clergy and laity as members as well as periodically include white speakers at the national convocation. Whites would regularly attend the national convocation held in Memphis in addition to state-wide convocations such as those in Texas.[18]

While most Church of God in Christ congregations in North America were racially homogenous, there were congregations across the continent during the first generation that were interracial.

Subverting Racial Hierarchies of Authority

The Pentecostal Assemblies of the World and the Church of God in Christ, along with the other black-led, interracial Pentecostal organizations, created a religious space where African Americans exercised religious authority over their white clergy and congregations. In these ecclesial spaces, white Christians were subject to the religious authority of an African American-led organization. These ecclesial innovations subverted racial hierarchies of authority.

By the 1920s, the majority African American General Assembly of the Church of God in Christ began to debate the propriety of white members voluntarily withdrawing from the denomination's interracial congregations to constitute white congregations within the denomination. Practical, ethical, and biblical arguments were mounted to address this challenge of accommodation to the dominant racial arrangement of the United States. First, the voluntary withdrawal of whites from interracial Church of God in Christ congregations was to be contemplated only under extraordinary circumstances such as local segregation laws. This would, then, be accepted as preserving the peace of the congregation and safety of the members in a hostile racial environment. Second, the freedom of association must be honored; whites should not be forced to attend interracial congregations. While the spirit of racial division was to be denounced as unbiblical, it was ruled appropriate for different races to have pastors of their own race. Although the decision did support the agenda of some white clergy and congregations, it was still decided through a process controlled by African Americans.[19]

By withdrawing from the dominant racial equation of white superiority and black inferiority, these black and white Pentecostals along with their black-led, interracial Pentecostal organization, engaged in the subversion of the racial hierarchies of authority. These white Pentecostal individuals put on hold the privileges granted to them by the exclusionary practices of racial segregation when they joined majority African American congregations and denominations. White Pentecostal congregations put on hold the privileges granted to them by the exclusionary practices of racial segregation when they joined predominately black Pentecostal denominations headed by African Americans and placed on hold the power distributed to them by their race. These white Pentecostal individuals and congregations placed on hold or even rejected the prejudices about black people that the American society inscribed into federal and states laws and that American Christianity structured into their church order.

At the joint session of Pentecostal Assemblies of the U.S.A., a predominately white religious body, and the Church of God in Christ, the racial hierarchies of authority were subverted in holding the interracial conference, in participating in interracial worship with preachers and choirs from both races, and in celebrating the event as interracial. In an account about the joint session, an author was pleased with the interracial worship; he said that "[i]t was blessed to see the different races who are all made of one blood shouting, dancing and praising God together in one Spirit." And the author noted that "we believe that the mingling of the saints [races] will prove a great blessing, an uplift to the work everywhere." Mason was praised for his spirituality: "All the saints were especially blessed by the deep spiritual ministry of Brother C. H. Mason. . . . They have seen the glory and wisdom of God manifested through his ministry." Additionally, the "freedom of the colored saints" was lauded as well as their humility— virtues of which whites were in need.[20]

While the author was clear that freedom and humility were needed by whites, what blacks in the Church of God in Christ needed was less clear. In the estimation of the white Pentecostals who were part of the bilateral agreement, the Church of God in Christ was the largest Pentecostal body by the 1920s, was led by some of the most phenomenal Pentecostal leaders, and exhibited prized virtues. The author concluded, "perhaps the Lord will help us to be some help and encouragement to them," since it was not evident what their black counterparts lacked.[21]

Transcending Racial Hierarchies of Authority

The black and white Pentecostals who participated in the subversion of the racial hierarchies of authority sought to transcend these structures. The whites might be accused of racial suicide by submitting to the authority of African American leaders, associating with African Americans as equals, borrowing from black Pentecostal culture, rejecting white supremacy, and crafting new racial practices. They could be seen as leveling the hierarchy of credibility and severing the link between credibility and race. The racial practice of black Pentecostal leaders was fashioned by the experience of having whites submit to their authority, being treated as equals by whites, having their religious culture recognized as worthy of adoption, and rejecting white supremacy. Together these black and white Pentecostals fashioned new ecclesial polity that prompted inclusionary racial practices as well as ecclesial structures.

The white Pentecostal leaders and congregations that joined black-led and interracial denominations constructed a racial politics of humility that challenged the racial politics of hubris, which shaped the "will to power" exercised by whites as a race. The politics of humility entails the people of the dominant race within the hierarchy of authority voluntarily displacing themselves from that position. Such displacement involves various maneuvers. First, they desist both from making the society in the image of their race and forcing other races to fit into their creation. Second, they dispossess themselves of the notion that their race is the "owners of truth and knowledge," and have the right to rule others, as well as that other races exemplify "ignorance." Third, by becoming open to the gifts and contributions of other races, they acknowledge the limits to their race's knowledge and join other races in "attempting, together, to learn more than" each race knows separately. Herein, the hierarchy of teachability is flattened: whites are willing to be taught by African American Christians as much as by white Christians. Fourth, they recognize the right of African Americans to possess religious authority, including exercising this right over white religious affairs.[22]

The black Pentecostal leaders and congregations that received white leaders and clergy into their denomination practiced a racial politics of hospitality that challenged the racial politics of deference, which shaped the ethic of servility imposed by whites as a race upon African Americans.

The racial politics of hospitality acknowledged that African Americans possessed the God-given authority to enter the arena of authority and exercised jurisdiction over white religious affairs. Framed also by an ethic of risk, the racial politics of hospitality involved African Americans figuring out the degree of authority that they would share with their white members and the corresponding amount of authority they would give up. Their racial politics of hospitality involved relinquishing a level of control. They had to learn to co-lead across races, without their racial group being solely in control. The fragility of black-led, interracial denominations exacerbated the risk of the black leaders in that their whole organization could implode; of course, this is what basically happened to the Pentecostal Assemblies of the World between 1932 and 1937 when they lost the majority of both black and white congregations that constituted the denomination at that time.[23]

Lacking the political and social power to change the racial order, the racial politics of hospitality and of humility generated enough power to interrupt the racial order within their religious territory and to erect an alternative interracial sector. Although neither racial politic could determine the longevity or social consequences of the interracial ecclesial experiments on their own nor remake American Christianity, these black and white Pentecostals still risked working toward the erection of denominational structures that embodied their ecclesial vision. They risked constructing a way of being church that appeared to be unrealistic and impractical and was actually illegal in many parts of the society. The racial politics of hospitality and of humility allowed Pentecostals to prize the relative lack of white control in these black-led or interracial religious organizations and informed the ethic of risk they practiced.

The racial politics of humility and of hospitality co-constituted themselves. Each politic mutually informed the other, fostering reciprocity. The recognition of black authority by whites, the sharing of authority with whites by African Americans, and efforts by both races to erect these new ecclesial communities spawned a new ecclesial reality on the margins of American Christianity.

In subverting the racial hierarchies of authority, these Pentecostals disrupted the center-margin equation, with whites constituting the center. These black-led, interracial Pentecostal denominations reconstituted the margins of Christianity as a third space, a haven infused with power not dependent on a center. They populated space on the margins as emancipatory sites. Subverting the center-margin binary with center as the locus of authority, these Pentecostals annunciated a church that transcended the exclusionary ecclesial practices of racial hierarchies of authority. This emancipatory zone on the margins of American Christianity subverted the racial hierarchies of authority and challenged the racial structure constituted by white supremacy. It countered a way of organizing religion that reproduced the racial hierarchies of race. By creating this emancipatory zone on the margins, it exposed how Christianity was implicated in reproducing exclusionary practices of racial hierarchies of authority as the center.[24]

Striving to transcend the exclusionary practices of racial hierarchies of authority, the black-led, interracial Pentecostal denominations focused on embracing the equal sharing of power and authority between Christians of different races. Inclusionary practices based on race were grounded in each race being recognized as a peer; all forms of racial subordination being rejected; and race being no longer a factor in the distribution of social, political, economic, or religious power. The racial hierarchies of authority that structure the Church and society were supplanted by an interracial order framed by the equality of the races.

The black-led, interracial denominations interjected an alternative to the racial hierarchies of authority. Taking the exclusionary practices and social reality of their times as an affront to the Christian gospel, they willingly violated racial segregation laws. This segment of Pentecostalism challenged the dominant racial assumptions, inverted the reigning racial categories, and invented race-crossing as an ecclesial practice. They chose to obey the Bible and not embrace the exclusionary practices of racial hierarchies of authority. They fashioned as a practice the choosing of being a Christian racial minority, a Christian racial minority based on theologically informed decisions and ecclesial visions. They reflected Pentecost rather than the political order; they anticipated God's future rather than accommodating themselves to the dominant social order. By resisting and countering exclusionary practices based on race, these Pentecostals, black and white, witnessed to a new ecclesiology.

Notes

[1] W. E. B. Du Bois. *Black Reconstruction in America* (New York: Russell and Russell, [1935], 1968), 695.

[2] For the hierarchy of credibility, see Howard S. Becker, "Whose Side Are We On?" *Social Forces* 14 (Winter 1967): 239–47. For Richard Dyer's concept of the racial hierarchy of desirability, see France Winddance Twine, *Racism in a Racial Democracy: The Maintenance of White Supremacy in Brazil* (New Brunswick, NJ: Rutgers University Press, 1998), 89.

[3] William J. Wilson, *Power, Racism, and Privilege: Race Relations in Theoretical and Sociohistorical Perspectives* (New York: The Free Press, 1973); Peggy McIntosh, "White Privilege: Unpacking the Invisible Knapsack," cited in Virginia Cyrus, ed., *Experiencing Race, Class, and Gender in the United States* (Mountainview, CA: Mayfield Publishing, 1993), 209–13. I was reminded of

the co-constitution of racism by racial privilege, prejudice, and power by David Esterline, director of the Institute of Cross-Cultural Theological Education, McCormick Theological Seminary, Chicago, Illinois.

⁴ David R. Roediger, *Working toward Whiteness: How America's Immigrants Became White* (New York: Basic Books, 2005), 138.

⁵ William B. Holt, compiler, *A Brief Historical and Doctrinal Statement and Rules for Government of the Church of God in Christ* (n.p., circa 1917), 9.

⁶ Ibid., 9.

⁷ See endnote 33 in David D. Daniels III, "Navigating the Territory: Early Afro-Pentecostalism as a Movement within Black Civil Society," cited in *Afro-Pentecostalism: Black Pentecostal and Charismatic Christianity in History and Culture*, ed. Amos Yong and Estrelda Alexander (New York: New York University Press, 2011), 62.

⁸ Jacob S. Dorman, *Chosen People: African Americans and the Rise of Black Judaism* (New York: Oxford University Press, forthcoming).

⁹ Frank Bartleman, *Azusa Street: An Eyewitness Account* (South Plainfield, NJ: Bridge Publishing, 1980 [1925]), 68–69, cited in Allan Anderson, *An Introduction to Pentecostalism* (Cambridge: Cambridge University Press, 2004), 249.

¹⁰ Bartleman, *Azuza Street*, 68–69.

¹¹ Holt, *A Brief Historical and Doctrinal Statement*, 9.

¹² Ibid., 9.

¹³ Miroslav Volf, "A Protestant Response," in *Pentecostal Movements as an Ecumenical Challenge*, ed. Jürgen Moltmann and Karl-Josef Kuschel, *Concilium* 1996/3 (Maryknoll, NY: Orbis Books, 1996), 41.

¹⁴ Holt, *A Brief Historical and Doctrinal Statement*, 9.

¹⁵ For a fuller discussion, see David D. Daniels, "Charles Harrison Mason: The Interracial Impulse of Early Pentecostalism," in *Portraits of a Generation: Early Pentecostal Leaders*, ed. James R. Goff Jr., and Grant Wacker (Fayetteville: University of Arkansas Press, 2002), 264–69.

¹⁶ Morris E. Golder, *History of the Pentecostal Assemblies of the World* (1973; reprint, Birmingham, AL: Faith Apostolic Church, 1993), 58–59, 70–72, 85; note that in 1937 almost all the African Americans who left the Pentecostal Assemblies of the World in 1932 returned back to the denomination; also see Daniels, "Navigating the Territory," 56–57.

¹⁷ Daniels, "Charles Harrison Mason," 264–69.

¹⁸ Ibid., 264–69.

¹⁹ Ibid., 268–69.

²⁰ *The Pentecostal Herald*, 6:11, February 1921, cited in Aaron M. Wilson, *Our Story: The History of the Pentecostal Church of God* (Joplin, MO: Messenger Publishing House, 2001), 94–95.

²¹ Letter from Evangelist C. E. Maness, *The Pentecostal Herald*, 7:4, June 1921, cited in Wilson, *Our Story*, 95.

²² A revision of Freire's concept of humility; see Paulo Freire, *Pedagogy of the Oppressed* (New York: Continuum, [1970], 2006), 90.

[23] For a theological study of hospitality, see Christine Pohl, *Making Room: Recovering Hospitality as a Christian Tradition* (Grand Rapids: Wm. B. Eerdmans, 1999); Sharon Welch, *A Feminist Ethic of Risk* (Minneapolis: Augsburg/ Fortress, 2000).

[24] For a discussion of ThirdSpace, see Edward Soja, *Thirdspace: Journeys to Los Angeles and Other Real and Imagined Spaces* (Cambridge, MA: Blackwell, 1996).

PART IV

EXCLUSION AND GENDER

Phyllis Zagano's *Women & Catholicism: Gender, Communion, and Authority*

An Introduction

Miriam Haar

Phyllis Zagano's recent book, *Women & Catholicism: Gender, Communion, and Authority*, was the starting point for the panel on "Women, Ministry, and Exclusion."[1] Zagano critically examines three areas in which questions regarding gender, communion, and authority are intertwined: (1) juridical authority, (2) sacramental authority, and (3) women's ordination. Her approach is fresh and inspiring: she discusses the rather abstract themes of juridical and sacramental authority and the breaking away from both the juridical and sacramental in the matters of ordaining women and married men by presenting three distinct situations as case studies. Each is related to the role of women in the Catholic Church and reflects the tension between communion and authority.

Zagano's first chapter addresses the area of juridical authority by presenting the case of Bishop Bruskewitz in Nebraska, the reactions of the U.S. Conference of Catholic Bishops, and the initiative "Call to Action." Her second chapter deals with issues related to sacramental authority, offering a careful analysis of the case of Archbishop Milingo from Zambia, the Vatican's reaction, and the initiative "Married Priests Now." A brief "Interlude" on "Ordained Women in the Underground Church" in former Czechoslovakia leads to the third and final chapter that combines questions regarding juridical and sacramental authority as it discusses women's ordination. Zagano's highly skilled and nuanced way of analyzing these three cases shows the complexity of the issues involved and alerts the reader to avoid easy answers and polemics.

In the first chapter, "Juridical Authority: Bishop Bruskewitz, the Bishops' Conference, and Call to Action," Zagano describes events in the Catholic

Diocese of Lincoln, Nebraska, where in 1996 Bishop Bruskewitz decreed automatic excommunication for members of twelve organizations because he considered them as attacking, skirting, or departing from Catholic teaching. At the same time, Bruskewitz refused to cooperate with the U.S. Conference of Catholic Bishops in investigating the priestly sexual abuse of minors, claiming his direct authority in communion with the See of Peter, and his only requirement to "respond to the bidding of Rome independent of what the U.S. Conference of Catholic Bishops does or says" (xii, 10). Zagano points out the important fact that as long as the bishop complies with canon law, he is the end of juridical authority within his diocese, so if the bishop is against women serving in legitimate liturgical roles or ordaining married men to the diaconate, he can refuse them. This juridical authority of a diocesan bishop will need to be remembered in our discussion about women and ministry.

In the context of discussing the case of Bishop Bruskewitz, Zagano asks the decisive question "At what point does a bishop's insistence on policy cause a break with the people of his diocese and with the rest of the bishops of his territory? Is he 'in communion' with the church, or has he removed himself from it?" (12). After a careful and detailed analysis and evaluation of the Bruskewitz case, Zagano concludes that, despite Bruskewitz's claims "to be operating with the authority of Rome," he "clearly did not join with other bishops in post-Vatican II moves to liberalize church practice without changing magisterial teaching," and thus, "clearly acted out of step with his fellow bishops" (12). Although the bishop is the end of juridical authority in his diocese, Zagano reminds us that "sometimes canonical rights collide with common sense and with the needs and desires of the church at large" (xiii).

Concluding the first chapter, Zagano makes the very important remark that it is a collision of views of "church" that is at the heart of the juridical impasse between "Call to Action-Nebraska" and Bishop Bruskewitz. Bruskewitz: "a 'strict constructionist' [who] rules above and beyond the sea change effected by Vatican II regarding the place of the 'laity'—the unordained—in the church," represents a "juridical" bishop and a purely hierarchical model of the church, whereas the educated laity advocates for a "communal" bishop and a model of church that includes more lay participation (40–42). Their respective views express two differing styles of governance as well as a different understanding of the role of the laity and the place and status of women in the church. Zagano's examination and conclusions are indispensable, but this discussion needs to be yet more deeply rooted in ecclesiology. Developing a theology of ministry and laity should be at the center of our attention here. However, given the aim of this book, extensive ecclesiological elaborations would go beyond its scope.[2]

Chapter 2, "Sacramental Authority: Archbishop Milingo, the Vatican, and Married Priests Now!" shows the global and truly catholic dimension of the book's title *Women & Catholicism*. Zagano analyzes the case of Emmanuel Milingo, former archbishop of Lusaka in Zambia, who was heavily involved in African faith healing and was forced to retire to Rome in 1983. In 2001, Milingo attended a group marriage blessing ceremony led by Rev. Sun Myung Moon, the leader of the Unification Church, now the Universal Peace Federation.

After Milingo was married, he created the movement "Married Priests Now!" and ordained two married men as priests and four married men as bishops in the United States. His followers are convinced that "Vatican II did not go far enough, in that it did not reinstitute the tradition of a married priesthood in the Western Church" (80). Milingo's is not the only such case; for example, Bishop Felix M. Davídek (1921–88) ordained married men as priests in the underground Czech church (81). In these cases, it is crucial to distinguish carefully between the sacramentality of the ordination and its liceity or legitimacy. As Milingo is—or at least when he performed the ordinations was—a Catholic bishop, the sacramentality of the ordination is not questioned, for according to Catholic teaching "a bishop (and only a bishop) is empowered to ordain individuals as priests" (63). However, if the ordaining bishop is not the diocesan ordinary of the person to be ordained, the "[l]iceity—legitimacy—requires that [he] . . . receive a dismissorial (permission) letter from the ordinand's bishop or religious superior" (85–88). As this has not happened, the legitimacy or liceity of these ordinations is open to question.

Despite the importance of questions of canon law and distinctions between liceity and validity in Roman Catholic contexts, as a Lutheran theologian with ecumenical interests, I would like to ask what the practices of Milingo and others mean for ecumenism, especially for ecumenical relations with churches that do ordain married men as pastors or priests and that have married bishops? What are the appropriate and ecumenically responsible responses from churches that practice the ordination of married men? These questions are not examined by Zagano but demand further exploration in order to build on the book's ecumenical potential.

A brief "Interlude" on "Ordained Women in the Underground Church" introduces the discussion about the ordination of women to the diaconate and the priesthood. Zagano presents results of her detailed study of events in the Czech Roman Catholic underground church in the 1970s. Czech Bishop Davídek not only ordained married men as priests and bishops but also women as deacons and priests, as "women had been excluded from ordination for only the past thousand years" and as there was "no dogmatic foundation for their exclusion," it was, in his view, "'neolithic thinking' about women [that] solidified objections to their ordination" (86).

The discussion about the ordination of women leads to the third and final chapter, "Juridical Authority, Sacramental Authority, and Women's Ordination." In this chapter, Zagano addresses various cases in which women have been ordained as deacons or priests and examines these ordinations in light of canon law.

In 2002, members of the Roman Catholic Womenpriests movement were ordained as priests on a Danube river tour boat by the Argentine Catholic priest Romulo Antonio Braschi who "had been twice ordained bishop by men claiming legitimate and valid provenance of episcopal orders" (xiv). Thus, two members of the Roman Catholic Womenpriests movement were ordained as bishops in Europe, possibly by a valid Catholic bishop. These bishops held ordination ceremonies in North America. Regarding the reaction of the Vatican, Zagano notes that the first women who were ordained were formally excommunicated by the Vatican but that relatively little action was taken against women who were ordained subsequently. However, the Congregation for the Doctrine of the Faith (CDF) issued a declaration that "stipulate[s] that anyone who participates in the ordination of a woman is *latae sententiae* excommunicated" (90) in May 2008. The CDF's decree was "entered into canon law" (xiv).

Here, the following questions must be asked again: What is the impact of these developments—both the ordination of women priests and bishops, and the declaration of the CDF—on ecumenical relations with churches that do ordain women? Is the consequence of the CDF's statement that the topic of women's ordination needs to be excluded from the agenda of ecumenical dialogues as has already happened, for example, in the Roman Catholic–Lutheran Dialogue on *The Apostolicity of the Church*[3] published in 2006? The preface to this document states that topics related to the ordination of women to the pastoral ministry and the episcopal office are not addressed in this dialogue.[4] Sometimes controversial issues do need to be bracketed in order to move forward in other areas of dialogue, but if the topic of women's ordination is simply excluded from ecumenical conversations, how can there be ecumenical progress with regard to the ordained ministry?

Is the exclusion of women's ordination from the dialogue agenda not a step back from *Baptism, Eucharist and Ministry*? In 1982, *Baptism, Eucharist and Ministry* urged the churches to complement "[t]he discussion of . . . practical and theological questions [regarding the ministry of men and women in the Church] within the various churches and Christian traditions . . . by joint study and reflection within the ecumenical fellowship of all churches."[5]

Zagano continues discussing skillfully the conflicting views about the question of infallibility regarding the authority of the church to ordain women and the main arguments for the ordination of male priests and bishops only (95–98). The restriction of priestly ordination to males is based mainly on two arguments: first, the iconic argument and second, the authority argument. After a brief critique of these two arguments, Zagano points out that the authority argument only applies to priests and bishops, not to deacons. Regarding the first argument, the iconic argument, Zagano chooses an approach one can find regularly throughout her book: she examines exhaustive historical evidence and then asks questions. In this case, she asks why the priest physically must represent Christ if the institution narrative is not required for a valid Eucharist as shown in some historical sources whose validity has now been affirmed by the Vatican.

In her argument for the ordination of women deacons, Zagano not only brings neglected historical evidence to the fore but also biblical sources such as Paul's letter to the Romans, where we find the deacon, not deaconess, Phoebe (Rom 16:1). While emphasizing that "[t]he humanity of Christ overcomes the limitations of gender," and highlighting church teaching about the equality of all persons, Zagano notes that "there is no church document that insinuates or states an ontological distinction among humans except among documents that address the question of ordination" (130). A further analysis of this finding would have been interesting. Zagano advocates clearly for the ordination of women deacons but distinguishes the ordination to the diaconate carefully from the ordination of women to the priesthood and the episcopate.

In regard to the latter, a reader supportive of women's ordination not only to the diaconate but also to the priesthood and the episcopate might want to see Zagano not only stretching existing boundaries within the Roman Catholic Church further but also expanding the debate and exploring more arguments for the ordination of women to the priesthood and the episcopate. It needs to be asked what kind of consequences the ordination of women deacons in the Roman Catholic Church would have for the ordination of women as priests and bishops.

Zagano's convincing arguments in favor of women deacons need to be further grounded in profound ecclesiological foundations. All types of ordination must be based on a theology of ministry with a strong foundation in sacramental theology. The consequences of our common baptismal priesthood need to be explored further, especially in regard to the role of women in the church. Such an exploration of our common baptismal priesthood might not only provide ecclesiological foundations for the ordination of women deacons but also possibilities for further ecumenical rapprochement in regard to ministry. This level of theologizing would go beyond the scope of the book, but it must be said that Zagano's argumentation already contributes greatly to deepening the ecclesiological debate regarding women's roles in the Roman Catholic Church.

Zagano concludes that "[i]t is not likely the Catholic Church will change its perspective on women priests or bishops," but that "[i]t is possible, even advisable, that the Catholic Church restore its older tradition of women deacons . . . [and] expands its acceptance of married priests. All of these are already present in one form or another within communions with a claim to Catholic legitimacy and validity. Women deacons and married priests are also present in churches in communion with Rome" (131). Thus, having women deacons and married priests in the Roman Catholic Church could also advance ecumenical relations.

Throughout *Women & Catholicism: Gender, Communion, and Authority*, Zagano's analysis is thorough, and her conclusions are constructive. The book provides an indispensable basis for the discussion about women in the Roman Catholic Church, but its significance goes far beyond the Roman Catholic context.

Notes

[1] Phyllis Zagano, *Women & Catholicism: Gender, Communion, and Authority* (New York: Palgrave Macmillan, 2011).

[2] Zagano does reference a few books that offer great contributions to further the ecclesiological discourse: Avery Dulles, *Models of the Church* (Garden City, NY: Doubleday, 1978), Yves Congar, *Lay People in the Church* (Westminster, MD: Newman, 1965), Paul Lakeland, *Liberation of the Laity* (New York: Continuum, 2004), and Paul Lakeland, *Catholicism at the Crossroads: How the Laity Can Save the Church* (New York: Continuum, 2007).

[3] Lutheran-Roman Catholic Commission on Unity, *The Apostolicity of the Church: Study Document of the Lutheran-Roman Catholic Commission on Unity [of] The Lutheran World Federation [and] Pontifical Council for Promoting Christian Unity* (Minneapolis: Lutheran University Press, 2006).

[4] Cf. "The Commission agreed from the beginning not to take up a point of serious difference between Lutherans and Catholics, namely, the ordination of women to the pastoral ministry and their appointment to the Episcopal office" (11).

[5] World Council of Churches, *Baptism, Eucharist and Ministry*, Faith and Order Paper no. 111 (Geneva: World Council of Churches, 1982), Commentary 18.

Implementing Vatican II's Eclesiology

Sandra Mazzolini

In the introduction to *Women & Catholicism: Gender, Communion, and Authority*,[1] Phyllis Zagano affirms that today the "Catholic Church is in trouble. Depending on which side of the altar rail you sit, women are either part of the problem or part of the solution" (xi). From the point of view of ecclesial life, the active and significant role of women in the ecclesial community has been and is unquestionable, but it still does not receive a suitably corresponding ecclesiastical acknowledgement. So, while the role is identified as essential by the ecclesiastic magisterium,[2] its enactment often seems to be temporary, optional, or voluntary, due in part to the shortage of priests and male religious.

One main issue arises from this fact. Can such lack of acknowledgement be linked solely to the exclusion of women from ordained priesthood? Or does it rather depend on a clerical model of church, which still survives despite the communion ecclesiological perspectives of the Second Vatican Council as well as on a continuing lack of recognition of a common baptismal dignity? I think that the latter is the deeper and more relevant issue. Even though the still persistent clerical model of church and the insufficient acknowledgement of a common baptismal dignity affect the ecclesial role of both laymen and laywomen, nevertheless their influence on the female ecclesial role is most evident and particular. The question of female ecclesial ministries is emblematic of these deeper matters.[3]

Analyzing three specific and "interrelated situations in the Catholic Church, each of which has further theological and ecclesiological implications," (xi) Zagano's book also refers to some fundamental ecclesiological issues whose meaning and implications are more universal. Three of them, which are implicated in the frame of this research, are relevant also in the reflection on the church and the female role in ecclesial life and mission: (1) church, communion, and sacrament, (2) divergent ecclesiological perspectives of Vatican II and those of the Code of Canon Law, and (3) the question of female ministries in the Catholic Church.

Church, Communion, and Sacrament

The relations inside any given local church, those between local churches and the universal church, the issues of ecclesial communion, sacramental and juridical authority, and the theme of ministries are the ecclesiological *fil rouge* (common thread) of the three cases analyzed by Phyllis Zagano. Her ecclesiological point of view attempts to integrate a heavily juridical approach with a more communional or relational one. In other words, she seeks to operate within the ecclesiological perspectives of Vatican II, in particular the model of church as communion and sacrament.

The Council distances itself from the so-called Gregorian model of church,[4] which distinguishes between active and passive subjects, by acknowledging the biblical and patristic traditions. The church as communion is a rather complex model of church. In fact, it implies the relations of the church with the triune God, the relations among the churches, those within each local church, and finally those with the world.[5] It is very important to note that the principle of ecclesial communion is not uniformity but rather the integration of differences.[6] The church communion, whose center is Christ, is an actual network of relations in which people interact and relate with each other. This communion model of church emphasizes, first of all, the common dignity of different ecclesial subjects, which is based on the reception of baptism.

Lumen Gentium 1 states that the church is in Christ as a sacrament of communion between God and human beings as well as a communion among human beings. The sacramentality of the church stresses its historical dimension, while recognizing its intrinsic correlation with the ecclesial mystical/spiritual dimension.[7] On the one hand, this qualification prompts consideration of the societal and institutional dimension of the church without overvaluing it. On the other hand, it permits the affirmation of the intrinsic necessity of ecclesial reform and transformation, according to both evangelical principles and the "signs of the time."[8] From this perspective, plurality, which enhances the diversity and specificity of ecclesial subjects, is not only wishful thinking but even a consequent necessity.

Divergent Ecclesiological Perspectives of
Vatican II and the Code of Canon Law

Phyllis Zagano highlights that in "the Catholic Church communion and authority formally understood are by definition and by law inextricably bound, each reflecting on the other in support of official, or 'magisterial,' teaching" (xi). In this regard, many theoretical, as well as practical, questions are still open, for example, those concerning the relation between the ecclesiological perspectives of Vatican II and those of the Code of Canon Law. According to some scholars, these perspectives are sometimes divergent.[9] This divergence can be highlighted by comparing the conciliar texts with the Code. This comparison could be made by first introducing some relevant gaps in the ecclesiological teachings of Vatican II and then calling into question the stated reception of Vatican II in the Code.

We can highlight four main gaps in the ecclesiological teaching of Vatican II: (1) the conciliar ecclesiological doctrine is characterized by a certain doctrinal atrophy; (2) the Council does not resolve the tension between preconciliar ecclesiology and the "new theology"; (3) Vatican II did not pay too much attention to the canonical dimension of the reforms, which it should have introduced; and (4) *Lumen Gentium* and *Gaudium et Spes* illustrate the relationship between church and world in a different manner, which is not entirely consistent.[10]

Concerning the reception of Vatican II in the Code, many scholars point out that, on the one hand, there are many elements of the conciliar ecclesiology in the Code, but, on the other hand, the reception of the conciliar perspectives has been insufficient. This insufficiency is clear if we consider the various levels of reception of Vatican II in the Code (meaning the epistemological level and that of content, analyzed from the point of view of the material and formal reception). On an epistemological level, the Code reproduces the twofold ecclesiological approach of the church as *communio* and the church as *societas* in a wider form than Vatican II did.[11]

From an ecclesiological point of view, the doctrinal atrophy of conciliar doctrine on the church, taken together with the divergent ecclesiological perspectives of Vatican II and those of the Code of Canon Law, could explain why the active and significant role of women in the ecclesial community still has not achieved a suitably corresponding ecclesiastical acknowledgement.

The Question of Female Ministries
in the Catholic Church

The ecclesiological perspectives of Vatican II provide the essential theological touchstones for the subsequent development of this theme. In the postconciliar era, the debate about ecclesial ministries has enlarged the previous perspectives. Paradoxically, this extension does not resolve the question of female ministries; in fact, we can note the problematic tendency to reduce the question of female ministries to the question of women priests. Today, however, it is necessary to enlarge the debate, as Phyllis Zagano especially highlights in the third part of her book where she examines the topic of "women deacons."[12] In my opinion, three perspectives, which are not only methodological, could be useful for developing the theme of female ministries in the Catholic Church.

1. The reflection on ministries of women has to be placed in a broader ecclesiological context because each determination of ministries and offices depends on a specific model of church. In fact, ministries are serving the church, so the church is the starting point for defining them more clearly.[13] In this perspective, the reference to the ecclesiological model of Vatican II as well as to an ecumenical model of church is an essential element also for rethinking the question of female ministries.[14] Consequently, communion, as founded on the principle of nonuniformity and the acknowledgement of differences, provides a significant key for understanding this issue.

2. Defining ministries more clearly implies having previously adopted an accurate methodology. In this regard, it should hardly be necessary to point out that ecclesiological investigation cannot prescind from historical data or vice versa.[15] Assessing the history of the church, we can note, first, the development of ecclesial ministries and structures.[16] On one side, various ministerial forms have been identified in the course of time; on the other, we can highlight some modifications that have concerned the form of some ecclesial ministries (the ministry of the bishop of Rome).[17] Second, we have no doubt that the ongoing process of ecclesiastical institutionalization has also changed and transformed the role of the women in the church as well as its acknowledgement.[18]

3. Some scholars refer to the church of the first centuries.[19] The early church recognized female ministries, but today it is very complex to determine exactly the sense, extension, and implications of this acknowledgement.[20] Nevertheless, the reference to the Christian sources of the first centuries is legitimate provided that scholars avoid one-sided interpretations by throwing modern perspectives, problems, etc., onto the past. In my view, the research on the thought and life of Christian origins must be carried out not to make a simple transposition of what was recognized or not recognized for women but to receive those fundamental perspectives that caused or favored both doctrinal and institutional changes and developments. Surely, the uncertain determination of female ministerial roles in the early church makes its reception more difficult today. This difficulty, however, does not exclude further development.

The issue of the acknowledgement of the female ecclesial role is still open. If the topic is considered from the point of view of ecclesiastic magisterium, there is no doubt that words of appreciation are insufficient without their being put into practice or without an actual acknowledgement of female presence in the church. But, from another point of view, there is also no doubt that to reduce the question to a mere claim of a right is analogously insufficient. In fact, this reduction implies entering a dead-end.

Zagano's focus on women deacons could represent a step beyond this impasse. This will appear even more likely as the underlying ecclesiological issues regarding the various roles of women, as well as the meaning of ministry and of the church itself, are developed further.

Notes

[1] Phyllis Zagano, *Women & Catholicism: Gender, Communion, and Authority* (New York: Palgrave Macmillan, 2011).

[2] In assessing the postconciliar magisterium, one can see the ecclesiastical teaching on the ecclesial role of women has developed according to two perspectives. The anthropological approach highlights female dignity, according to biblical data; a crucial moment is the debate about *gender*. The ecclesiological approach focuses attention on the female ministries. These perspectives are obviously correlated; both of them involve the question of the acknowledgement of the role of women in the church, albeit with different emphasis. See Sandra Mazzolini, "Donna," in *Dizionario di ecclesiologia*, ed. G. Calabrese, Philip Goyret, and Francesco Orazio Piazza (Rome: Città Nuova, 2010), 464–65.

[3] The issue of lay ecclesial ministries was also discussed by the Synod of Bishops dedicated to the *Christifideles Laici* (1987). The growing active presence of laymen and laywomen in ecclesial life and mission involved a clarification of the topic, in particular to avoid confusion between the lay pastoral role and the pastoral role of priests. The bishops reaffirmed that there was no theological reason to exclude women from those ministries, which were founded in baptism. At the same time, they had reservations about the putting into practice of this statement, because a huge number of them feared that the admission of women—especially in the liturgical field—could have strengthened their hope to be admitted to the ministerial priesthood. See Giovanni Caprile, *Il Sinodo dei Vescovi: Settima assemblea generale ordinaria (1–30 ottobre 1987)* (Rome: "La Civiltà Cattolica," 1989).

[4] This model accentuated the church's social-institutional profile in particular, identifying it progressively with the Pope. See Ghislain Lafont, *Immaginare la Chiesa cattolica: Linee e approfondimenti per un nuovo dire e un nuovo fare della comunità cristiana* (Cinisello Balsamo, Milan: San Paolo, 1998), 39–65; Paul Tihon, "La Chiesa," in Henri Bourgeois, Bernard Sesboüé, and Paul Tihon, *I segni della salvezza XII–XX secolo: Sacramenti e Chiesa, Vergine Maria* (Casale Monferrato, Italy: Piemme, 1998), 359–54.

[5] See Walter Kasper, *La Chiesa di Gesù Cristo: Scritti di ecclesiologia* (Brescia, Italy: Queriniana, 2011), 25–101.

[6] See C. René Padilla, "The Unity of the Church and the Homogeneous Unit Principle," in *Landmark Essays in Mission and World Christianity*, ed. Robert L. Gallagher and Paul Hertig (Maryknoll, NY: Orbis Books, 2009), 73–92.

[7] See Yves Congar, *Un popolo messianico: La Chiesa sacramenti di salvezza: La salvezza e la liberazione* (Brescia, Italy: Queriniana, 1976), 13–91; Otto Semmelroth, "La Chiesa come sacramento di salvezza," in Karl Rahner, *Mysterium salutis 7*, 377–436; Kasper, *La Chiesa di Gesù Cristo*, 231–91; Avery Dulles, *Modelli di Chiesa* (Padova, Italy: Edizioni Messaggero, 2005), 77–92 [New York: Image Books, 1987, 2002, 55–67]; Sandra Mazzolini, "La Chiesa sacramento del regno," *Gregorianum* 86, no. 3 (2005): 629–43.

[8] See Yves Congar, *Vera e falsa riforma nella Chiesa* (Milan: Jaca Books, 1972); Ignacio Ellacuría, *Conversione della Chiesa al Regno di Di: Per annunciarlo e realizzarlo nella storia* (Brescia, Italy: Queriniana, 1992), 29–37, 154–19.

[9] Sandra Mazzolini, "La recezione del Concilio Vaticano II come questione aperta: Una prospettiva ecclesiologica," in *La Chiesa è missionaria: La ricezione nel Codice di Diritto Canonico*, ed. Luigi Sabbarese (Vatican City: Urbaniana University Press, 2009), 236–39.

[10] Sandra Mazzolini, "La recezione del Concilio Vaticano II," 234–35.

[11] Ibid., 237–39.

[12] Recognizing that the "ecumenical dimension of the female diaconate is crucial to the resolution of the question in the Catholic Church," Zagano affirms that it "would seem logical that a decision by the Catholic Church to return to its tradition of ordaining women deacons might better foster Christian unity as well as help the Catholic Church regain its perceived lost authority in matters of human rights and equality" (Zagano, *Women & Catholicism*, 122–23).

[13] See Dulles, *Modelli di Chiesa*, 191–207 [English, 152–66]; Peter Hünnermann, "*Una cum:* Funzioni del ministero petrino dal punto di vista cattolico," in *Papato ed ecumenismo: Il ministero petrino al servizio dell'unità*, ed. Peter Hünnermann (Bologna: EDB, 1999), 108–09.

[14] See Sandra Mazzolini, "Soggettualità riconosciuta, soggettualità negata: le donne nelle chiese cristiane. Una prospettiva cattolica," in *Non contristate lo Spirito: Prospettive di genere e teologia: qualcosa è cambiato?*, ed. Marinella Perroni (San Pietro in Cariano, Italy: Il Segno dei Gabrielli Editori, 2007), 121–36; Sandra Mazzolini, "La Chiesa sacramento come orizzonte della partecipazione delle donne alla vita e alla missione della comunità ecclesiale," in *Il Vaticano II e la sua ricezione al femminile*, ed. Cettina Militello (Bologna: EDB, 2007), 209–26.

[15] See A. Antón, *La Iglesia de Cristo: El Israel de la Vieja y de la Nueva Alianza* (Madrid: La Editorial Católica, 1977), 707–49.

[16] See *I ministeri nella Chiesa antica: Testi patristici dei primi tre secoli*, ed. Enrico Cattaneo (Milan: Ed. Paoline, 1977); Wilhelm De Vries, *Orient et Occident: Les structures ecclésiales vues dans l'histoire des sept premiers conciles œcuméniques* (Paris: Cerf, 2011).

[17] See Klaus Schatz, *Il primato del papa: La sua storia dalle origini ai giorni nostri* (Brescia, Italy: Queriniana, 1996).

[18] See, for example, Susan E. Smith, *Women in Mission: From the New Testament to Today* (Maryknoll, NY: Orbis Books, 2007).

[19] See, for example, Elisabeth Schüssler Fiorenza, *In memoria: Una ricostruzione femminista delle origini cristiane* (Turin, Italy: Claudiana, 1990; in English, *In Memory of Her: A Feminist Theological Reconstruction of Christian Origins* [New York: Crossroad, 1983]); Carolyn Osiek and Margaret Y. MacDonald, *Il ruolo delle donne nel cristianesimo delle origini: Indagine sulle chiese domestiche* (Cinisello Balsamo, Milan: San Paolo, 2007; in English, *A Woman's Place: House Churches in Early Christianity* [Minneapolis: Fortress Press, 2005]).

[20] See Cattaneo, *I ministeri nella Chiesa antica*, 181–99.

The Viewpoint of an Orthodox Theologian

Vladimir Latinovic

Phyllis Zagano's *Women & Catholicism: Gender, Communion, and Authority*[1] provides excellent reading, not only for those who do not possess knowledge about the current discussion concerning the position of women in the Roman Catholic Church in general, but also for those who are more familiar with the matter.[2] The book is written in such form that every layperson can understand it, and we must admit that we are all laypeople in one way or another—at least in the "nonexpert" way, if not in the original "nonclergy" meaning of the word.[3]

Zagano analyzes the situation in the Roman Catholic Church in general by using two extreme positions as examples: Bishop Bruskewitz as the extreme conservative and Archbishop Milingo as (at least from the standpoint of the Vatican) the extreme liberal. Zagano exhibits both sides of the story and, for the most part, lets the reader decide how to feel about them. She simultaneously respects the official Roman Catholic teaching while stretching the boundaries.

In these first two parts of the book, Zagano deals with the problems that, in my judgment, come mainly from the application of a universalist ecclesiology on the local church. A universalist ecclesiology is one that automatically subordinates the local churches to the church universal, with the church universal being conceived as existing above and even detached from them. Zagano tells the story of a group of U.S. Catholics in the Diocese of Lincoln, Nebraska, who, in more or less legitimate ways, try to take part in making decisions in their local church. At first, their demands are concentrated on "women's legitimate participation in liturgy" (14). Bishop Bruskewitz was denying women even those liturgical and ministerial services that are allowed by the rest of the Roman Catholic Church and in some countries, such as Germany for example, are today considered to be something quite normal.

Zagano next deals with Emanuel Milingo, forcibly retired Archbishop of Lusaka (Zambia) and his "adaptations in service of inculturation of Catholicism in Africa" (49) in the form of a so-called faith healing practice. In this case it is the archbishop himself whose situation worsens as he hits a wall of nonunderstanding from the official Church authorities.

The first thing that is obvious from both these examples, that of Call to Action and that of Archbishop Milingo, is that the U.S. Christians and the African Christians view the same (Roman Catholic) Church in two different ways and that this is due to the simple fact that they do not necessarily share the same cultural values. What seems likely from my Orthodox perspective is that in both cases, Rome does not show sufficient understanding for either of these local variations/implementations of Catholicism. Instead, the official church is supporting persons such as Bishop Bruskewitz, who is implementing the Vatican's *current policy* without question. I say "*current policy*" here because even many Catholic theologians argue that the bishops' approach does not represent the official policy of the Roman Catholic Church as it has developed since the Second Vatican Council; instead, it is rather a step back into preconciliar ways of thinking.

From these two examples, one could conclude that, due to its centralization, the Roman Catholic Church cannot adequately respond to the particular demands and needs of each local diocese or region.[4] Nikolai Afanasiev, one of the official orthodox observers at the Vatican II, devoted his article, "The Church Which Presides in Love," precisely to the problem of the universalist ecclesiology and its negative aspects.[5] Participants of the Second Vatican Council were aware of this problem, and for this reason they started introducing an ecclesiological approach that Zagano calls the "'communal' (collegial, ecclesial) model against the 'juridical' (collaborative, political model)" (9). This "communal" model might also be labeled "communion ecclesiology" and has significant overlap, albeit with some distinction, with what Afanasiev depicts as "eucharistic ecclesiology."[6]

The reception of the Council is still not finished, and I think that, especially in the light of the ecumenical dialogue with the Orthodox Church, there is still a space for abandoning the universalist and overly centralized system and replacing it with a more suitable one, which does not necessarily need to be something entirely new.[7] Pope John Paul II can be interpreted as actually starting the process of jettisoning the universalist system with his encyclical letter *Ut Unum Sint* in which he expresses a desire "to find a way of exercising the primacy which, while in no way renouncing what is essential to its mission, is nonetheless open to a new situation."[8] Many churches responded very positively to this call, but Rome appears to have done little, if anything, as yet to put any of these ideas into practice.

Zagano addresses the problem of sacramental authority by considering several ordinations performed by the bishops who separated or had been excommunicated from the Catholic Church and then considers the question of whether these ordinations are sacramentally valid, as is claimed by those involved (70–71). From my Orthodox standpoint, the entire idea that the sacramental priesthood can never be lost, even after a bishop (or a priest) does not belong to the particular church anymore—the idea that he still possesses some kind of sacramental authority and that ordinations done by him could be considered as valid—is theologically and historically highly disputable, to say the least. In the apostolic times and in the early church priests (or bishops) were not so much different from any other church members, with the exception of the role that they had when they were presiding over the Eucharistic gathering.[9] It was precisely this presiding that constituted them as bishops. Following this logic, one has to conclude that a bishop can only be a bishop as long as he presides over the Eucharist of his local church. Seen from this perspective, Archbishop Milingo would not only have no juridical authority, a point not in dispute, but no sacramental authority as well. The same goes for all other bishops mentioned in the book as well as all of their alleged "ordinations." There is no magical power given through ordination to the bishop as an individual apart from his place in the ordering of a liturgical community, and *that* is why there cannot be any sacramentally valid ordination that takes place outside of a particular church.

The problem of a universalist ecclesiology arises in a different way in regard to Milingo's "faith healing" practices (68ff). Milingo saw himself as the person elected by God to heal the sick and the afflicted. He practiced his "powers" by conducting exorcisms and faith healings during or after his masses. Now, it is obvious that this form of piety looks strange to our "Western" eyes, but, on the other hand, it is also evident that there was insufficient appreciation for local practices on the part of the official church. Being aware that he was treading on a slippery slope, Milingo himself was ready to make some sort of compromise, but the universalist ecclesiology of Rome interfered.

Orthodox Experience with Married Priests

So far I have been trumpeting Orthodox views, but I would like to point out that Zagano is perhaps too kind in several places where she discusses Orthodox views by always placing them in a positive light. I do agree with her, though, that the Orthodox practice of ordaining married priests is something from which the Roman Catholic Church could learn, especially in the times when there is such a huge priest shortage. As Vatican II said, the "Churches of the East have had a treasury from which the Western Church has drawn extensively—in liturgical practice, spiritual tradition, and law" (*Unitatis Redintegratio* §14).

For the purpose of balance, Zagano also mentions the rather negative standpoint on this matter from Cardinal Nasrallah Pierre Sfeir that "married priesthood is problematic in Eastern Churches because a married priest's obligations to their families sometimes compete with their parish commitments or the bishop's ability to move him to another parish" (77). I completely disagree with the view of Cardinal Sfeir. Married priests' obligations to their family sometimes do compete with their parish commitments, but Orthodox priests are especially dedicated to their parishes. One also needs to take into consideration that Orthodox priests do not have to serve multiple parishes as many Roman Catholic priests do today. It can be argued, moreover, that married priests can have an advantage in understanding the daily problems of their flock because they are living more similar lives. Furthermore, the limited number of priest candidates in the Roman Catholic Church, which can be linked to the celibacy requirement, often does not leave much room for choosing the best possible person for the job.

Women Deacons in the Orthodox Church

On another matter I am not so proud of the record of my Orthodox Church as Zagano's description might otherwise make me feel. Zagano mentions several times that the Holy Synod of the Orthodox Church of Greece in 2004 reintroduced the service of women deacons. I feel obliged to give some more information on this point because the reality is not as spectacular as it might seem at first. What the Church of Greece did was to confirm one of the ancient church practices, one that was actually never forbidden; it had just not often been practiced. Saint Nectarios of Aegina (1846–1920), for example, ordained women deacons. Several theology professors and bishops from Greece whom I have consulted all said the same thing: yes, there is an official decision, but there is no implementation of this whatsoever. As of yet, there are very few women deacons in the Greek Church. It can even be argued that with this decision, the Orthodox Church of Greece actually *limited women deacon ordination* by allowing it only for either sisters living in remote monasteries or the ones ordained at the discretion of bishops, which are both rare exceptions.

Theological and Liturgical Aspects of Women's Ordination

Another question that Zagano raises in the book is whether women deacons were ever sacramentally ordained and if they took part in the liturgy. I do not attach great importance to this question, for even if women were never sacramentally ordained, there would be no reason why we should not start doing it now. Over the centuries, the church has been open to various innovations. Otherwise, we would not have monks; we would not have icons; and ultimately we would not have a pope—at least not in the form that we do today.

The official Orthodox position on this question is very clear: the liturgical role of deaconess was never the same as the role of deacons. The deaconess always had more of a baptismal role by assisting the bishop/priest during the baptism of female members to prevent misconduct. This position is the one with which even Prof. Theodorou, who was the initiator and driving force behind the decision of the Holy Synod of the Orthodox Church of Greece in 2004, agrees.[10]

The question of whether the deaconess ever belonged to the priesthood is from an Orthodox perspective also connected with the question of whether male deacons belong to the priesthood. From the Orthodox standpoint, deacons do not fully belong to the priesthood. For example, deacons are buried using the funeral rite for laypeople, unlike the burial of the priests and bishops who have their own special funeral rites. Also, their ordination is an Orthodox rite performed inside the liturgy but outside of the Eucharistic canon.

My main point in raising these historical difficulties is that I think that the most fruitful path in arguing for development in the ministerial roles of women lies more in the direction of supporting innovation rather than in the direction of finding historical precedents.

Orthodox View of Women's Ordination

Zagano advocates for the ordination of women as deacons. She does not push the question of the ordination of women as priests. I wish to comment, however, on why the question of women's ordination, whether as deacons or as priests, is really not on the table for most Orthodox theologians. This is not because we are uninterested in it but mostly because, in general, Orthodox women, for some strange and unexplainable reason, do not insist on the matter. It seems that most women in the Orthodox Church are still satisfied with their traditional role both in the church and in the family. One point of explanation for this is that, from an historical point of view, the position of women in Eastern Christian countries was not as bad as it was in the West. In the Byzantine Empire, for example, women had almost the same legal rights as men, and the empire was ruled by three different empresses over time.

The Orthodox Church always kept in mind that the first person who comes after God is a woman, Mary, and has used every opportunity to stress this, especially in hymnography. There is actually a saying in my country (Serbia) that describes the role of the women in Orthodox setting very accurately: *The man is the head of the family, but the woman is the neck and she turns the head in the direction she chooses.* Women were always some sort of *l'éminence grise* (gray eminence, or unofficial decison maker) in their families, and this is something that still survives today.

Another reason why Orthodox women do not demand to be ordained could be that in Orthodox tradition, motherhood was always considered to be some sort of counterpart to the priesthood. I have heard one old Orthodox priest say that the miracle of bringing new life into this world is something that belongs only to God and to the woman, and that men need to settle for the lesser service, that is, priesthood.

Although the ordination of women is not a burning theological question for Orthodox, one can still see some development in understanding in the Orthodox Church. For example, metropolitan John Zizioulas, who is considered to be one of the most prominent living Orthodox theologians, said once that there are actually no theological reasons for not ordaining women, only historical ones.[11] In my opinion, though, the Orthodox Church does not serve as a good example when it comes to the ordination of women. With all its rigidness in this matter, the Roman Catholic Church may still be much closer to ordaining women, even as deacons, than the Orthodox Church.[12]

Notes

[1] Phyllis Zagano, *Women & Catholicism: Gender, Communion, and Authority* (New York: Palgrave Macmillan, 2011).

[2] For those of you who are more interested in the topic of women's ordination, specifically as deacons, I would also recommend another Zagano book: *Holy Saturday: An Argument for the Restoration of the Female Diaconate in the Catholic Church* (New York: Crossroad, 2000), winner of the College Theology Society Annual Book Award (2002) and a First Place Book Award of the Catholic Press Association (First Place in Gender Studies).

[3] And this is exactly what this book is about: women not wanting to put up with the exclusion from the leading positions in the church, including those of a sacramental nature.

[4] On the other side, the Orthodox Church, because of its division in so-called national Churches, has problems in expressing its unity and superseding its limited ethnic and cultural dimension of existence.

[5] Nikolai Afanasiev, "The Church Which Presides in Love," in *The Primacy of Peter: Essays in Ecclesiology and the Early Church*, ed. John Meyendorff, new ed. (Crestwood, NY: St Vladimir's Seminary Press, 1992). Afanasiev (1893–1966)

was professor of theology at Saint Sergius Orthodox Theological Seminary in Paris.

⁶ Afanasiev, "The Church Which Presides in Love," 135.

⁷ We could simply use the old patriarchal system which at the same time guaranteed the unity of the church and freedom of expression of each local church.

⁸ John Paul II, *Ut Unum Sint*: On Commitment to Ecumenism, 95.

⁹ Cf. Zizioulas's doctoral dissertation: *Eucharist, Bishop, Church: The Unity of the Church in the Divine Eucharist and the Bishop during the First Three Centuries* (Brookline MA: Holy Cross, 2001).

¹⁰ Evangelos Theodorou, "*Das Amt der Diakoninnen in der kirchlichen Tradition: Ein orthodoxer Beitrag zum Problem der Frauenordination*," in *Una Sancta: Zeitschrift für Ökumenische Begegnung* (Meitingen Freising, Germany: Kyrios-Verlag, 1978), 169.

¹¹ Division of Studies, World Council of Churches, *Study Encounter* 4, no. 4 (1968): 193 §G.

¹² In the Roman Catholic Church, there is at least limited support for this from many scholars and from a sizable number of laity, which is not something you will find in the Orthodox Church.

Response:
Toward a Nonexclusionary View of Women

Phyllis Zagano

Thank you. I am deeply honored to be able to be with you and to be given the opportunity to think out loud with all of you about women and the Catholic Church, particularly about the church's vexed internal questions revolving around gender in relation to communion and authority. I indeed have been thinking about these precise matters for quite a while, first spurred, then encouraged by some of the good people who sit among us, especially Gerard Mannion, Paul Lakeland, and Dennis Doyle, and now encouraged and challenged even more by Miriam Haar, Sandra Mazzolini, and Vladimir Latinovic.

Women & Catholicism had its immediate start when the Catholic writer David Gibson, who lives in Brooklyn, called to ask me about excommunication. Fabian Bruskewitz, the Catholic bishop of Lincoln, Nebraska, had announced excommunication of all members of Call to Action, the lay Catholic group that blew into one of the Second Vatican Council's open windows. David, a member of the lay activist group Call to Action, wanted to know if he would be excommunicated if he went to a University of Nebraska-Lincoln basketball game. I studied what was going on, wrote a Religion News Service column about it, and began to put some pieces together.

Who is in? Who is out? And why?

The more I looked into Lincoln, Nebraska, the more I found an historical, reflexive distaste for secular (and in many cases religious) women in any ministry—in the ministry of the word, of the liturgy, even in the ministry of charity where it was a direct function of the diocese. I found this reflexive distaste not only on the part of the former bishop but among his presbyterate and even among the laity of his diocese. For Lincoln, Nebraska, the Second Vatican Council had not happened.

175

I learned that when Fabian Bruskewitz became bishop of Lincoln, a small group of lay Catholics—the core of a prior group interested in liturgical reform—asked about women in the church. Bruskewitz responded by requiring them, first, to read some bitter diatribes against the ordination of women as priests. But women's ordination was not on their minds. They were asking about women lectors and women extraordinary ministers of the Eucharist as well as for women to be more involved in the charitable endeavors of the diocese. Bishop Bruskewitz wasn't having any of it, and so the fight was on. He ended up excommunicating them. He had the juridical authority to do it. No one, really, could stop him from doing what he pleased inside the confines of Lincoln, Nebraska.

But, I thought, there must be bishops around who did not think that women cannot touch the holy or that touching a woman defiled a man so much that he could not touch the holy. So, enter Emmanuel Milingo, removed as archbishop of Lusaka, Zambia, because he was inculturating Catholicism in the wrong direction. He was adopting and incorporating African faith-healing practices in ways that made the majority of local priests—white European missionaries—more than nervous. Swept off to a do-nothing job at the Vatican, Milingo retained his salary—and his faith-healing ministry—in a suburb of Rome. When he turned seventy, Milingo lost his position. Not long after, he turned up in Madison Square Garden, New York, getting married to a Korean acupuncturist in a ceremony led by Sung Myung Moon, founder of the Unification Church. Then Milingo ordained four married men as bishops, a couple of others as priests, and proceeded to overstay his U.S. visa by a few days. I spent a few hours with him in the Tarrytown, New York, Moon headquarters, but he hasn't been to the United States since, failing on every visa attempt. Archbishop Milingo—now excommunicated and laicized—travels the world (most often to Africa) to ordain married men as priests.

But where did this lead? I was trying to understand who's in and who's out, and especially, what is the Catholic Church's problem with women? It seemed women could not speak in church, participate in liturgy, formally share governance or perform ministry, or touch the sacred—and for the most part anyone who "touched" women could not do those things either. That is, the restrictions on married clergy were deeply entrenched in both Catholicism and, at the episcopal level, Orthodoxy.

I think the exclusion of women is of a different order from the exclusion of racial or ethnic groups. Rather, the exclusion of women is a neuralgic response to ignorant beliefs about authority and about the sacred. The exclusion of women is caused by a defective view of God and a misunderstanding of the incarnation. The exclusion of women is because of people who cannot, who will not, understand that the God of philosophy is neither male nor female, and the God of theology is both. But it is more than simply misogyny.

I am not necessarily for or against the ordination of women so much as I am for a nonexclusionary view of women as fully human persons who happen to populate half the planet.

So I looked to Czechoslovakia, where the underground but recognized Catholic Bishop Felix M. Davídek ordained married men as deacons, priests, and bishops—and also ordained women as deacons and priests for *Koinótés*, the underground Catholic community he headed and that existed from approximately 1964 to 1989. Following the collapse of communism, the canonical back and forth was mostly resolved with the majority of the married priests becoming Eastern Rite (and some bi-ritual), and one married man only very recently reordained *sub-conditione* as a Roman Catholic priest. As for the one woman whom we know of ordained as a priest, Ludmilla Javarova, she affirms her priesthood as well as the juridical authority that denies her faculties to exercise it. But my study is more than about Ludmilla.

This book is constructed like a murder mystery. There is no smoking gun, but buried in the Davídek story, there is a "smoking bishop"—Dusan Spiner, ordained as bishop by Davídek in 1973 and who in 1992 agreed not to function as a bishop. Spiner is on the roster of official Catholic bishops.

And so I came to a fork in the road. What about other denominations and churches? What about the Anglicans? If nothing happens in Anglican ordinations, why is Rome so exercised about Anglican women priests and bishops? What about the Union of Utrecht Churches? Rome tentatively acknowledges the sacraments and orders of some of them, and one, the Old Catholic Church of the Czech Republic, only ordains women as deacons. And, what about the Orthodox? The Armenian Apostolic Church ordains women as deacons, and the Orthodox Church of Greece has recovered its tradition. It matters not how many there are or even what they do. The Catholic Church, overall, with the Second Vatican Council's Decree on Ecumenism, *Unitatis Redintegratio,* and again with individual mutual agreements, recognizes the sacraments and orders of the Armenians and the Orthodox.

So, if the Catholic Church recognizes the sacraments and orders of these other churches—I avoid the conflicted term "sister churches"—then what is the status of their women deacons? Are they "ordained" or not? The Catholic Church is silent on this. If it says "yes"—then that implies Catholic women can be ordained. If it says "no," it could force a fracture in ecumenical relations. So it says nothing.

And then there is the phenomenon of the Roman Catholic Womenpriests movement. Many believe the group began with priestly ordinations of seven women by vagrant Catholic bishops on the Danube River boat—ostensibly outside any bishop's jurisdiction—on June 29, 2002. Not quite. Prior to their ordinations as priests, six of the seven were ordained as deacons by Dusan Spiner, who is still a recognized Roman Catholic bishop.

So, what if anything has happened? Are these women the deacons of the Armenian and Orthodox Churches, the deacons, priests, and bishops of the Roman Catholic Womenpriest movement?

If nothing has "happened"—if none is validly (even if illicitly) ordained, what in Roman Catholicism keeps women on the other side of the altar rail? What in the Eastern Catholic churches keeps women outside the iconostasis?

What Miriam Haar has done so well is give you a précis of my argument in this book—an admittedly difficult task for a Lutheran not used to the Catholic canonical conundrums I like to formulate, but she has explained my underlying question: what are the implications of our common baptismal priesthood in all of these situations, not only the ordination of women (in my schema, as deacons), but also the questions of ministry? What is it about women that we are excluded from ministry and excluded from governance in the Catholic Church? And, what are the ecumenical implications of inclusion and exclusion? (Haar helpfully notes Archbishop Milingo's quite expansive use of the term "ecumenism," where he seems to include both followers of Sun Myung Moon and Muslims.)

For Catholicism, both questions and problems of validity and liceity are intertwined, and Haar asks what the impact of the various ordinations of women as priests and bishops and the subsequent declaration by the Congregation for the Doctrine of the Faith that such ordinations are offenses ("crimes") worthy of excommunication, especially on ecumenical relations. She further points out that the ordination of women does not seem to be an agenda item for Roman Catholic-Lutheran dialogue and asks, "if the topic of women's ordination is simply excluded from ecumenical conversations, how can there ever be ecumenical progress with regard to the ordained ministry?" Haar wonders whether the ordination of women as deacons would portend the ordination of women as priests and as bishops, and whether "an exploration of our common baptismal priesthood might not only provide ecclesiological foundation for the ordination of women deacons but also possibilities for further ecumenical rapprochement in regard to ministry."

It is clear that all churches and communions that subscribe to the first seven ecumenical councils ordain women to the diaconate or have done so. That the Roman Catholic Church has not recovered its tradition is both problematic and a starting point for further ecumenical dialogue on the questions of ministry that Haar develops.

So, with Professor Mazzolini's intervention, where does this exclusion come from? Is it linked to the exclusion of women from ordination? Is it because of a clerical model of the church that keeps the laity at a distance despite the ecclesiological perspectives of the Second Vatican Council? The problem she identifies is the underlying problem of the reception of the Second Vatican Council. As she writes, "the doctrinal atrophy of conciliar doctrine on the Church, taken together with the divergent ecclesiological perspectives of Vatican II and those of the Code of Canon Law, could explain why the active and significant role of women in the ecclesial community still has not achieved a suitably corresponding ecclesiastical acknowledgement."

As a Catholic theologian and ecclesiologist, Mazzolini agrees that the question of female ecclesial ministries is emblematic of the deeper matters. I greatly appreciate Mazzolini's pointing out what some other reviewers have already overlooked: in this work I operate strictly within the ecclesiological perspectives (and parameters) of the Second Vatican Council, in particular in the model of the church as communion and sacrament. I also recognize, as Mazzolini suggests, a divergence between the text of the Council and the Code of Canon Law as revised in 1983, which I demonstrate (and she points out) delays, if not deters, greater roles for women in the church and concomitant ecclesiastical authorization and acknowledgement. It is not enough, as she points out, to merely acknowledge the work of women without formalizing it.

The possibilities for authorization and acknowledgment of formal ministries for women have not been fully explored. Nor have they been properly distinguished. Unless one begins my study with a clear understanding that the diaconate and the priesthood are separate ministries, and that the one does not necessarily lead to the other, one cannot recognize the possibility of the restoration of women to the diaconate as a means of addressing a serious impasse in Catholic practice and ministry. I am grateful to Mazzolini for pointing out that a "focus on women deacons could represent a step beyond [the] impasse."

Vladimir Latinovic kindly tells us that my work is understandable, and I truly appreciate his perspective as an Orthodox theologian. He pulls the thread of distinct cultural values from this tapestry and I think underscores a good part of the essential argument that can carry the day on the matter of including women in ministry in whatever capacity—as lay ecclesial ministers, as lectors, as acolytes, as deacons. The essential argument is that the Catholic Church is an amalgam of ethnicities across time and place, which is, in the end, locally controlled, first, by the pastor and then by the bishop (through the cooperation of provincial episcopal conferences). And no bishop needs to do anything he does not want to do. So there is at least one U.S. bishop (Bruskewitz) who will not allow lay women to serve as acolytes despite the express provisions of law, and there are some bishops who support the concept of greater official recognition of women (women formally installed as lectors) and even the ordination of women as deacons.

Latinovic highlights an important point in this work: the problems evident in the cases of Bruskewitz and Milingo are the result of "the application of a universalist ecclesiology on the local church." But he does not review what causes the application of such an ecclesiology— an expanded decentralized media that allows nearly every corner of the world to have a look at other local churches. That women acolytes and lectors are permitted in some (but not all) local churches appears an uneven application of church practice, not an accommodation to local culture. Hence, expanded and decentralized media both cause and solve the same problems.

On the matter of Milingo (and other) illicit ordinations, I agree with Latinovic that ordination is tied to a local church, and that it is formally possible for Milingo to have no sacramental authority once he is detached as diocesan bishop from his local church, but Catholic practice is not coherent on this point. Further, if the Vatican was not concerned about his ability to ordain, why would it have both excommunicated and laicized him? Orthodox theology is clearer on this point, but I do not think it can be applied wholesale to the Catholic situation.

One point of difference I have with Latinovic is his discussion of women deacons, especially his assertion that women deacons of the early church in the East were never equivalent to men deacons. While the nascent church used women deacons to assist with baptisms of women, significant scholarship demonstrates their other roles—including liturgical—up to the twelfth century. Further, Latinovic asserts that Orthodoxy is not concerned with the question of ordaining women. This is perhaps true among the ranks of clergy and male theologians, but I can assure you there is (and has been for quite some time) significant discussion within Orthodoxy about a wider restoration of women to the diaconate.

Despite my book, and the fine interventions of Miriam Haar, Sandra Mazzolini, and Vladimir Latinovic, I think the questions raised by me and by them require deeper analysis if they are to be resolved. Quite simply, the topics of inclusion and exclusion of women in the Catholic Church are freight trains heading toward each other at tremendous speed.

Fine scholars, including and especially my kind colleagues here, are spending their time and talent to build an inclusive church that sees us all, each and every one, as made in the image and likeness of Christ, with all that that implies.

Exclusionists, I think, are faced with a tsunami of recognition of their—of our—belief that the word "church" means "neither slave nor freeman, neither male nor female, for we are all one in Christ Jesus" (Gal 3:28).

And I think that is a very, very good thing.

Church and Homosexuality:
Beyond Exclusion

Stefanie Knauss

Mark Jordan describes the situation of the church(es) regarding homosexuality with the image of the barred chapel, with homophobic Christians inside, and homosexual Christians outside, banging on the door to be let in.[1] Exclusion is, in the minds of many, the only way to think of this highly explosive issue that has the potential to pull apart ecclesial communities like few others. However, as Jordan himself and numerous studies on the issue suggest, the image of the barred chapel and the binary paradigm of exclusion vs. inclusion, them vs. us, inside vs. outside, might neither be the most true to reality, nor the most adequate and constructive way to think about homosexuality and ecclesial community. Instead there seems to be a very large grey area between being "inside" and "outside" the church as a homosexual Christian, and both homosexual believers and church communities appear to use various strategies to bridge the gap that is opened by official church pronouncements on the matter.[2] The experience of conflict between a person's religious and sexual identity can be dealt with in different ways in a process that might well last over a long time or one's whole life: leaving, remaining, hiding, looking for niches, groups where one feels welcome, compartmentalizing. While being a painful and potentially damaging experience,[3] sustaining conflict can also be the beginning of a process of integration, of coming to terms with one's being homosexual and Catholic in spite of negative magisterial feedback. Thus, while for many believers and nonbelievers alike, being homosexual and being Christian indeed appear mutually exclusive, many others have found ways to integrate these aspects of their identity.[4]

In this essay I suggest that integration, understood as a process both on the individual level of identity formation and on the social level of community formation, might be a more helpful paradigm for further reflection on the issue of homosexuality and/in the church. To prepare the ground, I will discuss first the more extreme paradigms of exclusion and inclusion, and then describe in more detail the paradigm of integration using psychological, sociological, and historiographical studies, before concluding with some suggestions for an agenda of ecclesiological reflections on the topic.

A methodological note is in order at this point: the empirical studies on homosexuals and faith all suffer from methodological limits due to the difficulties of having a random sample when researching homosexuality[5] and thus are not strictly generalizable. Their results are valid only for their sample of informants. Although comparisons between studies do suggest that there are certainly more general tendencies at work, for the moment any hypotheses remain unproven. Rather than relating to these studies as a set of facts, in the following I let myself be inspired by the experiences they report and analyze through my reflections on the current situation and through my imagination of a possible future for homosexuals to be a part of the ecclesial community.

Exclusion

The most extreme negative option is exclusion: in this view, homosexuality and church membership are simply incompatible. According to the magisterial teaching of the Catholic Church, homosexuality is objectively disordered, an anomaly, a sign of psychological immaturity, and can in no way be accepted as a form of living human relationality.[6] As a sin against the created order, a threat for human society, and an activity through which the individual causes damage to her/himself, homosexuality has to be condemned. The intransigent language[7] used by Vatican documents makes it clear that homosexuals are not welcome in the church: the same document might admonish Catholics to treat homosexuals with respect and sympathy only to call them severely damaged and a threat to society a few paragraphs later.[8] The comparison of homosexuals to persons with a contagious disease or the mentally ill is used to justify the limitation of their rights and their exclusion from the community in order not to put into danger the rest of the group.[9] Exclusion becomes, thus, a legitimate strategy of self-defense by the church. In the extreme case, this can mean that actively homosexual persons are denied the sacraments and that pastoral activities for homosexuals that do not explicitly agree with church teaching or do not aim at convincing homosexuals of their sinfulness are ousted from church property and denied support by dioceses or are forbidden to be discussed.[10] The apparently humane motto "Hate the sin, love the sinner" often appears to be used only to hide punitive actions of exclusion and discrimination[11] and to defend against accusations of the church for being exclusive: when homosexuals finally leave the church community, this is presented as self-exclusion on their part, a willful rejection of mother church,[12] who is prepared to include all repentant sinners. If a homosexual does not act on his/her orientation and receives frequently the sacrament of confession, he or she is, of course, welcome in the church. If they do not repent, however, and if they insist on equal rights to live their homosexuality, they cannot be a part of the community. The Letter on Pastoral Care of Homosexuals even implies that homosexuals or anyone else should not be surprised if they fall victim to discrimination and even violence if they insist on (impossible) equal rights.[13] This institutionally legitimated exclusion provides the basis for the handling of these issues on the level of parishes or dioceses, which depends very much on the line the responsible bishop or priest chooses to take.

A particular case is that of candidates to the priesthood. The Vatican's Congregation for Catholic Education dedicates an entire instruction only to this topic, in which it is made clear, yet again, that homosexuality is a sign of particular affective and psychological immaturities that render a candidate incapable for priesthood. Any candidate who admits to such tendencies, supports a homosexual culture, or practices homosexuality has to be excluded from the seminary; such a person could be ordained only if it has become clear that this was only a temporary "problem," which was overcome definitely three years before the ordination as a deacon.[14]

The exclusion of homosexual persons from the church through language, denial of pastoral care, inhospitality, and hostility is mirrored in the self-exclusion of homosexuals who disagree with doctrine on homosexuality and institutional authority structures, who cannot bear being discriminated against any more, or who do not want to hide any longer and thus resolve the conflict between being homosexual and being Catholic by leaving the church community. In many cases, this does not imply giving up on their faith or their spirituality as well: "The real difficulty is not with God but with the Church," says a Catholic gay man in Gross and Yip's study, "Living Spirituality and Sexuality."[15] Their study suggests that the dichotomy between "in" and "out" is particularly strong in the Catholic Church where church authority is attributed a higher value than in Protestant churches: the mechanism at work seems to be that if one disagrees with the magisterium on the issue of homosexuality, the only choice is to leave the church; there is no margin for compromise.[16]

Exclusion can also happen on a further level: the exclusion of Catholic homosexuals and faith groups from the LGBT movement. As Mark Jordan points out, these faith-based groups are, more or less, intentionally written out of the history of the homosexual movement, and their issues (such as same-sex blessings or requests of pastoral care) are perceived as irrelevant for the wider homosexual community; continued participation in a church characterized by its homophobic and discriminatory statements is seen as collaboration in homophobia. The result is that homosexual Christians are not able to live their identity as homosexuals and believers either in the church or in the homosexual community.[17]

Lesbians are one particular group that is excluded in multiple ways. They are excluded from the church and its offices because they are women, and because they are disordered and sinners; they are excluded from historiography because of the invisibility of female homosexuality (and its relative unimportance for moral and legal matters); they are invisible in the LGBT movement, which often says "gay" and pretends to mean "homosexual," but in reality does refer to male homosexuality; and they are also excluded from much of innovative theological writing about homosexuality, which concentrates on the more visible (and more problematic, for a patriarchal society?) male homosexuality, so that lesbians are deprived of the chance to find empowerment in a new theology that affirms the female lesbian body and its sexuality.[18] This is also unfortunate because empirical study suggests a significant gender difference in how the conflict between homosexual and religious identities is experienced and dealt with (less experience of conflict and a higher degree of integration in lesbians)—an aspect that might be fruitful to pursue for further reflections.[19]

A "soft version" of the exit strategy for those homosexuals who still want to be involved in the life of the church but do not want to face exclusion for being homosexual seems to be separation from the mainstream church and the formation of separate prayer, study, or Bible-reading groups. They are often characterized by a certain tension: while their members might still self-identify as Catholic, they do not share certain teachings or practices, do not celebrate the sacraments, or have to rely on priests who defy their authorities when they do so. They generally move outside the official Catholic sphere, being separated but still trying to stay in contact in an attempt to create inclusive communities that might serve as an example to the wider church, while being, at least for now, outside of, excluded, and separated from this church.[20] Their being in-between distinguishes these groups from gay-positive or inclusive churches that self-define as independent churches providing all the services and functions of a church for their members.[21]

Inclusion

We might think of inclusion as the opposite of exclusion: being, as a homosexual, a part of the community of the church. From an historical perspective, to be included in the ecclesial community as a homosexual is not quite as impossible as it might seem today. As John Boswell has shown convincingly, over long centuries, up until about the thirteenth century, homosexuals were considered as "distinguishable insiders" or "inferior insiders" within the church community: they were "different" and not necessarily equal, but they were a part of the church.[22] Various theological and social factors might be the reason for this; with sexuality being devalued in comparison to the highly esteemed life of celibacy, and with adultery (no matter with whom) being the central preoccupation, a homosexual was "just" a sinner like any other fornicator with just the same possibility to be redeemed. After all, do not all human beings live in a state of sin to various degrees and for various reasons and thus have to trust in Christ for their salvation?[23]

It seems likely that religious orders in medieval Europe were a valid and accepted alternative for persons who did not identify with heterosexual marriage and family life, and it can be presumed that a large number of members of religious orders were homosexuals. Homosexual love poetry, more or less open homosexual relationships, possibly even the liturgical celebration of same-sex unions[24] were thus not unknown to the church and contemporary culture, and there was not much of a preoccupation about it. Apparently, a so far unexplained change in social attitudes in the fourteenth century forced the church to take a stricter stance so that homosexuality became the most horrible of sins.[25]

In the premodern and modern era, the metaphors changed, and now homosexuality is understood as a disease, an unchangeable condition, innate, and potentially contagious—a change that is also reflected in contemporary magisterial documents, as seen above. The historical perspective thus complicates the image of the "barred chapel"; for a considerable span of time, homosexuals were "in" with a certain margin of living their homosexuality openly and expressing it in their literature and theology. Boswell writes, "It is poignantly ironic that a group as marginalized and despised as gay people should have exerted such an influence on Christian society within the ranks of its spiritual elite."[26] This is probably still true today as anecdotal evidence suggests that the number of homosexuals among the clergy and in religious orders is higher than the social average.[27] Jordan also draws attention to the fact that it is with regard to the gay members of the clergy whose inclusion in the church (and often in positions where they themselves can or have to decide about who is to be included and who is not), is an open, unspoken secret, that it becomes most clear that theological and magisterial discourses on homosexuality have always been more about church power and authority, and not about sexual morality. At play is, indeed, the power over identities and lives, over inclusion and exclusion, and over being and not being.[28]

As mentioned before, the magisterium argues that the desire of the church is, in fact, to include persons with homosexual orientation under the condition that they affirm church teachings on the issue and that they give up any homosexual activities or support of such actions.[29] Inclusion thus comes at a cost, and this makes it a very ambiguous paradigm for thinking about homosexuality and church: it means inclusion in a community that has its preset rules and doctrines condemning homosexuality and holding up the heterosexual ideal, which have to be accepted, while an important part of one's identity has to be denied.[30] Is inclusion thus really what a homosexual believer might hope for when it means that the church's opinion, its language, its moral theology and its theology in general, its values, its forms of celebrating faith and community life in the liturgy are to remain unchanged, and this means, at the present state of affairs, exclusive of homosexual persons?

Compartmentalization might thus be considered the "soft version" of inclusion, a way to bolster the demands on one's identity when seeking inclusion. Through this strategy, conflict between one's faith and sexuality is avoided by keeping them in different compartments without overlap and with different systems of values, norms, and behaviors. Two Catholic informants of Gross and Yip's study confirmed this saying, "I hide the fact that I am gay," and "I keep my sexuality separated from my church involvement. It's not worth it, I think."[31] This strategy does not require the full acceptance of church teaching on sexuality and thus the denial of one's sexual orientation because one is not perceived to be relevant for the other; however, this means also that one does not (and cannot) attribute religious value to one's sexuality and sexual relationships and vice versa because these are kept in separate realms.[32]

Martine Gross points out that individuals do not only compartmentalize their identity but also the church itself by drawing a clear line between the hierarchy (or the institution and its pronouncements) and their local parish, between the magisterium and the people of God.[33] While they reject the official institutional stance against homosexuality, many homosexuals still report feeling included in the Catholic community as they experience it locally and in their everyday lives, in positive encounters with clergy and other believers, in participation in church activities and liturgies, in being welcomed, in finding the occasion to give religious meanings to their life choices. As one informant puts it, "Religious community . . . is different from religious institution."[34] This attitude is possible because of a shift in the attribution of authority: now it is less an institution (like the magisterium) that is trusted with authoritative decisions about one's own life; instead, people attribute more value to personal experience and establish their own view on the matter, drawing on innovative Bible interpretations, new images of God, or the reevaluation of central evangelic values such as love, tolerance, and faith.[35]

Inclusion remains thus an ambiguous concept. It can mean having to denounce one's identity in order to be a part of the community; it can mean having to remain closeted and subject to power games; it can mean having to adapt to forms of worship and church life that do not acknowledge one's existence; it can mean having to separate sexuality from religion and to distinguish between hierarchy and community within the one church. However, it can also mean being a full and equal member of a particular parish and experiencing in this context the community of the church in one's life.

Integration

Both inclusion and exclusion thus seem to be of little use to reflect the reality of Christian homosexuals or as constructive paradigms for further ecclesiological reflection. Instead, a new paradigm has come up in studies on how homosexual believers live their faith and their sexuality: integration. Rather than being an externally attributed psychological category, this term or semantically related forms are used by homosexual informants themselves to describe the processes through which they live.[36]

In place of the dichotomy of being in or out, of complete disagreement or loyalty, compartmentalization or separation, this concept suggests the reconciliation of these two parts of one's identity (among the many others as well) as a process that continues over time[37] and that is influenced and shaped by a number of factors.[38] The most important factors are trust in one's personal experiences, an emphasis on God's love, and the fact that the magisterium's authority over doctrine is no longer uncontested.[39] Integration also seems to be related to a higher level of involvement in church activities and to openness about one's sexuality.[40] While being an individual process of identity formation, integration is also dependent on interaction with other people who can support the development.[41] This is certainly an incomplete list of the factors involved in the process of identity integration; as Rodriguez and Ouellette point out, the concept of integration as a process, rather than as a "product" or "construct," requires still much more research regarding the triggering of this process and its development as well as detailed research of the factors that might impact it and how they interrelate.[42]

The concept of integration can also usefully be transferred from the context of individual identity to the level of group dynamics. On this level, integration does not simply mean an addition, an insertion of some individuals that are different into a majority that sets the rules (this would be what I called "inclusion" earlier), but rather it means that both sides will change in the process to result in something new. Thus, the church community will not be able to continue in the same vein; it simply will not be the same community as before, since new experiences have been added.

Many theologians of homosexuality have pointed out that the discussion of homosexuality does raise other issues that are far removed from and maybe even more important than genital activities and touch the church at its core:[43] such issues include power structures and authority, the sources and methods of moral theology and of theology in general, the weight of tradition, the relation between the hierarchy and the people of God, questions of how we live our faith in a diverse community and how the structures of the church can sustain this community, of how we understand the sacramental practice of the church (in particular with regard to the sacraments of marriage and ordination, but not only), how we conceive of the relevance of history and tradition for ecclesiology, in how far we see the church as an historical and changing reality, and so on. Thinking of homosexuality and church in terms of a process of integration means also that this is a development that will require time and that can take on different forms at different points, a process that will most likely continue for as long as there is a church consisting of changing, diverse human beings.

Some Suggestions for
Further Ecclesiological Reflection

Looking beyond magisterial pronouncements and taking inspiration from psychological and sociological studies, historical research, and personal testimonials have opened the perspective to move beyond the paralyzing dichotomy of "in" or "out" with the concept of integration, which is not an alternative to exclusion or inclusion but rather transcends both in a new way of thinking about church and homosexuality as both being in a process of change and coming together in this development as something new. Without pretending to know the answers, I would like to conclude with suggesting some issues for an agenda of ecclesiological reflection that is inspired by this paradigm, taking seriously the contemporary situation and trying to imagine the future in a constructive way.

First of all, the studies show the importance of listening to the experience of the people concerned: we might presume that the image of the "barred chapel" is valid because it seems quite natural given the position of the church in relation to homosexuality, but testimonials show that this is not true, either for the homosexuals who feel welcome and can live their faith in various forms in church communities or for many local parishes who do not bar their chapel doors in front of their homosexual brothers and sisters. In listening to how these people tell their stories, where they experience conflict, how they deal with it, and where they find support, new images of the church as a diverse but integrated community can emerge that can serve as guidance for ecclesiological reflections.

The fact that many homosexuals compartmentalize the church itself and perceive a considerable gap between the hierarchy and the people of God, that is, between the church as known through the pronouncements of the magisterium and in its hierarchical power structures, and the church as experienced as a community of people sharing their faith in ritual and community life, and the fact that for many the "real" church seems to be this concrete local community, suggests that the concept of the people of God should be brought back to the center of ecclesiological reflections from where it seems to have disappeared at some point after the Second Vatican Council.

This is connected to another issue that requires serious reflection: the relationship between the authority of the church and of tradition, and the authority attributed to one's own experience and reflection. The shift in importance from the first to the second might well be perceived as a threat and lead to negative reactions that try to retain the church's (the institution's) power; but it should also be taken seriously and valued positively as a sign of people's trust in the strength of their religious experience and of the reflective maturity of their faith.

Finally, the many realities in which homosexuals live their faith show that there are different forms of "church" understood as the community of the faithful, each with its own functions, strengths, and weaknesses. Thus, a homosexual person might go to mass in his or her local parish because the celebration of the sacrament and the familiar rite are important to feel as a member of the church, but he or she might then move on to a Bible study group or prayer group that might represent a very different position regarding matters of sexual ethics. In this situation, it appears important to reflect upon the many faces of the church, upon how they are characterized, and how they can sustain each other. In this context, the idea of individual identity as a dynamic and multifaceted process that continues throughout one's life, which is presupposed by the paradigm of integration, can also be of help to understand the identity of the church in the contemporary situation in a new way, so that change will no longer be perceived as a threat but as a part of the church's reality in history.

The paradigm of integration as a process can be helpful in thinking through these issues (and likely many more) with regard to homosexuality and the church on the various levels of individual identity and group formation, in order to imagine new realities of the church as the people of God.

Notes

[1] Cf. Mark D. Jordan, *Blessing Same-Sex Unions: The Perils of Queer Romance and the Confusions of Christian Marriage* (Chicago: University of Chicago Press, 2005), 5.

[2] Although I will mostly refer to the Catholic Church and theology in this paper, this is by no means the only Christian or religious community that condemns homosexual activity as unnatural and perverse, excluding homosexuals from its community. Cf. Eric M. Rodriguez, "At the Intersection of Church and Gay: A Review of the Psychological Research on Gay and Lesbian Christians," *Journal of Homosexuality* 57 (2010): 5–38, 26. See also Martine Gross and Andrew K. T. Yip, "Living Spirituality and Sexuality: A Comparison of Lesbian, Gay and Bisexual Christians in France and Britain," *Social Compass* 57, 1 (2010): 40–59, 55.

[3] In many cases the dissonance between these two aspects of one's identity can drive a person close to suicide or actually be the cause of suicide; cf. the testimonial cited by Martine Gross, "To Be Christian and Homosexual: From Shame to Identity-Based Claims," *Nova Religio: The Journal for Alternative and Emerging Religions* 11, no. 4 (2008): 77–101, 95.

[4] Mark Jordan actually claims that for Christian homosexuals, the Christian and the homosexual dimension of identity might be interdependent for their formation. Cf. Mark D. Jordan, *The Silence of Sodom: Homosexuality in Modern Catholicism* (Chicago: University of Chicago Press, 2000), 229–30. The question of how to classify a homosexual and a believer is not undisputed; the studies I use for my reflections work with self-definitions; religiosity is measured with regard to various aspects such as church attendance, community activity, activities like prayer or Bible reading.

[5] Cf. Eric M. Rodirguez and Suzanne C. Ouellette, "Gay and Lesbian Christians: Homosexual and Religious Identity Integration in the Members and Participants of a Gay-Positive Church," *Journal for the Scientific Study of Religion* 39 (2000): 333–47, 338.

[6] Cf. Congregation for the Doctrine of the Faith, *Persona Humana: Declaration Regarding Certain Questions of Sexual Ethics* (1975), no. 8.

[7] As Mark Jordan's analysis shows, the rhetorical means applied in Vatican documents in fact render impossible any reasonable and constructive discussion of these topics; linguistically, homosexuals are excluded through either persistent silence about the sin that cannot be named, the use of negatively marked ter-

minology or through hysterical chatter that makes communication impossible, because it tends to provoke equally hysterical responses. Cf. Jordan, *The Silence of Sodom*, 111, 114.

[8] Cf. Congregation for the Doctrine of the Faith, *Considerations Regarding Proposals to Give Legal Recognition to Unions between Homosexual Persons* (2003), nos. 4 and 9.

[9] Cf. Congregation for the Doctrine of the Faith, *Some Considerations Concerning Response to Legistlative Proposals on the Non-Discrimination of Homosexual Persons* (1992), no. 12.

[10] Cf. Congregation for the Doctrine of Faith, *Letter to All Catholic Bishops on the Pastoral Care of Homosexual Persons* (1986), no. 15. Cf. the cases of Sr. Jeannine Gramick and Robert Nugent.

[11] Cf. Janet R. Jakobsen and Ann Pellegrini, *Love the Sin: Sexual Regulation and the Limits of Religious Tolerance* (Boston: Beacon Press, 2004), 1.

[12] Cf. Jordan, *The Silence of Sodom*, 46.

[13] Congregation for the Doctrine of Faith, *Pastoral Care of Homosexual Persons*, no. 10.

[14] Cf. Congregation for Catholic Education, *Instruction Concerning the Criteria for the Discernment of Vocations with Regard to Persons with Homosexual Tendencies in View of Their Admission to Seminary and to Holy Orders* (2005), no. 2.

[15] Gross and Yip, "Living Spirituality and Sexuality," 49. Later in their study the authors write, "Myriad reasons were reported for non-participation in the local church community. This ranged from general disillusionment with institutional authority structures to more specific disappointment with the lack of progress in the area of affirming LGB people within the community. Interestingly, these non-participants still maintained the Christian identity, not only as a cultural marker but also as a religious identity that could be nurtured despite their disassociation from the Church. In other words, leaving the institutional Church does not equate to losing one's spirituality" (51). It might even be necessary to leave the church to be able to continue to believe, as one informant says.

[16] Cf. Gross and Yip, "Living Spirituality and Sexuality," 47; see also 54: "We found that the French sample, who were more compliant with Church teachings, experienced a greater degree of psychological dissociation from the institutional religion, as well as social dissociation in the form of non-participation in church communities." For Gross's study of the French situation, cf. Gross, "To Be Christian and Homosexual," 82.

[17] Cf. Jordan, *Blessing Same-Sex Unions*, 15–18. See also Gross and Yip, "Living Spirituality and Sexuality," 51. An informant in David Shallenberger's study says, "if I talk to people within the church, they're easy and quick to bash the gay community. If I talk to my gay friends, they feel like it's very easy to bash the church community" (David Shallenberger, "Reclaiming the Spirit: The Journeys of Gay Men and Lesbian Women Toward Integration," *Qualitative Sociology* 19, no. 2 [1996]: 195–15, 209).

[18] Cf. Jordan, *The Silence of Sodom*, 10; see also Jane M. Grovijahn, "Reclaiming the Power of Incarnation: When God's Body Is Catholic & Queer (with a Cunt!)," in *Queer and Catholic*, ed. Amie M. Evans and Trebor Healey (New York: Routledge, 2008), 249–61. Cf., for a rare study concentrating on lesbian women, Melissa Wilcox, *Queer Women and Religious Individualism* (Bloomington: Indiana University Press, 2009).

[19] Cf. Rodirguez and Ouellette, "Gay and Lesbian Christians," 344–45.

[20] Examples of such groups are maybe more frequently found in countries with a strong denominational identity, such as France or Italy (predominantly Catholic), because in these contexts, leaving the church entirely might be more difficult to imagine. This means also that inclusive gay-positive churches can find it more difficult to strike root (cf. Gross, "To Be Christian and Homosexual," 94–97, for the French context). The marginality of these groups can be perceived as the core of a new kind of ecclesiology that draws strength and meaning exactly from its experience of exile and dislocation. Cf. Dan Spencer, "Church at the Margins," in *Sexuality and the Sacred: Sources for Theological Reflection*, ed. James B. Nelson and Sandra P. Longfellow (Louisville, KY: Westminster John Knox Press, 1994), 397–401.

[21] Cf. Rodriguez and Oullette, "Gay and Lesbian Christians," for a study of the gay-positive Metropolitan Community Church of New York and its (positive) impact on identity integration.

[22] Cf. John Boswell, "Homosexuality and Religious Life: A Historical Approach," in *Sexuality and the Sacred: Sources for Theological Reflection*, ed. James B. Nelson and Sandra P. Longfellow (Louisville, KY: Westminster John Knox Press, 1994), 361–73, 361.

[23] Boswell, "Homosexuality and Religious Life," 362.

[24] Cf. John Boswell, *Same-Sex Unions in Premodern Europe* (New York: Vintage Books, 1995).

[25] Ibid., 262.

[26] Ibid., 372.

[27] Cf. Jordan, *The Silence of Sodom*, 159. A study of gay clergy with a statistically relevant sample is still outstanding.

[28] Cf. Jordan, *The Silence of Sodom*, 82; this is not a pun: many homosexual Catholics, clergy and not, have been driven close to or into suicide because of the perceived conflict between their desires and the position of the church they love (cf. for one story among many: Marco Politi, *La confessione: Un prete gay racconta la sua storia* [Rome: Editori Riuniti, 2000]).

[29] Cf. Congregation for the Doctrine of Faith, *Pastoral Care of Homosexual Persons*, no. 3.

[30] Indeed, the major aim of pastoral care of homosexuals is to make sure that homosexuals agree on church teaching on homosexuality; cf. Congregation for the Doctrine of Faith, *Pastoral Care of Homosexual Persons*, no. 8.

[31] Gross and Yip, "Living Spirituality and Sexuality," 53.

[32] Whether they had experienced conflict or not, for some people it also seems to be simply understood that religion and sex cannot be part of the same realm; an informant in Gross's study states, "I think my faith has no link whatsoever with my sexuality. . . . Faith came one day and has never left; what a funny idea to want to pair it with my sexuality!" (Gross, "To Be Christian and Homosexual," 86).

[33] Cf. Gross, "To Be Christian and Homosexual," 93.

[34] Gross and Yip, "Living Spirituality and Sexuality," 52. What informants told Gross and Yip in their study "is incontrovertible evidence that there could be a discrepancy between the institutional stance and treatment at grassroots level; or to put it differently, between doctrinal prescriptions and pastoral practice" (54).

[35] Cf. Gross, "To Be Christian and Homoscxual," 89.

[36] Rodriguez and Ouellette mention the following: "entangled, melded, reconciled, combined, congruence, fusion, together, and wedded" ("Gay and Lesbian Christians," 340).

[37] Cf. Rodriguez, "At the Intersection of Church and Gay," 17.

[38] This concept presupposes an idea of identity as dynamic and multi-facetted, sometimes even self-contradictory, a life-long process of identity formation rather than a fixed and stable state; cf. Kathryn Woodward, "Concepts of Identity and Difference," in *Identity and Difference*, ed. Kathryn Woodward (London: Sage, 1997), 7–50.

[39] Many informants in Gross and Yip's study state that they ignore certain church teachings or develop their own ideas on the matter: "God loves us as we are with an infinite love. . . . This is how I managed to reconcile homosexuality and Christian [Protestant] faith. I distanced myself from the official discourse of traditional churches that condemns homosexuality" (Gross and Yip, "Living Spirituality and Sexuality," 45, cf. also 55). Cf. Rodriguez, "At the Intersection of Church and Gay," 16.

[40] Cf. Rodriguez and Ouellette, "Gay and Lesbian Christians,"344, and Gross, "To Be Christian and Homosexual," 85.

[41] Cf. Shallenberger, "Reclaiming the Spirit," 208–9; Gross mentions that while the importance of individual religious experience has increased, it is still important for believers to come together in a community that "strengthens and legitimizes—through the sharing of ritual practices with others like oneself—this new integration of two formerly contradictory identities." (Gross, "To Be Christian and Homosexual," 97).

[42] Cf. Rodriguez and Ouellette, "Gay and Lesbian Christians," 345. Also a comparison between different denominations or religions regarding the correlation between community activity and integration might be interesting.

[43] Cf. Jordan, *The Silence of Sodom*, 80.

PART V

EXCLUSION AND THE CHURCH

Inclusion and Exclusion in the Ecclesiology of the New Catholic Movements

Massimo Faggioli

Especially during and after the pontificate of John Paul II, it is beyond dispute that the "new Catholic movements" have a central place in the contemporary Catholic Church. By new Catholic movements I mean, of course, such institutions as Communion and Liberation, the Community of St. Egidio, Focolare, Neocathecumenal Way, Cursillos de Cristiandad, the Regnum Christi movement of the Legionaries of Christ, and others. The deeper history of the "movements" in twentieth-century Catholicism, however, begins with the "reform movements" (biblical movements, liturgical movement, patristic renewal, ecumenical movement) that renewed Catholic theology and made possible the crucial changes of Vatican II.[1] These movements developed much of what would become the theology of Vatican II, but they were eventually absorbed by Vatican II: most of their protagonism and vitality in pre-Vatican II Catholicism was transformed (or, according to some, got lost) during the implementation of the reforms of the council.[2]

It is therefore difficult to map out the genes of the pre-Vatican II "theological movements" and find those genes in the "new Catholic movements." In the "new Catholic movements," whose date of birth predates Vatican II (such as Opus Dei and the Legionaries of Christ, both a product of the 1920s–1930s), it is clear that they reject the new impulses coming from the Council, for example, collegiality in the church and church reform, ecumenism, and interreligious dialogue.

For other movements, the issue of their conciliar identity is more complex and spread along a very wide spectrum of attitudes (enough here to say that Communion and Liberation and the Community of St. Egidio are on the two opposite extremes of this spectrum). For other movements still (such as the Focolare) the acceptance of the issues *"ad extra"* of Vatican II (ecumenism and interreligious dialogue) is not accompanied by the acceptance of the issues of participation and collegiality in the church. There is thus a clear difference between the pre-Vatican II theological movements and the contemporary new Catholic movements: worldview, internal structure, ways to become a member and to leave the movement, and the relationship between the movement and the ecclesiastical hierarchy.[3]

Sociologically the main difference is in the organizational principles of the two different movements: at the beginning of the twentieth century, the old "reform movements" were made up of the theological elites of Catholicism working mostly underground and trying to open the field to new ideas and involve the whole church and the laity in embracing these new theological developments in spite of or against the lack of official ecclesiastical approval for these ideas. With the "new Catholic movements," we now have *a new kind of movement* whose primary goals are not to "move" new ideas in the church but rather to rally particular sections of the church (ordained and lay people together) around a charismatic founder and his/her message, and/or around a particular issue (social, cultural, or otherwise) that defines the activity of the members, with the number of members being crucial for the movement's survival in the market of contemporary Catholicism.

This need for strong visibility (particularly evident in events like the 1997 World Youth Day in Paris for the movement "L'Emmanuel") is a result of the fact that the new Catholic movements somehow were given the task to replace, in the structure of the church, the role played by Catholic Action in the first half of the twentieth century. It is important to remember that until the 1980s, the very survival of the Catholic movements within Catholicism was an important issue, nobody being sure about the "juridical grounds" on which the Catholic movements could survive at the end of the benevolence of one pope after his death (especially in the passage between Paul VI and John Paul II and between John Paul II and Benedict XVI).

Once the monopoly of Catholic Action on laity in the church was over, the market was divided between different brands competing for their share of Catholic laity—but now a very different kind of Catholic laity. If the pre-Vatican II laity belonging to Catholic Action had an immediate commitment to the parish priest and the bishop, and only an indirect one to the pope in Rome, with the new Catholic movements, the relationship between these different points of reference has changed direction: the pope has become the first and most important direct channel of identification with the church.

In this sense, it is accurate to define the new Catholic movements as "postconciliar movements" and not as "conciliar movements" given the gap between the ecclesiology of the laity of Vatican II and the later developments—more faithful to a certain "spirit of Vatican II" than to its "letter."[4]

In distinction from the local churches and the unaffiliated Catholics in the Western hemisphere, it is certainly true that the new Catholic movements did not go through the uncertain and trying times of the post-Vatican II period—at least publicly.[5] The vertically structured and charismatic-leader-driven structure preserved the new Catholic movements from the culture of "collegiality" in the church—but with a price. The price was, in some cases, the refusal of the impulse of Vatican II for a new synthesis between tradition and modernity, substituting now the theological culture of some of these movements as built *per oppositionem* to modernity—theological and otherwise. For each and every one of the new Catholic movements it is clear, on the other hand, that the defining dimension is the refusal to update ecclesial culture according to the ecclesiology of Vatican II.

Weltanschauung

In terms of worldviews, it can be said that the new Catholic movements are more a product of 1968 than of Vatican II.[6] That is to say, their worldviews reflect a variety of cultural and political elements that are not only theological.

A first element, quite new if compared with the culture of the origins of the Catholic movement in the early twentieth century, is the *centrality of the founder and/or leader of the movement*. The worldview of the founder is the worldview of the members of the movement, and the attitude of the movement toward inclusion/exclusion is driven by the word of the founder or his/her successor, usually elected in order to perpetuate the fidelity of the movement to the charism of the founder.

A second element, relevant for the issue of inclusion and exclusion, is the drive to rebuild Catholicism *around the sociological idea of "community"* more than on the theological concept of "communion."[7] This element is sustained, in many cases, by a negative worldview in which the rejection of the Rahnerian term "world Church"[8] couples with an idea of the world as inherently negative and threatening to the Christian identity. It is clear that the inclusiveness of the "political theologies" of the early postconciliar period are no longer part of the theological identities of the new Catholic movements, given that their self-definitions no longer attach to any political reading of the historical-social reality of the world.[9]

A third element relevant for the issue of inclusion and exclusion, and part of the *Weltanschauung* of the most important new Catholic movements "imported" from Spain (Opus Dei, Cursillos de Cristianidad, Neo-Catechumenal Way), is a "spirituality of the reconquista" that drives these movements' indifference or hostility towards ecumenism, their marked clericalist identity, and their aggressive relationship with the local churches in which they operate.[10]

A fourth element of their theological culture, which can be seen as a perversion of Vatican's II's theological *ressourcement*, is the conspicuous nostalgia for a premodern world or for a modernity tamed by ecclesiastical ideology, a sort of *regressus ad uterum*[11] that longs for a pure origin in the pre-Vatican II period or in the pre-French Revolution period, or in the council of Trent—more rarely in the patristic era or in early Christianity for theologically obvious reasons.[12] The material (if not formal) rejection of the liturgical reform by some of the new Catholic movements is nothing but a visible way to reject the ecclesiology of Vatican II, especially its *ressourcement* and *rapprochement*.[13]

These cultural-theological options reveal a basic "apologetics of enmity" that receives its theological justification from a fundamentally negative worldview.[14] Interesting is that the negative prejudice against the modern world affects also the new Catholic movements' perception of the universal dimension of contemporary Catholicism that they see as theologically sustainable only if closely identified with the Roman identity and that therefore they judge at grave risk when associated with "inculturation."

Membership and Relationship
with the Ecclesiastical Institution

The presence of the new Catholic movements in the church has to be understood also in light of their institutional behavior and of the response of the church institution (in relation to which the movements should be "dialectical," at least from a semantic point of view). Their activism has provided contemporary Catholicism with an element of further centralization and "fragmentation" of the church at a global level creating a kind of new version of the old motto "*duo genera christianorum*"—"in the Church there are two different kinds of Christians": once the parting criterion was the belonging (or not) to the clerical order, now it is about belonging (or not) to a Catholic movement.

This new consequence coming from the existence of the new Catholic movements has been encouraged by a kind of "spoils system" adopted by the institutional church when it comes to ecclesiastical appointments (especially appointments of bishops) and to the prominence awarded on the occasion of particular global church events. The existence of the new Catholic movements provided the Catholic Church with a new kind of disciplined and organized laity, not at all willing to enter the stage with a distinct voice as laity, but available to present themselves as the "elite troops" of the papacy. The new Catholic movements' visibility, fidelity, and readiness to mobilize for the defense of the institution have proved difficult to beat in recent decades, especially since the beginning of John Paul II's pontificate.

It is true that here we deal with visible and invisible movements, but the trend in the vast world of the new Catholic movements in the last two decades has been to give more emphasis to the visibility and to receiving an official endorsement by Rome and less to the development of a real dynamic as a "movement in the Church-institution." Such institutional dynamics of the life of the movements in the church has forced the movements to accept or to embrace the official doctrinal policies of the church or of the pontificate, thereby giving up the chance to develop a genuine theological identity. On the other side, weakened local churches often feel compelled to accept the offer (new members, seminarians, resources) coming from these thriving new Catholic movements.

In a way, the present danger of the development of the competition between movements in the church or between certain movements and bishops in a given area (like for the Neo-Catechumenal Way in Asia) is that the movements become a recruiting tool for the new ruling elite in the church—in some cases as a local church faction opposed to the authority of the bishops. In this respect, John Paul II's definition of the new Catholic movements as "schools of communion" must be read as an encouragement more than as an actual description of how they are perceived in the church.[15]

All of this has to be seen together with the recent tendency of the new Catholic movements to "clericalize" their structures and to build their own seminaries separately from diocesan seminaries.[16] After John Paul II's attempt to appeal to the movements to use diocesan seminaries for the formation of their candidates to the priestly ministry (apostolic exhortation *Pastores dabo vobis*, 1992),[17] the trend of the last few years has been to grant the movements the chance to build and run their own formation institutions.

The Impact of the Movements on the Issue of Inclusion and Exclusion

One of the reasons for the success of the new Catholic movements is the immediacy of the experience of Christian faith within that kind of Catholicism. Also at work, however, is a problematic connection between the praxis of this new kind of Catholic experience and the relationship of these groups with the Catholic Church at large, at the level of both the local and the universal church.

Inclusiveness in the Local Church

The new movements have made the Catholic Church more *plural* and less *pluralistic* at the same time. This can be seen in the local churches where the movements are more rooted and active (the example of the

United States is not as telling as some examples in secularized areas, like Western Europe, or in "mission countries" or former mission countries like Japan and Southeast Asia).

The epoch-making shift made possible by Vatican II from a hierarchical, institutional ecclesiology to one centered on *communio* implied a new pattern of relationship between pope, bishops, clergy and laity, and between Rome and the local churches. At the local level, the new ecclesiology meant not only the resurgence of synods, provincial councils, and plenary councils, the need of which had been ignored for four centuries, but also the creation of a series of new councils and boards at the diocesan and parish level. The goal of the creation of these new institutions for the governance of the church was to *include* more of the Christian people and give way to some "representation" of the laity in modern Catholicism (even if without features typical of liberal democracy such as elections).[18]

In the vision expressed at Vatican II, these institutions were supposed to redress the balance of power within the local church by stressing the ordinary powers of bishops alongside the pope's extraordinary powers in the government of dioceses and enabling the participation of laity in the life of local churches, not just through liturgy and social action, but also through taking part in the theological reception of Vatican II. In the vision of Vatican II, the faithful were invited to take part in the life of the local church as individuals and families building a community not only at the parish level but also at the diocesan level. Participation in this local level was encouraged for individual Catholics through liturgy, parish life, and evangelization.

This ongoing process has been influenced by some important and still little considered factors. On one side, the secularization and the new self-consciousness of the laity gave a considerable push to the weakening of the power of clergy and bishops. On the other side, the rise of the new movements was not only a reaction against secularization along the lines of John Paul II's slogan of "new evangelization" but also a reaction of the new laity as *parvenus* against the old elite within the Catholic Church— being the old elite formed on one side by the bishops (heirs of a European tradition in which being a bishop was a class symbol just like having land and real estate) and on the other side by the "old school" laity formed along the *théologie du laïcat* of the 1930–1950s.[19] It is time to notice that this pivotal shift in the life of Catholicism had a fairly negative impact on the ability of achieving "inclusion" at the local level. In the last three decades, the practical ecclesiology of the movements has initiated the end of the "bishop- and clergy-led local Church."

Even if one considers that the relative decline of bishops in the overall balance of church power has a positive side, this situation is not immune to deep consequences and not only for the sake of the ecclesiological tradition that recognizes in the episcopacy a necessary link to the *paradosis* of Christian faith.

The end—or crisis—of a "bishop- and clergy-led local church" has not been in the direction of a more participatory local church. Rather, the movements have replaced the inclusive model opened by Vatican II with a more leader-driven model of Christian community where inner diversity is paradoxically far less present and less welcome than in the past. For example, in Italy after the post-Vatican II initial wave of diocesan synods, the celebration of such events within the local churches has become very uncommon in the last twenty years. The need for debate between laity and clergy—so strongly felt in the 1960s and 1970s—has been replaced by the creation of strong, personal ties between ever weaker bishops and ever stronger leaders of the movements at the diocesan level. This partition of the local church is graphically represented in liturgies celebrated separately behind closed doors by different communities (especially the Neocatechumenate).

Within the movements, the need for free speech inside the public sphere of the church—strongly represented not only by the twenty-centuries long tradition of local councils and synods and by the very example of Vatican II but also by the late institutional and theological development of Catholic Action—is often dismissed by the movements as a concession to current social and political taste, and is seen as jeopardizing their new Catholic way of living within the social community.[20]

This negative and pugnacious *Weltanschauung* has peculiar effects on the shape of the new movements. Given the emphasis on the coherence of the group and on its success in perpetuating itself in the face of a world perceived as secularist and hostile, the spiritual needs of the less "employable" members of the community easily become marginal both within the movement and within the local church, with obvious consequences for the inclusiveness of contemporary Catholicism.

Offered this new model of obedient and active Catholicism, local bishops rarely grasp the movements' long-term challenge to the "catholic" (in the sense of plural and inclusive) setup of the local church. Driven by the need to fight back secularization at all costs, bishops and clergy tend to perceive the movements as "the real church," as the ultimate asset for the counterattack against the crisis of authority of Catholicism: a crisis that they see related to its inclusive character. In this sense, the new Catholic movements provide the example of a new kind of Catholicism that is clustered in separate and noncommunicating cells: a Catholicism whose diversity is now much more limited than the diversity that could show up from a more representative look at the intellectual and spiritual identities of Catholicism.

The creation of networks of Catholic welfare and the protection of the vested interests attached to this volunteerism give the movements active in this arena a political, economic, and moral power that few people dare to question, especially in regard to its relations with the role of individual Christians in the church and in society at large. The rest of the local church and the Catholics not active in the movements are left in a sort of a "dead zone" between this new, front-page Catholicism and the outer world. In a sense, the rise of the movements has re-created within the Catholic Church the medieval *duo genera christianorum* ("two types of Christian faithful"): a church where the distinction between the power holders, on one side, and the subjects, on the other side, is crystal clear. The movements' founders and their successors are held up as an example of the new *ecclesia docens* over against a once again patronized lay church supposed to be the *ecclesia discens*.

At the local and diocesan level, the important distinction is no longer between clerics and lay people but between "movement-belonging Catholics" (where the individualism of contemporary Western culture is accommodated through the creation of a variety of different movements for different tastes) and "ordinary, loose Catholics" (whose cultural, social, and moral subjectivity is considered as the definitive victory of secularization over the old, comforting, yet gone "shepherd-leading-sheep Catholicism").[21]

The coexistence of the ecclesiological role of the local church and the "globalized character" of the new Catholic movements is still a building site, in part overlapping the theological debate of the early 2000s on the relationship between local church and universal church. But it is clear that if, at the beginning, the rise of the new Catholic movements represented a direct accusation against the effectiveness of the pastoral life in the local churches, now their role in some local churches puts at risk the very life of a local church existing independently from the activity of a new Catholic movement. In some areas of the world there is an evident competition between "territorial Catholic Church" and "the Church of the movements": in this fight, the first casualty is inclusiveness and diversity in the church.

Strange as it may seem, inclusiveness and diversity are much better protected in a church that works under the leadership of a bishop willing to enact the procedures and governing bodies created by Vatican II—much better than in a church led by movements whose procedures and governing bodies are part of the *arcana imperii* (secrets of the rulers).[22]

The Impact at the Level of the Universal Church

At the universal level the effects of the new movements on inclusion within the Catholic Church are no less critical. One of the roots of the success of the movements is their embrace of the "ecclesiology of the universal church" (pushed by Cardinal Ratzinger from the mid-1980s) and their rejection of the "ecclesiology of the local church." Besides all the elements that distinguish one movement from another, one key point constitutes the basic ecclesiology of most of them: the ideological acknowledgement of the pope as their only and real pastor, the *episcopus episcoporum* or *episcopus universalis*.

This "globalized ecclesiology," which acts as an undeclared disowning of Vatican II collegiality and goes far beyond Vatican I-style infallibility, is at the core of the new movements' identity. It has heavy implications for the issue of inclusion in the church. The twentieth-century struggle to rediscover the ancient, patristic conciliar and synodal tradition in the church has had a short life. The post-Vatican II, antimodern anguish embodied by the movements has contributed to the failure of the conciliar and synodal institutions in the church and to the suppression of subsidiarity in the relations between Rome and the local churches in favor of a modernistic presidential style of leadership that is neither traditional nor Catholic.

This latter element derives neither from the development of ecclesiology in the twentieth century nor from the great ecclesiological tradition from the late second century on. Rather, it represents the appropriation of some features of antiliberal political culture by the Catholic Church in Europe. This "Jacobin attitude"[23] of the new elites within the Catholic Church explains the movements' refusal to address the most debated issues in the church today (sexual ethics, inculturation, ecumenism, interreligious dialogue) and reflects their and their leaders' refusal to enter a theological debate not only about the Vatican's policies and their enforcement but also about the theological agenda of global Catholicism now.

Their increasingly important presence in the institutions of the Roman Curia and their effort to establish institutions for higher education in Rome tells much about their success in creating a "Roman nest" that is necessary in order to have a voice and a face inside the very heart of universal Catholic Church government. Some movements' apparently unlimited financial resources and the esteem in which they are held in the Catholic mainstream are creating inside the Vatican a fierce market of vocations. The most prestigious universities, such as the Gregorian, are now fighting with the new movements' academically anemic but politically stronger universities and seminaries that educate priests for the movement's needs around the world.

Surprisingly, the ecclesiology of the movements embodies identitary papalism but at the same time embodies a more "horizontal" conception of the church as a community rich in charisms but with no intermediate level (episcopate, clergy, theologians) between the founder-leader (the pope) and the base (the individual faithful). In this respect, it is unlikely that the new European-based Catholic movements will contribute to the vitality of theological debate within a church facing the intellectual challenges of bringing the gospel to the contemporary world.

The institutionalization of the movements in the body of the Roman Church has come a long way. The juridical status of each of them differs. They represent the richness and the variety of the spiritual traditions within contemporary Catholicism, and in this sense they are a true manifestation of freedom. But it is a freedom that is given only to the members of the movements, and it comes at the expense not only of the old church elites but also at the expense of the unorganized laity. It is fair to say that the role the movements have acquired in the Catholic Church is not helping to foster debate within the church but, on the contrary, is strengthening anti-intellectual sentiment and rebuffing calls for the freedom of individual, "unlabeled" Catholics within Catholicism.

A Setback for Inclusiveness in the Church?

There is no doubt that the phenomenon of the new Catholic movements represents a new face of the relations between the faithful and the ecclesiastical hierarchy. The blessing currently given by the papacy and the bishops to the new movements should not cause us to forget how, at the beginning of their history in the 1960s and 1970s, the founders and members of these movements struggled with the hierarchy in order to get permission to act as Catholics outside of the institutional and recognized Catholic lay associations. The new style of leadership, the lay identity of the leaders, their mission to reach out to a new society, and their early independence from clerical authority made for an uneasy relationship between the movements, the bishops, and the Vatican—at least until the mid-1970s. Carried on the wave of 1968 in Europe and America, the movements represented the long-awaited chance (in Italy especially) for a revolutionary *prise de parole* (opportunity to speak) inside the Catholic Church.

But this fight for freedom inside the Catholic Church, waged by the new movements *against* the institutional establishment and *for* a new model of organized Catholicism, soon turned into the slow but steady development of a new kind of "movement Catholicism" that has given this network of communities and movements the same kind of power in the church that they questioned and fought against immediately after Vatican II. For the movements and for some of the members of the movements, freedom in the church has expanded significantly. Since they are no longer under ecclesiastical surveillance, their members enjoy considerable liberty in terms of self-government and independence from the institution, liturgical creativity, autonomy of pastoral projects, and social and economic entrepreneurship. On the other hand, the movements tend to form inner communities, in order to maintain "spiritual warmth" and to meet their spiritual and material needs, causing a selection of the members on the basis of their ability to protect the group identity and to perform the group's mission.

The need for these movements to compete aggressively in the dynamic "market" of Catholic identities manifests itself within the call for an intense and high-cost activism in order to carry out the mission of the community inside the church. This process comes frequently at the price of the spiritual and intellectual freedom of the members as well as the diversity and inclusiveness of their community. The selection of the members of these movements and communities involves not only the ideological and theological personality of the faithful but also their willingness to devote their entire life—family life, social relations, job opportunities, *Weltanschauung*—to the movement's mission. The very minor role of theological reflection in these communities and in the members' education reflects this attitude, as do the refusal to share the language of the old Catholic elites and the adoption instead of an idiom of social action, allegiance to the community, and proud obedience to the pope and the official teaching of the church.

The rise of many of the "new Catholic movements" is a sign of the path "from the open Church to neo-exclusivism," as it has been accurately put by Gerard Mannion.[24] This lay mobilization of the Catholic Church for the *reconquista* of the contemporary world leaves little room for the exercise of freedom inside the movements. While the movements have enhanced the new media-friendly face of world Catholicism, their "community Catholicism" is quite different from "Catholicism as a communion." It is enacted in a church made up of small communities highly committed to sharing their members' faith and in making their faith visible and effective but also to silencing the voices that put in jeopardy the "ticket mentality."[25] Harmony becomes far more important than pluralism; obedience to the leader overrides spiritual freedom; a "sound-bite" theology replaces the daily contact with the Bible and with theology as an intellectual effort to read the gospel in the world as it is.

Vatican II is the council that introduced religious freedom as correlated both to human dignity and to the freedom of the church. The Council's ecclesiology opened the gates toward the future, toward a church capable of addressing the issue of balance of power within itself and of solving the contradictions between its liturgical-communional identity and an overwhelmingly inherited Ancien Regime institutional framework.

After Vatican II the institutional framework has somehow changed, and the supremacy of bishops and clergy has been reduced; this change, however, did not create new balances and new room for freedom in the church. After the shock of 1968, Catholicism has seemed to become more and more afraid of freedom in the church. A major part of the new Catholic movements embodies reaction to this shock manifested in a spirit of fear.

The rise of the new movements is leading to a church that is effectively no longer run by bishops and clergy (as in Tridentine Catholicism) but that is not renewed by a participatory and theologically educated laity either (as the mid-twentieth-century theology of the laity dreamed). Rather, we see a new alliance between a hyperactive papacy and a highly motivated and mobilized spectrum of movements strongly tied to the pope as the symbolic badge of theological orthodoxy. This could mean the precipitous end of Vatican II's attempt to reconcile Catholicism with the ancient tradition of councils and synods governing the Catholic Church, on one side, and with democratic, human-rights-based and participative culture, on the other side.

Their "political" option for an ecclesiology based almost exclusively on obedience to the pope and to the culture of their community, applied through an intense communitarianism that almost completely bypasses communion with the local churches (their bishops and parishes), has heavy implications for the issue of freedom and dialogue in the church.[26] Accessibility and inclusion in the church are witness to the accessibility of God, "the gate" (John 10:9): it is time to ask whether the accessibility of the church has been increased by the "new Catholic movements" or if these new movements have introduced new filters for the accessibility of God.[27]

The new Catholic movements have gained a special legitimacy within Catholicism, one that seems above criticism—until the secrecy of their inner life becomes a problem for the public relations of world Catholicism. The mobilization brought about by the "new Catholic movements" in the church offered, in the first decades of their rise, hospitality to a more diverse population of Catholics. Now, after the biblical forty years of their life in the church have elapsed, it is time to recognize that from an ecclesiological point of view, serious problems are posed by the present outcome of this new phenomenon.

Notes

[1] For an overview of the history of the "new Catholic movements," see Massimo Faggioli, *Breve storia dei movimenti cattolici* (Rome: Carocci, 2008; Spanish translation: *Historia y evolución de los movimientos católicos: De León XIII a Benedicto XVI* (Madrid: PPC, 2011). On the history of the debate on Vatican II, see Massimo Faggioli, *Vatican II: The Battle for Meaning* (Mahwah, NJ: Paulist Press, 2012).

[2] A fundamental difference exists between the "new Catholic movements" and the "basic ecclesial communities": see Richard R. Gaillardetz, *Ecclesiology for a*

Global Church: A People Called and Sent (Maryknoll, NY: Orbis Books, 2008), 122–26.

[3] See Massimo Faggioli, "Il movimentismo cattolico e l'apologetica dell'inimicizia» nella chiesa post-conciliare," in *Tutto è grazia. In omaggio a Giuseppe Ruggieri*, ed. Alberto Melloni (Milan: Jaca Books, 2010), 441–56.

[4] See Massimo Faggioli, "Council Vatican II between Documents and Spirit: The Case of the New Catholic Movements," in *After Vatican II: Trajectories and Hermeneutics*, ed. James Heft and John W. O'Malley (Grand Rapids, MI: Eerdmans, 2012).

[5] There is a serious lack of objective and independent studies on the new Catholic movements such as Opus Dei, Communion and Liberation, and the Legionaries. One exception is Thomas Masters and Amy Uelmen, *Focolare: Living a Spirituality of Unity in the United States* (Hyde Park, NY: New City Press, 2011).

[6] See Massimo Faggioli, "The New Elites of Italian Catholicism: 1968 and the New Catholic Movements," *Catholic Historical Review* 98, no. 1 (January 2012): 18–40.

[7] The cultural relationship between new Catholic movements and "communitarism" are still to be explored.

[8] See Karl Rahner, "Basic Theological Interpretation of the Second Vatican Council," in Karl Rahner, *Concern for the Church* (New York: Crossroads, 1981), 77–90.

[9] The new Catholic movements fit the current trend of a Catholicism that has undermined "l'engagement politique au profit d'une revalorisation concurrentielle des pratiques chrétiennes de charité": see Catherine Fino, "L'autorité des pratiques chrétiennes de la charité en contexte de pluralisme: L'impulsion de Vatican II et le travail à poursuivre," in *L'autorité et les autorités: L'herméneutique théologique de Vatican II*, ed. Gilles Routhier and Guy Jobin (Paris: Cerf, 2010*)*, 211.

[10] For the history of the "Neocatechumenal Way" between Rome and Japan, see Massimo Faggioli, "The Neocatechumenate and Communion in the Church," *Japan Mission Journal* 65, no. 1 (Spring 2011): 31–38. The Focolare movement and Sant'Egidio are two exceptions here.

[11] See Mircea Eliade, *Myth and Reality*, trans. Willard R. Trask (New York: Harper & Row, 1975 [1963]); Shmuel Noah Eisenstadt, *Fundamentalism, Sectarianism, and Revolution. The Jacobin Dimension of Modernity* (Cambridge: Cambridge University Press, 1999).

[12] For the "primitivist" mindset in the theology of and after Vatican II, see Ormond Rush, *Still Interpreting Vatican II: Some Hermeneutical Principles* (Mahwah, NJ: Paulist Press, 2004), 69–85.

[13] See Massimo Faggioli, "*Sacrosanctum Concilium* and the Meaning of Vatican II," *Theological Studies* 71 (June 2010): 437–52.

[14] See Giuseppe Ruggieri, "Chiesa e mondo," in *Cristianesimo, chiese e vangelo* (Bologna: Il Mulino, 2002), 307–38.

[15] See Piero Coda, "Movimenti ecclesiali e chiesa in Italia. Spunti ecclesiologici," *Communio* 149 (September–October 1996): 64–73.

[16] See Jean Beyer, "Movimento ecclesiale (Motus ecclesialis)," in *Nuovo Dizionario di Diritto Canonico*, ed. Carlos Corral Salvador, Velasio De Paolis, Gianfranco Ghirlanda (Cinisello B., Milan: Paoline, 1993), 707–12. See the example of the seminaries "Redemptoris Mater" of the Neo-Catechumenal Way (the first one was founded in Rome in 1990).

[17] See John Paul II, apostolic exhortation *Pastores dabo vobis,* March 25, 1992, 68.

[18] About this, see Massimo Faggioli, *Il vescovo e il concilio: Modello episcopale e aggiornamento al Vaticano II* (Bologna: Il Mulino, 2005); *Synod and Synodality: Theology, History, Canon Law and Ecumenism in New Contact*, ed. Alberto Melloni and Silvia Scatena (Munster, Germany: LIT: 2005); *Repraesentatio: Mapping a Keyword for Churches & Governance*, ed. Alberto Melloni and Massimo Faggioli (Berlin: LIT, 2006).

[19] For the historical ties between the episcopate, the clergy and the social elites in Europe, see Joseph Bergin, "L'Europe des Évêques au temps de la réforme catholique," *Bibliothèque de l'École des chartes* 154 (1996): 509–31; *Power Elites and State Building*, ed. Wolfgang Reinhard (Oxford: Oxford University Press, 1996); Christoph Weber, *Senatus divinus: Verborgene Strukturen im Kardinalskollegium der frühen Neuzeit (1500–1800)* (Frankfurt am Main, Germany: Peter Lang, 1996).

[20] See Massimo Faggioli, "Chiese locali ed ecclesiologia prima e dopo il concilio di Trento," in *Storia della Chiesa in Europa tra ordinamento politico-amministrativo e strutture ecclesiastiche*, ed. Luciano Vaccaro (Brescia, Italy: Morcelliana, 2005), 197–213.

[21] See Danielle Hervieu-Léger, *Le pèlerin et le converti: La religion en mouvement* (Paris: Flammarion, 1999).

[22] See Alberto Melloni, "Movimenti: De significatione verborum," *Concilium* 2003/3, *I movimenti nella chiesa*, ed. Alberto Melloni: 13–34; Jean Beyer, "De motu ecclesiali quaesita et dubia," *Periodica*, 78 (1989): 437–52; Gianni Ambrosio, "Cammino ecclesiale e percorsi aggregativi," *La Scuola Cattolica* 116 (1988): 441–60; Agostino Favale, *Movimenti ecclesiali contemporanei: Dimensioni storiche, teologico-spirituali ed apostoliche* (Rome: LAS, 1982, 1991); Piersandro Vanzan, "Elementi comuni e identificativi dell'attuale fenomeno movimentista intraecclesiale con cenni a rischi e speranze," in *Fedeli Associazioni Movimenti* (Milan: Glossa, 2002), 187–206.

[23] See Shmuel N. Eisenstadt, *Fundamentalism, Sectarianism, and Revolution: The Jacobin Dimension of Modernity* (Cambridge: Cambridge University Press, 1999).

[24] See Gerard Mannion, *Ecclesiology and Postmodernity: Questions for the Church in Our Time* (Collegeville, MN: Liturgical Press, 2007), 43–74.

[25] See Theodor W. Adorno et al., *The Authoritarian Personality* (New York: W. W. Norton, 1950); Elias Canetti, *Masse und Macht* (Hamburg: Fischer, 1960).

[26] See Bradford Hinze, *Practices of Dialogue in the Roman Catholic Church: Aims and Obstacles, Lessons and Laments* (New York: Contimuum, 2006), esp. 238–67.

[27] See Jürgen Werbick, *Grundfragen der Ekklesiologie* (Freiburg im Breisgau, Germany: Herder, 2009), 243–46.

Ecclesiology and Exclusion:
Setting Boundaries for the Church

Neil Ormerod

The question of who is in and who is out of the church has been present from the beginning.[1] As the Matthean Jesus states, "Whoever is not with me is against me, and whoever does not gather with me scatters" (Mt 12:3), noting, of course, the variants in Luke and Mark, "whoever is not against me is for me." Within the New Testament witness there are clear examples of heterodox belief and practice being excluded from church boundaries. Paul attacks those who seek to impose circumcision (Gal 2, 5), he excludes from the community those who are living blatantly immoral lives (1 Cor 5), and he criticizes those who deny the resurrection (1 Cor 15). The author of the Second Letter of John labels those who deny that Christ has come in the flesh as the "anti-Christ": "Many deceivers have gone out into the world, those who do not confess that Jesus Christ has come in the flesh; any such person is the deceiver and the anti-Christ" (2 John 7).

The establishment of boundaries is to be expected because one role of the church is to preserve the practices taught by Jesus, as well as the meanings and values that preserve those practices, including the meaning and value of Jesus' own person as the definitive act of God in history. For as Paul notes, "God was in Christ reconciling the world to himself" (Col 1:20); God is then acting in Jesus to do something new, something not previously present in human history, yet something that is definitive for the salvation of the whole of human history, "the world" that is to be reconciled in Christ. If this process is itself an historical process bound in with the existence of an historical community, then inevitably such a community will require structures of authority that operate to determine the scope and placement of the boundaries that define the nature of Christian identity.

Once we go beyond the immediate New Testament era, the two movements that immediately test the nature of those boundaries are those movements scholars refer to as Judaeo-Christianity (and the correlate problem of the "parting of the ways") and Gnosticism. In terms of their response to the new thing that God is doing in Jesus, we might think of these in the following terms: firstly, in the case of Judaeo-Christianity as a failure to appreciate the newness of what God is doing and so attempting to constrain Christian faith to Jewish expectations and categories; and secondly, in the case of Gnosticism as being so caught up in the newness of God's action that it loses contact with the historical continuity of Christianity with its Jewish roots. Here I shall focus on the question of Gnosticism and certain responses to the Gnostic movement within contemporary scholarship.[2]

Gnosticism

Few terms are as disputed in relation to early church history as the term "Gnosticism." Much of the problem lies in the diverse nature of those groups labeled as such. From our perspective it is possible to view the groups generally identified as "Gnostic" as involving overreaching both the cultural and the social implications of the new thing God is doing in Jesus.[3] Some will retain some Jewish social and cultural elements; some will become increasingly anti-Jewish; all will engage in a process of mythologizing the Christian message, taking it out of the realm of history and into the realm of an increasingly elaborate religious myth cut off from its historical roots. This type of analysis also confirms theoretically the increasing historical evidence that "Gnosticism" is of Christian and not Jewish origin.[4] It is a specific response to the new thing that God is doing in Jesus.

While Judaeo-Christianity failed to do justice to the new thing God was doing in Jesus, these groups are captured by the newness. So where does Gnosticism go wrong? In simple terms, Gnosticism reduces faith to knowledge. Moreover, it is a knowledge no longer grounded in any tradition, neither the cosmological myths of paganism nor the soteriological history of Israel, including the Jesus event itself.[5] Its increasingly bizarre speculations rest solely on the authority of the teacher who claims to have the special knowledge (*gnosis*) required for salvation. It is not surprising that the early church sought to distance itself from such a reformulation of the Christian message and to exclude those who held such views.

A Counterposition

It is worth comparing this suggestion with that of those found in modern literature on Gnosticism to see where differences may lie. As is the case with much of this modern literature, the key question is the meaning of the term "Christian" and its applicability to various groups and movements.

This problem is not unique to the ancient world, and indeed one can ask the same question about various modern movements that claim the title "Christian" but are not necessarily accepted as such by mainstream churches as represented for example by the World Council of Churches.[6] Does one adopt an "empirical" understanding of the term such that any group that self-designates as Christian is therefore Christian, or is there some normative account of what constitutes Christianity by which such claims are to be judged? The problem of establishing ecclesial boundaries is constant throughout history.

In his study on the validity of the category of Gnosticism, Michael Williams introduces his reader to material from the Apocryphon of John, commonly identified as Gnostic and found in the Nag Hammadi collection. Williams devotes six pages to present a summary of this document, which consists of a fantastical myth of the divine realm, of creation and redemption.[7] We learn of the mythical divine entity "Barbelo," who mediates between the "Invisible Spirit" and all else. Barbelo and the Invisible Spirit give birth to "Child" as some sort of parody of the Christian Trinity. Other divine entities emerge, "an entourage of mythopoetically personified eternal divine attributes ('aeons')."[8] There follows a complex myth of material creation involving a monstrous child of a self-willed Wisdom named Ialdabaoth. Adam and Eve get thrown into the mix as part of the redemption story. Significantly, the role of Jesus of Nazareth is diminished as "only one mode of true divinity's self-revelation."[9] Williams concludes with the comment, "But if [the Apocryphon of John] does represent the doctrines of a specific community, that community's precise identity, *except for the fact that it was Christian*, is not certain."[10] It is difficult to know in what sense such a group can be called "Christian." Clearly we are light years away from a normative understanding of the term grounded in some sort of orthodoxy.

One might argue that there is an ideological agenda at work here. As Ben Meyer has noted, there is a concerted effort among some scholars to make "Gnosticism" simply another legitimate expression of Christian faith, which was obliterated by an "orthodox" elite asserting their dominance.[11] For a theologian the issue remains one of a faith commitment. The set of beliefs expressed in the Apocryphon of John are not in the same ball park as orthodox Christianity but show all the characteristics of cutting Christianity off from its historical roots and so moving away from a commitment to the historical person of Jesus.

Where then do we locate an orthodox Christianity in this picture? There is a center that seeks to move forward, respecting limitation (its Jewish roots and grounding in the historical Jesus) but transforming itself both socially and culturally to accommodate the new thing that God is doing in Jesus.

And so it continued to uphold the Jewish sacred writings but read them in a new light, finding in them a prefiguration of Christ. It denied the necessity of circumcision but still followed some Jewish food laws, not eating meat offered to idols. Paul, of course, knew that the idols do not exist and that he was free to eat such foods, but for the sake of the "weak," he did not eat such food lest they be scandalized (1 Cor 8). In all, it sought to maintain the unity of the group, a unity of faith in Jesus, a unity threatened by forces that would pull them off in any one of the directions given by movements such as Judaeo-Christianity and Gnosticism. This was no mean task as is evidenced by the multiplicity of groups and their persistence during these first few centuries. Again, an evaluation of the success of the early Church in maintaining some semblance of unity of faith, of orthodoxy, will depend on how one views the origins and purpose of God's action in Jesus.

It is apparent that the precise boundaries of that orthodoxy are not clear. But a concern for such boundaries is clearly present within the New Testament itself. The center moving forward was fuzzy around the edges without doubt, but it strove for a unity of faith within an emerging new cultural and social identity. Within that center there was an awareness of both identity and difference with Israel, a change but not a break from the past. They were a new "Israel," a new "people of God" (1 Pt 2:10) created through a new covenant in Jesus (1 Cor 11:25; 2 Cor 3:6). There were still many disputed questions, notably about the status of Jesus himself and the implications of that status for a Christian understanding of God. These were not trivial matters and would take most of the following centuries to resolve. The boundaries are not so much set as sensed, and there would be many false paths along the way to a clearer demarcation of the issues.

Suppression of Gnosticism and the Legitimacy of Authority

I would suggest that the central question here is the possibility of legitimate authority being exercised within the emerging church. The question of the legitimacy of authority has been examined by Max Weber, who defines authority as legitimate power.[12] Weber's definition, however, suffers from being unable to identify a normative stance concerning what constitutes legitimation. Without some normative understanding of legitimation, he falls back to an empirical stance, that "legitimate" means "legitimated," that is, its acceptance by those over whom authority is exercised. On the other hand, one may seek to define legitimacy normatively in terms of the authenticity of those who exercise power—as suggested by Lonergan[13] and Komonchak[14]—and so distinguish between legitimate authority and authority that is merely legitimated but not legitimate. Without some such distinction, there is no genuine legitimate authority, only power accepted as legitimate. And if power is then the basic reality, there can only be winners and losers in a game of power. Orthodoxy then becomes a matter of a powerful elite rejecting the competing claims of others and suppressing legitimate diversity.

As we noted initially, the problem of authority and exclusion goes back to the New Testament itself. It is there from the very beginning, not some strange or alien offshoot. But if we recognize a legitimate authority to that apostolic witness and acknowledge that this needs to be extended through this whole life of the church, our evaluations of the exercise of that authority will be very different. In fact, the prevalence of a hermeneutic of suspicion with regard to the exercise of authority present in modern scholarship is more a reflection of our own contemporary problems with the whole notion of legitimate authority rather than some superior critical historical approach to the topic.

One may speculate that those who apply a hermeneutic of suspicion toward such an approach itself are more concerned with legitimizing current theological and dogmatic pluralism within contemporary Christianity by projecting it onto Christian origins than with a disinterested reading of the past. The instability of the approach is evident in that if there had been a different set of "winners," for example, if Gnosticism had won out over an orthodox Christianity, then contemporary authors might be railing against them as the "orthodox," the elites, the winners, over the losers who sought to keep some sense of continuity with the historical events of the gospel. Apart from suspicion of winners and sympathy for losers, they can offer no clear criteria for evaluation.

Conclusion

Discussion concerning boundaries, exclusion, and identity needs to be embedded in a larger framework of the forces of social and cultural transformation and stability present in any society and how these work themselves out in the life of the church. It needs to move beyond essentialist accounts of identity and recognize how processes of transformation shift identity over an historical timeframe, producing what Richard Lennan calls a "change *in* but not *of* identity."[15] Theologically the new thing God is doing in Jesus provides principles of both identity and transformation of that identity. The tensions between the options of Judaeo-Christianity, on the one hand, and Gnosticism, on the other, serve as a good illustration of this process at work in the early church.

Notes

[1] Material in this paper is drawn from a larger research project on systematic historical ecclesiology currently under review for publication.

[2] For the issue of the parting of the ways, see Adam H. Becker and Annette Yoshiko Reed, *The Ways That Never Parted: Jews and Christians in Late Antiquity and the Early Middle Ages* (Tübingen, Germany: Mohr Siebeck, 2003).

[3] While the term remains problematic for scholars, our approach has not been to find a definition of Gnosticism that then might prove problematic but to define from general categories four antitypes and note that what some scholars call Gnosticism has features in common with two of these antitypes.

[4] A. H. B. Logan, *Gnostic Truth and Christian Heresy: A Study in the History of Gnosticism* (London: T & T Clark, 2004). Also on empirical sociological grounds, Rodney Stark, *The Rise of Christianity: A Sociologist Reconsiders History* (Princeton, NJ: Princeton University Press, 1996).

[5] The terms cosmological and soteriological in this context are derived from Eric Voegelin, *The New Science of Politics: An Introduction* (Chicago: University of Chicago Press, 1952). They are given more explanatory precision in Robert M. Doran, *Theology and the Dialectics of History* (Toronto: University of Toronto Press, 1990).

[6] For example, are groups such as "Christian Scientists" really Christian? Or Mormons? Or Jehovah Witnesses? What criteria do we use to decide? Some would ask whether there is adherence to the Creed of Nicaea, for example.

[7] Michael A. Williams, *Rethinking "Gnosticism": An Argument for Dismantling a Dubious Category* (Princeton, N.J.: Princeton University Press, 1996), 8–13.

[8] Ibid., 10.

[9] Ibid., 9.

[10] Ibid., 13. Emphasis added.

[11] Ben F. Meyer, *Reality and Illusion in New Testament Scholarship: A Primer in Critical Realist Hermeneutics* (Collegeville, MN: Liturgical Press, 1994), 186.

[12] See Anthony Giddens, *Capitalism and Modern Social Theory: An Analysis of the Writings of Marx, Durkheim and Max Weber* (Cambridge: Cambridge University Press, 1971), 154–63, for a discussion of Weber's account of authority.

[13] Bernard J. F. Lonergan, "The Dialectic of Authority," in *A Third Collection*, ed. F. Crowe (New York: Paulist Press, 1985), 5–12.

[14] Joseph Komonchak, "Authority and Magisterium," in *Vatican Authority and American Catholic Dissent*, ed. W. May (New York: Crossroad, 1987), 103–14.

[15] Richard Lennan, *The Ecclesiology of Karl Rahner* (Oxford: Clarendon, 1995), 60.

The Prophetic Mission of the Local Church: Community Organizing as a School for the Social Imaginary

Bradford Hinze

Faith-based community organizing in the United States is often traced back to 1939 in Chicago with the formation of the Back of the Yards Neighborhood Council, a group composed of workers from Slavic enclaves, especially Poles, Czechs, Lithuanians, and Slovaks, each with their own ethnic parishes, schools, and social clubs catering to the needs of individual ethnic communities. With the Great Depression and the exploitation of workers in the stockyards at the hands of owners and government officials, there was a need to forge a coalition of these parish groups to fight for economic and community development. Since then, community organizing has evolved, becoming more multi-issue, interracial, and nonpartisan, and has played an integral role in the life of local churches in the United States and around the world.

In this essay I will explore how faith-based community organizing serves as a school for the social imaginary of the local church as it advances its prophetic mission.[1] This collective endeavor offers a unique version of Catholic Action associated with the method of see-judge-act, which was closely associated with the Second Vatican Council's teaching on the people of God. I wish to emphasize that faith-based community organizing promotes lay and clergy leadership and collaboration in the local church that is rooted in parish and diocesan settings and branches out into social and political arenas of public life. The resolutely parish-based character of these groups distinguishes these efforts from some liberation theologies that accentuate the importance of base Christian communities operating outside of parish structures and those New Catholic Movements that foster communities aligned with papal and curial priorities, which can circumvent the leadership and pastoral priorities of the local church, such as Opus Dei, the Neocatechumenal Way, Communion and Liberation, and Focolare.[2]

My interest in the role that community organizing plays as a school of the social imaginary for the prophetic mission of the local church initially dawned on me while investigating synodal and conciliar structures of discernment and governance at the level of parishes and dioceses, both national and international.[3] Although introduced to the work of Saul Alinsky in the 1970s during my college years when I was enlisted to participate in a campaign against the "redlining" practices of banks and lending institutions guilty of racial exclusion in housing loans, my research helped me to see how influential Alinsky's methods were not only among people who worked directly with him in Chicago and in the Midwest but also nationwide among the Catholic Committee on Urban Ministry (CCUM) that included Msgr. Jack Egan and through their work those involved in the first Call to Action Convention held in Detroit in 1976. Community organizers taught many in the U.S. church to practice a certain type of dialogical discernment and decision making when considering the local mission of the church.

More recently I have been examining three faith-based community organizations in the Bronx in the extended neighborhood of my academic residence, Fordham University: the Northwest Bronx Community and Clergy Coalition, the South Bronx People for Change, and South Bronx Churches. As I will argue in subsequent writings, these three groups offer valuable illustrations of the reception of the people of God ecclesiology of Vatican II in the Archdiocese of New York. They demonstrate how parish priests and lay women and men can collaborate in the parish and surrounding neighborhoods to develop the skills necessary to promote social justice in civil society and in the process revitalize their parish.

These parish-centered community organizations that take their inspiration from the people of God ecclesiology need to be appreciated in relation to the ecclesiology of communion as articulated in the documents of Vatican II, which has increasingly become the governing ecclesiological paradigm since the pontificate of John Paul II. The official ecclesiology of communion centers on the mission of the church in the administration of sacraments, proclamation of the gospel, catechesis, and the prominence given to the exercise of hierarchical and clerical authority, while carefully restricting lay leadership in decision-making matters of mission and ministry. Communion ecclesiology has occasionally been pitted against the people of God ecclesiology that accentuates the full and active participation of all the faithful in the mission of the church, including social and political engagement and the need for creativity in the local inculturation of the gospel. It should be noted, however, that even though the people of God ecclesiology has often been minimized or passed over in official Catholic documents since the mid-1980s, it has not been repudiated. It is my contention that communion ecclesiology has over the last twenty-five years eclipsed but not destroyed the resources offered by the people of God ecclesiology. The ongoing work of faith-based community organizing in parishes supports this claim.

The promotion of faith-based community organizing among Catholics and other Christian churches and groups offers important evidence of the light, grace, and power offered by the people of God theology in our own day. There are two recent examples. In October 2010, a conference was held on community organizing sponsored by the Campaign for Human Development at the University of Notre Dame. This event provided an opportunity to take the pulse of local support for community organizing across the United States and to highlight trends in the field and by so doing to promote their significance. A second noteworthy phenomenon is the development over the last few years of the parish-based Justfaith formation program developed by Jack Jezreel and his team at Justfaith Ministries sponsored by Catholic Relief Services, the Campaign for Human Development, Pax Christi, Maryknoll, Bread for the World, and Catholic Charities.[4] Community organizing is fostered through this program as a central ingredient in the advancement of a justice-oriented spirituality.

The simple argument I am advancing here about community organizing and the prophetic character of the church offers a distinctively theological approach that builds on and can be contrasted with two recent works. The first is *Blessed Are the Organized: Grassroots Democracy in America* by philosopher of religion Jeffrey Stout. Building on his previous defense of the importance of religious discourse and reasoning in democratic societies,[5] Stout explores in this book how faith-based community organizing offers a means for promoting social change through grassroots democratic processes. His research agenda is described in the preface:

> [O]ne needs to look away from the centers of elite power and ask ordinary citizens what they are actually doing in their own communities to get organized, exert power, and demand accountability. How do they build an organization? How do they analyze power relations? How do they cultivate leaders? What role does religion play in the organizational process? What objectives are being sought? What concerns, passions, and ideals lie behind those objectives? What have concerned citizens actually achieved and how have they achieved it? What have their setbacks been? Who are their allies and their opponents? What obstacles stand in their way? By answering these questions, we can strengthen our grasp on what grassroots democracy is.[6]

Stout wants readers to appreciate how faith-based community organizing among Catholics, Protestants, Jews, and Muslims provides impressive resources to advance democratic practices in the public realm. However, he also expresses no real interest in exploring the impact this has on the vitality of the parish or congregation and none at all in the theological and specific ecclesiological issues that are at stake. Such issues are simply beyond his research agenda, but they are at the center of mine.

The second research project I wish to draw upon is the sociological work of Richard L. Wood and his particular collaboration with Mary Ann Ford Flaherty in *Faith and Public Life: Faith-Based Community Organizing and the Development of Congregations*. This text has as its goal to identify various ways that faith-based community organizing contributes to congregational development. The authors break down congregational development into the following ingredients:

> Congregational development ... means the growth of members as multi-faceted leaders within their congregations, and the strengthening of congregations as institutions. For individual congregation members, this development includes gaining leadership skills, deepening engagement in congregational life, and strengthening understanding of the connections between the faith traditions' call to social justice and the work of faith-based community organizing. For congregations, such development includes strengthening relationships within the congregation, creating connections to other congregations and organizations, deepening linkages between the worship life and the wider social world, transforming con-gregational culture to become more relational and accountable, and increasing memberships.[7]

Wood and Ford Flaherty draw the conclusion that faith-based community organizing offers the best hope for the development of congregations in four areas: relationships (which they describe in terms of bonding and bridging social capital), leadership development, faith links (cultural connections between religious commitment and public life), and power and public presence of clergy and lay leaders of their congregation in the community. The purpose of my paper is to advance this argument further in a theological and specifically ecclesiological idiom. My approach, to reiterate, is different from Stout's and Wood and Ford Flaherty's works, because it is explicitly theological: I am proposing that faith-based community organizing offers a school for the social imaginary that contributes to developing the prophetic mission of the local church.

What do I mean by the social imaginary? Here I draw on the work of Charles Taylor. Inspired by the work of Benedict Anderson,[8] Taylor uses the phrase "social imaginaries" to identify "the ways in which [people] imagine their social existence, how they fit together with others, how things go on between them and their fellows, the expectations which are normally met, and the deeper notions and images which underlie these expectations."[9] Social imaginaries are first of all "the way ordinary people 'imagine' their social surroundings . . . often not in theoretical terms, [but] in images, stories, legends . . . ; secondly, they provide a collective vision that is persuasive for groups of people; and thirdly, they provide a 'common understanding which makes possible common practices, and a widely shared sense of legitimacy.'"[10] Taylor's agenda, like that of Anderson, is to explore the realization of social imaginaries at the macrohistorical level, as these are found in various groups in societies in diverse periods in history. By contrast, I wish to emphasize that a social imaginary can also be operative at grassroots or mediating levels where leaders and groups articulate a vision of life that can motivate collective action.

To translate Taylor's formula about the social imaginary into the language of community organizing, let us consider a saying that is associated with the Industrial Area Foundation, one of the main centers of training in community organizing in the United States that goes back to Saul Alinsky. The saying is "You can't organize what you can't imagine."[11] You need to help people to imagine or reimagine their neighborhood or a particular area of social life. As Stout rightly recognizes, community organizing is as much a work of memory, mourning, and anger as it is of the creative and productive imagination. In fact, this hypothesis could be extrapolated to argue that lamentation, memory, and the imagination are operative in every new ecclesial movement, in every instantiation of Catholic Action, as well as in the formation of religious orders in the past and present. For our purpose we need to explore how this is operative in faith-based community organizing.

Faith-based community organizing has become a school for the social imaginary across the United States. This is in evidence in the four large national networks that operate in this country: (1) the Industrial Area Foundations or IAF (started in 1940 by Saul Alinsky); (2) People Improving Communities through Organization (formerly Pacific Institute for Community Organization—or PICO, 1972); (3) the Gamaliel Foundation (1986); and (4) Direct Action and Research Training Center or DART (1982).[12] They have developed 133 ecumenical and interfaith confederations in cities across the country. These federations have about four thousand institutions as official members. About 3,500 (or 87 percent) of those institutions are religious parishes and congregations.[13] Besides religious congregations, federations include labor unions, schools, and other community organizations.[14] These confederations are characterized as broad based (because they are composed of various types of groups and organizations); they are locally constituted; they focus on a variety of issues; they are staffed by professional organizers and are political but nonpartisan.[15]

As influential as Saul Alinsky's own viewpoint and methods have been, contemporaries of Alinsky and his heirs held contrasting convictions about the overriding aims of community organizing. During Alinsky's lifetime, a friend of his, Myles Horton, the founder of what came to be called the Highlander Research and Education Center, espoused a North American version of the pedagogy of the oppressed associated with Brazilian educator Paulo Freire.[16] Horton and the Highlander Center were primarily interested in building relationships and educating people to promote human agency in contested social situations in contrast to Alinsky's focus on issues-based organizing oriented toward winning victories often championed by charismatic leaders.[17] Alinsky and Horton respected the strengths of each other's positions, but they were clear about their differences. As Horton stated the difference,

> I think [one should] use organizations to educate people. . . . I am less concerned about whether you win in your goal. If you don't educate people regardless of how many little victories you have, nothing is ever going to happen. To me organizations are for the primary purpose of educating people because most of them do not bring about any kind of changes that are significant anyway. So you might as well use them for something worthwhile. I've always taken a position that Highlander was not in the business of organizing, or even of training organizers, but in education for action, and trying to help develop people who would become activists.[18]

Using insights not unlike Horton's points, some of Alinsky's most influential heirs brought about an evolution in his aims and methods: from a strict issue-based approach to organizing to one that was also oriented toward building relationships; from an approach focusing on victories to one focusing on the building of a culture of civic relationships, responsibility, and accountability. Moreover, instead of avoiding cultural factors, including religious, racial, and ethnic identities that marked Alinsky's approach, the students of Alinsky grew to respect and capitalize on these factors in forming multiracial and multiethnic ecumenical and interfaith organizations. This transition occurred at the Industrial Area Foundation through the influence of a group of Catholic leaders: Ed Chambers and Ernesto Cortes in organizations influenced by Alinsky trainee Tom Gaudette, who also went on to influence the formation of the networks

Gamaliel, the Pacific Institute for Community Organization (which became associated with the leadership of Jerry Helfrich, S.J., and subsequently John Baumann, S.J.), and the National People's Action (NPA).[19]

For the remainder of this essay, I wish to identify five basic lessons that have been learned from faith-based community organizing for the mission of the local church.

How Is Faith-Based Community Organizing a School for Developing the Social Imaginary of a Prophetic People of God?

First, community organizing teaches the central role of forming close relationships by means of one-on-one conversations to develop a community oriented for mission. People must learn to listen carefully to each other to identify their aspirations and desires and what disturbs them, their laments, and what angers them about society (and the church) so as to determine the legitimate interests of individuals and eventually the common interests of the community. Community organizers, the clergy, and lay leaders should not tell people what they are concerned about and what disturbs them. Rather they need one-on-one conversations with members of the community to learn these things. This was the bedrock conviction of Saul Alinsky's method. As Alinsky put it,

> The first thing you've got to do in a community is listen, not talk, and learn to eat, sleep, breathe only one thing: the problems and aspirations of the community. Because no matter how imaginative your tactics, how shrewd your strategy, you're doomed before you even start if you don't win the trust and respect of the people; and the only way to get that is for you to trust and respect them. And without that respect there's no communication, no mutual confidence and no action. That's the first lesson any good organizer has to learn.[20]

Second, faith-based community organizations advance a multilayered approach to institutions and cultivate leadership intent on identifying collective interests and issues that need to be addressed by the local community. In community organizing there are three levels of group formation. One is at the congregational level. For Catholics this means parishes that have their parochial mission influenced by the lay leadership exercised in parish pastoral councils and social action committees. A second group is an ecumenical clergy caucus frequently composed of Catholic and Protestant clergy, but it is sometimes an interfaith clergy caucus of leaders of Christian and other faith traditions such as Jews, Muslims, or other religious groups. The members of this clergy group share their deepest convictions based on their distinctive faith traditions as they pertain to pressing issues in their communities. In the process they also identify shared beliefs to begin to articulate an ecumenical and interfaith vision and mission that will offer a framework for addressing their concerns and inspiring their collective actions. The third kind of group is a federation of groups of people from various institutions, predominantly faith-based congregations, but also unions as well as school and tenant associations among others. Representatives from the groups are convened on a regular basis to discuss their collective concerns and priorities. Each of these groups cultivates certain practices.

- Leaders are trained to form relationships within and between congregations and among congregation members and people in the neighborhoods, to lead a meeting with a group decision-making process, and to engage in social and political analysis.[21]
- Clergy and lay leaders are challenged and held accountable: there is internal organizational discipline cultivated in order to build up the political culture of the group. People are challenged and held accountable one-on-one and in groups.
- The actions of the leaders and groups are evaluated: after public events there is a thorough evaluation of whether the objectives were met, what worked, and what didn't work.

Third, community organizing teaches the staff of the community organization how to identify a mission target and strategy based on the information learned from the one-on-ones and discussions in parish-based groups. To break this down into steps, the staff of the community organization (1) "cuts an issue" that can be acted upon by finding out the necessary information about the issues of concern and identifies strategic and tactical choices, (2) determines a "target" person who makes the decisions pertaining to the prioritized issue, and (3) develops ways to hold this person "accountable" by identifying a particular "demand" that needs to be met to respond to the problems being raised.[22]

One mode of social action takes place when representatives of the federation, clergy, organizers, and lay leaders meet with individuals with decision-making authority to talk about the concerns and demands of the people. If the targeted person is not receptive and does not take action in response to the concerns raised by the group, another mode of collective speaking and action is considered in which members from the congregations are mobilized through rallies, prayer vigils, and public demonstrations. Some rallies serve to foster the resolve of the group. Others provide occasions for a dramatic presentation of concerns before selected officials (business leaders or government officials) who are asked publicly to take a stand on the issue. Another mode of social action is to find a tactic that draws attention to the issue in the public arena.[23]

Fourth, community organizing invites ongoing reflection on how power operates in the public realm and in institutions. The exercise of power by the leaders and institutions of governments and economic activity affect policies and practices in the various realms of society, in the economy, housing, education, health care, and the environment. The exercise of power in these areas needs to be evaluated in terms of the vested interests of those who use it, whether it is unjust and discriminatory and serves individuals or select groups, or whether it promotes the common good. People must not be deceived about the exercise of power in society. Analogous lessons can also be applied to the use of power in religious and ecclesial settings.

Saul Alinsky conceived of civic life as a battlefield on which those who abuse economic and political power are engaged by those who are regularly exploited by them. This latter group needs to join forces to gain sufficient power to work for change. His 1945 book *Reveille for Radicals* put the matter simply: "the building of a People's Organization is the building of a new power group . . . [, which is] an intrusion and a threat to the existing power arrangements. . . . A People's Organization is dedicated to an eternal war. It is a war against poverty, misery, delinquency, disease, injustice, hopelessness, despair, and unhappiness."[24]

In his 1971 book, *Rules for Radicals*, he differentiated life-giving powers and destructive powers: "Power is the very essence, the dynamo of life. It is the power of the heart pumping blood and sustaining life in the body. It is the power of the active citizen participation pulsing upward, providing a unified strength for a common purpose. Power is an essential life force always in operation, either changing the world or opposing change. Power, or organized energy, may be a man-killing explosive or a life-saving drug."[25] People and institutions exerting destructive power can only be effectively challenged by means of the dispossessed and marginalized joining forces to identify the sources of their collective grief and anger and by exercising their collective power to advance their collective interests for the common good of all.

The heirs of Alinsky built upon his basic convictions to develop a multidimensional approach to power analysis. Greg Galuzzo from Gamaliel begins his day-long leadership training session by saying that in the United States many working-class and poor people get the message that their involvement in civic life doesn't really matter. It may be shocking that among the over one hundred democracies in the world, the United States is the fourth worst in terms of the percentage of citizens that exercise their right to vote.[26]

Galuzzo contends that people with political and economic power try to discourage those without power from using their power or confuse them from exercising their power wisely by means of intimidation, bribery, violence, propaganda, or other forms of deceitful communication.[27] Alinsky's conviction is in evidence in Galuzzo's formulation: there are two groups with power, power elites who exploit others and those who need to get organized to exercise their collective power to challenge the power elites to bring about meaningful change. In this framework, two views of power come into view: on the one hand, power can be described in terms of power over others or control by one means or another; on the other hand, power is an ability to act, to do something, a capacity to effect a change. Ed Chambers, who took over the leadership of the IAF after Alinsky's death, augments Galuzzo's approach when he writes that "from one perspective, power is neutral. It may be used for evil or for good. From another, it is ambiguous because any employment of power by finite human beings, no matter how well intended and successful, will lead to unexpected consequences for self and others."[28]

In the 1980s, over a decade after Alinsky died, Ed Chambers and others in the IAF, in conversation with Leo Penta and Michael Cowan, began to utilize certain writings by Hannah Arendt and Bernard Loomer to differentiate power in terms of a unilateral approach and a relational approach. It stands to reason that Hannah Arendt served as a valuable resource for the IAF, since she too was greatly concerned about the diminishment of civic involvement of people in democratic societies. She chose not to speak of two kinds of power but preferred to contrast a unilateral exercise of violence, force, or strength with a relational view of power. She understood relational power as something that happens between people in the public realm through communication and action in civic engagement. As she phrased it, "Power is what keeps the public realm, the potential space of appearance between acting and speaking men, in existence."[29]

In an analogous fashion, Loomer, who was trained in process philosophy and theology, describes a linear approach to power as "the capacity to influence, guide, adjust, manipulate, shape, control, or transform the human or natural environment in order to advance one's purposes." By contrast, relational power is "the ability [of groups] to produce and to undergo an effect. It is the capacity of both to influence others and to be influenced by others. Relational power involves both a giving and a receiving."[30] Arendt and Loomer provided the descendants of Alinsky a conceptual framework and justification for criticizing the use of power by economic and political elites to take advantage of people in society for their own purposes, while recommending a relational approach to power to motivate people to get organized to participate collectively in the public realm in civil society.

Organizing people offers an alternative way of exercising power in the public realm by claiming one's role as a citizen in civil society. People who live in democratic societies or in societies that aspire to be democratic need to learn how to exercise their power in the public realm. In the public realm, people exercise their power as citizens by voting, by making their voices heard by those with institutional power, through public discourse, and through collective action.[31] As Richard Wood explains, the public realm is not only composed of the systems of government and economic activity but also includes agents in political society and in civil society. Political society is identified with organizations with political goals: "political parties, lobbyists and political action committees, labor unions and business associations."[32] Civil society is associated with "all those organizational settings that are not part of political society or government and in which members of society reflect upon and form values and attitudes regarding their life together, social problems, and the future of society."[33] Civil society includes churches, ethnic associations, and civic groups.[34] Here is the arena for the prophetic mission of the church in society.

Fifth, one of the paramount lessons taught by community organizing that has relevance for the prophetic mission of the church is that there will inevitably be conflict in communities when holding people in authority accountable, but conflict need not rule out the possibility of forming partnerships with power elites. As the prophetic tradition frequently attests, when one is wrestling with destructive powers operative in social bodies, one can expect conflict as people voice grievances and call for significant change. There is agitation in society when members of the group hold official representatives accountable for their action, just as there is conflict in religious communities when we challenge our own members to live up to the demands of the gospel and the call to work for justice. Catholic theology and pastors have a track record of being conflict averse. Catholics have often been taught and too often subscribe to the belief that conflict and agitation in society and in the church are unworthy of the disciples of Jesus. This mentality contradicts the public ministry of Jesus in the gospels: the one who is put to death on a cross is suffering the consequences of responding to the voices of the Spirit of God in the laments of the people of God by agitating the religious and political leaders of his day.

It is not only people in the church who object to conflict. Sometimes academics who champion the virtues of dialogue or open mutual discourse in the public realm are unwilling to admit the important role played by conflict. As Saul Alinsky said, "this general fear of conflict and emphasis on consensus and accommodation is typical academic drivel. How do you ever arrive at consensus before you have conflict? In fact, of course, conflict is the vital core of an open society; if you were going to express democracy in a musical score, your major theme would be the harmony of dissonance. All change means movement, movement means friction and friction means heat."[35] Faith-based community organizing is a crucial way to promote nonviolent direct action against the forces of injustice in society. Conflict is not the antithesis of a social program that fosters dialogue and consensus as the means to promote peace and reconciliation; rather, there is a creative tension between them. People who do not have power in the public realm must mobilize, organize, and often contentiously speak up and act out "to have their voices heard in the public realm."[36]

There is a need to walk a fine line between working for concessions and toward some acceptable negotiated consensus, as theorized by John Rawls and Jürgen Habermas, while acknowledging the agonistic character of democracy as explored by William E. Connolly. Faith-based community organizations cannot shrink from conflictive strategies that challenge institutions, policies, and practices but must also create opportunities for antagonists present in these institutions to become partners and collaborators in the work for justice and human flourishing.

In an interview, a respected woman in the Bronx, who has long been involved in community organizing on issues in education and housing, lamented that more parish priests weren't trained as community organizers. This paper has tried to offer a preliminary theological rationale for the judgment implicit in her grief. Faith-based community organizing provides priests and lay people with the skills needed to articulate and advance the prophetic mission of the local church. In other words, community organizing offers a school for the social imaginary. The cultivation of this particular kind of social imaginary is based on face-to-face dialogue about the laments and aspirations of those in one's community and neighborhood and provides a process of collective discernment and decision making to advance a prophetic course of action. The prophetic character of this undertaking has not been sufficiently delineated here, but what differentiates community organizing that is prophetic in character is that it takes its inspiration from the laments of God's people and that it has no illusions about the importance of power and conflict in matters religious and social.

Notes

[1] Portions of this essay have appeared in "Faith-Based Community Organizing and the Prophetic Mission of the Local Church," *Eastern Journal of Dialogue and Culture* 4 (2011): 87–106.

[2] Massimo Faggioli, "The Neocatechumenate and Communion in the Church," *Japan Mission Journal* 65 (2011): 31–38; Massimo Faggioli, "The New Catholic Movements, Vatican II and Freedom in the Catholic Church," *Japan Mission Journal* 62 (2008): 75–84.

[3] Bradford E. Hinze, *Practices of Dialogue in the Roman Catholic Church: Aims and Obstacles, Lessons and Laments* (New York: Continuum, 2006).

[4] For information about Justfaith Ministries, see http://www.justfaith.org.

[5] Jeffrey Stout, *Democracy and Tradition* (Princeton, NJ: Princeton University Press, 2005).

[6] Jeffrey Stout, *Blessed Are the Organized: Grassroots Democracy in America* (Princeton, NJ: Princeton University Press, 2010), xiii–xiv.

[7] Mary Ann Ford Flaherty and Richard L. Wood, *Faith and Public Life: Faith-Based Community Organizing and the Development of Congregations*, 2004, http://repository.unm.edu/bitstream/handle/1928/10664/faith%26Publiclife.pdf?sequence=1, 3.

[8] Benedict Anderson, *Imagined Communities: Reflections on the Origin and Spread of Nationalism* (London: Verso, 1983, 1991), 1–19.

[9] Charles Taylor, *A Secular Age* (Cambridge: Harvard University Press, 2007), 171.

[10] Ibid., 172.

[11] Leo Penta introduced this saying to me in a personal conversation. He thought it may go back to Saul Alinsky or possibly the Industrial Area Foundation. See the article by Marion Mohrlok, "*Die Politik Beginnt bei den Leuten! Organizing im Stile der Industrial Areas Foundation,*1996, http://www.foco.info/politik_beginnt_bei_den_leuten.htm.

[12] On the Industrial Area Foundation, see Edward T. Chambers, *Roots for Radicals: Organizing for Power, Action, and Justice* (New York: Continuum, 2003); on Ernesto Cortes, Industrial Area Foundation (IAF) and the particular IAF group, Communities Organized for Public Service (COPS), see Mary Beth Rogers, *Cold Anger: A Story of Faith and Power Politics* (Denton: University of North Texas Press, 1999), and Mark R. Warren, *Dry Bones Rattling: Community Building to Revitalize American Democracy* (Princeton, NJ: Princeton University Press, 2001); on the Gamaliel Foundation, see Dennis A. Jacobsen, *Doing Justice: Congregations and Community Organizing* (Minneapolis: Fortress Press, 2001); on Pacific Institute for Community Organization (PICO), see Richard L. Wood, *Faith in Action: Religion, Race, and Democratic Organizing in America* (Chicago: University of Chicago Press, 2002).

[13] This data can be found in Mark R. Warren and Richard L. Wood, *Faith-Based Community Organizing: The State of the Field*, http://comm-org.wisc.edu/papers2001/faith/faith.htm, Part III. This is estimated to be about 1 to 1.5 percent of all congregations in the country, which experts on civic participation in American history say is as good as any group has achieved numerically and being broad based.

[14] Wood, *Faith in Action*, 68.

[15] Warren and Wood, *Faith-Based Community Organizing*, I.

[16] See a late in life exchange between Myles Horton and Paulo Freire, *We Make the Road by Walking: Conversations on Education and Social Change* (Philadelphia: Temple University Press, 1990).

[17] Sanford D. Horwitt, *Let Them Call Me Rebel: Saul Alinsky, His Life and Legacy* (New York: Vintage, 1992), 246.

[18] *The Myles Horton Reader: Education for Social Change*, ed. Dale Jacobs (Knoxville: University of Tennessee Press, 2003), see 264–66.

[19] For descriptions of this shift as developed by Ernesto Cortes, see Mark R. Warren, *Dry Bones Rattling: Community Building to Revitalize American Democracy* (Princeton, NJ: Princeton University Press, 2001), chaps. 2, 4, 5, 7; and Rogers, *Cold Anger*. See Nicholas von Hoffman, *Radical: A Portrait of Saul Alinsky* (New York: Nation Books, 2010), 35–40, 164–67; see also Horwitt, *Let Them Call Me Rebel*, 545–48; Stout, *Blessed Are the Organized*, 36–38.

[20] Interview with Saul Alinsky, *Playboy Magazine*, 1972, http://www.progress.org/2003/alinsky9.htm, Eighth of Thirteen Parts, Success Versus Co-optation.

[21] My delineation here is indebted to Richard Wood's discussion in *Faith in Action*, 34–49, 164–71; he also includes the role of credentialing the leaders as religious in public gathering, which I have not treated here.

[22] Wood, *Faith in Action*, 104. These methods are discussed in a variety of sources. Jeffrey Stout gives special attention to accountability in his book *Blessed Are the Organized*.

[23] Saul Alinsky was a master of finding tactics that would provide a threat, but may not need to be employed because those in official positions back down before the tactical action takes place. The threat of an action may be as effective as the action itself.

[24] Saul D. Alinsky, *Reveille for Radicals* (New York: Vintage Books [1946], 1969), 132–33.

[25] Saul Alinsky, *Rules for Radicals*, 51.

[26] Economist Intelligence Unit, *Democracy Index 2010: Democracy in Decline* http://graphics.eiu.com/PDF/Democracy_Index_2010_web.pdf.

[27] Greg Galuzzo, Leadership Workshop on Community Organizing, October 16, 2010, St. Nicholas of Tolentine Church. For more about the approach taken by Galuzzo, see Dennis A. Jacobsen, *Doing Justice: Congregations and Community Organizing* (Minneapolis: Fortress Press, 2001).

[28] Edward T. Chambers with Michael A Cowan, *Roots for Radicals: Organizing for Power, Action, and Justice* (New York: Continuum, 2003), 28.

[29] Hannah Arendt, *The Human Condition* (Chicago: University of Chicago Press, 1998), 200.

[30] Bernard Loomer, "Two Conceptions of Power," originally appeared in *Process Studies* 6 (Spring 1976): 5–32.

[31] Citizenship includes the public arena where public officials, public decision makers, deliberate about economic policy, finances, military and security policy, heath care, education, housing, and environmental policy. Various groups of ordinary citizens are also involved through religious congregations and other organizations, such as unions and nonprofit organizations. Families and friends also are involved in civic life through their engagement with issues in the public arena.

[32] Wood, *Faith in Action*, 127.

[33] Ibid., 127.

[34] Stout comments on Michel Foucault's earlier analysis of power and raises a relevant question: "whether the agents of power highlighted in [the IAF] power analysis—namely, individuals, groups, and institutions—are the only sources of socially significant effects worthy of consideration, or even the most important one" (*Blessed Are the Organized*, 302, n.33). Foucault discovers two "anonymous sources of power: . . . The first is the array of propositions that people living in a given place at a given time are in a position to entertain, accept, or reject. The second is the array of possible social identities that people living in a given place at a given time can acquire, adopt, or attribute." These are not the result of intentional agents, personal, social, or institutional, but "simply . . . unintended by-products of earlier similar configurations of effects, interacting with historical contingencies without necessarily needing much direct help from intentional human agency." Stout believes that Foucault's contribution can supplement without contradicting the agency-oriented approach of community organizers. "Agents need not be disempowered by learning how they have been shaped by the vocabularies and identities lodged in their discursive and formative social practices. To the contrary, such knowledge can and should inform deliberate choices concerning which social practices to support, how to embed them in institutions, and how the norms and identities embodied in them should be revised." Nevertheless, Stout believes that Foucault is wrongly inclined to reduce domination to any form of power-over people, rather than "the defining trait of relationships in which one person or group is in a position to exercise power *arbitrarily* over others. . . . Exercising power over someone is not necessarily a bad thing, but domination is" (303, n.33). While this might be true, Stout concedes he has not explored the later works of Foucault that may nuance his earlier position, insights important in the work of Judith Butler and Giorgio Agamben.

[35] Interview with Alinsky, *Playboy Magazine*, Part Ten, After World War Two.

[36] Wood, *Faith in Action*, 127.

PART VI

EXCLUSION AND SACRAMENTAL PRACTICES

Ecclesiology, Exclusion, and Sacraments

Mary McClintock Fulkerson

In my Protestant experience, the Eucharist, or what we call "communion," has been explicitly open and welcoming. Although some denominations require baptism, I have not been aware of strong restrictions on access to the table. As a sacrament rooted in images of Jesus' radical hospitality, the Eucharist certainly has profound associations. In light of this kind of welcome, I want to explore a form of "exclusion" that is operative in most Protestant communion practice that calls this sacrament's profundity into question—an exclusion connected to serious forms of obliviousness. I will address first the growing attention given to the ritual and then offer my challenge.

The importance ascribed to the Eucharist—or "communion"—seems to be growing. Many Protestant churches in my area have shifted from celebrating once a month to every Sunday. Contemporary New Testament scholarship highlights the significance of Eucharist by recovering Jesus' patterns of table fellowship. With his commitment to "outsiders," Jesus' patterns disrupted the function of meals to mark off purity/impurity distinctions and social status. According to this scholarship, Paul writes of the function of the Lord's Supper to contest just such "rituals of division, practices set up to distinguish between insiders and outsiders, clean and unclean, honored and shamed."[1] Drawing upon John Dominic Crossan's reading of Jesus' practices, Catholic theologian Shawn Copeland says, "Jesus demanded of his hearers and disciples personal conversion and new body practices of solidarity. Chief among these practices was the inclusion of new and 'other' bodies at the table."[2] Homilitician Charles Campbell describes his own experience with homeless men as they sat around outside preparing to sleep in boxes one night. One of the men shared doughnuts, and Campbell says he realized immediately that they were sharing communion.

Jesus—now a black Jesus, a homeless Jesus, an oppressed Jesus—feeding the five thousand with a few loaves and fish. . . . And in that odd circle of strangers—rich and poor, black and white, housed and homeless—Jesus was present, and we shared food as equals. It was a joyful, thankful, Eucharistic celebration, a foretaste of that great banquet when all God's children will sit together at table in shalom.[3]

There are other examples of these alternatives to the nice sedate practice I experienced growing up Presbyterian,[4] but, in short, prominent themes for the Eucharist are "hospitality," the welcoming table, and table fellowship with outsiders, which we might understand to represent Christ's bodily presence.

Another way the significance of the Eucharist has increased is its enhanced role in Protestant ecclesiology. My colleague Geoffrey Wainwright invokes *"lex orandi, lex credendi"* to ground reflective theology in doxology.[5] After all, liturgical traditions greatly preceded creeds and a biblical canon. Some theologians now grant sacraments the center stage for what used to be called "ethics." In his book *Political Worship: Ethics for Christian Citizens*, Bernd Wannenwetsch claims that "[i]t is *in worship itself* that the ethical in-forming of human acting and judging comes about."[6] Eucharist is definitely not a secondary (or optional) ritual. Stanley Hauerwas puts it baldly: sacraments "are the essential rituals of our politics"; "liturgy *is* social action."[7]

The importance of such claims is heightened by the increasing focus on the embodied character of lived religion by religious studies scholars Robert Orsi and David Morgan and sociologist Paul Connerton.[8] These scholars' focus is on the affective, the visual, the aural in the formation of religious faith, *and* the function of bodily knowledge/communication. Such work represents a significant challenge to theology's overemphasis on ideas/beliefs. Although the theologians who valorize worship/rituals are not in conversation with materialist theories, the latter underscore such theologians' insistence that worship is the primary place for formation—we are ethically "in-formed" *in worship itself*—*such practices as communion shape our "acting and judging."* And, as materialist theories insist, our bodily perceptions are crucial to that ethical "in-forming."

So what *kind* of "social action" is being narrated and performed by this welcoming table fellowship; *how* are we being "formed?" Given the primary significance attributed to this practice, its affective formation certainly merits scrutiny over and above what the creeds and sermons purport. Bodies clearly matter, both epistemologically—ritual practice entails bodily knowledge and communication—and with respect to *which* bodies gather around the table. One obvious failure is in duplicating Jesus' meals with outsiders—Campbell's meal with the homeless is not a widespread practice. However, except for the doctrinal prescriptions in churches such as the Roman Catholic Church, most church patterns are not devised for *intentional* exclusion. Most churches understand themselves to be welcoming communities; a mantra for "inclusiveness" is found in many of their mission statements. Indeed, (white) churches have so "moved on" from one of our most egregious exclusions—our historic sins of slavery and racial segregation—that, like most (white) Americans, they claim to be "color-blind," intending to see all persons, regardless of color, as God's children.

However, this narrative merits more scrutiny. If Christ's presence has to do with bodies—his and ours as the "body of Christ"—perhaps the bodies at the table matter. A conspicuous American narrative is the view that we have resolved the injustices of racism. We are a "color-blind" society. "I don't see color, I just see people," as the saying goes. According to sociologists, a common claim by most whites is that "I treat [or view] people the same whether they are white, black, pink, or green."[9] Through color blindness, whites intend to proclaim that we are what Martin Luther King Jr. envisioned, a nation where his children would "not be judged by the color of their skin but by the content of their character."

Despite the popular theme of color blindness, change in the social, material, and embodied realities of race relations in the United States is less significant than King would have desired. As many sociologists insist, the mostly white habit of "not seeing" the realities of racism, both what we have inherited and new forms, dominates contemporary culture and, however well-intentioned, this "I don't see any" is, in reality, a fiction—what I will call "obliviousness."[10] Basically, this habit assumes that racism was "fixed" by legislation.[11] Widely documented "color blindness" assumes that any racism that does exist is a malicious racist act by or intention of an individual. As such, this "analysis" gets most of us whites "off the hook," for we do not have to acknowledge the structural/institutional complexities of racism that still exist.[12] As Andrew Hacker says, most white Americans say they are in favor of racial integration and equal opportunity, but "[w]hat has changed in recent years" is only "the way people speak in public," not living patterns.[13] Much of the violence of racism, then, occurs as obliviousness and denial in our culture.

Now we *could* say that church is different from that wider "secular" context due to our traditions of confession, sin, reconciliation, and so on. But is it? Or is this American color blindness narrative being performed by white Eucharistic habits? Color-blind welcome is the story of many churches. While our sacramental enactments of the body of Christ are framed with Jesus and other biblical narratives, in mainline white denominational churches the other bodies at the table are overwhelmingly white. Only 7 percent of American churches are significantly interracial—communities in which no more than 80 percent of the membership identifies as the same race.[14] Narrating this table as a place where all of God's people from all nations, all tongues, come to sing God's praises, the invoking of welcome and inclusion in the body of Christ is basically a *symbolic gesture* when it comes to those who are "other."

Now, some objections to my criticisms can be entertained: this color-blind inclusiveness is well intentioned. It can and will bear fruit when we whites go out into the world and work for racial justice. Furthermore, it would be wrong to make "multiracial" a requirement for the faithful church, something akin to a new form of "works righteousness." What about other forms of brokenness within white communities that need attention? And don't African American churches have good reasons for wanting to stay predominantly black?

Although all these issues deserve attention, I can only take on the first, the question of whether good intentions carry out into the world. Theologians' insistence that we are ethically formed in ritual practices pushes the following question: what kind of "knowledge formation" happens when we worship in "color-blind" (white) churches? According to the materialist theories, it matters that our bodily experience is primarily of bodies racially similar to our own—with class similarities as well. Sociologist Mark Chaves complicates the significance of bodily "knowledge" even more, insisting that we cannot assume congruence between religious beliefs and values.[15] In short, typically there is not consistency between our beliefs and our practices. Rather than congruence—where beliefs take the form of a "logically connected, integrated network," or "religious and other practices and actions follow directly from those beliefs and values," or beliefs expressed in such contexts as religious space "are consistently held and chronically accessible across contexts, situations, and life domains"—there is a "ubiquity of religious incongruence."[16] As Chaves puts it, "what happens in Las Vegas, stays in Las Vegas"—that is, what happens in church, stays in church. While Chaves's primary audience is sociologists of religion who continue to mistakenly assume these congruencies, his critique also has implications for theologians. We cannot assume that the commitments to welcome the "other" as proclaimed in liturgies will travel outside of the church space and be enacted in the welcoming of strangers.

So if the sacraments are central to the faith, not simply optional rituals that are secondary to real ethics in "the world," and if, as Hauerwas claims, "liturgy *is* social action" (emphasis mine), and if worship is "the happening which shapes practical knowledge,"[17] it may be that our social action is essentially to simply say good things about caring for the "other" as we continue to be with people like ourselves.

However we want to interpret this, the focus on liturgy as formative requires attention to bodily proprieties, communications, and habituations. The harsh interpretation would say that predominantly white churches are doing bodily rituals or performances of the dominance of whiteness as our "social action." What these rituals do *not* do is challenge the larger culture, and while its racial imaginary is changing, it is nevertheless still dominated by stereotypes of African Americans (for example, welfare queens, gang members, and so on) and the narratives that typically frame media messages. Because whites still rarely have sustained relationships with a significant number of persons of color of equal status, media images continue to impact the white imagination. Even a black president counts as "an exception."[18]

What we cannot do is pretend that bodily knowledge/communication does not matter. Our practical knowledge, a knowledge that is never simply cognitive/reflective, is typically formed by ecclesial relations with others who are racially like us (and, typically, of the same class.).[19] Chaves's account has, therefore, an important implication, namely, that statements made and sentiments preached about those different from ourselves do *not* automatically travel outside church space. Chaves says that what is most likely to influence what is taken outside of worship is first of all, an intensely purposeful focus on enacting belief, especially authoritarian versions of what Christians must believe. No surprise there. The second condition for congruence between belief and practice heightens the significance of our bodily habituations. It is our prereflective, deeply habituated practices that also "carry" outside of that sacred space.[20] So whatever else ritual shapes as a bodily practice, in most white churches it most likely habituates us into continuing to associate the sacred liturgy with bodies like our own or to be most comfortable with other whites. Thus, it is the habit of segregating cultural space that most likely travels outside sacred space. At the very least, it is not challenged.[21]

So what constructive outcomes might come from the Eucharist? Such issues are much too complicated to take on here. And I am only speaking of middle- and upper-class white communities, not taking up the complexities of poor whites, black churches, and other ethnicities. However, based upon my initial explorations of attempts to dismantle racism as well as literature on whiteness, my sense is that the symbols, narratives, and the means and ends of the Lord's Supper could be deeply significant for real alternatives to color blindness and the avoidance strategies that fail to address forms of privilege. The high level ecclesial rhetoric of churches *should* make faith communities different from the color-blind "secular" culture. I close with two such resources from our traditions: (1) ecclesial relations and (2) ecclesial memory.

First, ecclesial relations: loving your neighbor as yourself, traditions of hospitality, prophetic justice, confession, eschatological hope—these traditions should compel honest acknowledgement and self-scrutiny by whites. The alternatives are not simple "inclusion" or assimilation; the residuals of racism must be named and addressed, not continually denied or overlooked. Race is not simply about people of color. The privilege of whiteness (class) has to be surfaced, acknowledged, and explored in ecclesial terms of social sin. Redemptive alteration merits face-to-face community, relationships that are ongoing and honor the *imago Dei* of all, and call for honesty and confession. This must be a safe space for whites to be able to acknowledge that race remains an issue that matters, that whiteness still functions to grant privilege, that historically whites have played a role in racial injustice, and that today that role continues. It must also be a space for persons of color to be honest, to be other than victims—a space where resilience is valued and new wisdom can be gained by all. We need alternatives to victims vs. oppressors. Ecclesial traditions are ripe for nurturing spaces for such relations to develop.

Bodies matter for the body of Christ, including which bodies are at the meal whose end is radical hospitality. But we need the second resource as well: what it means for the body of Christ to "remember Jesus." Johann Baptist Metz's view on the remembering that is central to Eucharist is compelling. It must function as "dangerous memory," not simply as reiteration of Bible passages. To treat the *memoria passionis, mortis, et resurrecitonis Jesu Christi* as "the paradigm" of ecclesial dangerous memory is not to romanticize the past, or to simply reproduce the church as an institution, but to connect us with "the world's suffering and the demand to do something about it."[22] As Shawn Copeland argues, "*anamnesis*—the intentional remembering of the dead, exploited, despised victims of history" is crucial to the Eucharist, and black bodies are a signal.[23] Eucharistic memory must reflect the insight of Truth and Reconciliation movements, namely, the imperative that societies recover memory of trauma/social injustice—both social and individual. As Martha Minow expresses it, "The failure to remember, collectively, triumphs and accomplishments diminishes us. But failure to remember, collectively, injustice and cruelty is an ethical breach. It implies no responsibility and no commitment to prevent inhumanity in the future. Even worse, failures of collective memory stoke fires of resentment and revenge."[24] Whites need to acknowledge our role in the historical and ongoing situations of racial injustice, and we need to understand what that role has to do with white privilege, not only the malicious racist acts that we typically disavow. Ecclesial traditions, Eucharistic narratives, invite us to move ahead in new ways.

In closing, I do not mean to suggest that the "fix" is to force interracial churches just so I can share communion with more bodies of color. That is obviously simplistic and could function as avoidance (there is much literature on multiracial churches that avoid the power dynamics).[25] I am raising the epistemological issue of bodies for all ecclesiology and the face-to-face ecclesial practices ecclesiology entails. Bodies are racialized, classed, sexualized, and gendered—all of which occur as social habituations that come with deeply embedded markers of power and "lessness." The Eucharist and its best narratives represent a ritual that should—must—foreground these issues for further discussion and action. We cannot continue to be oblivious of the kind of homogeneous communities too many churches continue to reproduce.

Notes

[1] Stanley P. Saunders and Charles L. Campbell, *The Word on the Street: Performing the Scriptures in the Urban Context* (Grand Rapids: Eerdmans, 2000), 51.

[2] M. Shawn Copeland, *Enfleshing Freedom: Body, Race, and Being* (Minneapolis: Fortress Press, 2010), 61f. See also John Dominic Crossan, *Jesus: A Revolutionary Biography* (New York: Harper & Row, 1994).

[3] Saunders and Campbell, *Word on the Street*, 39.

[4] See Sara Miles, *Take This Bread: A Radical Conversion* (New York: Ballantine Books, 2007).

[5] Geoffrey Wainwright, *Doxology: The Praise of God in Worship, Doctrine, and Life: A Systematic Theology* (New York: Oxford University Press, 1980).

[6] Bernd Wannenwetsch, *Political Worship: Ethics for Christian Citizens*, trans. Margaret Kohl (Oxford: Oxford University Press, 2004), 6.

[7] Stanley Hauerwas, *The Peaceable Kingdom: A Primer in Christian Ethics* (Notre Dame, IN: University of Notre Dame Press, 1983), 108.

[8] Manuel A. Vásquez's recent book exemplifies this shift, *More Than Belief: A Materialist Theory of Religion* (New York: Oxford University Press, 2011).

[9] Joe Feagin and Eileen O'Brien, *White Men on Race: Power, Privilege, and the Shaping of Cultural Consciousness* (Boston: Beacon Press, 2003), 17.

[10] Donald R. Kinder and David O. Sears, "Prejudice and Politics: Symbolic Racism versus Racial Threats to the Good Life," *Journal of Personality and Social Psychology* 40 (1981): 414–31; Eduardo Bonilla-Silva, *Racism without Racists: Color-Blind Racism and the Persistence of Racial Inequality in the United States*, 2nd ed. (Lanham, MD: Rowman & Littlefield, 2006; 2010).

[11] See Leslie G. Carr, *"Colorblind" Racism* (Thousand Oaks, CA: Sage, 1997), ix–x.

[12] Feagin and O'Brien, *White Men on Race*, 30–65.

[13] Andrew Hacker, *Two Nations: Black and White, Separate, Hostile, Unequal* (New York: Scribner, 2003), 52.

[14] Michael Emerson, e-mail message to author, October 23, 2001. See also Michael O. Emerson and Christian Smith, *Divided by Faith: Evangelical Religion and the Problem of Race in America* (New York: Oxford University Press, 2000), 10.

[15] Mark Chaves, "SSSR Presidential Address: Rain Dances in the Dry Season: Overcoming the Religious Congruence Fallacy," *Journal for the Scientific Study of Religion* 49 (2010): 1–14.

[16] Chaves, "Rain Dances in the Dry Season," 2.

[17] Wannenwetsch, *Political Worship*, 21.

[18] See Robert M. Entman and Andrew Rojecki, *The Black Image in the White Mind: Media and Race in America* (Chicago: University of Chicago Press, 2000).

[19] Gender, sexual orientation, and other markers of difference matter, but to use one significant historic marker of difference for the United States is to make a broader theological point.

[20] Chaves, "Rain Dances in the Dry Season," 7f. I am expanding Chaves's claim of what gets internalized as an automatic response, but I think it fits.

[21] For white bodily proprieties as "white ownership of space," see my *Places of Redemption: Theology for a Worldly Church* (Oxford: Oxford University Press, 2007), 42–52.

[22] Johann Baptist Metz, *Faith in History and Society: Toward a Practical Fundamental Theology,* trans. J. Matthew Ashley, with Study Guide (New York: Crossroad, [1992] 2007), 18–19.

[23] Copeland, *Enfleshing Freedom*, 100.

[24] Martha Minow, "Memory and Hate: Are There Lessons from around the World?" *Breaking the Cycles of Hatred: Memory, Law, and Repair*, ed. Martha Minow (Princeton, NJ: Princeton University Press, 2002).

[25] A recent example is Korie L. Edwards, *The Elusive Dream: The Power of Race in Interracial Churches* (Oxford: Oxford University Press, 2008).

Whose Exclusion?
Which Inclusion?

Barry Harvey

The question that has bounced around my head since I was first told of the topic of ecclesiology and exclusion is whose exclusion, which inclusion? Is exclusion *always* a bad thing? Should all things and everybody be included? Excluded from or included in what? I doubt that there exists a social group of any consequence that, whether explicitly or implicitly, does not exclude some people, prohibit some forms of conduct, or rule out of bounds some ideas and ideologies (there are few people more dogmatic than an antidogmatist). If everything and everyone is included, if nothing and nobody is excluded, what if anything is really at stake? If there is something at stake, what is it? To repeat, then, whose exclusion, which inclusion?

What if it were the case that a church that does not possess a certain kind of exclusivity could not act as an agent of divine transformation? In other words, what if the church needed to cultivate a kind of exclusivity, not for its own sake, but for the sake of a greater inclusivity? My thesis is that to affirm the notion that the church is a sacrament of Christ requires a certain, very specific type of distinction or separation from the world, not to maintain an imagined moral or intellectual purity in contrast to the great unwashed mob that might infect us with some sort of contagion, but precisely for the sake of the world, as that place created by God where we live, move, and have our being, and as that damaged in all sorts of ways yet still cherished by its creator.

The sort of separation to which I refer is not necessarily spatial (though at times it might demand that), nor is it in any case a disengagement with the world. In a very real sense disengagement from the world is not an option; even the Old Order Amish engage "the world" in all sorts of ways. I mention the Amish, descended from the sixteenth-century Anabaptists, because they are commonly described as having "withdrawn" from the world and thus represent either a mere curiosity or an enthusiastic anachronism existing into the present on false pretenses. What few "English" (as we are called by the Amish) seem willing to consider is that their community might just be a gift of divine grace in all sorts of ways that we ignore to our own peril.

Before I unpack my thesis, however, allow me to give a little personal background. By serendipity of parentage and upbringing I belong to the ecclesial community called Baptists, who first appeared on the scene in seventeenth-century England. Baptism, and specifically infant baptism, formed the ground of contention between my forebears and the Church of England because they recognized that "Baptism was the sacrament that set the boundary situating and giving proper significance to all bodies— individual, communal, political."[1] What this suggests, first, is that the significance of bodies is not self-evident. One often hears allusions to Paul's comments in his letter to the churches in Galatia that in Christ there is no longer Jew or Greek, slave or free, male and female. What is usually not noted is that this affirmation is part of a baptismal confession that implies that prior to baptism, these categories do indeed apply: "[I]n Christ Jesus you are all children of God through faith. As many of you as were baptized into Christ have clothed yourselves with Christ. There is no longer Jew or Greek, there is no longer slave or free, there is no longer male and female; for all of you are one in Christ Jesus" (Gal 3:26–28).

This is not a statement of radical egalitarianism, which would have made no sense in its first century setting, but a matter of divine grace, setting aside one set of social identities mandated by dominant power in the form of family, tribe, nation, empire, and race, and the conferral of a new identity, which conveys new roles to play within the *politeia*, the *res publica* of Christ. This is a matter of no little importance, for as the issue of migration brings to our attention, it makes a great deal of difference whether we describe a particular body as an "illegal alien" or as a sister or brother, or potential sister or brother, in Christ.

To be sure, Baptists were neither the first nor the last group to recognize the political function of baptism. Albert Raboteau, in his classic book *Slave Religion: The "Invisible Institution" in the Antebellum South*, notes that one of the primary reasons plantation owners did not want their slaves to be instructed in the Christian faith "was the fear that baptism would emancipate their slaves."[2] And Dorothy Day acknowledged a dual significance of baptism, first, when she realized, though thankfully only after the fact, that the baptism of her daughter into the mystical body of Christ denoted a real separation from her, and secondly, that baptism is a sign not only for those who are members of that body but also a reminder that all human beings are potential members.[3]

Baptism, when performed as an ecclesial rite, supersedes (and may very well undermine) all other markers of identity and, in particular, those of tribe and language and people and nation. The early Baptists thus sought to exclude themselves from a very inclusive church, arguing as Thomas More had a century earlier, that the king has no authority over the church and thus no authority over the conscience. In their own ways, Raboteau, Day, and early Baptists understand that this sacrament relativizes all other social expressions of identity, thus constituting what might be called "baptismal anarchism."[4]

What infant baptism accomplished in seventeenth-century England, by contrast, was to bring everyone "by the lump," as one Baptist of the time colorfully described it,[5] into the Church of England. Such a baptism effectively transvalued the sacramental rite into an instrument of control of the British crown, which conferred a very different identity on bodies. All of the colonial powers of Europe, not just England, recognized the social and political significance of baptism as a principal means to bring alien bodies under the control of their laws, especially those relating to labor and property. The history of colonialism reminds us that exclusion and inclusion are not simple, mutually exclusive categories but rather concepts that interpenetrate each other at many different levels. There is no exclusion that does not presuppose a prior inclusion at some point.

We should, of course, distinguish between inter- and intracommunal exclusions and inclusions. In what follows, I shall focus primarily on intercommunal relations, but I do want to offer a word or two about the other. Perhaps because these are "family" fights, intracommunal exclusions lend themselves to inflamed passions and inflated rhetoric, resulting in all sorts of suspect analogies (how many times have the parties in a moral dispute compared their adversaries to the Nazis) and rigid dichotomies that vilify some and valorize others. One need not look further than the debate over same-sex marriages to witness these social dynamics.

I have no standing to critique, either positively or negatively, the intramural debates within the Roman Catholic Church, not because there is nothing at stake for me in them (indeed, I think I shall be impacted greatly no matter how things progress), but because we lack a meaningful institutional framework within which I as a Protestant might engage in them. Instead I shall mention once more the Amish, in particular, the community located at Nickel Mines, Pennsylvania. If that name sounds familiar to you, it should, for there in the autumn of 2006 the world learned what costly grace and forgiveness actually involve. A deranged man charged into an Amish school and shot ten young girls, five of whom died of their wounds. To the surprise of most of the world, the members of that community did not react in anger or call for vengeance but reached out in the midst of their grief and mourning to forgive the perpetrator and embrace his family in their shock and disgrace. Central to Amish life is a rigorous discipline that involves a form of exclusion called shunning, which they do, again, for the sake of the identity and integrity of their way of life. Without validating everything about Amish life, would the witness they offered in the aftermath of that horrible day, which in many ways may have shocked the world more than the atrocity that provided the occasion for their astounding display of forgiveness, have been possible without the communal integrity provided by their discipline for which the practice of shunning is a key element?[6]

With respect to the interactions between inclusion and exclusion in the relationship between the church and all that is not church (I put the contrast this way because the church by its very nature as a sacrament is an engagement with the world of which it is inextricably a part), we can fairly easily eliminate the extremes, but after that, the going gets difficult. Surely most would agree that the world is not evil, nor would many think that grace is a commodity or service for which the church is the exclusive vendor. At the same time, I hope that not many would say that every aspect of the world participates to the same manner or degree in grace, for that would reduce the divine presence to something like "a hydraulic apparatus, with its allotted equal weight on each square inch."[7] In like manner, virtually all Christians would agree that the church exists not for itself but for the world, for others. But if the church has nothing distinctive to offer, if, on the basis of a doctrine of creation or incarnation or pneumatology or the sacraments, it posits a close fit between its life, thought, and worship and an abstract conception of "the world" or "human culture," then it is in danger of sounding like the campaign of the 1940 Republican presidential candidate, Wendell Willkie, who was essentially reduced to promising that he would run the New Deal better than Franklin Roosevelt did.

I am especially persuaded that we are in need of a better understanding of how dominant power works if we are to make progress on the question of exclusion and inclusion. Anthropologist Talal Asad contends that such power does not always suppress or exclude differences, in order to impose the unity of its governance, or that it always shies away from ambiguity. He writes, "To secure its unity—to make its own history—dominant power has worked best through differentiating and classifying practices." He cites, in particular, India's colonial history as evidence, stating that in that setting, one can clearly see that power is constructive, not repressive, working largely through mechanisms of inclusion. The ability of dominant power to distinguish and classify differences in ways that will serve its ends and interests depends on exploiting both the dangers and the opportunities that present themselves in ambiguous situations. Indeed, says Asad, ambiguity is one of the factors that gives dominant power its immense improvisational quality.[8]

Asad contends, in particular, that the concepts of culture and religion, so often simply taken for granted by theologians and other theorists, were key elements "of a language of controlled reconstruction . . . according to the dictates of liberal reason" ("liberal" here used to describe modern democratic polity as initially articulated by John Locke). Its aim was to identify, study, and normalize the traditions and *mores* of subject peoples for the purpose of integrating them into modern (in other words, Western) civilization by way of "amalgamation" and "persuasion." Talk of an "amalgam," says Asad, implies the myth of original, "pure" cultures coming into contact with each other to create a new, emergent, and more progressive historical identity. The dynamics of this mode of social reconstruction involves the proper theoretical and practical coordination of dominant (meaning, North American and European) and subordinate (native) cultures. On the one hand, there is to be equal respect and tolerance for all ("multiculturalism"), but, on the other, the realities of political and economic power require the subordinate, who is less "progressive," to adjust to the dominant and more progressive culture.[9] Recent assertions, both in academic publications and the popular press, for example, that the Islamic world needs its own "Renaissance," only serve to reinforce Asad's observations, as, once again, European life and thought establish the baseline for what constitutes a genuinely civilized or cultured form of life.

Put simply, every act of inclusion comes with a price, or more precisely, a tacit or explicit set of terms. In his book *Beyond Anthropology*, Bernard McGrane contends that Europeans and North Americans have changed the way they describe and interpret non-Western peoples. They are no longer demonized as pagans, or described derisively as primitive and superstitious, or relegated to an earlier step in the process of social evolution, surviving, as Zygmunt Bauman puts it, into the present on false pretenses and ultimately doomed to extinction.[10] The dominant paradigm has become "culture." According to McGrane, "We think under the hegemony of the ethnological response to the alienness of the Other; we are, today, contained within an anthropological concept of the Other. Anthropology has become our modern way of seeing the Other as, *fundamentally and merely*, culturally different."[11] In a word, difference has been "democratized" such that the non-European other is no longer a relic of another time. The radical democratization of difference permits us to make space for the other into "our" present, to welcome her or him as "our" contemporary but always, of course, on "our" terms: "The non-European 'other' is still 'different' of course, but now (s)he is *merely* 'different.'"[12] Or as Slavoj Žižek puts it, the concept of culture names "all those things we practice without really believing in them, without 'taking them seriously.'"[13]

In like manner, classical democratic liberalism invents the category of the "religious" and juxtaposes it to the "secular," the former being irrational and therefore dangerous, and, thus, if it cannot be eradicated, it must be constantly reined in by "rational," that is, secular power. Delimiting the human condition in this manner establishes the other as those who are essentially irrational, fanatical, and violent, which in turn authorizes coercive measures against them. In our time, says William Cavanaugh, "the Muslim world especially plays the role of religious Other. *They* have not yet learned to remove the dangerous influence of religion from political life. *Their* violence is therefore irrational and fanatical. *Our* violence, by contrast, is rational and peacemaking, and sometimes regrettably necessary to contain *their* violence."[14] The not-so-subtle message is that the only good religion is one in which everyone acts like good cultural Protestants, that is, as those who do not take their religion seriously (John F. Kennedy comes to mind here). And, thus, we see Muslims all over the United States scrambling to prove to their neighbors that they really are no different than the Presbyterians or Methodists down the street, who, in turn, are really no different than their nonreligious neighbors.

I shall conclude by returning to my initial thesis, whether it might be the case that, for the sake of a greater inclusivity, the church needs to practice a kind of exclusion. Rowan Williams has argued that the church, as the cruciform sacrament of the reign of God, properly exists at an angle to the forms of human association that dominant power would have us treat as givens: family, language, territorial state, people, culture, nation, and civilization.[15] He contends that the extent to which the church ceases to cultivate its own distinctive communal life, which requires that adult men and women commit themselves to a shared form of life that they did not design, the more it will be assimilated into the forms of inclusion configured by dominant power.

Williams points out that many of the theological rationales for talking about our engagement with the world—for example, the doctrines of creation, incarnation, pneumatology, and the sacraments (which in themselves are good things)—are frequently carried out with a marked degree of abstraction from the actual story of God incarnate. There is a specific shape to the life, death, and resurrection of Jesus, says Williams, narrated in a story that is marked time and again by conflict, discontinuity, and costly separation: "The gospels make it harshly clear that belonging with Jesus upsets other kinds of belonging—of family, of status, even of membership of the children of Abraham." In other words, Christian forms of sociality, as depicted in scripture and continuing into the early centuries of the church, stand over against other kinds, with little sense that they disclose the true nature or rationale of these other forms. The "society of the Church in its origins creates considerable tension with the society around because it will not take for granted . . . the finality and authority of the socially prevailing accounts of status and power."[16]

At times the severity of the angle lessens, and the opportunities for collaborative action in pursuit of shared goods, thankfully, become numerous and substantial; at other times it will, regrettably, become more acute. The Archbishop of Canterbury concludes, in terms that he acknowledges are heavily loaded, by insisting that "a church which does not at least possess certain features of a 'sect' cannot act as an agent of transformation." Beginning with baptism the church must, therefore, keep before it its distinctiveness and separateness, not from the human race as such, but from all societies and kinships, the limits of which fall short of the human race.[17] Here is a form of exclusion practiced for the sake of a larger, more truthful inclusion.

Notes

[1] Philip E. Thompson, "Religious Liberty, Sacraments, God Image, and the State in Two Periods in Baptist Life and Thought" (unpublished paper presented to the Forty-Sixth Annual Convention of the College Theological Society, Philadelphia, PA, June 4, 2000), 15.

[2] Albert Raboteau, *Slave Religion: The "Invisible Institution" in the Antebellum South* (New York: Oxford University Press, 1978), 98.

[3] Dorothy Day, *The Long Loneliness: The Autobiography of Dorothy Day* (New York: Harper & Row, 1952), 139, 144; Dorothy Day, *Dorothy Day: Writings from Commonweal* (Collegeville, MN: Liturgical Press, 2002), 151.

[4] Thompson, "Religious Liberty," 14.

[5] Thomas Grantham, *The Prisoner against the Prelate, or A Dialogue Between the Common Goal [sic] and Cathedral of Lincoln, Wherein the True Faith and Church of Christ Are Briefly Discovered and Vindicated by Authority of Scripture, Suffrages of Antiquity, Concessions and Confessions of the Chief Oppressors of the Same Church and Faith*, cited by Thompson, "Religious Liberty," 15.

[6] To those wishing to gain further insight into this tragedy in particular, or the Amish in general, I recommend Donald B. Kraybill, Steven M. Nolt, and David L. Weaver-Zercher, *Amish Grace: How Forgiveness Transcended Tragedy* (San Francisco: John Wiley & Sons, 2007).

[7] Hugh Ross Mackintosh, *Types of Modern Theology: Schleiermacher to Barth* (London: Collins, 1964), 85.

[8] Talal Asad, *Genealogies of Religion: Discipline and Reasons of Power in Christianity and Islam* (Baltimore: Johns Hopkins University Press, 1993), 17.

[9] Asad, *Genealogies*, 248–53.

[10] Zygmunt Bauman, *Postmodern Ethics* (Cambridge, MA: Blackwell, 1993), 39.

[11] Bernard McGrane, *Beyond Anthropology: Society and the Other* (New York: Columbia University Press, 1989), x.

[12] Kenneth Surin, "A Certain 'Politics of Speech': 'Religious Pluralism' in the Age of the McDonald's Hamburger," *Modern Theology* 7 (October 1990): 74, author's emphasis.

[13] Slavoj Žižek, *The Puppet and the Dwarf: The Perverse Core of Christianity* (Cambridge, MA: MIT Press, 2003), 7–8.

[14] William T. Cavanaugh, "Sins of Omission: What 'Religion and Violence' Arguments Ignore," *Hedgehog Review* 6 (Spring 2004): 35, author's emphasis.

[15] Rowan Williams, *On Christian Theology* (Malden, MA: Blackwell, 2000), 235.

[16] Ibid., 229, 284–85.

[17] Ibid., 233, 284–85.

A Case of Ecclesial Exclusion: Eucharistic Sharing

Susan K. Wood

The pain is real; the embarrassment is profound; the experience of exclusion is wrenching. To be denied at table is to be cut off from the sustenance of life. The symbol of rejection around the Eucharistic table awakens primordial emotions associated with starvation. Such emotions are appropriate because they accurately reflect the meaning of communion and the high cost of ecclesial disunity.

The Eucharist as celebrated within a concrete community is a sign of that community's unity in faith, worship, and community life. In addition to being a sign of unity, the Eucharist is also a means for achieving unity and building up the community. Thus, the Eucharist is not only the presence of the risen Christ among us and our union with him as individuals and as faith communities; it is also inseparably linked to the expression of ecclesial community. Sometimes in our concern to emphasize the presence of Christ with us in the Eucharist, as well as in our individual communing with him in the sacrament, we miss its ecclesial meaning.

In the *Directory for the Application of Principles and Norms on Ecumenism* (1993) issued by the Pontifical Council for Promoting Christian Unity, two principles that relate to Eucharistic sharing and exclusion are held in tension. First, a sacrament's celebration in a concrete community is "the sign of the reality of its unity in faith, worship, and community life." However, in addition, "sacraments—most specially the Eucharist—are sources of the unity of the Christian community and of spiritual life, and are means for building them up."[1] This means that Eucharistic communion is inseparably linked to full, ecclesial communion and its visible expression. According to this principle, Eucharistic sharing between two ecclesial traditions not in full, ecclesial communion would be excluded. This is why the Catholic Church ordinarily permits access to its Eucharistic communion, penance, and anointing of the sick only to those who share in its oneness in faith, worship, and ecclesial life.

The Catholic Church also teaches, however, that members of other churches and ecclesial communities are brought into a real, even if imperfect, communion with the Catholic Church by baptism and that "baptism, which constitutes the sacramental bond of unity existing among all who through it are reborn . . . is wholly directed toward the acquiring of fullness of life in Christ."[2] The Eucharist helps the baptized to overcome sin, to live the very life of Christ, and to be incorporated more profoundly into Christ and the church.[3] This principle would seem to recommend sacramental sharing on the basis of a common baptism and imperfect ecclesial communion. This is why the Catholic Church "recognizes that in certain circumstances by way of exception, and under certain conditions, access to these sacraments may be permitted, or even commended, for Christians of other churches and ecclesial communities."[4]

To summarize the two tensions, an understanding of the Eucharist as simultaneously both a sign of unity and a means of unity constitutes the first tension. Further, there exists a second tension between a shared baptism that is oriented to the Eucharist and the inability of churches acknowledging a common baptism to share in the one Eucharist.

The contemporary distress over a lack of unity at the Eucharistic table is a sign of ecumenical progress. The 1917 Code of Canon Law outlawed the administration of sacraments to non-Catholics: "It is forbidden that the sacraments of the church be administered to heretics and schismatics even if they ask for them and are in good faith, unless beforehand, rejecting their errors, they are reconciled with the Church" (can. 731, para. 2). Nor was it licit "for the faithful actively to assist, that is, to take part in 'sacred functions' of non-Catholics" (can. 1258). Only a passive or purely material presence was tolerated. According to canon 2316, anyone who "communicates in divinis with heretics against the prescription of canon 1258 is automatically suspect of heresy."[5] In 1960, at the first plenary meeting of the Secretariat for Christian Unity, the first ecumenical dilemma discussed was whether a Catholic could licitly recite the Lord's Prayer together with a Protestant.[6]

During and after Vatican II, of course, much progress has been made. Even though the Council articulated the twofold tension described earlier, saying that while the lack of unity generally forbids common worship, still the grace to be obtained sometimes commends it, it left concrete practices to the prudent decisions of the local episcopal authority unless the bishops' conference has determined otherwise (*Unitatis Redintegratio*, §8). As for the liturgical actions of our separated Christian brothers and sisters, it affirmed that "these liturgical actions most certainly can truly engender a life of grace and . . . are capable of giving access to that communion in which is salvation" (*Unitatis Redintegratio*, §7). The *Catechism of the Catholic Church* (1994), unfortunately, steps back from affirming such a causal relationship between these liturgical actions and salvific grace, and refers only to the sign value of these actions, saying they "profess that it [the Holy Supper] signifies life in communion with Christ."[7]

The Secretariat for the Promotion of Christian Unity[8] gave four conditions for a separated Christian to receive the Eucharist from a Catholic minister if the danger of death is present or some other grave necessity urges it:[9]

> The person be unable to have recourse for the sacrament desired to a minister of his or her own Church or ecclesial community;
> Ask for the sacrament of his or her own initiative;
> Manifest Catholic faith in this sacrament;
> Be properly disposed.[10]

Subsequent papal teaching essentially repeats these conditions but with no reference to accessibility to one's own minister. For example, John Paul II says,

> It is a source of joy to note that Catholic ministers are able, in particular cases, to administer the sacraments of the Eucharist, Penance, and Anointing of the Sick to Christians who are not in full communion with the Catholic church, but who greatly desire to receive these sacraments, freely request them, and manifest the faith which the Catholic church professes with regard to these sacraments.[11]

He repeats these words verbatim in *Ecclesia de Eucharistia*.[12] Catholics, on the other hand, are permitted to receive penance, Eucharist, and anointing of the sick "whenever necessity requires it or true spiritual advantage suggests it," from non-Catholic ministers in whose churches these sacraments are valid if error or indifferentism is avoided and they are physically or morally unable to approach a Catholic minister.[13] This would allow communion, for example, with the Orthodox, the Assyrian Church of the East, and the Polish National Catholic Church, although the disciplines of these churches may not permit it.

The Catholic Church does not permit Catholics to share the Eucharist with ecclesial communities derived from the Reformation and separated from the Catholic Church because they "have not preserved the proper reality of the Eucharistic mystery in its fullness, especially because of the absence of the sacrament of Holy Orders."[14]

Observations

A few observations are now in order with respect to the following difficulties: too little attention given to the ecclesial meaning of the Eucharist, the interpretation of "grave necessity" and nonaccess to one's own church, the challenge of mixed marriages, and the problem of reciprocity. These are areas requiring further theological development in order to manage better the inherent tensions posed by the problem of Eucharistic sharing.

An Undue Emphasis on Individual Spirituality Rather Than Ecclesial Meaning

A primary and central difficulty arises from an overemphasis on the individual spirituality surrounding the Eucharist at the expense of its ecclesial meaning. The Eucharist represents not only the presence of Christ under the species of bread and wine but also the unity of the baptized in the body of Christ and the communion of churches. Admission or nonadmission to the Eucharist is not only a statement about the presence or absence of grace or of incorporation into the dead and risen body of Christ; it is also a statement about the relationships between and among ecclesial communities.

These relationships, however, are not usually experienced in the pain occasioned by the absence of Eucharistic hospitality between our churches. Even though we are baptized into specific concrete faith communities, our experience of the Eucharist is not usually one of asking to be admitted to communion with another local community because we have lost the ecclesial meaning of the Eucharist. In contemporary theology and practice, our sense of universal communion in Christ generally eclipses our sense of the relationship between Eucharistic communions. The pain of exclusion at the Eucharistic table serves as a helpful reminder that Eucharistic communion creates a relationship both with Christ and the church, and that much work remains to be done to achieve full ecclesial communion.

The Meaning of "Grave Necessity" and the Issue of Nonaccess

What constitutes "grave necessity," aside from the danger of death, needs clarification.[15] The Latin is "*alia urgeat gravis necessitas.*" A more grammatically precise translation reads, "If there is danger of death or in the judgment of the diocesan bishop or the conference of bishops, another grave need would urge it."[16]

Nonaccess includes both physical and moral forms. Physical nonaccess, mentioned in the 1972 instruction, is defined as living in an area in which one does not have access to one's own minister. In other words, those who lack access are those who live day and night in a residence of any kind where they do not have regular access to their own minister.

The current interpretation of physical nonaccess is that the non-Catholics do not have access to a church of their own denomination. However, many non-Catholics identify their church first as a local congregation and then as a denomination. The issue for Lutherans, for example, is frequently not whether there is an Evangelical Lutheran Church in America in town but whether they have access to Good Shepherd Church. The principle of discernment should be that the Protestant, not the Catholic, determines whether he or she has access to what he or she identifies as "my church."

Moral inaccessibility, although mentioned in the code, has not been broadly explored in the literature on Eucharistic sharing. The principle refers to subjective reasons why a Christian may not have access to his or her own minister. One example given in a commentary on canon law is extreme inconvenience.[17] However, a spiritual condition may also be sufficient to establish moral impossibility to have access to one's minister.[18] A number of situations in the literature on interchurch marriages may apply to this category.[19] For example, the strain on a marriage separated at the Eucharistic table may become intolerable. The Canadian Conference of Catholic Bishops' Commission for Ecumenism recommended to the bishops of Canada as a case of grave need an Anglican or Protestant party in a mixed marriage who has a serious spiritual need for the Eucharist. In this instance, the commission recommended that such a person be allowed to receive communion on special occasions, "such as principal anniversaries, funeral of family members, on Christmas and Easter if the family attends Mass together, and other occasions of ecclesial or familiar significance."[20]

The restriction of Eucharistic sharing to times of inaccessibility can have a positive dimension. Huels points out that the requirement for Eucharistic sharing that other Christians be unable to go to a minister of their own community is ecumenically sensitive. It avoids the impression of proselytism by the Catholic Church. It also takes seriously the fact that God's grace operates through sacraments that the Catholic Church judges to be "invalid":

> If the Protestant sacraments were inefficacious, it would be immoral for the Catholic minister to refuse the request of a Protestant for a sacrament in danger of death when his or her minister is available. Yet, the requirement of canon 844, §4, that the non-Catholic be unable to approach a minister of his or her own community, applies even if the person is in danger of death. On the basis of this requirement, one can only conclude that the Catholic Church implicitly considers the sacraments of ecclesial communities to be effective in preparing the

dying person for eternal life, and thus not devoid of sanctifying grace.[21]

The Challenge of Interchurch Marriages

Marriage between two Christians creates a relationship to the church. The couple in an interchurch marriage shares two sacraments: baptism and marriage, both of which are strongly ecclesial. Baptism initiates a Christian into the one church of Christ. Marriage is a sign of the union between Christ and the church (Eph 5:22–33). Marriage has been called "a domestic church." The partners are called to a unity that reflects the union of Christ with the church. The family itself is "a little church" and is called in a similar way to the church itself to become a sign of unity for the world."[22] Cardinal Willebrands asks "whether the time has now come to study afresh the possibility of admitting the non-Catholic partners in mixed marriages to Eucharistic communion in the Catholic Church, obviously in individual cases and after due examination."[23] The theological argument is that when a non-Catholic enters into a marriage with a Catholic, the sacrament also creates a bond with the Catholic Church because of the sign value of the marriage vows themselves witnessing to the union between Christ and the church.

For any of the situations indicated above, the application of the norms for Eucharistic sharing requires balancing values, namely the Eucharist as expressing unity and the Eucharist as a means to grace, and differentiating between a practice representative of the relationship between ecclesial communities or a practice responding to the spiritual need of an individual.[24]

The Problem of Reciprocity

The teaching of the Catholic Church is that when a Catholic goes to a Protestant service, reception of the Eucharist is always excluded.[25] A Catholic may not ask for the sacraments except from a minister who has been validly ordained. The reasoning is that since Protestant churches do not have valid ordinations, they therefore have not preserved the proper reality of the Eucharist in its fullness.

The reason given for the invalidity of the ordination of Protestant ministers and thus the invalidity of the Eucharist is usually the lack of apostolic succession, generally interpreted as ordination by a tactile succession of laying on of hands by bishops in apostolic succession. However, this interpretation does not adequately represent the status of contemporary scholarship on apostolicity or the complexity of the issue for the following reasons: "It cannot be substantiated biblically or historically that all the presbyter-bishops received their office in this manner from the apostles. The office of bishop did not exist at the time of the apostles, so the practice of a tactile succession of laying on of hands only developed after the office existed."[26]

There were two theologies regarding the relationship between presbyteral ordination and episcopal ordination, one requiring ordination of presbyters by bishops and the other permitting ordination by presbyters. Whereas Catholics have traditionally held that presbyteral ordination by a bishop is necessary, Lutherans followed the teaching of Jerome, who held that there was no essential difference between a presbyter and a bishop. Lutherans practiced presbyteral ordination because on the continent no Catholic bishops went over to the Reformed side to ordain their ministers. In doing so, they appealed to Jerome's theology. There is also historical evidence of presbyteral ordinations in the Catholic Church, particularly in monastic communities, which were sanctioned by the pope. Thus, it would seem that presbyteral ordinations in these historical contexts would not, in and of themselves, constitute invalidity, although other factors may require evaluation in determining the validity of orders.

A contemporary understanding of apostolic succession explicitly recognizes that the whole church embodies apostolicity, not just the ordained minister.[27]

Further study is needed on the meaning of *defectus* as applied to ordination. A *defectus* of orders has traditionally been translated as "lack." Round X of the U.S. Lutheran-Catholic dialogue (2005) recommended that this term be translated as "defect," insofar as Protestant orders are not in communion with the ministry of other churches and thus do not witness to the unity of the church.[28] Cardinal Walter Kasper has expressed agreement with this proposed translation of *defectus* stating, "On material grounds, and not merely on the basis of the word usage of the Council, it becomes clear that *defectus ordinis* does not signify a complete absence but rather a deficiency in the full form of the office."[29]

The issue of women's ordination further complicates the recognition of orders. The Catholic Church does not consider itself authorized to ordain women and has determined that attempted ordinations of women in the Catholic Church are invalid and not only illicit. How this affects mutual recognition of ministry in other ecclesial traditions remains to be worked out.

To solve issues of reciprocity, much work remains to be done on the mutual recognition of ministry and its relationship to Eucharistic sharing. This need not, however, be constrained by questions of validity. Ratzinger wrote to a Bavarian bishop that we must get beyond the category of validity when speaking of orders:

I count among the most important results of the ecumenical dialogues the insight that the issue of the Eucharist cannot be narrowed to the problem of "validity." Even a theology oriented to the concept of succession, such as that which hold in the Catholic and in the Orthodox Church, need not in any way deny the salvation-granting presence of the Lord in a Lutheran Lord's Supper.[30]

Conclusion

The Eucharist is never a sign of perfectly achieved unity but one of imperfect unity seeking to become more perfect.[31] Different denomination churches see themselves as one in Christ, despite their structural and doctrinal divisions. Avery Dulles in 1976 suggested that "granted, then, that one should normally receive communion in a service of one's own confession, occasional acts of intercommunion may be seen as an appropriate sign of the partial but growing unity among separated churches and as an appropriate remedy for their present separations."[32] He identifies the following necessary conditions for Eucharistic sharing: (1) a basic unity in faith, expressed by common creeds understood in a similar way; (2) a sense of somehow belonging, notwithstanding all the divisions, to the one church of Christ; (3) the will to a more perfect union; (4) a basic agreement about the nature and meaning of the Eucharist; (5) a shared conviction about what is transpiring at the particular Eucharistic service being conducted.[33]

The inability to sacramentalize the unity we share in baptism around a common Eucharistic table represents a deep incongruence and self-contradiction. The pain we experience as a result is an impetus to work for church unity so that the unity we express within the Eucharist reflects the unity we practice and celebrate among our churches. It is also an impetus to move beyond an individualized theology of the Eucharist to a more communal one and to do the theological and pastoral work to clarify our theology of the Eucharist and ministry so that we can articulate a common faith and implement pastoral practice that reflects the faith we share.

In the meantime, episcopal leadership would be well advised to develop guidelines to implement the policy already in place as articulated in the Code of Canon Law and the *Ecumenical Directory* (1993). This would provide a more uniform practice and correct the "all or nothing" approach sometimes practiced by clergy and laity alike, which does not reflect actual church teaching and the best pastoral practice of the Catholic Church.

Notes

[1] Pontifical Council for Promoting Christian Unity, *Directory for the Application of Principles and Norms on Ecumenism* (Washington, DC: United States Catholic Conference, 1993), §129 (hereafter, *Directory*).

[2] Vatican II, *Unitatis Redintegratio,* §22.

[3] *Directory*, §129.

[4] Ibid.

[5] For a detailed history, see George H. Tavard, "Praying Together: *Communicatio in Sacris* in the Decree on Ecumenism," in *Vatican II by Those Who Were There*, ed. A. Stackpoole (London: Geoffrey Chapman, 1986), 202–19.

[6] Ibid., 204.

[7] *Catechism of the Catholic Church*, §1400.

[8] Now the Pontifical Council for the Promotion of Christian Unity.

[9] Can. 844, §4. This canon repeats the conditions listed in the *Directory,* but adds the phrase "some other grave necessity urges it."

[10] *Directory*, §131.

[11] John Paul II, *Ut Unum Sint* (25 May 1995), §26.

[12] John Paul II, *Ecclesia de Eucharistia* (2003), §46.

[13] Code of Canon Law (1983), Can. 844 §2; *Directory*, §134.

[14] *Catechism of the Catholic Church*, §1400, citing UR 22, para. 3.

[15] Can. 844, §4.

[16] John M. Huels, O.S.M., "A Policy of Canon 844, §4 for Canadian Dioceses," *Studia Canonica* 34 (2000): 91–118, 96.

[17] John P. Beal, James A. Coriden, Thomas J. Green, eds., *New Commentary on the Code of Canon Law* (New York: Paulist Press, 2000), 1025.

[18] See Myriam Wijlens, *Sharing the Eucharist: A Theological Evaluation of Post Conciliar Legislation* (New York: University Press of America, 2000), 319. Here she refers to the impossibility of a Catholic to have access to a Catholic minister, but the same may apply to the inaccessibility of a Protestant to a Protestant minister.

[19] See, for example, George Kilcourse, "Ecumenical Marriages: Two Models for Church Unity," *Mid-Stream* 26, no. 2 (April, 1987): 189–214.

[20] Cited in Heuls, "A Policy of Canon 844," 94–95.

[21] Ibid., 107.

[22] Cardinal Willebrands, "Mixed Marriages and Their Family Life: Cardinal Willebrand's Address to the Synod of Bishops, October, 1980," *One in Christ*, 78–81, citing the *Instumentum Laboris*, 956.

[23] Willebrands, "Mixed Marriages and Their Family Life," 80.

[24] Wijlens, *Sharing the Eucharist*, 321–23.

[25] *Directory*, §132; *Catechism of the Catholic Church*, §1400.

[26] Raymond Brown, *Priest and Bishop* (New York: Paulist Press, 1970); Lutheran-Roman Catholic Commission on Unity, *The Apostolicity of the Church* (Minneapolis: Lutheran University Press, 2006), 31–34.

[27] The Dogmatic Constitution on Revelation (*Dei Verbum, 1965*) says that "the church, in its doctrine, life and worship, perpetuates and transmits to every generation all that it itself is, all that it believes" (*DV*, §8).

[28] U.S. Lutheran-Roman Catholic Dialogue, Round X, *The Church as Koinonia of Salvation* (Washington, DC: United States Conference of Catholic Bishops, 2005), §100.

[29] Walter Kasper, "Die apostolische Sukzession als ükumenisches Problem," in *Lehrverturteilungen-kirchentrenend?*, vol. III, ed. Wolfhart Pannenberg, Theodor Schneider, Karl Lehmann (Göttingen, Germany: Vandenhoeck & Ruprecht, 1997), 345.

[30] "Briefwechel von Landesbischof Johannes Hanselmann und Joseph Kardinal Ratzinger über des Communio-Schreiben der Römischen Glaubenskongregation," *Una Sancta* 48 (1993): 348, as cited in *Church as Koinonia of Salvation*, §107.

[31] Avery Dulles, "Intercommunion between Lutherans and Roman Catholics," *Journal of Ecumenical Studies* 13, no. 2 (1976): 250–55, 250.

[32] Ibid., 250.

[33] Ibid.

Eucharist at a Divided Table

C. Pierson Shaw Jr.

On October 31, 2017, the Western church will mark the five hundredth anniversary of the event that led to the most significant and widespread call for the reformation of the church. While Luther was by no means the first to call for reform, this Augustinian friar's request for a colloquy to debate the sale of indulgences on the Eve of All Saints sparked such a firestorm that our nearness to that anniversary is worth noting. The voices of Waldo, Wycliffe, and Huss had issued calls for reform in the centuries that had preceded Luther's, but the crisis in Wittenberg demonstrated that reform movements can take on a life of their own when equipped with the right technology, namely, the printing press. Printing would spell both the beginning of a monumental reform and, at the same time, a seeming irreconcilable division experienced up to the present within Christ's church.

Thus, all who are "citizens with the saints and also members of the household of God, built upon the foundation of the apostles and prophets, with Christ Jesus himself as the cornerstone" (Eph 2:19–20) remain a divided household. Nowhere is this division more clearly felt than around that which the Apostle Paul calls "the Supper of the Lord" (1 Cor 11:20). For nearly five centuries, Western Christians have experienced the often painful separation from their Christian brothers and sisters around the sacrament of the Eucharist. Such separation and sense of exclusion still exists, despite decades of conversation both among and between many Protestants and Roman Catholics. This separation is made even more profound when one has witnessed the liturgical and theological convergence from the late twentieth century to the present. Many have hoped that this sacrament itself could lead to the very unity that Christians seek. Yet, antithetically, the Eucharist has often become a barrier to a long hoped-for unity.

It is my contention in this essay that among the many steps necessary toward ultimately removing ecumenical barriers stands the imperative that the complex historical and theological reasons that those barriers have come to exist, as well as the complicity on all sides in their origin and sustenance, be acknowledged and appreciated. In the interest of long-range ecumenical progress, I wish to speak from the Protestant side about the need for all of us to own up to our own faults as we more fully come to grips with the whys and wherefores as well as the real opportunities present in the ecumenical situation of our time.

One should be especially mindful that Protestants themselves have historically practiced varying degrees of exclusionary Eucharistic practice. In the parlance of many in the church, open invitations to the Eucharist of a given community are often said to be "pastoral." To in any way seem exclusionary with respect to open reception of those from other communions is often described as "not being pastoral." Yet in ages gone by, among varying Protestant communions, the practice of not receiving congregants from across denominational lines was, in fact, seen as the more "pastoral" approach. In a postmodern society, obsessed with avoiding any hint of exclusivity, some practices around Eucharistic hospitality seem foreign and seem to convey a meaning that would seem to go against the very gospel itself and against the mission of *ecclesia*.

Ecumenical conversation in the past decades has continued to enrich the theology of the Eucharist, not just for Roman Catholics, but for Protestant ecclesial communities as well. One of the biggest advancements has been in the area of a recovery of rich Eucharistic symbols, decorous ritual, and the poetic language in the liturgy of the mass. Much has also been gained from the richness of ecumenical reflection on the various theologies of the Eucharist expressed in the New Testament and the Eucharistic images in the Hebrew scriptures. Much has been gained as well from the *bikat-ha-mazon* table blessings in first-century Palestinian Judaism that were offered at the conclusion of meals. While it is appropriate to speak of the sacrifice of the mass, it is helpful to remember that this sacrifice is the liturgical action of the mass itself, not just the sacerdotal activity within the mass. The minimalist controversies that marked late scholasticism often resulted in Eucharistic theologies that centered on the words and actions of the priest and not upon the participation of the whole people of God. The work of Thomas Aquinas and his systematic reflections in the *Summa Theologica* helped to combat the crass realism that perpetuated stories of bleeding hosts and mysterious visions connected to the consecrated and reserved *corpus*.[1]

It must be remembered that the Reformers' primary reason for arguing that the sacrament is *not* efficacious *ex opere operato* is because of perpetual private, daily, priestly celebrations of the mass apart from the faithful.

Further, Lutherans wanted to affirm the need for the communicant to trust in the promises before eating and drinking. Thus, Philip Melanchthon in article XIII of the Latin edition of the "Augsburg Confession" or *Augustana*, polemically asserts against the Church of Rome that the Wittenberg Reformers "also condemn those who teach that the sacraments justify *ex opere operato* and do not teach that faith, which believes that sins are forgiven, is required in the use of sacraments."[2] However, if we follow the reasoning of Aquinas, who understands that the sacrament is truly *the sacrament as it is offered in the midst of and on behalf of the faithful*, then it would be truthful to argue that the sacrament is, in fact, efficacious *ex opere operato*, and, as such, one avoids the main objections of those who followed Luther.

The difficult word "transubstantiation" used by the scholastics came to be criticized by many of the Protestant reformers, since by the time of the Reformation it had come to be used as a way of explaining *how* Christ came to be present in the Eucharist. Interestingly enough, at Session 13 of the Council of Trent, which met in 1551, the fathers specified how the term "transubstantiation" should properly be understood. In the first of the "canons on the most holy Sacrament of the Eucharist," they stated,

> If anyone denies that in the most holy Sacrament of the Eucharist there are contained truly, really and substantially, the body and blood of our Lord Jesus Christ together with the soul and divinity, and therefore the whole Christ, but says that he is present in it only as a sign or figure or by his power: let him be anathema.[3]

Thus, the Council of Trent took a very circumspect approach in the matter. The real concern here was clearly establishing the doctrine of the real presence such that the true Body and true blood of Jesus may be understood to be truly present in the Eucharist. When understood with theological nuance, the word "transubstantiation" offered the most apt theological description of this *doctrina catholica*.

Building upon the canons of Session XIII of Trent, *Mysterium Fidei*, an encyclical letter of Pope Paul VI in 1965, offered three major areas of teaching on the Eucharist: (1) the understanding that the sacramental sacrifice perpetuates the benefits of the sacrifice of the cross; (2) that the Eucharist is also a memorial of the paschal event; and (3) that the Eucharist is a banquet, which is a foretaste of the eschatological feast to come. Paul VI recognized the helpfulness of the new terms offered by some theologians in the 1960s, such as "transignification" and "transfinalization," but he called for an integration of the old and the new, not a simple replacement of the old term with new ones. The new terms were not substitutes for Trent's teachings concerning the substantial presence of Christ in the Eucharist and transubstantiation.[4] More recently, Reformed theologian George Hunsinger has offered a fresh look at the theologies of the Eucharist inherent in the liturgy of the East, the Eastern Fathers, and the theologies both pre- and post-Reformation in the West. He has suggested using "transelementation" or *metastoicheiosis* as a term that could bring about ecumenical convergence among divided Christians.[5]

Hunsinger's work offers new insights, and its use in dialogue is potentially extremely helpful. In light of Paul VI's letter, however, the use of another term, such as "transelementation," will not serve as a replacement for the term "transubstantiation." For Protestant ecumenists, it will be necessary to seek convergence, albeit with differences in the matter of interpreting "transubstantiation" as that term seeks to describe the real presence of Christ in the Eucharist.

For their part, Lutherans have historically operated out of a high doctrine of the "real presence." Twenty-nine years after the Council of Trent issued its Decree on the Eucharist and seventeen years following the close of the twenty-fifth and final session of the Council of Trent, the descendants of Luther's Wittenberg reform met to iron out numerous differences that had arisen in their ranks. At issue concerning the doctrine of the Eucharist was the Council of Trent's anathematizing anyone who did not hold to the conviction that this substantial change in the substance of the body of Christ was properly to be called "transubstantiation." As we have noted, the Reformers had understood this term as a way of attempting to define how Christ comes to be substantially present in the forms of bread and wine.

In 1580, in the "Solid Declaration of the Formula of Concord," the descendants of Luther affirmed,

> The reason for using the formula "under the bread," "with the bread," "in the bread" alongside the words of Christ and of St. Paul that the bread in the Supper "is the body of Christ" [Mt 26:26; Lk 22:19; Mk 14:22; 1 Cor 11:24] or "the sharing of the body of Christ" [1 Cor 10:16] is to reject the papistic transubstantiation and to point to the sacramental union of the unchanged essence of the bread and the body of Christ. In the same way, this expression, *verbum caro factum est* ["the Word became flesh"], is repeated and explained in several ways, through phrases with the same meaning: "the Word lived among us" [Jn 1:14], or "in Christ the whole fullness of deity dwells bodily" [Col 2:9], or "God was with him" [Acts 10:38], or "God was in Christ" [2 Cor 5:19], and similar phrases. They all mean that the divine essence is not transformed into the human nature, but

that the two unaltered natures are personally united. Many of the foremost ancient teachers—Justin, Cyprian, Augustine, Leo, Gelasius, Chrysostom, and others—used this comparison for the words of Christ's testament, "This is my body." Just as in Christ two distinct, unaltered natures are inseparably united, so in the Holy Supper two essences, the natural bread and the true natural body of Christ, are present together here on earth in the action of the sacrament, as it was instituted.[6]

At the same time, there was substantial concern over Crypto-Calvinism. Philipp Melanchthon, in an effort to reach substantial convergence with Martin Bucer and the Calvinists, sought to reduce the presence of the Lord's body and blood strictly to the moment of the reception of the elements. Even during Luther's lifetime, Melanchthon had become reluctant to identify the bread and wine with the body and blood of Christ. For Luther, since Jesus had promised to be present, believers could be assured that the Words of Institution, during which the presider spoke the words of Jesus, effected the presence of Christ's body and blood at the altar.[7]

In "The Formula of Concord" the early Lutherans went on to express their rejection of the Philippist or Crypto-Calvinist position on the Eucharist when they said,

> This union of Christ's body and blood with the bread and wine, how-ever, is not a personal union, as is the case with the two natures in Christ. Rather, as Dr. Luther and our people called it in the Articles of Agreement of 1536 (mentioned above) and in other places, it is a *sacramentalis unio* (that is, a sacramental union). With this expression they wanted to indicate that, although they also use the *formae* "*in pane*," "*sub pane*," "*cum pane*" (that is, these various ways of speaking: "in the bread," "under the bread," "with the bread"), nevertheless, they accept the words of Christ in their proper sense, as they read. In the *propositio* (that is, in the words of Christ's testament) "hoc est corpus meum" ("this is my body"), there is not *figurata praedicatio* (that is, not a figurative, embellished expression or a metaphorical formulation) but an *inusitata* [unique expression]. As Justin says, "We do not receive this as ordinary bread and as an ordinary beverage, but just as Jesus Christ, our Savior, became flesh through God's Word and had flesh and blood for the sake of our salvation, so we believe that the meal consecrated by him through Word and prayer is the flesh and blood of the Lord Jesus Christ."

Likewise, Dr. Luther in his *Great Confession*, and especially in his *Brief Confession on the Supper*, defended the formula that Christ used in the first Supper with great zeal and seriousness. Because Dr. Luther must deservedly be regarded as the foremost teacher of the churches that subscribe to the Augsburg Confession, since his entire teaching in sum and content was set down in the articles of the Augsburg Confession and presented to Emperor Charles V, the actual intention and meaning of the Augsburg Confession should not and cannot be derived more properly and better from any other place than from Dr. Luther's doctrinal and polemical writings. In the same way, the position of Luther recounted here is based upon the unique, firm, immovable, indubitable rock of truth from the Words of Institution in the holy, divine Word, and was so understood, taught, and propagated by the holy evangelists and apostles and their disciples and hearers (FC, SD, 599ff).

The formula had made it abundantly clear. Confessional Lutheranism would speak of real presence in very specific terms. While Lutherans would not speak of *how* Jesus came to be present, the faithful could trust in the specificity of the Lord's presence in the chalice and on the paten. One received the true body and blood of Christ. As far as venerating the blessed sacrament in the tabernacle, in a monstrance and in procession, these are often foreign practices to Lutheran pieties. The Lutheran Confessions resisted such practices, instead focusing on the eating and the drinking, through which the one receiving in faith could be confident that the sacrament was efficacious. Yet Lutherans have also held to such a stringent view of the presence of Christ in the Eucharist that they came often to be accused in the sixteenth century by Calvinists and others of believing that Jesus was present all the way, to what today we would call the toilet. For Lutherans, Christ remained truly present even after consumption. Such a high view of real presence distinguished Lutherans even from their Roman Catholic counterparts.

In 1533, Philipp Melanchthon had published a revised version of the German text of the Augsburg Confession, and subsequently the Latin versions were published in 1540 and 1542. The altered Augsburg Confession or the *Variata* that spoke of Christ only as *"cum pane"* (with the bread), while it had sought convergence with Calvinists, had at the same time caused a major rift within Lutheranism. The wording in the *Variata* has continued to halt Lutherans over the past five centuries. In 1817, on the three hundredth anniversary of Luther's call for a colloquy in Wittenberg, King Frederick Wilhelm III of Prussia urged his subjects to abandon using separate reformed and Lutheran liturgies. No longer would communicants in Lutheran congregations in Prussia hear quoted "take, eat, this is the true body of our Lord Jesus Christ." Pastors would use the alternate formula,

"Jesus Christ says, this is my body." By 1831 anyone refusing to use the new liturgy would be seen as being flagrantly disobedient to the crown.[8]

In the 1830s, an American Lutheran by the name of Samuel Simon Schmucker, who had founded a seminary in the quiet rolling hills of southern Pennsylvania, sought to bring greater unity to American Protestantism. His own views favored less specificity than contained in the unaltered Augsburg Confession. However, his personality and his propensity for teaching a doctrine of the Eucharist, which sounded a great deal like the *Variata*, elicited strong reactions among Lutherans living in a new and independent country. American Lutherans began to align themselves into two predominant camps. Those synods and conferences that had supported Schmucker aligned themselves with the General Synod. Congregations and pastors who opposed Schmucker's leadership style and theological positions formed separate synods and conferences.

Many of these splits and alignments still remained present, although to a minor degree, in 1987 when the predecessor bodies to the Evangelical Lutheran Church in America (ECLA) organically merged and formed a new American denomination. Schmucker had hoped that his seminary would be set apart from the conflicts and concerns of the world. Like the General Synod, the Lutheran Theological Seminary at Gettysburg, despite Schmucker's hopes, would become a victim of its own history. Far from being removed from the ways of the world, it became the general headquarters of Robert E. Lee as he attempted to move his southern Army into the North during the American Civil War. The General Synod would become a symbol of disunity and distrust among American Lutherans for generations. Certainly, neither the seminary nor the General Synod moved in the directions for which Samuel Simon Schmucker might have hoped.

In 1872, in Akron, Ohio, several Lutheran synods in Midwestern states adopted what became known as the Akron Rule, later to be reaffirmed in 1875 and dubbed the Galesburg Rule. One of the major principles of the Akron and Galesburg Rule was that "Lutheran pulpits are for Lutheran ministers only. Lutheran altars are for Lutheran communicants only." Communion was to be considered a privilege not a right, and any exceptions to this rule were to be granted on a case-by-case basis by the local pastor.

The Akron and Galesburg Rule was not significantly different from the policies of American Anglicanism during the same period. However such an ecclesiology of exclusion and what came to be understood as "close communion" became ways of assuring the integrity of the Confessional doctrine of "real presence." As a result of the Akron and Galesburg Rule, and based on the principles of Article VII concerning the church as found in the Augsburg Confession, Lutherans in the ECLA have eagerly entered into full communion relationships with other denominations. In a real sense an ecclesiology of exclusion around the Eucharist has borne the fruit of numerous ecumenical agreements between the ELCA and other denominations. These "full communion" relationships include the Reformed Church in America, United Churches of Christ, the Presbyterian Church USA, the Northern and Southern Provinces of the Moravian Church, the Episcopal Church in the United States, and most recently the United Methodist Church.

Often such "ecclesiologies of exclusion" as articulated in the Akron and Galesburg Rule and as professed in the Lutheran confessions and contained in the *Book of Concord* seem to be an affront to the inclusiveness craved by postmodern society. For this same reason many Protestants find the ecclesiology of exclusion around the Eucharist as celebrated in the Roman Catholic Church as an affront to postmodern sensibilities of inclusivity. However, given Protestant history surrounding ecclesiologies of exclusion around the Eucharist, greater tolerance may be in order on the part of Protestants.

At the Second Vatican Council, the Dogmatic Constitution on the Church, *Lumen Gentium*, spoke of the unity extended to all Christians in holy baptism. However, the current Code of Canon Law speaks of admission of non-Catholic Christians to the Eucharist in this way:

> If there is a danger of death or if in the judgment of the diocesan bishop or the bishop's conference, there is some other grave and pressing need, Catholic ministers may lawfully administer these same sacraments to other Christians not in full Communion with the Catholic Church, who cannot approach a minister of their own community and who spontaneously ask for them, provided they demonstrate Catholic faith in respect of these sacraments and are properly disposed. (Canon 844 § 4)

Clearly, while the canons of the Roman Catholic Church recognize exceptional occasions when, as a matter of "necessity," non-Roman Catholics may commune in the Roman Catholic Church, the norm is that one who has not been confirmed in the Roman Catholic Church and has not completed the sacraments of initiation is not welcome to commune. Protestants and Catholics alike may easily find such an "ecclesiology of exclusion" distasteful and problematic in light of ecumenical convergences over the last several decades. Yet here Protestants might remember our Lord's admonition, "Why do you see the speck in your neighbor's eye, but do not notice the log in your own eye?" (Mt 7:3; Lk 6:41). For Protestants the "log" is their own history of "ecclesiologies of exclusion" around the sacrament of the altar as they have historically sought to maintain scriptural and confessional integrity.

In addition to the concern of having not been received into the Roman Catholic Church through the sacrament of confirmation, clearly one of the major impediments to the unity of the church remains in the area of the sacrament of holy orders. While the ordination of women complicates the issue not just for Roman Catholics but also for some Protestants who as yet have not begun ordaining women, the question remains whether the Roman Catholic Church might come to a place where those ordained in the historic episcopacy may be recognized as possessing valid orders. Here some historical perspective is helpful. The following citation appears in Ludwig Ott's the *Fundamentals of Catholic Dogma,* which seems to offer an historical precedence for Roman Catholics to accept the orders of Protestants that have been considered *defectus* since the time of the Reformation:

> In regard to the sacramental Order grades of diaconate and presbyteriate, most theologians, with St. Thomas, hold the opinion that a simple priest cannot validly administer these, even with plenary power from the Pope. But there are grave historical difficulties with regard to this opinion: Pope Boniface IX, in agreement with the teaching of numerous medieval canonists (for example Huguccio, 1210), by the Bull "*Sacrae religionis*" of the 1st February, 1400, conferred on the Abbott of the Augustine monastery of St. Osytha at Essex (Diocese of London) and his successors, the privilege of administering to those subject to them of the Minor Orders and those of the sub-diaconate, diaconate, and priesthood. The privilege was withdrawn on 6th February, 1403, on the instance of the Bishop of London. But the Orders conferred on the ground of the privilege were not declared invalid. Pope Martin V, by the Bull "*Gerentes ad vos*" of 16th November, 1427, conferred the privilege on the Abbott of the Cistercian Monastery of Alzelle (Diocese of Meissen) of promoting all his monks and others subject to him for the term of five years, to the higher Orders also (Sub-diaconate, Diaconate, and Presbyteriate). Pope Innocent VIII, by the Bull "*Exoscit, tuae devotionis*" of 9th April, 1489, conferred on the four Proto-Abbots of the Cistercian Order and their successors the privilege of ordaining their subordinates to the Sub-diaconate and the Diaconate. The Cistercian Abbots were still using this privilege in the 17th century without hindrance.

> Unless one wishes to assume that the Popes in question were victims of the erroneous theological opinions of their times (this does not touch the papal infallibility, because an *ex cathedra* decision was not given),

one must take it that a simple priest is an extraordinary dispenser of the Orders of Diaconate, and Presbyteriate, just as he is an extraordinary dispenser of confirmation. In this latter view, the requisite power of consecration is contained in the priestly power of consecration as *"potentas ligata"* For the valid exercise of it a special exercise of the Papal power is, by Divine or Church ordinance, necessary.[9]

Michael Root has used this citation before members of the Catholic Theological Society of America to make the same argument that we are making here. In addition, he argued that the Latin *defectus* means not "lack" or "absence," as it has been translated, but rather "defective."[10] He and others on the ecumenical scene, especially those involved in *U.S. Lutheran Roman Catholic Dialogue X "The Church as Koinonia of Salvation, Its Structures and Ministries,"* suggest that Protestants and Roman Catholics alike are "deficient" insofar as we remain in a state of disunity and brokenness. As stated in the dialogue document,

102. The same must be said of the Lutheran churches and their ministries. Lutherans understand their ministries to be realizations of the one ministry of the one church, and yet they cannot manifest communion in this one ministry with many other churches. This woundedness provides a helpful basis for a new understanding of the Catholic assertion of *defectus* in the sacrament of Order in Lutheran churches (§§108–109).

103. We recommend a mutual recognition that:
our ordained ministries are wounded because the absence of full communion between our ecclesial traditions makes it impossible for them adequately to represent and foster the unity and catholicity of the church; and our communities are wounded by their lack of the full catholicity to which they are called and by their inability to provide a common witness to the gospel.

109. We recommend that Roman Catholic criteria for assessing authentic ministry include attention to a ministry's faithfulness to the gospel and its service to the communion of the church, and that *defectus ordinis* as applied to Lutheran ministries be translated as "deficiency" rather than "lack."[11]

In light of Ott's historical analysis and the conclusions of the *U.S. Lutheran Roman Catholic Dialogue X*, we are compelled to continue conversation with persistence and consider the possibilities.

Lumen Gentium also speaks of ecclesiologies of "the new people of God" and the "new Israel." It speaks of the church as sacrament and also speaks of the local church (diocese, but also Eucharistic assembly) as the church of Christ. It speaks of the charisms of God's people, the collegiality of laity and clergy within the church, and degrees of communion among churches and ecclesial communities.

The faithful are called in the waters of baptism to live out their priestly and prophetic offices in Christ, empowered by the gifts of the Holy Spirit for the building up of the church. One may see this office in ordained ministry or in an institute for the consecrated life in religious communities. The role of bishop is maintained as crucial for the maintenance of visible unity. But *Lumen Gentium* also uses the word "subsists" in a way that has often confused many Protestants and Roman Catholic alike. The famous passage §8 reads as follows:

> This is the one Church of Christ which in the Creed is professed as one, holy, catholic and apostolic, which our Savior, after His Resurrection, commissioned Peter to shepherd, and him and the other apostles to extend and direct with authority, which He erected for all ages as "the pillar and mainstay of the truth." This Church constituted and organized in the world as a society, subsists in the Catholic Church, which is governed by the successor of Peter and by the Bishops in communion with him, although many elements of sanctification and of truth are found outside of its visible structure. These elements, as gifts belonging to the Church of Christ, are forces impelling toward catholic unity.

One helpful way of understanding this term, which appears only once in *Lumen Gentium*, is to remember that in the mass, Christ subsists in the Eucharist. Throughout all peoples of the world, it is the word that subsists in human nature. There is a subtlety in the use of this one word "subsists" that is often overlooked. *Lumen Gentium* does not say "This Church constituted and organized in the world as a society, *is contained* in the Catholic Church." The distinctions between "subsists in" and "is contained in" are deceptively enormous. The distinction is one of exclusion and not inclusion. Although the meaning of the phrase is hotly debated, one can argue that "This Church . . . subsists in the Catholic Church" does not necessarily imply that the church may not also subsist in ecclesial communities. As *Lumen Gentium* reminds us, "many elements of sanctification and of truth are found outside of its visible structure. These elements, as gifts belonging to the Church of Christ, are forces impelling toward catholic unity." It should therefore be the impassioned work of theologians, both Protestant and Catholic, to help us to see how and where Christ "subsists in" one another's communions in order that we might see the day when in dialogue we may adequately discern such a level of subsistence that together all might be in communion with "the successor of Peter and . . . the Bishops in communion with him."

Once again, in *Lumen Gentium* we are reminded that the faithful are called in the waters of baptism to live out their priestly and prophetic offices in Christ, empowered by the gifts of the Holy Spirit for the building up of the church. One may see this office in ordained ministry or in an institute for the consecrated life in religious communities. For those involved in ecumenical dialogue, the prophetic ministry to which we all have been called in holy baptism should include careful discernment as to whether adequate convergence exists in the doctrines and praxes of "ecclesial communities" such that these dialogue partners can come to be regarded as "Churches in the proper sense."[12] Amid the present situation, Protestants dialoguing with Roman Catholics need work in the hope that some Catholic ecumenists are doing what they can, within and sometimes in tension with official constraints, to actively discern such convergence. When and if Roman Catholic dialogue partners are regarded as "churches," it would then become incumbent on Catholic dioceses to invite their congregants to commune when they have occasion to worship in newly recognized "sister churches."

Currently, Protestants might consider their present inadmissibility to the Eucharist celebrated in the Roman Catholic Church not as an exclusion and rejection of their having been initiated fully into the Christian faith but as a painful, yet necessary reminder of Christian division. Too often Protestants may see the Eucharist as a common Southern potluck supper at which a dinner bell should be rung, and the call go out "Y'all Come!" Instead this is the Supper of the Lord, not a common free-for-all picnic. At the same time, both Protestants and Roman Catholics might view the present "crisis" as an opportunity to practice reciprocal fasting and necessary asceticism, until such a time when there exists full mutual recognition, when both Protestants and Roman Catholics may come to the table of our Lord together.

Notes

[1] David N. Power, "Eucharist," in *Systematic Theology: Roman Catholic Perspectives*, 2nd ed., ed. Francis Schüssler Fiorenza and John P. Galvin (Minneapolis: Fortress Press, 2011), 515–41.

[2] Timothy Wengert and Robert Kolb, eds., *The Book of Concord: The Confessions of the Evangelical Lutheran Church* (Minneapolis: Fortress Press, 2000).

[3] Norman P. Tanner, S.J., ed. *Decrees of the Ecumenical Councils*, vol. 2 (*Trent to Vatican II)* (Washington, DC: Sheed & Ward and Georgetown University Press, 1990), 697.

[4] Power, "Eucharist," 528.

[5] George Hunsinger, *The Eucharist and Ecumenism* (New York: Cambridge University Press, 2008), 12.

[6] Wengert and Kolb, *Book of Concord*, 599.

[7] John R. Stephenson, "The Lutheran View," in *The Lord's Supper: Five Views*, ed. Gordon T. Smith (Downers Grove, IL: IVP Academic, 2008), 41–58, 46.

[8] H. George Anderson, "The Early National Period 1790–1840," in *The Lutherans in North America*, ed. E. Clifford Nelson (Philadelphia: Fortress Press, 1975), 81–144, 131.

[9] Ludwig Ott, *Fundamentals of Catholic Dogma* (Rockford, IL: Tan Books and Publishers, 1974), 459.

[10] Michael Root, "Bishops, Ministry, and the Unity of the Church in Ecumencial Dialogue: Deadlock, Breakthrough, or Both?" *Catholic Theological Society of America Proceedings* (2007): 19–35, 29.

[11] *"The Church as Koinonia of Salvation: Its Structures and Ministries," Dialogue X: U.S. Lutheran Roman Catholic Dialogue.* (Washington, DC: United States Conference of Catholic Bishops, 2003).

[12] Congregation for the Doctrine of the Faith, Dominus Iesus, *On the Unicity and Salvific Universality of Jesus Christ and the Church* (Vatican City, 2000), 17.

Rethinking the Sacrament of Reconciliation/Healing in the Light of Postmodern Thought

Stephen Annan

I experienced most deeply the challenges of sacramental exclusion and ostracism of Christian faithful when I worked as a Catholic associate pastor in a parish in Ghana (Diocese of Sunyani). Not only were some denied the reception of the basic sacraments of initiation, but also many were refused the sacraments of reconciliation and anointing of the sick. To rub salt into the wounds, such people were equally denied fitting Christian burial. The overarching reason accounting for these deprivations was the lack of sacramentalized marriages on the part of people who, practically speaking, have no other choice. The reactions of such disenchanted groups were twofold: either a "positive defiance" whereby many would go on to receive communion or approach the confessional saying, "Father, even though I am not a communicant, I would like to confess my sins and receive *forgiveness from God*," or a "negative defiance" whereby most of these Christian faithful would leave the Catholic Church and join any other Christian church.

The foregoing existential problematic is pastorally and theologically challenging. At the last Synod of Bishops for Africa, Bishop Matthew Gyamfi, who is my local ordinary, could not help but address it head on. In his remarkable intervention, he observed that in some parts of Africa, some women find themselves in polygamous marriages through no fault of their own, as a result of which they are denied the sacraments of initiation, reconciliation, and marriage. As a pastorally-minded bishop, he gave his candid opinion that such women be given the opportunity to receive the sacraments:

The church needs to address this painful and unpleasant situation in Africa by giving some special privileges to women, who have been the first wives with children and through no fault of their own have become victims of polygamous marriages, to receive the sacraments of initiation and others. The reception of these trying women to the sacraments will enable them to share in the peace and reconciliation offered by the compassion and peace of our Lord Jesus Christ who came to call sinners and not the self-righteous.[1]

A similar pastoral concern was expressed at the First National Catholic Pastoral Congress in Ghana when the participants observed that

[T]hese sacraments [Eucharist, reconciliation, and anointing] are as of now reserved for only communicants. Unfortunately, non-communicants outnumber communicants in many of our communities. When we consider that many illnesses in our day are linked with tensions, crises, upsets, emotions, guilt, remorse, and unforgiving spirit, then the question of the importance of the Sacrament of reconciliation in the healing process needs to be revisited (cf. Mk 2: 1–2; John 5:14).[2]

A Burning Question:
Is It (Im)possible to Receive the Sacrament of
Reconciliation and Healing in "Mortal Sin"?

The demanding issues that such existential pastoral and ecclesiological discriminations impose on us are not hard to fathom. Preeminently, is it (im)possible for a baptized Catholic to receive the Eucharist without sacramental marriage? Since noncommunicants are, like other church members, prone to sin, fall sick, and are in need of healing, how can they receive the fullness of forgiveness and reconciliation? For in the eyes of the church, "the first conviction is that for a Christian the sacrament of penance is the *primary way* of obtaining forgiveness and the remission of serious sin committed after baptism."[3] If these sacraments of healing are positively denied to noncommunicants, then our perplexities continue: Is a sacrament a reward for the righteous or a medium through which God encounters feeble humanity? To what extent might the church allow these members to receive the sacraments without being seen as too liberal or as "cheapening" the sacraments? Granted that those who are barred from communion are "sinners," and noting that indeed, Martin Luther (echoing Augustine) once referred to the church as the "infirmary of the sick,"[4] is it not possible for them to receive the sacraments of healing? What would be the ecclesiological reverberations if the victims of this exclusion were to be admitted to the sacraments of reconciliation and anointing irrespective of their sacramental circumstances?

The undergirding thesis in all these questions, which I propose in this paper, is that *an appropriation of the postmodern understanding of sacramental theology is an ecclesiological prerequisite for overcoming sacramental exclusion in the church*. Otherwise stated, a contemporary understanding of the theology of the sacraments would open up possibilities for those who have been sacramentally disenfranchised by the church to receive the sacraments.[5] Thus understood, a sacramental proclivity for the "*(self)-righteous*" is disavowed. In what follows, I will focus mainly on the sacraments of reconciliation and healing, making references to the Eucharist where necessary. I shall refer to both reconciliation and healing as sacraments of reconciliation/healing and tackle the foregoing questions in three broad strokes. The first section clarifies the background of the problematic and the ramifications of ecclesiological exclusion through the prism of a postcolonial theory/victim perspective. Having taken up the general understanding of the sacraments in the church's understanding in the second section, I will conclude with a hermeneutical recontextualization of the sacraments of reconciliation/healing.

Sociological Analysis of Exclusion

As a sociological category, the term (social) exclusion is defined by the Harvard sociologist Hilary Silver as "*a multidimensional process of progressive social rupture, detaching groups and individuals from social relations and institutions and preventing them from full participation in the normal, normatively prescribed activities of the society in which they live.*"[6] Among other factors, she outlines three key characteristics of social exclusion that we deem noteworthy for our discussion. First, social exclusion is context specific. That is to say, it always implies a context-dependent definition of social belonging such that what applies in a particular context may not necessarily apply in another. Second, it is relational. As a relational concept, it has two parties, namely, the excluders and the excluded. Lastly, it is multidimensional; in other words, it cuts across different aspects of their (the excluded) lives: social, psychological, economic, and so on, leading to further forms of exclusion.[7] Social exclusion is manifested mainly within the domain of the material and external.

Ecclesiological Analysis of Sacramental Exclusion

Mutatis mutandis, ecclesiological exclusion could be explained *as a multidimensional process of ecclesiological rupture that detaches groups and individuals from ecclesial relations and positively prevents them from full participation in the normal, normatively prescribed activities of ecclesial life and structure in which they divinely and rightfully belong*. It is, indeed, a process whereby some Christian faithful who have been called through the power of the Holy Spirit in baptism to live in the love of Christ as a church to glorify God are consistently denied, discriminated against, and deprived of what is characteristically constitutive and spiritually nourishing in their faith-seeking journey, in this case the sacraments. What is more characteristic of sacramental exclusion, in contrast to social exclusion, is that it does not derive from the institutional structure of the church, but rather informs its very life/charism.[8] In other words, it precludes some members of the church from the spiritual life of the church but not necessarily from its external or administrative structure.

Specifically in sub-Saharan Africa, many of the faithful are deprived of the reception of the sacraments of initiation and reconciliation/healing on the basis of their marriage. This marriage could be monogamous or polygamous. For most traditional African monogamous partners, it is superfluous to undergo a second marriage in the church. According to them, this marriage *in facie ecclesiae* is an added element to the customary marriage and therefore seen as a formality[9] to be fulfilled in order to receive the sacraments. Due to lack of this "second marriage" in the church, they are sadly denied the sacraments, notably the Eucharist and reconciliation/healing, since most of the victims in this category might have been baptized (mostly as infants) prior to their customary marriage.

The plight of those in the second category, who sometimes fall into polygamy without their volition, is not different. Often this will be a woman who marries a man who later marries one or more other women. The major obstacle is that they are thought to be living in "mortal sin" because of their polygamous marriage. Without endorsing polygamy, many substantial arguments have been raised in favor of tolerating it, positing that polygamous marriages are not intrinsically sinful but congruent with African cultural life and with a theological understanding of marriage. If such analysis is upheld, then what prevents them from the reception of the sacraments? Another related category of Catholics excluded from receiving the sacraments includes those who either live in courtship, marital engagement, or have given birth outside of wedlock. Because the cultural traditions frown upon such practices, people in these categories are equally prohibited from the sacraments, even though, comparatively, it would be very normal for such categories of people to receive the sacraments in the Western world.

Another context-related factor that feeds into ecclesiological exclusion is the attitude of some of the clergy. Some exclusions originate as a result of the (in)actions of the excluders. Most of the bishops, priests, and pastoral leaders in the sub-Saharan African region not only endorse what Rome says but they implement its decisions without the proper application to their local contexts. There are conciliar and ecclesial teachings that give them authority in their local churches to act in a proactive manner, though. Indeed, the instructions given in the *Introduction to the Rite of Marriage* (#12–16) give each bishops' conference the right to completely draw up new marriage rites. Herein lies the potential pastoral alternative of local churches, with which they either willingly or inadvertently refuse to act. In some cases excluders have positively restrained other faithful from receiving the sacraments either through insufficient knowledge about the authentic teachings of the church or by the lackadaisical use of pastoral judgment.

Lastly, sacramental exclusion is multidimensional. Those in so-called irregular situations can receive neither the Eucharist nor the sacraments of reconciliation/healing, although, fundamentally, baptism is the portal to all the other sacraments. Ultimately, this sacramental exclusion includes a lack of fitting Christian burial.

Ecclesiological Effects of Sacramental Exclusion

Pastorally, the situation has provoked a massive exodus of Catholic Christians to the Protestant and Pentecostal churches where traditional African marriage is not perceived as a "mortal sin" and is therefore not an obstacle to receiving communion. Current statistics prove how dire the consequences of inaction are for the Catholic Church in sub-Saharan Africa.

A second pastoral effect derives from the fact that ecclesiological exclusion, as a process and as multidimensional, goes on to affect the moral image of the victim. This has become the case because, for most of the people, those who do not receive the sacraments, especially the Eucharist, are seen as "sinners." As a result, they are looked down upon by other members of the church, are not elected as lay leaders in the church, and sometimes even their parents could be punished with excommunication.

To respond to some of these pastoral concerns, notably, the sacraments of healing, many Catholic faithful resort to the "sacramental ministries" in the charismatic renewal. Here, everybody is invited for "counseling" (actually in some cases it is "confession of sin" and inner healing before deliverance) or the application of anointing oil for everybody who is in need of healing. In spite of the appearance that this practice is addressing real needs, most Catholic pastors and pastorally mandated leaders criticize this practice.

Not the least among these pastoral effects is the fact that it deprives the victims from appropriating a "we feeling" in the church. This sociological category applied in the ecclesial sense leads to a lethargic attitude on the part of the excluded on the grounds that they do not feel "full belongingness" in the church.

Theologically, such exclusive practices undermine the goals of communion ecclesiology. If the church as the family of God is seen as the palpable offshoot of a focus on communion, then it stands to reason that such sacramental exclusion undercuts and obfuscates this most African of ecclesial images. As Appiah Kubi pointed out, in the African family, even the worst person is not denied food.[10] By extrapolation, why should we deny baptized Catholics reconciliation/healing, which is the salve of all human frailties?

Another theological implication of exclusive practices is that they give the impression that, whereas those who do not receive the sacraments are in the category of the "sinful church," those who do receive them constitute the elect, the "holy church." In spite of its mark of holiness, the church is also a community of sinners and continues to battle with the inevitability of sin and scandals. All members of the church must be in continuing search for conversion and struggle forward as the "holy Church of sinners."[11]

It can be argued that those who are not worthy should not approach the altar. But certain critical questions still need to be asked. If the church is deemed as the sacrament of salvation and reconciliation, is it not contradictory when it fails to accept and reconcile itself with those whom it judges as sinners and outcasts? If it does not concern itself with those who find themselves in this unfortunate state, does it not give a countertestimony when it baptizes the children of those who find themselves in this unfortunate condition, claiming to accept them into the bosom of Christ in the name of the church? Here, we should recall that there was a point in time that the church was not baptizing children of *illegitimi*. If the church has been able to rethink this exclusivism and marginalization in the course of its history, is it still (im)possible to rethink the inclusion of all in the sacraments of reconciliation/healing?

Holiness in Relation to the Instrumentality of the Sacraments

In what follows, I take my lead from the French theologian Louis-Marie Chauvet. In his introduction to *The Sacraments: The Word of God at the Mercy of the Body*, Chauvet analyzes three theoretical models of sacramental understanding and challenges us to move beyond their frontiers.

In the objective model,[12] which corresponds to scholastic theology, Chauvet observes that the sacraments are seen less as *revelatory signs* than as *operative means* of salvation. The sacraments are considered as instruments of causality that work *ex opera operato* and through which God deposits some sort of "a spiritual germ" into the soul. The concomitant effects arising from such understanding of the sacraments are that the priest is seen less as a pastor than as a bridge. The celebration of the sacraments becomes individualistic and "interioristic" in that it neglects the role of the church and focuses on the soul of the individual. By insisting on the objective efficacy of the sacraments, the importance of the concrete existential subject is not taken into consideration. Chauvet explains that the only way in which the objective model takes the recipient into account consists in the requirement that they not place any obstacle in the way of their reception of the grace of the sacrament.[13]

A contrasting type of sacramental analysis is found in the subjective model. Chauvet points out that, under its myriad forms, this model tends to sacrifice objective truth to the criterion of subjective sincerity and the quality of faith to that of generosity. The value of the sacraments is linked with the *subjective sincerity* of every person. This model leads one to see the sacraments as a "celebration of lived experience." Chauvet teases out the problematic with this model thus: "where[as] the objective model emphasized their function as operative means, and therefore as source of salvation, this model on the contrary stresses their function as revelatory signs and therefore as summit of the salvation already given at the risk of erasing more or less their character as instruments."[14] In effect, if the objective model sees the sacraments as the *production* of grace, the subjective model sees it as the *transmission* of grace already given to human subjects (hence its subjective character).

Chauvet discusses also a third approach, the Vatican II model, which mainly follows Aquinas while making some important emendations. Chauvet asserts that, even though Vatican II did not formally develop a sacramental model, it did try to broaden the perspectives of the scholastics. The Council endorsed understanding the church as the universal sacrament of salvation (*Lumen Gentium* #1). The operative nature of the sacraments is always God working through Christ in the Spirit.[15] In effect, the council recognized the pneumatological dimension of sacraments as well as their nature as signs and instruments (*LG* #1). Thus understood, Vatican II's attempt to counterbalance the theology of sacraments as instrumental means by emphasizing their role as *signs* is unmistakable.

As Chauvet sees it, though, this presentation is not without its own Achilles heel in that it is still fraught with Aristotelian categories, the effect of which is still evident in the celebration of the sacrament of reconciliation. An overly mechanical stress on causality gives way to a contemporary sacramental onto-theology that personifies God as a being who causes in the way that creatures cause. Regarding onto-theology, Chauvet questions, "How did it come about that, when attempting to comprehend theologically the sacramental relation with God expressed most fully under the term 'grace,' the scholastics . . . singled out for privileged consideration the category of 'cause'?"[16] This leads us to see a danger that the church can unconsciously move back toward the Tridentine perspective if it is not carefully consistent with its language and concepts across a range of issues.

Hard on the heels of such a causal analysis of the sacraments, John Paul II wrote specifically on the sacrament of reconciliation thus: "[T]he church can only invite her children who find themselves in these painful situations [the excluded] to approach the divine mercy by other ways, not however through the sacraments of penance and the Eucharist until such time as they have attained the *required dispositions.*"[17] It seems unavoidable to see a connection between John Paul II's approach and the sacramental onto-theology about which Chauvet is warning. As an alternative to the onto-theological[18] understanding of the sacraments, Chauvet opines for an understanding of the sacraments not as "instrument" or "cause" but as *symbol*[19] understood in terms of symbolic exchange, drawing upon an understanding of the dynamics of interhuman communication and language. In this case, language becomes a *medium* and not an instrument.[20] Sacramental communication is less a process of mechanical causality and more a relational gift exchange between God and human beings.

Rethinking the Sacraments of Healing/ Reconciliation in Postmodern Categories

The postmodern consideration of the sacraments is paramount because, in its checkered history, the sacrament of reconciliation/healing has had the common elements of confession, repentance, and forgiveness.[21] In this vein, the eminent historian of the sacraments, Joseph Martos, concludes that the ritual through which divine forgiveness was sought changed with the changing circumstances. Attention to the signs of the times should always be in reference to Jesus who was a sacrament of divine forgiveness and healing to many who met him. He called people to repentance and embraced sinners. In the same broad sense, the church is called to be a sacrament of reconciliation today as in the fecund early years of Christianity.[22] That is to say, the church should not be squirreling away its sacramental tradition but rather making it an "open tradition under the inspiration of the Holy Spirit, wherein continuity with the past as well as creativity in an eschatological perspective are both operative."[23]

Rethinking sacramental theology begins fundamentally with a postmodern understanding of God, which exposes the lacunae of an onto-theological vision of God, a god of our thoughts and projections and not the true relational God who gives god self to us as a gift. At the heart of Chauvet's fundamental sacramental theological discourse is his insistence on changing our perspectives of God: "*God reveals God in what is different from God.*" God reveals God as human in God's very divinity. Jean-Luc Marion's philosophy, drawing insights from Heidegger, corroborates this view when he opposes the true God against the god of metaphysical thought (*idole conceptuelle*). The true God is to be found in the evangelical message of God's self-revelation in Jesus as the image of the invisible God as an unsolicited gift (*don*), to the abandonment (*abandon*) of his Son, for the forgiveness (*pardon*) of evil.[24] This gratuitous communication of God with believers is the salient point of the sacraments, Chauvet asserts: "Any weakening of this affirmation . . . would rob the sacrament of its essential originality."[25]

Applying this unsolicited gift of God to the sacrament of reconciliation, the Belgian theologian Lambert Leijssen clarifies it in Paul Ricoeur's hermeneutical terms: "a certain 'figure' is identifiable in the act of reconciliation[/healing], prefigured (*préfiguré*) in fundamental patterns from the biblical message and history. These form the basis for a new figure for our contemporary thought-world (*configuration*) that fulfills the real intention of this sacrament, namely, the conversion and reconciliation of the faithful (*réfiguration*)."[26]

Herein lies the mystery of the sacrament of reconciliation. This "figure" who was "disfigured" by our sins/weakness (Is 52:14) is not ashamed to "configure" sinners/the weak to himself through the Spirit to grant them reconciliation and healing (Is 53:5).

A postmodern analysis of the sacraments thus helps us to overcome the weaknesses of the three theoretical models discussed earlier. By the anthropological categories of language and symbols, Chauvet overcomes the major onto-theological category of "cause," which is seen as the bane of a proper understanding of the sacraments. Without falling into the subjective model, a postmodern understanding of the sacrament of healing equally stays clear of a one-sided christological emphasis by integrating it with a pneumatological principle within a trinitarian framework.[27] Leijssen can thus characterize the sacraments as the "silent glimmer of the Spirit." In other words, contrary to the Aristotelian "matter-form" pattern, a postmodern perspective focuses on the fact that it is "the language of the self-giving God, as a renewed gift of the Holy Spirit, that illuminates the inner heart of the believer, invites him or her to conversion, and offers God's reconciliation as a gratuitous gift."[28]

In effect, it could be suggested that within the current exigencies of church life, the sacrament of reconciliation is seen less as a *process* and more as an *end result* of conversion. A postmodern analysis recommends that in whatever form it takes, either as communal or individual celebration, reconciliation should not exclude categories of people in the church whom "we" deem as "sinners."[29]

Is Permissiveness for All a Form of Liberalism?

From what I have been arguing thus far, some might think they detect a liberal attitude toward the sacraments. As one priest puts it, the sacraments are not for us to deny people, but when it comes to its application, we need to be very strict. But those who argue in favor of liberalism *a priori* construe the sacraments as a reward for good behavior and holiness. Before arguing that such a stance is pure liberalism in the church, we need to cast our minds back in history to understand that in the New Testament times, on the basis of the forgiveness preached by Jesus, he who died for "our sins," a very open sort of attitude was taken toward forgiveness. It was increasingly from the second century onward that a more rigorous attitude to reconciliation was put in place. Thus, in line with the early fathers, who emphasized God's mercy and forgiveness to the sinner who converts, we equally think that in the light of sacramental *ressourcement* both components can be maintained in our time, namely, the holiness of life as an evidence of genuine conversion but also a trust in the merciful God who forgives sins.

Moreover, we are of the view that allowing the excluded to be beneficiaries of the sacrament of healing more or less cements the notions of *communion* ecclesiology and of the church as family of God. More inclusive practices will lead to a situation where people will trust in the Catholic Church and recognize the outstretched hand of God in an open believing community over and against antiquated forms of exclusivism. The ecclesial community must be an inviting community where "sinners" are welcome and where they are supported on their journey of conversion to God.

Conclusion

In the practical existential life of the church, the gap between classical sacramental theology and contemporary ecclesial culture puts the very plausibility and relevance of the sacraments under enormous pressure. While many Christians are gradually distancing themselves from the ecclesial sacramental life of the church, a preponderance of those who remain within it are sadly denied access to the sacraments of reconciliation/healing. The provenance of such marginalization is due largely in part to the church's clinging to onto-theological understanding of the sacraments as well as to some pastoral discriminations and indiscretions. A sacramental understanding of the church itself should aid in grasping the sacraments as means of grace through which a deeper relationship with one's God is attained.

Even though postmodern theologians, particularly Chauvet, urge us to overcome onto-theological categories, vestiges of this causal, instrumental, and productionist understanding are operative in the church. By appreciating more deeply the symbolic character of the sacraments, it is possible to admit all members of the Christian faithful to the sacramental celebration of the reconciliation/healing irrespective of their marital status. The existential condition of human beings, who always experience brokenness in their lives irrespective of their "sinful condition," still accompanies them as they knock at the door of the church. It is up to the church to open up its doors. The acceptance of all people to these sacraments will not detract from the holiness of the church but rather make it grow in works of "grace." As Karl Rahner has well argued, "grace can no longer be seen as an external entity that is infused into our souls, but rather as God's self-communication (*Selbstmitteilung*) of love to the entire world."[30] This grace is a participation in the love bond of the triune God. Thus understood, the admission of all Christian faithful to the sacrament of reconciliation/healing or of the Eucharist within the terms of our consideration is not simply *out of charity or privilege* but *constitutive of their rights* as Christians faithfully baptized in the Spirit.

To take this challenge of approaching the sacraments of reconciliation/healing in this way, the church community must draw from the faith conviction that its sacraments are borne and encompassed by the trans-sacramental, namely, by that which precedes and transcends sacraments. The first *and* final word is left to the communicative grace of God, to the wholly other who offers blessing, strength, and a future to all the baptized. If indeed Jesus is the *Ursakrament* who excludes neither "perceived sinners" nor "real sinners" but accepts them irrespective of their situation and condition, then it stands to reason that the *Grundsakrament*, the church, must accept all its members who are seeking the salvific touch of the *Ursakrament* through the sacraments of reconciliation and healing.

Notes

[1] See Bishop Matthew Gyamfi's "Intervention at the Seventh Congregation of the 2nd Synod of Bishops for Africa," http://www.zenit.org/rssenglish-27130.

[2] Catholic Bishops' Conference of Ghana, *Ecclesia in Ghana: On the Church in Ghana and Its Evangelizing Mission in the Third Millennium* (Cape Coast, Ghana, 1997), 73.

[3] John Paul II, *Post Synodal Apostolic Exhortation Reconciliation and Penitence*, no. 34.

[4] Martin Luther, *Lectures on the Romans*, trans. Wilhem Pauck (Philadephia: Westminster, 1961), 130.

[5] For a contemporary understanding of the sacraments, I draw mainly from the works of Louis-Marie Chauvet on the sacraments, which try to reconstruct a hermeneutics of the sacraments from the Christian existential condition of faith

and practice as a Christian in the postmodern context. See Louis-Marie Chauvet, *Symbol and Sacrament: A Sacramental Reinterpretation of Christian Existence*, trans. Patrick Madigan and Madeleine Beaumont (Collegeville, MN: Liturgical Press, 1995), 1–4; see also Lieven Boeve, "Theology in a Postmodern Context and the Hermeneutical Project of Louis-Marie Chauvet," in *Sacraments: Revelation of the Humanity of God, Engaging the Fundamental Theology of Louis-Marie Chauvet*, ed. Philipe Bordeyne and Bruce T. Morrill (Collegeville, MN: Liturgical Press, 2008), 5–23.

[6] Hilary Silver, *Social Exclusion: Comparative Analysis of Europe and Middle East*, The Middle East Working Initiative Paper No. 1 (Washinton, DC: Wolfeson Centre for Development, 2007), 15.

[7] See ibid., 5–6.

[8] On the institutional aspect of the church, it is important to underscore the various shades of meaning. It seems natural to make a distinction between two levels among all these institutional structures. Following Yves Congar, for example, we can distinguish between the *essential structures* and *occasional structures*. Similarly, Hervé Legrand differentiates between what results from *fundamental institutionality* of the church and what comes from the *organizational right* as *ecclesia semper reformandum*. For a recent analysis of the relationship between structure/life, charism/institution etc., see Remi Chéno, *L'Esprit-Saint et L'église: Institutionalité et pneumatologie, vers un dépassement des antagonisme Ecclésiologique* (Paris: Cerf, 2010), 24. In fact, Chéno prefers the terms "couple" (*couple*) or "binomial/binary" (*binôme*), which avoids pitting the categories of charism and institution against each other, instead of the term "opposition."

[9] Based on the church's understanding of customary marriage, it is actually a formality to undergo a "second marriage." This is because the Code of Canon Law's understanding of natural marriage permits situations whereby the customary marriage of couples who were hitherto non-Christians (natural marriage) is upheld as "true marriage," and a second marriage is not performed subsequent to their conversion and baptism.

[10] Francis Appiah Kubi, "The Church as the Family of God: Theological and Pastoral Challenges," Lecture given at Leuven, INTAMS Conference March 10–13, 2010.

[11] Ibid.

[12] On the objective analysis, see also Louis-Marie Chauvet, "L' Institution ecclésiale et sacramentalle dans le champ du symbolique," *Raisons Politiques* 4, no. (2001): 97.

[13] Louis-Marie Chauvet, *The Sacraments: The Word of God at the Mercy of the Body* (Collegeville, MN: Liturgical Press, 2001), xvi.

[14] Ibid., xix.

[15] Ibid., xxv.

[16] *Symbol and Sacrament*, 7.

[17] Cf. Pope John Paul II, *Post Synodal Apostolic Exhortation Reconciliation and Penitence no. 34*, my emphasis.

[18] Chauvet takes his cue from Heidegger in criticizing onto-theology; see Lieven Boeve, "Method in Postmodern Theology: A Case Study," in *The Presence of Transcendence: Thinking "Sacrament" in a Postmodern Age*, ed. Lieven Boeve and J. C. Ries (Leuven, Belgium: Peeters Press, 2001), 19–39.

[19] Louis-Marie Chauvet, "Parole et Sacrement," *Recherche de Science Religieuse* 2 (2003): 203–22.

[20] Cf. Chauvet, *Symbol and Sacrament*, 45.

[21] See Joseph J. Martos, *Doors to the Sacred: A Historical Introduction to Sacraments in the Catholic Church*, rev. ed. (St. Louis, MO: Liguori Publications, 2001), 276.

[22] Ibid., 279.

[23] Lambert Leijssen, *With the Silent Glimmer of God's Spirit: A Postmodern Look at the Sacraments* (Mahwah, NJ: Paulist Press, 2006), 62.

[24] Jean-Luc Marion, *Being Given: Toward a Phenomenology of Givenness*, trans. Jeffrey L. Kosky (Stanford, CA: Stanford University Press, 2002).

[25] Chauvet, *The Sacraments*, xiii. On the perceptions and understanding of God, see also Uche Bede Ukwuije, "Thinking God Differently: Christian Theology and Postmodernity," in *God, Bible, and African Traditional Religion: Acts of SIST International Missiological Symposium 2009*, ed. Uche Bede Ukwuije (Enugu, Nigeria: SNAAP Press, 2010), 196–211.

[26] Leijssen, *With the Silent Glimmer of God's Spirit*, 62.

[27] See Chauvet, *Symbol and Sacrament*, 492–509.

[28] Leijssen, *With the Silent Glimmer of God's Spirit*, 63.

[29] See Patrick Cogan, "The Sacrament of Reconciliation: Issues, Praxis and the Future," *Proceedings of the Canon Law Society of America* 66 (2004): 81–92.

[30] Karl Rahner, "Concerning the Relationship between Nature and Grace," in *Theological Investigations*, vol. 1 (Baltimore: Helicon Press, 1961), 296–318; George Wandervelde, "The Grammar of Grace: Karl Rahner as a Watershed in Contemporary Theology," *Theological Studies* 49 (1988): 445–59.

PART VII

EXCLUSION AND ECUMENICAL REALITY

Inclusion and Exclusion in the Anglican Communion:
The Case of the Anglican Covenant

Mark D. Chapman

It would be fair to say that the Anglican Communion developed in a piecemeal and somewhat accidental way. What began as a national church of the Reformation limited to the boundaries of England and Wales has mutated into a worldwide communion of some eighty million members. But it was not always like this; at the beginning there was not an Anglican Communion. When Thomas Cromwell boldly declared in 1534 that "This realm of England is an Empire" and Henry VIII made rapid use of that sort of imperial power in matters ecclesiastical, this meant that the church *in* England became the Church *of* England. At least at the beginning of the Church of England, it was impossible for Anglicanism to be anything other than a *local* phenomenon. One of its principal defining characteristics was that it was not Roman Catholic.

While the ultimate authority in the Church of England might be the gospel of Jesus Christ, there could be no appeal to "any foreign prince or potentate, spiritual or temporal" in the interpretation or implementation of that gospel. The Church of England expressed what can be called a kind of "contained catholicity"—that is, it considered itself catholic, but such catholicism was expressed more in terms of its inheritance from the past rather than spatially through its international relations. In theory at least, the Church of England, as it developed through the Elizabethan settlement, claimed to include everybody in England. Thus, in a famous statement, Richard Hooker declares, "There is not any man of the Church of England but the same man is also a member of the commonwealth; nor any man a member of the commonwealth which is not also of the Church of England."[1]

Without trying to cram in four hundred years of the history of missions into a few sentences, it is this idea of "contained catholicity" that became the key principle of Anglican ecclesiology as it expanded overseas. Although there were obviously many connections with the English Crown in the early years of missionary endeavor, the example of the American church clearly displays this form of independent ecclesiology: the Crown could have no authority over a church when it had completely lost control over the American colonies. What was adopted at the General Convention in 1789 was a democratic constitution modeled on the new political arrangements for the United States. The Episcopal Church was as equally independent as the Church of England from any other church. By the end of the nineteenth century, there were many separate churches throughout the Anglican Communion governed by their own constitutions, often with quite different structures from the Church of England. While most were still united with the mother church in terms of culture, and even though England still provided most of the leaders, the different national churches were independent of direct control from England.

By the 1860s, there were serious conflicts between these new national churches, and many bishops, especially from Canada and New Zealand, asked the Archbishop of Canterbury to convene a meeting to solve the problem of Bishop Colenso in South Africa whose opinions were regarded as heretical by Bishop Robert Gray of Cape Town. Archbishop Longley responded to the call with the First Lambeth Conference in 1867. Yet it was very tentative—even the archbishop of York refused to go, since he could not see how any foreign bishop could have any authority over the Church of England. Although there was a clamor for firm leadership and strong decision-making powers, what emerged was quite the opposite: there could be no canons or laws or even excommunications of errant bishops. Those who sought a strong centralized authority in the Anglican Communion exercised by bishops modeled on the so-called primitive episcopate were thwarted, as a completely different approach to Anglicanism was adopted at the next Lambeth Conferences, especially in 1888.

What emerged was not a strongly doctrinal Anglicanism rooted in English formularies but an extraordinarily inclusive denominational identity, exercised through independent churches with virtually no central authority. This meant that under the influence of the American church, as well as the reluctance of the Archbishops of Canterbury to expand their claims, a completely different sense of catholicity from the post-Vatican I Roman model developed. Instead of becoming a centralized communion focused on Canterbury, the communion mutated into a loose collection of churches that shared common histories but that had begun to go their own separate ways with very little holding them together.

William Reed Huntington: The National Church
and the Anglican Communion

Crucial in the shaping of the inclusive theology of the Anglican Communion was William Reed Huntington (1838–1909),[2] rector of All Saints' Church, Worcester, Massachusetts (1862–83), and then of Grace Church, New York (from 1883), and one of the leading theological voices in the Episcopal Church in the last three decades of the nineteenth century. Although he had been deeply influenced by the work of F. D. Maurice and other English defenders of a broad national church, Huntington was working in the very different context of a society divided by the disastrous Civil War, which remains one of the bloodiest wars in history. In his most important work, *The Church-Idea* (*CI*) of 1870, he was concerned first and foremost to promote unity through what he called the "Anglican principle," which would allow the church to become "the reconciler of a divided household."[3] The word "Anglican," however, was used as a synonym for catholicity rather than Englishness. The growing awareness of the independence of the American church was established in part on an anti-Englishness that resembled the anti-Britishness of the founding myths of the American republic. For Huntington, the creation of an American Catholic Church was central for it to fulfill its national vocation.[4]

Huntington begins *The Church-Idea* by describing the dissatisfaction that "best expresses the state of mind in which Christendom finds itself to-day. . . . Unrest is everywhere. The party of the Curia and the party of the Reformation, the party of orthodoxy and the party of liberalism, are all alike agitated by the consciousness that a spirit of change is in the air" (*CI* 1). It was in this period of rapid change that he sought to redefine catholicity: "Clearly we have come upon a time for the study of first principles, a time to go down and look after the foundations upon which our customary beliefs are built. The more searching the analysis, the more lasting will the synthesis be sure to be" (*CI* 2).

This analysis leads him to develop what he calls the "Anglican principle," which moves beyond any tendency to sectarianism or provincialism by pointing toward a universality: "Anglicanism stands, as Wellington's squares of infantry stood at Waterloo, firm, patient, dogged, if we must call it so, but true,—true as steel" (*CI* 124). On this basis, he asked, "What are the essential, the absolutely essential features of the Anglican position?" His answers were both radical and provocative. Thus, in a famous passage, he develops an understanding of Anglicanism shorn of its Englishness:

When it is proposed to make Anglicanism the basis of a Church of the Reconciliation, it is above all things necessary to determine what

Anglicanism pure and simple is. The word brings up before the eyes of some a flutter of surplices, a vision of village spires and cathedral towers, a somewhat stiff and stately company of deans, prebendaries, and choristers, and that is about all. But we greatly err if we imagine that the Anglican principle has no substantial existence apart from these accessories. Indeed, it is only when we have stripped Anglicanism of the picturesque costume which English life has thrown around it, that we can fairly study its anatomy, or understand its possibilities of power and adaptation.

The Anglican principle and the Anglican system are two very different things. The writer does not favor attempting to foist the whole Anglican system upon America; while yet he believes that the Anglican principle is America's best hope. At no time since the Reformation has the Church of England been in actual fact the spiritual home of the nation. A majority of the people of Great Britain are to-day without her pale. Could a system which has failed to secure comprehensiveness on its native soil, hope for any larger measure of success in a strange land? (*CI* 124–25)

Having thus removed Anglicanism of its dependence on its English origins, he develops the idea still further by using the analogy of a "quadrilateral" derived both from Augustine as well as the four great fortress cities of Mantua, Verona, Peschiera, and Legnano, which had become famous during the Austro-Prussian War of 1866.

The true Anglican position, like the City of God in the Apocalypse, may be said to lie foursquare. Honestly to accept that position is to accept,—
  1st. The Holy Scriptures as the Word of God.
  2nd. The Primitive Creeds as the Rule of Faith.
  3rd. The two Sacraments ordained by Christ himself.
  4th. The Episcopate as the key-stone of Governmental Unity.
  These four points, like the four famous fortresses of Lombardy, make the Quadrilateral of pure Anglicanism. Within them the Church of the Reconciliation may stand secure. Because the English State-Church has muffled these first principles in a cloud of non-essentials, and has said to the people of the land, "Take all this or nothing," she mourns to-day the loss of half her children. Only by avoiding the like fatal error can the American branch of the Anglican Church hope to save herself from becoming in effect, whatever she may be in name, a sect. Only by a wise discrimination between what can and

what cannot be conceded for the sake of unity, is unity attainable. (*CI* 125–26)

Thus, in a manner highly reminiscent of F. D. Maurice, Huntington sees the church as an agent of reconciliation founded on four simple points. The identity of the church is rooted in history, as well as the visible sign of unity in the episcopate, although he does not limit the form of episcopacy solely to that inherited by his own church.

Huntington thereby sought to move the Episcopal Church onto a higher level: its denominational identity was to be found not in a vague recollection of Englishness but in the identity of the Catholic Church itself in which Englishness did not feature except as a nostalgic recollection. Episcopalianism was thus less Anglican than national as it sought to embrace all Christians prepared to adopt the minimal definition of what constituted the church. Thus, even if it might not, in practice, become the sole national church, it could at least aspire to the ideal. Toward the end of *The Church-Idea*, he spoke candidly of the problems of Episcopalianism, which was always in danger of becoming little more than a respectable sect. This would be a denial of its true catholicity. Instead, Huntington held up a very different vision of the church:

> If we aim at something nobler than this, if we would have our Communion become national in very truth, . . . then let us press our reasonable claims to be the reconciler of a divided household, not in a spirit of arrogance (which ill befits those whose best possessions have come to them by inheritance), but with affectionate earnestness and an intelligent zeal. (*CI* 169)

Huntington continued to develop his ideas of a national church throughout the remainder of his life. As he says in his book, *A National Church* (*NC*), while he might have hoped for an ultimate "federation of the world," he held that at present "the Sovereign Commander of all the world has use for nations," in which the national church played a crucial role, even if it was a "temporary expedient, . . . forced upon us by the necessities of the present, and destined in due time, . . . to merge in the larger *ecclesia* in which are to be gathered all the nations of the earth" (*NC* 14, 16).

The national church was especially important in providing an alternative ideal from that of the infallibilist. For Huntington, the national church offered something quite different from the absolutism of what he called Vaticanism. Recognizing that "in this world of dimmed eyes and wayward wills, absolutism has a charm all its own," he nevertheless sought a model of ecclesiastical authority based on consent and open to the future (*NC* 31–33). "Would you be a good Catholic?" he asks, and answers "Be a good Nationalist first" (*NC* 36). This meant that an American Catholic Church would resist simply mimicking its English antecedent: "The English ivy is a beautiful plant, and nothing is one-half so becoming to church walls; but unfortunately the English ivy does not flourish in all climates, and to insist that it shall be 'Ivy or nothing' in a land where the woodbine and other fairly presentable vines are indigenous is a mistake" (*NC* 51).

While the churches of America obviously owed a great deal to England, Huntington urged his audience not to be drawn to "the fool's paradise of those who fancy that American Christianity in its entirety can be Anglified" (*NC* 52). Instead it would be as diverse as American society. "Why should it be any greater hardship to dwell in the same Church with a man who dotes upon candles and incense, than to dwell in the same town as him?"(*NC* 66). Now that the Episcopal Church had come of age, he claimed, it needed to move toward a new vision of national inclusivity. Thus he concluded, "Surely an American Catholic Church worthy of the name ought to have godlier words for those whom it is her duty to gather and include, than the cold, hard, stolid *Non possumus* of absolutism, or sharp apothegm, This people which knoweth not the rubrics is accursed" (*NC* 71–72).

The Chicago-Lambeth Quadrilateral

Huntington's four points were taken as constitutive of the identity of catholicity at the General Convention held at Chicago in 1886: again the aim was to promote national unity and reconciliation. There was, however, little sense of spatial catholicity contained in the quadrilateral; it was, after all, concerned more with national unity than with global communion. For Huntington, as for the General Convention, the point of the quadrilateral was to promote an inclusive national church to which the scattered denominations might be invited to join. To this was added an understanding of the primitive or historic episcopate that was seen as the best way of representing this unity.

The Anglican Principle of a national unified church for all people was expressed in the broader resolution adopted at Chicago that was addressed "especially to our fellow-Christians of the different Communions in this land, who, in their several spheres, have contended for the religion of Christ."[5] The entry requirement into the church was simply baptism, while in "all things of human ordering or human choice, relating to modes of worship and discipline, or to traditional customs, this Church is ready in the spirit of love and humility to forgo all preferences of her own." Unity was to be established by a return to the undivided church of the past. Before affirming the quadrilateral, the convention asserted "that the Christian unity can be restored only by the return of all Christian communions to the principles of unity exemplified by the undivided Catholic Church during the first ages of its existence; which principles we believe to be the substantial deposit of Christian Faith and Order committed by Christ and his Apostles to the Church unto the end of the world, and therefore incapable of compromise or surrender by those who have been ordained to be its stewards and trustees for the common and equal benefit of all men."[6] The Chicago Quadrilateral was aimed principally at reconciliation at home and as an invitation to other denominations to unite, rather than as a definition of international Anglicanism.

When applied to the broader sense of catholic unity between the national churches of the Anglican Communion, however, Huntington's quadrilateral had very different consequences. The pressing question for the Anglican Communion was what sort of unity a group of churches established on the basis of national independence could adopt at a transnational level. Archbishops after Longley continued to resist calls for centralization and for a firm executive body that could make hard and fast decisions, including exclusions and excommunications. So tightly bound up was the archbishop's authority with the English establishment that it was impossible to see how it could extend beyond national boundaries. Thus, whatever sort of catholicity the communion might adopt would be highly circumspect and decentralized. Archbishop E. W. Benson (1829–96), for instance, who presided over the 1888 Lambeth Conference, maintained that the unity displayed by the church did not imply uniformity (which, he held, was the failing of what he called "Roman Unity").[7] Instead, he held that all unity had to be sensitive to its cultural setting, and ultimate unity was located in a hidden future rather than a visible institution. Unity resided with God and was always a hope rather than a fact:

> If we wish to prepare a future for our people and our children, we must make provision for an active, realised unity in the Church. . . . But we must avoid a common fancy. We cannot recur to the past for unity. External unity has not existed yet, except superficially. *Unity is not the first scene, but the last triumph of Christianity and man.* Christ himself could not *create* unity in His Church. He could pray for it, and his prayer most movingly teaches us to work for it. On earth it is not a gift, but a growth. If any vision of it is granted us we must work both in and towards what we have seen that "although it tarry, it may be for an appointed time," but rather still that "it may come and *not* tarry."[8]

The unity of the church, according to Benson, could thus never be a completely undifferentiated unity imposed from above but had to respond to local circumstances. A failure to be responsive to the cultural conditions and "to seek to build up a like Church, stone by stone as it were, spiritually, out of the utterly different characters, experiences, sentiments of another race, is to repeat without excuse the error of the great Boniface, in making not a Teutonic but an Italian Church in Germany. It is to contradict the wise axioms with which Gregory tried to save Augustine from the error."[9] The crucial question for the Anglican Communion was over precisely how it could function as a catholic church without adopting the alternative model of a centrally imposed uniformity.

The question of unity was addressed at the 1888 Lambeth Conference over which Benson presided, where the bishops adopted a slightly revised version of the Chicago Quadrilateral as the basis "on which approach may be by God's blessing made towards Home Reunion."[10] A crucial difference, however, was that instead of simply seeing the four points as inherent parts of the deposit of faith and order, the Lambeth Resolution regarded them as "articles," presumably akin to the Thirty-Nine Articles, and therefore as constitutive of both Anglicanism and the Christian faith.[11] The Anglican principle became less a clamor for reconciliation and more a description of the churches that could be accepted as the members of the Anglican Communion. For the first time, an international definition of what constituted Anglicanism was given. Furthermore, the basis in Home Reunion was soon forgotten. Thus, instead of serving the project of ecumenical reconciliation and as an invitation to move beyond denominationalism through applying what was effectively a temporal criterion for catholicity rooted in scripture and tradition, the Lambeth Quadrilateral served the opposite purpose of creating a definition of worldwide Anglicanism as a particular denomination. Beyond this, specific statements of doctrine were left to the national churches, partly because it was assumed that the English formularies would continue to be accepted.

The Covenant

The inclusive model served the Anglican Communion well through most of the twentieth century, as the different national churches were united in common missionary endeavor and huge growth. But the last years of the century revealed levels of conflict that simply could not be contained by the extraordinarily weak structures of the communion. Several key events have highlighted the questions of unity and diversity in the communion and the virtual absence of any central authority. While women's ordination stretched the bonds of communion, there were two main pressing issues:

firstly, some Asian and African bishops started setting up missionary bishops to work across the boundaries of other churches, and, secondly, the Episcopal Church ordained Gene Robinson, a partnered homosexual man, as bishop of New Hampshire.

Homosexuality has been high on the Anglican agenda since Lambeth 1998, when an amendment to a resolution was passed by an overwhelming majority of the bishops condemning homosexuality as incompatible with scripture. While the Lambeth Conference had always claimed to be nothing more than advisory, Resolution 1.10 was treated very differently. It raised questions both about the authority of the Bible, as well as the authority of the Lambeth Conference, over the national churches. If it is considered to be a requirement of the faith revealed in scripture that bishops should not live in same-sex partnered relationships, then those churches that do not accept this would no longer be maintaining the catholic faith. As things stand, this latter view is currently the majority view in the Anglican Communion as a whole, and even within those provinces that have taken a different line, there are significant numbers who disagree. But what is lacking is any means of adjudication: the national church ideal and the absence of centralism or dogmatic unity has stretched inclusivity to the breaking point.

In May 2003, shortly after Robinson's election, matters were complicated still further when the Canadian Diocese of New Westminster authorized rites for same-sex blessings. These actions meant that the new archbishop of Canterbury, Rowan Williams, was immediately faced with threats by some provinces to excommunicate the American and Canadian churches. A number of bishops from Africa and Asia began to intervene in other churches across the Atlantic. This meant that there was an urgent need to examine the nature of relationships between the provinces. The Archbishop of Canterbury summoned the primates to an emergency meeting and set up the Lambeth Commission on Communion, chaired by Robin Eames, which produced *The Windsor Report* in October 2004.[12] It was a lengthy document that tried to clarify the nature of communion and authority in the Anglican Communion, especially the constraints, restraints, and discipline necessary to ensure that the greatest degree of communion between provinces could be maintained: it contained the seeds of the idea of a covenant, or an agreement by the constituent churches to restrain their actions. For the first time it spoke of sanctions for those who were not to be restrained. Exclusion, as well as inclusion, was spoken of for the first time. The report proposed a method of "mutual reciprocity and forbearance" that would be policed by what was called a "Council of Advice," acting as an extension of the office of the Archbishop of Canterbury.

Tension remained high. The Council of Anglican Provinces of Africa (CAPA) issued a statement that they would "definitely not attend any

Lambeth Conference to which the violators of the Lambeth Resolution are also invited as participants or observers." At the meeting of the primates in Dar es Salaam in February 2007, eight primates refused to receive communion at a service at which Katherine Jefferts-Schori, the recently elected presiding bishop of the Episcopal Church, was present. They nevertheless considered a first draft of a covenant: what is most significant is that the first use of the word "covenant" is as a verb (§1).

After ruling out any communion-wide canon law, further drafts have stressed the idea of a voluntary commitment by the autonomous churches of the Anglican Communion to be prepared to limit their autonomy for the sake of the communion as a whole. Churches of the Anglican Communion would remain as free as they always have been to amend their canons and to make changes to their practices, but where up to now this has led to a piecemeal and somewhat anarchic series of actions by churches and dioceses across the world (and even within the same church), what is proposed is a mechanism that would provide some sort of structure for dealing with change and possible conflict. The covenant principle is that certain actions may need to be restrained for the sake of the relationships of trust, respect, and commitment. The particular church thus needs to relate to the universal, which is not simply historical as with the quadrilateral but also spatial.[13]

On the covenant model, the church is established on the notion of a freely entered into agreement to abide by a somewhat more developed set of Anglican principles and methods (parts one to three) and also to limit those actions that might be controversial. Under the covenant there is a voluntary commitment from all churches to listen to others before acting. And there is also a recognition of the need for mediation and conflict resolution, which has been conspicuously absent in the past few years. After listening has occurred and when disagreement persists, a standing committee would then rule: its only sanction is exclusion from the Anglican Communion, a sanction that would make no difference to the national independent churches except in their relations with other national churches. This could not affect the legal autonomy of each church, unless, of course, it were to change its own canons to give the committee legal recognition— akin to the European Court—something that would be almost unthinkable given the strength of the national church model. It would amount to expulsion from some modest structures from which many have already absented themselves. Where a church felt it was more in accord with its understanding of the gospel to act, despite the recommendation of the standing committee, nothing would be able to prevent it from doing so. The only sanction would be to lose its representation on the various instruments of communion. But even that would not mean that churches would cease to be in communion with one another—this would be for each church to decide for itself.

Overall, I think the covenant is a kind of "tepid constitutionalism" that could allow for greater ecclesial coherence, although it is highly unlikely that all thirty-eight churches will adopt it. While there may well be tough decisions and splits ahead, it seems to me that these are already happening in an unstructured and sometimes highly acrimonious way, and it is unlikely that a covenant will make things worse. Obviously it may well turn out that the standing committee, which is supposed to administer the sanctions, will not be able to gain the trust and authority that is required for its decisions to be effective, in which case the Anglican Communion will mutate into a much looser federation of churches rooted in an historical Anglican identity. For many, this may not be an undesirable development.

Perhaps the Anglican Communion's contextual model of catholicity with its decentralized interactive pluralism cannot hold together except through more informal dialogue and discussion between those who are prepared to listen to one another and agree to disagree. The covenant will not work unless there is a desire to make it work, and that requires far more than any modest constitutional document can achieve. To succeed, the common mind of Anglicanism will need to be tempered by the humility to acknowledge human fallibility, even among the leaders and decision makers of the church. The fact that a number of primates have absented themselves from recent meetings and that a new parallel communion structure is developing does not augur well.

Notes

[1] Richard Hooker, *Laws of Ecclesiastical Polity*, bk. VIII, chap. i.2.

[2] See Robert Prichard, *A History of the Episcopal Church* (Harrisburg, PA: Morehouse, 1999), 188–90. On the origins of the national church idea, see Paul T. Phillips, "The Concept of a National Church in Late Nineteenth-century England and America," *Journal of Religious History* 14 (1986): 26–37, esp. 31–32.

[3] William Reed Huntington, *The Church-Idea: An Essay Towards Unity* (New York: E. P. Dutton, 1870; 4th ed., Charles Scribner's Sons, 1899), 169 (hereafter as *CI*).

[4] William Reed Huntington, *National Church* (New York: Charles Scribner's Sons, 1899), 52–53 (hereafter as *NC*).

[5] Resolution of the General Convention 1886, http://anglicansonline.org/basics/Chicago_Lambeth.html.

[6] Ibid.

[7] "Growing Unity" in Edward White Benson, *Living Theology* (London: Sampson Low, Marston, 1893), 131–45, 139.

[8] Ibid., 133.

[9] This passage from Benson's "Visitation Charge of 1885" is found in his biography, *The Life of Edward White Benson: Sometime Archbishop of Canterbury*, by his son, Arthur Christopher Benson (London: Macmillan and Co., 1899) vol. II, 465–66.

[10] Resolution 11 of the Lambeth Conference of 1888. Cf. Roger Coleman, *Resolutions of the Twelve Lambeth Conferences* (Toronto: Anglican Book Centre, 1992), 13; Alan M. G. Stephenson, *Anglicanism and the Lambeth Conferences* (London: SPCK, 1978). Cf. Jonathan Draper, ed., *Communion and Episcopacy: Essays to Mark the Centenary of the Chicago-Lambeth Quadrilateral* (Oxford: RCC, 1988).

[11] Gillian R. Evans, "Permanence in the Revealed Truth and Continuous Exploration of Its Meaning," in *Quadrilateral at One Hundred*, ed. J. Robert Wright (London: Mowbray, 1998), 111–25, esp. 114–15.

[12] *The Windsor Report* (2004), http://www.anglicancommunion.org/windsor2004/index.cfm.

[13] *Draft Covenant*, Intro, sec.4, and sec. 3, http://www.anglicancommunion.org/commission/covenant/final/text.cfm.

The Arduous Journey from Exclusion to Communion: Overcoming Relationships of Distrust between Orthodox and Catholics

Peter De Mey

As an ecumenist I am more used to reflecting on notions such as "ecumenism" and "communion" rather than on notions such as "exclusion," "division," "disunity," and "schism," especially when dealing with ecumenical relations with the Orthodox Church, which Roman Catholics consider as their "sister church" par excellence.[1] The 1967 address of Archbishop Vitaly of Montreal and Canada to the Sobor of bishops of the Russian Orthodox Church Outside Russia, however, already makes one aware that Orthodox-Roman Catholic relations are not always free from exclusivist tendencies:

> Ecumenism is now at the doors of our Church. . . . If until today ecumenism has not been dangerous for us, now the situation has changed somewhat, first of all because we have remained the only Church in the whole world that has not entered the WCC, and in all probability special steps will be undertaken for us, a special tactic will be employed. We must be ready for this. Second, unquestionably a strong attack will be made on the mass of our believers, among whom there are not a few souls, some of whom will yield, being seduced by the thought of union, fearing their isolation, and others being tempted by advantages, a better situation, in a word by the golden calf.[2]

The Orthodox-Roman Catholic dialogue also came into my mind because its point of reference is known as "the great schism" of 1054. Those specialized in the history of the great schism know that it is important to pay attention to a great amount of cultural, historical, and political—often called "nontheological"—factors if one wants to better understand the reasons for the gradual separation of East and West.[3] In the same vein, if one wants to better understand why the theological dialogue between Orthodox and Catholics in our time moves on rather slowly and even has known a long period of standstill, a study of the theological divergences alone is not sufficient. There are a lot of church politics and difficult relations involved as well.

At the time of the Second Vatican Council, there was great hope that the restoration of the communion between both churches would be an event of the near future. After the Catholic Church had developed an ecclesiological understanding of the notion of catholicity that allowed for a great amount of inner-Catholic theological, spiritual, liturgical, and canonical diversity, the Council could declare the existing diversity among the churches of the East as something that they would not lose in case of an eventual reunion:

> To remove all shadow of doubt, then, this synod solemnly declares that the churches of the east, while mindful of the necessary unity of the whole church, have the right to govern themselves according to the disciplines proper to themselves, since these are better suited to the character of their faithful, and more for the good of their souls. (*Unitatis Redintegratio*, § 16)

The great expectations of the bishops of the Catholic Church toward the Orthodox are also clearly expressed in the final words of this section of the Decree on Ecumenism: "If this cause is wholeheartedly promoted, the synod hopes that the barrier dividing the church between east and west will be removed, and that at last there may be but the one dwelling, firmly established on Christ Jesus, the cornerstone, who will make both one" (*Unitatis Redintegratio*, §18).

Here I will not focus so much on the current ecclesiological discussions between Orthodox and Catholics; this dialogue is still ongoing and will require a long period of further deliberations. After all, the 2007 Ravenna document *Ecclesiological and Canonical Consequences of the Sacramental Nature of the Church: Communion, Conciliarity and Authority* was only the result of a modest redaction of a text that had basically been ready in 1990.[4] I will take the Orthodox-Roman Catholic international dialogue as the framework to highlight two areas of tension and exclusion. Because it pertains to a relatively well known and not so recent issue, we will only briefly recall the so-called problem of uniatism and will, in that context, refer to the 1993 Balamand document. The more recent Ravenna document will be the occasion to speak about the tensions between the autocephalous and autonomous Orthodox churches and the ecumenical patriarchate.

Tensions around Uniatism: The Balamand Document

After the collapse of the Communist regime, especially in the Western part of Ukraine and in certain areas of Romania, the Greek Catholic Church proved to be much stronger than the Orthodox majority had foreseen. The relations between both churches soon became extremely loaded because of fierce disputes around the property rights of church buildings. For many Orthodox, who consider their country as their "canonical territory," even the existence of a church that shares the same faith and celebrates the same liturgy, while accepting the jurisdiction of the bishop of Rome, is a problem. It was unthinkable that the Orthodox-Roman Catholic international dialogue could stick to its ecclesiological agenda and disregard this burning issue. For the Orthodox, the "problem" of uniatism first had to be solved in an acceptable way.

After three years of preparation and in the absence of six of fifteen Orthodox churches, the international commission in 1993 released a new statement entitled *Uniatism: Method of Union of the Past, and the Present Search for Full Communion.* In this Balamand statement, uniatism was rejected as an ecclesiological method in favor of the ecclesiology of sister churches. The document also contained a clear condemnation of proselytism, but at the same time it stated that the Oriental Catholic Churches deserve further pastoral care and support from Rome. Whereas the Balamand document has been well received in the Roman Catholic Church and in some Greek Catholic and Orthodox churches, important negative reactions were issued by the Greek Catholic Church in Romania and by the Orthodox Church of Greece.

Seven years passed before the next plenary commission of the international dialogue was convened. In this 2000 meeting, however, the Catholic delegation refused to qualify the existence of Greek Catholic churches as "anormal." This refusal led to a rupture of the official relations between both churches until the Ecumenical Patriarchate, shortly after the start of a new pontificate in 2005, finally agreed to continue the dialogue. A lasting solution of this "problem" will require that the different countries involved engage in a common and profound rereading of history in view of a healing of memories. The Catholic Church also needs to further clarify its ecclesiological views on the relation between the universal church and the particular churches *sui iuris*. On the occasion of the recent election of a new major archbishop, the willingness of the Ukrainian Greek Catholic Church to help overcome the tensions with the different Orthodox jurisdictions in Ukraine has been firmly stated. It remains possible, however, that the "problem" of uniatism will still be able to disturb Orthodox-Roman Catholic ecumenical relations in the future as well.[5]

Inner-Orthodox Tensions: The Ravenna Document

The tensions on the role of the ecumenical patriarchate in the Orthodox Church can be highlighted by referring first to the events around the 2007 meeting in Ravenna and then to the document itself.

After the delegation of the Moscow Patriarchate, headed by Metropolitan Hilarion Alfeyev, had noticed that the ecumenical patriarchate had invited representatives of the Estonian Apostolic Orthodox Church to the meeting, they felt forced to leave, because staying would, in their opinion, have been identical with recognizing the legitimacy of this church, which the Moscow Patriarchate denies.[6] After the departure of the Russians, those who remained were able to discuss and approve the Ravenna statement. Still, in the perception of the Moscow Patriarchate, the departure of their delegation raises questions about the validity of the document. The following criticism, which Bishop Hilarion Alfeyev issued on February 19, 2008, seems to represent the Moscow Patriarchate's official opinion:

> I do not share the optimism of Cardinal Walter Kasper concerning the Ravenna document and consider his statement about this document as a "real breakthrough in Orthodox-Catholic dialogue" unjustified premature [*sic*]. First of all, the Russian and the Bulgarian Churches, as well as the Orthodox Church in America were absent in Ravenna. The total membership of these three Orthodox Churches exceeds the membership of all other Orthodox Churches taken together. Consequently, the Ravenna document cannot be regarded as an agreement between the Catholics and the Orthodox. As it stands now, it is an agreement between representatives of the Roman Catholic Church and representatives of some, but by no means all Orthodox Churches.[7]

One should also realize that this is not the only example of important tensions among individual Orthodox churches and the ecumenical patriarchate. Another well-known example is the crisis in the Diocese of Sourozh and the decision of Bishop Basil of Sergievo in 2006 to go over to the Patriarchate of Constantinople. The long-awaited panorthodox council has been postponed many times because of disagreements about the order of the holy diptychs.

One also can find traces of the tensions among the Orthodox churches in the Ravenna statement itself. For example, when it comes to maintaining communion among churches on the universal level, the document stresses, first of all, the importance of the ecumenical councils. Whereas the 1990 text enumerated four essential conditions for an ecumenical council to be truly ecumenical, following the definitions of the Second Council of

Nicea in 787, the revised document prefers to indicate that the "special characteristics" of ecumenical councils have "to be studied further in our future dialogue, taking into account the evolution of the ecclesial structures during recent centuries in the East and the West" (§37). The document sadly admits that "the break between East and West rendered impossible the holding of Ecumenical Councils in the strict sense of the term" but that "both Churches continued to hold councils whenever serious crises arose." The 1990 version spoke about "general councils," but during the final redaction the authors decided to somehow take into account the objections formulated by Bishop Hilarion of the Moscow delegation, who had observed that the Orthodox churches had since 787 never succeeded in convening such a "general council."[8]

The Moscow delegation also had profound difficulties concerning the next line. The final version reads as follows: "These councils gathered together the bishops of local Churches in communion with the See of Rome or, although understood in a different way, with the See of Constantinople, respectively." Compared to the 1990 document, the words "although understood in a different way" (§39) have been added to the text to indicate that the ecumenical patriarchate does not enjoy the same kind of authority as the See of Rome for the Orthodox sister churches. On the other hand, the document did not follow the suggestion of Bishop Hilarion to remove any reference whatsoever toward relations of communion of local churches with the See of Constantinople.

From Exclusion to Communion

By way of conclusion, I suggest a way to make progress in the arduous journey from exclusion to communion by listening to the voice of one Orthodox and one Roman Catholic theologian, Nicholas Afanasiev (1893–1966) and Anton Houtepen (1940–2010), respectively. In his famous article "Una Sancta," published in *Irénikon* in 1963 and extensively commented on among the fathers of the Second Vatican Council, Nicholas Afanasiev, one of the major Orthodox theologians of the twentieth century, contrasted two types of ecclesiology, universal ecclesiology and Eucharistic ecclesiology.[9] The author criticized both Catholic and Orthodox theology for subscribing to the universal ecclesiology of St. Cyprian of Carthage, according to which only one true and universal church can exist. According to such an ecclesiology, the church that claims to be in the truth necessarily has to excommunicate all other churches. To quote Afanasiev, "How do the catholic church and the orthodox church mutually regard each other? From the point of view of the universal ecclesiology, common for both, each regards the other as a schismatic and even heretical community, having lost completely or in part its ecclesial nature, the cause of this being separation from the true Church."[10]

According to a Eucharistic ecclesiology, "the Church is where the Eucharistic assembly is."[11] Even if one would prefer a form of Eucharistic ecclesiology that is less focused on the parish and more on the diocese,[12] Afanasiev's conclusions about the implications of a Eucharistic ecclesiology for our topic of exclusion remain valid: "From the perspective of Eucharistic ecclesiology, such 'excommunications' are impossible. There is no power superior to the union of churches above the local churches themselves as manifestations of the Church of God. A local church could not amputate another church from the Church because this would mean that the Church would be excommunicating herself."[13] According to this paradigm, (local) churches can only interrupt relations of communion with one another: "The halting of fraternal communion between the union of local churches on the one hand and one or more churches on the other is nothing more than a matter of 'cessation of relations,' with this or these churches. Above all there is the cessation of Eucharistic communion."[14]

Afanasiev hoped that if both the Orthodox Church and the Roman Catholic Church would give up their universalist pretensions and would operate from within the framework of a Eucharistic ecclesiology, then, "by an effort in Love, the orthodox church *could* re-establish communion with the catholic church, the dogmatic divergences notwithstanding and without demanding that the catholic church renounce the doctrines that distinguish her from the orthodox church."[15] But he adds, "Certainly, to attain this the effort in Love is necessary, a great sacrifice, an element of self-renunciation."[16]

This is certainly not an easy program for the Orthodox Church. As Andrew Louth made clear in the first receptive ecumenism conference some years ago, "We are eloquent about our wonderful Eucharistic ecclesiology: but what sign is there of it in our practice?"[17] The Roman Catholic Church too, however, needs to reflect upon whether it is willing to develop a Eucharistic ecclesiology more fully. Certain passages from Vatican II invite us to do that. One can think here of *Sacrosanctum Concilium* 41–42 and *Lumen Gentium* 26. But does the same third chapter of *Lumen Gentium* (20–22) not also contain an account of collegiality that reflects, as Richard Gaillardetz argues, "a 'universalist' ecclesiological framework that begins with the bishops' membership in the college and the college's share, with and subordinate to the pope, in supreme authority of the whole church?"[18]

The situation became even worse in postconciliar magisterial teaching and culminated in an outright critique of Eucharistic ecclesiology in the famous 1992 *Letter to the Bishops of the Catholic Church on Some*

Aspects of the Church Understood as Communion: "The rediscovery of a *eucharistic ecclesiology*," it is said in §11 of the Congregation for the Doctrine of Faith document, "though being of undoubted value, has however, sometimes placed unilateral emphasis on the principle of the local Church. It is claimed that, where the Eucharist is celebrated, the totality of the mystery of the Church would be made present in such a way as to render any other principle of unity or universality non-essential." In my opinion, Roman Catholic magisterial teaching urgently has to re-receive its earlier rediscovery of Eucharistic ecclesiology in the documents of the Second Vatican Council.[19]

In November 2004 my departed Dutch colleague Anton Houtepen dedicated his valedictory lecture, which unfortunately only exists in Dutch, to our theme. The lecture received the title: "Anatomy of the Anathema: On Exclusion and Reconciliation, Dividedness and Reunion in the Ecumenical Process."[20] Houtepen was aware that structures that promote exclusion rather than communion and acceptance of the other exist in all churches and religions. He preferred no longer to call such structures "nontheological factors" because the tendency to exclude others from being in partial or full communion with oneself is in most cases theologically motivated. His anatomic lesson not only focused on the past—discussing rules and procedures of excommunication in the Old and New Testament, the early church, the medieval period, and the Council of Trent—but also on the future.

Houtepen considered the mutual exclusion from the Eucharist as the modern version of the anathemizations of the past. If one realizes that the Catholic Church in its latest council decided to address the other Christians no longer as *fratres separati* but as *fratres seiuncti*, to develop an ecclesiology of sister churches, to focus on the different degrees of communion, which already exist among churches, then it is a paradoxical situation that the rules to allow non-Catholic Christians to share at the Eucharistic table remain so strict, even if they are theologically motivated by pointing to the necessary link between Eucharistic fellowship and unity in faith and doctrine. My colleague saw reasons to be hopeful, however, in the theses on Eucharistic hospitality, which the ecumenical institutes of Tübingen, Strasbourg, and Bensheim had formulated together in 2003 and especially in the first thesis, stating that what needs to be justified is not the admission of baptized Christians to the Eucharistic table but the refusal thereof.[21]

Afanasiev's focus on a local, Eucharistic ecclesiology and Houtepen's focus on an ecclesiology of sister churches can work hand in hand as we struggle to move forward from exclusion to communion.

Notes

[1] Cf. Emmanuel Lanne, "Églises unies ou Églises soeurs: Un choix inéluctable," *Irénikon* 48 (1975): 322–42.

[2] Cf. http://orthodoxinfo.com/ecumenism/vitaly.aspx.

[3] See Theodor Nikolaou, ed., *Das Schisma zwischen Ost- und Westkirche 950 bzw. 800 Jahre danach (1054 und 1204)* (Münster, Germany: LIT, 2004); Yves Congar, "Neuf cents ans après: Notes sur le 'Schisme oriental,'" in *1054–1954. L'Eglise et les Eglises. Neuf siècles de douloureuse séparation entre l'Orient et l'Occident. Etudes et travaux offerts à Dom L. Beaudouin* (Gembloux, Belgium: Éditions de Chevetogne, 1954), I:3–95; Henry Chadwick, *East and West: The Making of a Rift in the Church: From Apostolic Times until the Council of Florence* (Oxford: Oxford University Press, 2005).

[4] Interesting studies include Eva M. Synek, "Konziliarität und Autorität in der Kirche'—Orthodox-katholischer Dialog: Das so genannte Ravennadokument," *Österreichisches Archiv für Recht und Religion* 55 (2008): 55–78; Joseph Famerée, "'Communion ecclésiale, conciliarité et autorité': Le document de Ravenne," *Revue théologique de Louvain* 40 (2009): 236–47; Ansgar Santogrossi, "The Ecclesiology of the Ravenna Agreed Statement: Analysis and Correction," *The Thomist* 73 (2009): 435–454; Paul McPartlan, "The Ravenna Agreed Statement and Catholic-Orthodox Dialogue," *The Jurist* 69 (2009): 749–65; Kallistos Ware, "The Ravenna Document and the Future of Orthodox-Catholic Dialogue," *The Jurist* 69 (2009): 766–89.

[5] A few important essays on Balamand include Waclaw Hryniewicz, "Uniatismus einst und jetzt: Reflexionen zum Dokument von Balamand" (1993), *Ostkirchliche Studien* 43 (1994): 328–39; John H. Erickson, "Concerning the Balamand Statement," *Greek Orthodox Theological Review* 42 (1997): 25–44; Mircea Basarab, "Die Problematik der unierten Kirche aus orthodoxer Sicht," *Orthodoxes Forum* 12 (1998): 21–50; Benoît Bourgine, "La réception de la Déclaration de Balamand," *Irénikon* 74 (2001): 538–60. An important collection of articles is found in Comité mixte Catholique-Orthodoxe en France, *Les enjeux de l'uniatisme: Dans le sillage de Balamand* (Paris: Cerf, 2004).

[6] The conflict is related to the existence of two Orthodox jurisdictions in Estonia. The Estonian Orthodox Church operates under the Moscow Patriarchate and is the second largest church in Estonia, following the Lutheran Church. It has around 170,000 faithful. The smaller one, the Estonian Apostolic Orthodox Church, has around 20,000 faithful. In 1923, with the agreement of the Moscow Patriarchate, which was then virtually paralyzed by Communist persecution, the ecumenical patriarchate had offered this church autonomous status under its guidance. After the Soviet annexation of Estonia in 1940, the control of the church reverted de facto to Moscow, which was recognized by Constantinople in 1978 by suspending its 1923 *tomos*. The independence of Estonia in 1991 cancelled for Constantinople the basis of the 1978 action, and, therefore, in 1996 it reactivated the canonical measure that it had taken in 1923. This measure was

highly criticized by Moscow, which even broke the Eucharistic communion with the ecumenical patriarchate during some months. Cf. Huub Vogelaar, "Ecumenical Relationships in Estonia," *Exchange* 37 (2008): 190–219.

⁷ http://orthodoxeurope.org/page/14/140.aspx.

⁸ Synek, "Konziliarität und Autorität in der Kirche," 74.

⁹ Nicolas Afanasiev, "Una Sancta," *Irénikon* 36 (1963): 436–75. The article is found in English translation in *Tradition Alive: On the Church and the Christian Life in Our Time: Readings from the Eastern Church*, ed. Michael Plekon (Lanham, MD: Rowman & Littlefield, 2003), 3–30. See also Nicolas Afanasiev, *The Church of the Holy Spirit*, ed. Michael Plekon (Notre Dame, IN: University of Notre Dame Press, 2007).

¹⁰ Plekon, *Tradition Alive*, 8–9.

¹¹ Ibid., 14.

¹² Cf. John Zizioulas, *Eucharist, Bishop, Church: The Unity of the Church in the Divine Eucharist and the Bishop during the First Three Centuries* (Brookline, MA: Holy Cross Orthodox Press, 2001).

¹³ Plekon, *Tradition Alive*, 17.

¹⁴ Ibid., 17.

¹⁵ Ibid., 26.

¹⁶ Ibid.

¹⁷ Andrew Louth, "Receptive Ecumenism and Catholic Learning—An Orthodox Perspective," *Receptive Ecumenism and the Call to Catholic Learning: Exploring a Way for Contemporary Ecumenism*, ed. Paul D. Murray (Oxford: Oxford University Press, 2008), 361–72, 365–66.

¹⁸ Richard R. Gaillardetz, *The Church in the Making: Lumen Gentium, Christus Dominus, Orientalium Ecclesiarum* (New York: Paulist Press, 2006), 78–79.

¹⁹ Cf. Peter De Mey, "An Investigation of the Willingness to Develop a Eucharistic Ecclesiology in Roman Catholic Magisterial Teaching on the Church and in the Orthodox-Roman Catholic Ecumenical Dialogue," *ET Bulletin* 19 (2008): 78–99.

²⁰ Anton Houtepen, *Anatomie van het anathema: Over uitsluiting en hereniging in het oecumenisch proces* (Utrecht, The Netherlands: Universiteit Utrecht/ Faculteit Godgeleerdheid, 2004).

²¹ Institut für Ökumenische Forschung (Tübingen), Centre d'Etudes Oecuméniques (Strasbourg), Konfessionskundliches Institut (Bensheim), *Abendmahlsgemeinschaft ist möglich: Thesen zur eucharistischen Gastfreundschaft* (Frankfurt am Main, Germany: Lembeck, 2003).

Toward a New Dayton Momentum?
Exclusion, Sociocultural Identities,
and the Ecumenical Movement

E. A. J. G. Van der Borght

Dayton Revisited

Dayton, Ohio, is a wonderful place for a conference on the theme of ecclesiology and exclusion because the place has witnessed a landmark event in the fight against exclusion politics and has given its name to an important agreement. On November 21, 1995, after three weeks of intense negotiations, an agreement was reached at the Wright-Patterson Air Force Base near Dayton. A full and formal agreement would be signed three weeks later, on December 14 exactly, this time in Paris, but the agreement would become known as the Dayton Agreement for Peace in Bosnia and Herzegovina, nicknamed the "Dayton Peace Accords." The Dayton Peace Accords made an end to the war in Bosnia and outlined a General Framework Agreement for Peace in Bosnia and Herzegovina. The Bosnian war (April 1992–December 1995) had come about as a result of the breakup of Yugoslavia. It preserved Bosnia as a single state made up of two parts, the Bosniak-Croat federation and the Bosnian Serb Republic, with Sarajevo remaining as the undivided capital city. Through this event and the name of the agreement, Dayton was put on the global map.

The list of witnesses present at the signing ceremony in Paris illustrates the importance attached to the Dayton agreement at that time: French President Jacques Chirac, American President Bill Clinton, UK Prime Minister John Major, German Chancellor Helmut Kohl, and Russian Prime Minister Viktor Chernomyrdin all came to Paris. Also, the names of the signers of the agreement make us aware of what was at stake: President Alija Izetbegovic signed for the Republic of Bosnia, Herzegovina President Franjo Tudman signed for the Republic of Croatia, and President Slobodan

Milosevic signed for the Federal Republic of Yugoslavia. The last signer, Milosevic, would die in 2006 in The Hague awaiting the verdict of the International Criminal Tribunal for the former Yugoslavia where he was indicted for crimes against humanity. Tudman had died in 1999. If he had lived longer, he would also have been indicted for crimes against humanity. These indictments of presidents remind us of the cruelty of the Bosnian War, which was characterized by bitter fighting, indiscriminate shelling of cities and towns, ethnic cleansing, systematic mass rape, and genocide. It was a territorial war based on nationalist claims. Or to put it in the terms of "Ecclesiology and Exclusion," this war was about exclusion of people from territories on the basis of nationalist agendas. The Bosnian War illustrates the violence that can accompany identity politics.

Many were surprised by the resurgence of nationalistic violence and practices of ethnic cleansing in the heart of Europe after the end of the Cold War. The use of religions as identity markers in these post-Communist societies that had been thoroughly secularized under state control for over forty years was even more highly unexpected. Serbs, for example, presented themselves as Orthodox, Croats as Roman Catholics, and Bosnians as Muslims.

Religions were abused for political purposes, but religions also made use of the opportunity to present themselves as key players in the public sphere. In this heated atmosphere, religious leaders knew and used the Christian peace and reconciliation vocabulary, but, more importantly, many religious leaders, theologians, and lay believers defined themselves in terms of national or ethnic identities without reserve. For many Christians, the loyalty to their faith and the love for their country or people were, and still are, almost self-evidently, like the two sides of one coin.

Christian churches like to present themselves as agents of reconciliation and peace in conflict, but in situations such as in the former Yugoslavia, one observes that in the case of violence and war, Christian traditions tend to become parties that identify themselves with one side in the conflict and, as such, become agents of exclusion themselves. As a consequence, Christian communities can become part of the problem.

ETHNAT: A Project of Faith and Order

In 1997, the Board of Faith and Order (F&O) of the World Council of Churches (WCC) showed that it was aware of this problem and launched the ETHNAT project, abbreviating the full title of the project "Ethnic Identity, National Identity and the Unity of the Church." The project was finalized in 2006 with the publication of *Participating in God's Mission of Reconciliation: A Resource for Churches in Situations of Conflict.*[1]

At the 1997 meeting of the Board of F&O, Thomas Best and Alan Falconer, then secretary and director of F&O, presented a paper to introduce the discussions on the implementation of the new project.[2] This document goes beyond the common position that nationalism and ethnicity challenge the churches to reflect theologically more deeply on their reconciling mission.[3] The paper identified issues that need further preparation as well as specific questions to be addressed. The text mentioned as topics for preparation papers ethnicity and nationalism in ecumenical documents; the relation of nationalism to the unity of the church (questions of catholicity and unity, diversity, the local and the universal enculturation); the role of nationalism and ethnicity within denominationalism; and the role of Christianity in relation to ethnicity and nationalism in the various continents.

In addition, the following specific questions were listed as needing to be addressed through the consultation: the nature of human identity (anthropology), the nature of the church as local and universal, the theology of election, the cultural captivity of the churches, the concept of memory/the nature of tradition, the role of religious symbols in community building and conflict, a hermeneutic of otherness/embrace, the relation of majority and minority groups in society, the impact of missionary endeavor on ethnic identity, and finally Christian formation/malformation. It is evident that Falconer and Best wanted the focus to be on the nature and the mission of the church in dealing with issues of ethnic and national identity.

In March 2005, a drafting group drew the various inputs of the study process together into one study document with the title *Participating in God's Mission of Reconciliation: A Resource for Churches in Situations of Conflict.* The Standing Commission made its final remarks in the 2005 meeting.[4] It became clear that this was not going to be a consensus text but merely the record of a study process. It was offered to the churches and interested parties for their use in addressing these issues in their context.[5] It had the intention of providing sources for the local churches to engage each other ecumenically. Finally, at the Standing Commission meeting of 2006, the publication was presented.[6] Apparently, there was no money to send it to all member churches of the WCC.[7] But churches, theological faculties, and ecumenical bodies would be invited to send responses. There are currently no further plans to initiate a new project directly related to this one.[8]

Thus, after the 2004 plenary meeting, this study that had been dragging on since 1997 was speedily brought to a conclusion with the publication of a study document in 2006. It is clear that in 2004 the decision was taken to finish the project as soon as possible. No further effort was made to mold the different aspects together into a more consistent text that would have challenged churches to reconsider their local ethnic and/or national identities in relation to the visible unity of the church. The material that was the result of the study sessions in the previous years was collected and put together. The original plan to include extra case studies had been abandoned. As an observer, I had the impression that F&O wanted to get rid of a controversial project. The altered title expresses the change of purpose. The question of the unity of the church is no longer central. Instead, the issue now is how churches can be assisted in reconciliation work in situations of conflict. The focus has shifted from the ecclesiological dilemma to an ethical challenge. Movement toward visible unity of the churches has been replaced by a belief simply in the reconciliation potential of churches in the context of national and ethnic strife.

The Sociocultural Deficit of Faith and Order

After reading the history of the long decision process to start the project, the shift during the drafting process, and the evaluation of the final result, one might come to the conclusion that if this was supposed to be the new dawn of ecumenical reflection on unity, the effort was aborted before it had really started. Indeed, this was one of the less successful projects of F&O. At the same time, it showed that the input of social sciences and of recent results of biblical studies have a strong potential for contributing to a new discourse on sociocultural identities in relation to the unity of the church.

In one additional way, the ETHNAT project and its result are eye-openers on the way to developing a more successful exploration of the unity of the church in the twenty-first century. The strong resistance to the original aim of the project challenges us to dig deeper into the question of what is at stake. The initial enthusiasm for the project in the F&O Board soon waned and gave way to expressions of hesitation, warnings, subtle threats, and finally a redefinition of the project away from identity issues toward a reconciliation approach. The outspoken negative reactions came from representatives from regions such as the Middle East, Africa, and South-East Europe, regions with a long history of tense sociocultural relationships. Apparently they had been able to convince those who liked the original plan of the ETHNAT project to reorientate the proposal. They had an important historical argument: this project contradicts the F&O approach toward the unity of the church up until now because F&O had spoken against this approach before World War II.

In 1937, both Life and Work and F&O, the two organizations that would merge into the WCC, organized a world conference in Great Britain. Life and Work under the inspirational leadership of J. H. Oldham gathered in Oxford around the theme of "Church, Community and State."

If one translates "community" into the German "Volk," the link with the nationalistic sentiments all over Europe, and most of all in Nazi Germany, becomes evident. This world conference offered theological input in relation to the concepts of nation, "Volk," and race, and it suggested to churches how to react to the challenges of aggressively nationalistic states.

F&O organized a conference in the same year in Edinburgh, but it did not deal with issues such as nation and race in relation to the unity of the church. The conference only briefly mentioned the national churches under the heading "non-theological factors that hinder church unity."[9] It indicated that issues related to the division of people along racial or national lines were problems of the secular world, not of the church. The conference suggested that if such issues were a stumbling block on the way to church unity, they were of a practical, nonessential nature and implied that it might be easy to resolve them once the essential theological differences were solved.

This attitude toward those so-called nontheological factors would continue after the war. At the Second General Assembly of the WCC at Evanston in 1954, under the theme of "Christ the Hope of the World," intergroup relations and especially the race issue were very prominent as topics of one the sections.[10] F&O provided its own report to that assembly, unrelated to the theme of group relations and race issues.

In the following decades, F&O would restrict itself to traditional theological—that is, confessional—differences that caused divisions that undermined the unity of the church. As a consequence, the well-known involvement of the WCC with the struggle against apartheid in South Africa was essentially a Life and Work approach, even when the consequences for the churches became evident through the division of the church according to racial lines. So, the proposal to start ETHNAT represented a rupture with the traditional F&O definition of theological issues. It implied that the thinking about the relationship between the one catholic church and sociocultural identities was fundamentally of a theological nature. Against this background, it is not so strange that quite a lot of resistance developed against ETHNAT, since it had no tradition to build on.

Toward a Theological Dayton Momentum?

The 2004 F&O plenary meeting revealed that the theme of sociocultural identities as developed in the first draft of *Participating in God's Mission of Reconciliation* did not resonate in some regions of the world. Latin America indicated preoccupation with socioeconomic issues and Asian representatives referred to interreligious dialogue. The observations are correct: not in every region in the world are sociocultural identities the main cause of societal tensions. These reactions could be expected, however, because of the reorientation of the ETHNAT project. The shift from a focus on sociocultural identities as a theological challenge to the unity of the church to a focus on the reconciliation potential of churches in relation to sociocultural identity issues in society had a consequence: those Christians who lived in a society that did not suffer from identity politics found it difficult to identify with the project.

For this reason, when in the future the issue of sociocultural identities is raised again as a theme deeply affecting the understanding of the nature of the church, it will be important to explain more explicitly that this is a fully ecclesiological topic that touches the heart of the theology of the church. In the first discussion paper on ETHNAT, Falconer and Best related the project to questions of the unity of the church, the catholicity of the church, the church local and universal, and diversity and unity. If presented in this way, it becomes clear that these issues are not reserved to regions in the world with difficult ethnic relations.

Once one has become aware that our human sociocultural identities do not self-evidently fit in with the confession of the one catholic church, one discovers how the issue has bothered the church from its beginnings. According to the New Testament, the first major church conflict focused on the entrance conditions for non-Jews to the Christian community (see Acts 15) and the centrality of church unity as a theme (as emphasized also in the Pauline letters to the Galatians, to the Colossians, and to the Ephesians). Major splits in the global church during the history of the church were often, if not always, linked to questions of the local and universal church, and thus to recognition of local cultural identities, as was the case in both 1054 with the schism between Eastern and Western Christianity and in 1517 with the start of the division between Roman Catholicism and Protestantism in Western Christianity in Europe.[11]

In the following era of confessionalization, the ecclesiological concept of transconfessional and transnational unity was not developed due to external circumstances—that is, the state formation and territorialism (*cuius regio eius religio*).[12] The emergence since then of national churches and of auto-cephalic churches mainly in the nineteenth century highlights the way sociocultural identities have influenced and shaped the structures of many denominational churches within Protestantism and Orthodoxy, respectively. It helps to explain the reticence from the side of some Protestant and Orthodox leaders to discuss the unity of the church in relation to sociocultural identities.

The Roman Catholic Church has experienced the force of national identities as well. From an ecclesiological perspective, the whole evolution within the Roman Catholic Church in the nineteenth and the twentieth centuries can be explained as a balancing exercise between the universal expressed by the definition of papal infallibility at Vatican I and the local church expressed in terms of the authority of the bishops at Vatican II.

The influence of sociocultural identities is also visible today in many ecclesial practices all over the world. It is an issue in Amsterdam as much as it is in all European cities where new migrant congregations are established daily. Most Ghanaian Presbyterians in Amsterdam, for example, do not join Dutch Reformed congregations but start their own Ghanaian Presbyterian Church. It is an issue in the United Protestant Church in Belgium of how to help the French-speaking members and the Dutch-speaking members relate to one another in one united church. In Central and Eastern Europe, where mostly Orthodox churches consider themselves guardians of the national identity of their nations, it is also an issue. Sociocultural realities and dynamics are likewise an issue in American churches where the national American identity—symbolized by the American flag next to the cross at the front of the church—has become as important as their Christian identity. Similarly, all over Africa, churches tend to be ethnically or tribally structured. In all these examples, a similar ecclesial and ecclesiological problem must be solved: how the contextual expressions of Christian faith interact with the confession of the church that its body is one, holy, catholic, and apostolic. How can the contextual expression in a diversity of cultures relate to the universal nature of Christianity?

If one becomes aware of the way sociocultural identities have challenged the ecclesial practices and the ecclesiological theories of the church right from the start through the history of the churches until today, the hesitation experienced within F&O to deal with this issue is put in perspective and becomes understandable. At the same time, it is obvious that this is not just a challenge for some regions in the world but that it calls on all churches, on all confessional traditions, to bring together the best of their theological traditions to find new solutions to the urgent questions.

For this reason, I plead for a new approach to ecumenical work on the unity of the church, a new vision that transcends the traditional confessional contrasts. The urgency of the times calls all churches to think outside of the box and to make a new start. I am convinced that an approach to the unity of the church through theological work on the place of sociocultural identities will make that fundamental shift possible.

I end with a last reference to the Dayton Peace Accords. Why did they come to Dayton, of all places, after so many unsuccessful attempts to come to an agreement? Luxury hotels in major European cities had been the venues of the previous failed attempts to reach an agreement. This time they chose a place where they could isolate the participants and keep them away from the spotlight. In this way, they were unable to manipulate public opinion. It was clear for all participants: no more holidays, no more games. Opposing sociocultural identities is a hard and tough issue with a potential danger for violence when leading to exclusion. Remembering the outcome of that Dayton conference, I wondered whether the time has not come for theologians to surf on the symbolic power of the place of Dayton and the growing awareness that sociocultural identities challenge the nature and the mission of the church.

Notes

[1] *Participating in God's Mission of Reconciliation: A Resource for Churches in Situations of Conflict*, Faith and Order Paper no. 201 (Geneva: WCC Publications, 2006).

[2] T. Best and A. Falconer, "Ethnicity and Nationalism in Relation to Christian Unity," *Minutes of the Meeting of the Faith and Order Board, 8–15 January 1997, Abbaye de Fontgombault, France*, Faith and Order Paper no. 178 (Geneva: WCC Publications, 1997), 38–47.

[3] Ibid., 38.

[4] *Minutes of the Standing Commission on Faith and Order Aghios Nikolaos, Crete, 14–21 June 2005*, Faith and Order Paper no. 200 (Geneva: WCC Publications, 2005), 18–21.

[5] Ibid., 18.

[6] *Participating in God's Mission of Reconciliation*.

[7] *Minutes of the Standing Commission on Faith and Order, Faverges, Haute-Savoie, France 14–21 June 2006*, Faith and Order Paper no. 202 (Geneva: WCC Publications, 2006), 76.

[8] Ibid., 107.

[9] After examples of obstacles due to historical factors, we read about churches agreeing on doctrinal matters but having different cultural origins: "These Churches are not conscious of any obstacles to such union because of mutually exclusive doctrines. They are, however, kept apart by barriers of nationality, race, class, general culture, and, more particularly, by slothful self-content and self-sufficiency" (L. Hodgson, ed., *The Second World Conference on Faith and Order held at Edinburgh*, August 3–18, 1937 [London: 1938], 258–59).

[10] W. A. Visser't Hooft, ed., *The Evanston Report: The Second Assembly of the World Council of Churches 1954* (London: SCM Press, 1955). The report of the section "The Churches amid Racial and Ethnic Tensions" is to be found on pages 151 to 160.

[11] See the subtitle "Europe's House Divided" of Diarmaid MacCulloch's famous volume *The Reformation* (London: Allan Lane, 2003).

[12] W. Janse, "Church Unity, Territorialism, and State Formation in the Era of Confessionalisation," in E. Van der Borght, *The Unity of the Church: A Theological State of the Art* (Leiden, The Netherlands: Brill, 2010), 33–42.

Retrospective

Vincent J. Miller

Within the diversity of topics and methods through which conference participants addressed the theme "Ecclesiology and Exclusion," two central concerns appeared. First, human division is a fundamentally ecclesial problem, not merely an ethical one. Second, ours is an age particularly prone to division.

Human division, whatever its source, is a challenge to the church's unity. Thus, while racism, nationalism, and the treatment of immigrants and other social outcasts are profound moral issues, the church's responses to them are much more than matters of individual or communal moral responsibility. They implicate the church's faithfulness to its own nature and mission.

Participants lamented the fact that unity is not widely understood to be a serious ecclesiological obligation or Christian virtue. This is evident on a range of levels—from the stalling of high-level ecumenical dialogues to the widespread acquiescence of Christians in the social divisions that rend society and church.

Theologians must navigate between uncritical assumptions that there are intraecclesial causes for all ecclesial problems and a distinction that places such "facts" outside of the church in some secular realm beyond our obligation to engage. Eddy van der Borght cited a telling example of this tendency in the 1937 Faith and Order statement that characterized the churches' complicity in virulent nationalism as "non-theological facts that hinder unity." Even though such divisions do not necessarily arise from within the church or its theology, they appear there and thus pose an ecclesiological challenge.

A second shared theme was awareness that our current cultural context is particularly susceptible to division, polarization, and sectarian and identity politics. Human division is, of course, a primordial problem that did not begin with any particular schism, reformation, or political arrangement. Nevertheless, the papers in this volume sketch a divisive leitmotif across issues and communities. Debora Spini outlines scholarship on the decline of homogenizing national spaces, the return of "tribalism," and the replacement of justice by identity conflicts in postmodern civil society. Gerard Mannion's argument about "neo-exclusivism" stresses that this is not merely the nostalgic return to some previous homogeneity but a distinctly new set of theological inclinations. Several comments shared by scholars in the conference sessions were particularly telling. One noted the curious enthusiasm for the line drawing of *Dominus Iesus* that thrives among communities on the other side of the line of exclusion inscribed by that document. Another was troubled by the renewed enthusiasm for a dichotomous theology of nature and grace that resonates with a sharp boundary between the church and the world.

I have argued elsewhere that globalization and technology fuel a cultural ecology of polarization.[1] Far from producing one homogenous global culture, globalization heightens awareness of cultural difference. Unlike twentieth-century mass communication technologies that helped consolidate homogenous national cultures, twenty-first-century communication technologies enable the proliferation of subcultures. This fragments civil society, communities, and religions into enclaves, where groups define themselves over against others but do not have to engage them. As culture fragments, it also floats free of space. Communities cease to be bound by geography and, at the same time, they lose their ties to particular territory. As communities lose the ability to influence the economy, politics, and society, their sense of responsibility is transformed. Traditional means of translating dogmatic commitments into practice, such as casuistry and religious systems of jurisprudence, are discarded in favor of apocalyptic and prophetic denunciations of the sinful world. In this cultural ecology, all cultural and religious practices are in constant danger of being reconfigured in service to a more fundamental cultural practice: projecting an identity, not as a positive practice of distinctive commitment, but as a negative contrast with competing groups. We live in an age when "countercultural" has become a cultural norm and imperative.

In this cultural context, Christians face not only the challenge but also the temptation to allow God's gift of the church to be reduced to just another social group engaged in boundary maintenance and oppositional identity. This is hard to discern because of the aura of integrity that surrounds such words as "identity" and "countercultural witness." These tendencies disarm the church's witness against the sinful exclusions of the age—racism, nationalism, xenophobia, economic disparities, and exploitation—and threaten to pervert the gospel into supporting them.

The true witness of the church is positive, borne of God's trinitarian love at work in the salvation of the world. Ecclesiological work is urgently needed to discern the true divine mission of the church and its proper ways of proceeding so that it may bring God's salvation to an age threatened with epochal divisions in and between societies and religions. This requires theological work to carefully attend to the complexities of doctrines likely to be ignored or drawn into the task of boundary maintenance such as creation, revelation, Christology, ecclesiology, and eschatology. This also requires social scientific analysis of the workings of exclusion and division. The essays collected in this volume mark a significant beginning of this task.

Notes

[1] Vincent Miller, "Where Is the Church? Globalization and Catholicity," *Theological Studies* 69 (2008): 412–32.

Contributors

Stephen Annan is a priest of the Diocese of Sunyani, Ghana. Currently a *doctorandus* at the Katholieke Universiteit Leuven, Belgium, his research interests include pneumatology, ecclesiology, ecumenism, and sacramental theology. He is currently preparing a dissertation tentatively entitled "What Is Wrong with Us?" A Critical Analysis of Pneumatological Ecclesiology in the Context of Increased Charismatic Christianity in Ghana."

Pascal D. Bazzell is a professor of intercultural theology and and coordinator of the Mission Department at Koinonia Theological Seminary, Davao City, Philippines, and currently a Ph.D. candidate at Fuller Theological Seminary. From Switzerland, he has been doing mission service in the Philippines since 1998. Currently serving with the Overseas Missionary Fellowship, he co-leads with his wife Karina Faye Ravello the Silingan [Neighbors] Outreach (SO) team that serves various street-level communities.

Gioacchino Campese is a Scalabrinian missionary from Italy currently pursuing doctoral studies in missiology at Urbaniana University in Rome. He has ministered with migrants in Tijuana and Chicago. Among his publications are *Migration, Religious Experience, and Globalization* (coedited with Pietro Ciallella in 2003); *A Promised Land, a Perilous Journey: Theological Perspectives on Migration* (coedited with Daniel Groody in 2008); and *Hacia una Teología desde la Realidad de las Migraciones: Métodos y Desafíos* (2008). He now lives and works in Siponto (Puglia, Southern Italy).

Mark D. Chapman is vice principal at Ripon College Cuddesdon, a reader in modern theology, University of Oxford, and a visiting professor at Oxford Brookes University. He is author and editor of a large number of books in modern theology, church history, ecclesiology, and Anglicanism, including *Anglicanism: A Very Short Introduction* (Oxford University Press) and *Bishops, Saints and Politics* (T & T Clark).

David D. Daniels III is Henry Winters Luce Professor of World Christianity at McCormick Theological Seminary. He has served as the president of the Society for Pentecostal Studies and is the current cochair of the Reformed-Pentecostal International Dialogue. The author of over twenty book chapters and journal articles, he has served as a member of seven research projects funded by various foundations, including the Eli Lilly Endowment, the Luce Foundation, and the Pew Charitable Trust. Daniels has lectured at over twenty colleges and seminaries in the United States and other countries along with presenting academic papers at conferences in Nigeria, Senegal, Switzerland, Sweden, Great Britain, Lebanon, South Korea, the Philippines, and Malaysia.

Peter De Mey teaches Roman Catholic ecclesiology and ecumenism at Katholieke Universiteit. He is past president of Societas Oecumenica, the European society for ecumenical research, and cochair of the new Vatican II Studies Group of the American Academy of Religion. He is a member of the international Catholic-Reformed Theological Dialogue and is author of "The Church in a European Perspective" in the 2007 Routledge Companion to the Christian Church.

Dennis M. Doyle has taught at the University of Dayton for twenty-eight years. He is the author of numerous articles and two books, *The Church Emerging from Vatican II: A Popular Approach to Contemporary Catholicism* (Bayard, updated 2002) and *Communion Ecclesiology: Vision and Versions* (Orbis, 2000).

Mark Ensalaco is the founding director of the Human Rights Studies program at the University of Dayton. As a human rights researcher, educator, and advocate, he has lectured and written on a wide range of human rights issues, including torture, disappearance, violence against women, human trafficking, and immigration.

Massimo Faggioli is an assistant professor in the Department of Theology at the University of St. Thomas (St. Paul, MN). Among other publications, Dr. Faggioli is the author of *Il vescovo e il concilio: Modello episcopale e aggiornamento al Vaticano II* (Il Mulino, 2005); and *Breve storia dei movimenti cattolici* (Carocci, 2008 and in Spanish, PPC, Madrid 2011). He has two books forthcoming in 2012: *Vatican II: The Battle for Meaning* (Paulist Press) and *True Reform: Liturgy and Ecclesiology at Vatican II* (Liturgical Press).

Mary McClintock Fulkerson is an ordained minister in the Presbyterian Church (U.S.A.) and teaches at Duke University Divinity School. She is the author of *Changing the Subject: Women's Discourses and Feminist Theology* (Fortress, 1994); and *Places of Redemption: Theology for a Worldly Church*

(Oxford, 2010). Her most recent publication is *The Oxford Handbook of Feminist Theology* (Oxford, 2012), coedited with Sheila Briggs. She is currently involved in the "Pauli Murray Project: Activating History for Social Change," a Duke Human Rights Center project on racial healing and reconciliation in Durham County through history-telling.

Timothy J. Furry's academic research brings theological, philosophical, historical, and biblical issues into conversation as a framework for retrieving the ancient practice of figural exegesis in our contemporary intellectual milieu. A revised version of his dissertation will be forthcoming from Brill, and he has published articles in *New Blackfriars* and the *Scottish Journal of Theology*. Tim also works part time in ministry at his local Lutheran parish in Dayton.

Richard R. Gaillardetz is the Joseph McCarthy Professor of Catholic Systematic Theology at Boston College. He has published numerous articles and authored seven books while coediting an eighth. In addition, most recently, he has coauthored with Catherine Clifford *Keys to the Council: Unlocking the Teaching of Vatican II* (Liturgical Press, 2012). Gaillardetz is currently the president of the Catholic Theological Society of America.

Miriam Haar is completing the Ph.D. program at the Irish School of Ecumenics, Trinity College, Dublin and is writing her dissertation on the ecumenical debate about the apostolicity of the church. She was a Ph.D. research scholar at Yale Divinity School in 2010/11. Active in ecumenical dialogue, she has been involved in the "Young Dialogue" between the Evangelical Church in Germany (EKD) and the Romanian Orthodox Church as well as the study process of the Community of Protestant Churches in Europe on "*Ecclesia semper reformanda*: Ecclesiological Reflections on the Renewal of the Protestant Churches in Europe."

Barry Harvey is a professor of theology in the Honors College at Baylor University in Waco, Texas. He is the author of three books, *Politics of the Theological* (Peter Lang), *Another City* (Trinity Press International), and *Can These Bones Live?* (Brazos), and coauthor of a fourth book, *StormFront* (Eerdmans). He has published numerous articles in collections and scholarly journals. Harvey serves on the Board of the International Bonhoeffer Society, and the Editorial Board of the Dietrich Bonhoeffer Works, and is an active member of the Ekklesia Project.

Bradford Hinze is a professor of theology at Fordham University. His most recent publications include *Practices of Dialogue in the Roman Catholic Church: Aims and Obstacles, Lessons and Laments* (Continuum, 2006) as well as a variety of articles in books, proceedings, and reference works.

David L. Johns is an associate professor of theology at the Earlham School of Religion, Richmond, Indiana. Much of his work focuses on intersections between Quaker thought and the wider church catholic. Dr. Johns is interested in ecclesiology, liberation theology, culture, and the contextualization of theology at the margins of class and poverty. He has also taught at the Instituto Colegio Jorge Fox in Honduras and the Instituto Teológico de los Amigos de El Salvador.

Stefanie Knauss has worked as a research fellow at the Center for Religious Studies of the Fondazione Bruno Kessler (Italy). Recent publications include *L'enigma corporeità: Sessualità e religione*, coedited with A. Autiero (EDB, 2010) and *Fascinatingly Disturbing: Interdisciplinary Perspectives on Michael Haneke's Cinema*, co-edited with A. Ornella (Wipf and Stock, 2010).

Paul Lakeland is the Aloysius P. Kelley S.J. Professor of Catholic Studies and the director of the Center for Catholic Studies at Fairfield University in Connecticut. His most recent books are *Church: Living Communion* (Liturgical Press, 2009) and *Yves Congar: Essential Writings* (Orbis, 2010).

Vladimir Latinovic was born in Serbia. He is currently engaged in doctoral studies at the University of Tübingen under Prof. Dr. Bernd Jochen Hilberath. The subject of his Ph.D. work is "Christology and Communion: The Consequences of Anti-Subordinationism of Late Antiquity and the Early Middle Ages on the Frequency of Communion." Since 2011 he has been working as a research fellow at the Institute for Ecumenical and Interreligious Studies in Tübingen.

Gerard Mannion is a professor of theology and religious studies and director of the Center for Catholic Thought and Culture at the University of San Diego. He has published widely in the fields of both ecclesiology and ethics and has authored, edited, and coedited some twelve books to date, including *Ecclesiology and Postmodernity: Questions for the Church in Our Time* (2007), *The Routledge Companion to the Christian Church* (2008), and *The Ratzinger Reader* (2010). He serves as chair of the Ecclesiological Investigations International Research Network and editor of the Continuum Series, "Ecclesiological Investigations."

Bryan N. Massingale is a priest of the Archdiocese of Milwaukee and professor of theological ethics at Marquette University. His research focuses on Catholic social thought, liberation theologies, African American religious ethics, and racial justice. He is the author of *Racial Justice and the Catholic Church* (Orbis, 2010) and more than seventy articles, book chapters, and book reviews. He is the convener of the Black Catholic Theological Symposium and the immediate past president of the Catholic Theological Society of America.

Sandra Mazzolini is an Extraordinary Professor and holder of the chair "Church and Mission" (Faculty of Missiology, Pontifical Urbanian University, Rome). She has published various contributions to academic journals, reviews, and collected works. Her most recent book is *Chiesa e salvezza, l'"extra Ecclesiam nulla salus" in epoca patristica* (Urbaniana University Press, 2008).

Vincent J. Miller holds the first Gudorf Chair in Catholic Theology and Culture at the University of Dayton. He is author of *Consuming Religion: Christian Faith and Practice in a Consumer Culture* (Continuum, 2003) and is currently working on a book about how globalization is affecting religious belief and communities.

Neil Ormerod is a professor of theology at the Australian Catholic University. Published widely in Australia and overseas, his recent books include *Creation, Grace, and Redemption* (Orbis, 2007) and with Shane Clifton, *Globalization and the Mission of the Church* (T&T Clark, 2009). He has also published widely in international journals including most recently "Transposing Theology into the Categories of Meaning," *Gregorianum* (2011). He is currently completing a manuscript on systematic historical ecclesiology.

Agbonkhianmeghe E. Orobator is a Nigerian Jesuit priest, currently the provincial of the Eastern Africa Province of the Society of Jesus (Jesuits), and a lecturer at Hekima College Jesuit School of Theology, Nairobi, Kenya. He is the editor of *Reconciliation, Justice, and Peace: The Second African Synod* (Orbis, 2011), author of *Theology Brewed in an African Pot* (Orbis, 2008), and of three books published in Africa. He writes and speaks on ethical and theological issues in African church, religion, and society.

Giovanni Pernigotto teaches Catholic social teaching and theology of religions at the Centre for Religious Studies, Bruno Kessler Foundation of Trento (Italy).

Leslie H. Picca is a professor of sociology at the University of Dayton. She has published in the areas of racial relations and adolescent sexuality. She is coauthor, with Joe Feagin, of *Two Faced Racism: Whites in the Backstage and Frontstage* (Routledge, 2007). Her research on racial relations has been nationally recognized by CNN, the Associated Press, *Congressional Quarterly*, National Public Radio, the *Journal of Blacks in Higher Education*, and the *Dayton Daily News*, among others.

C. Pierson Shaw Jr. is currently a Ph.D candidate in systematic theology at the University of St. Michael's College in Toronto. He is an ordained pastor in the Evangelical Lutheran Church in America (ELCA).

Debora Spini teaches in the Department of Humanities and Social Sciences at Syracuse University in Florence where she is also the academic internship coordinator. She recently coedited *Civil Society and International Governance* (Routledge 2010).

E. A. J. G. Van der Borght holds the Desmond Tutu Chair on Reconciliation at the Faculty of Theology, VU University, Amsterdam. His research focuses on ecclesiology, and he is currently writing a monograph on the challenge of sociocultural identities such as race, nation, and tribe for the unity of the church in the ecumenical movement. He is editor-in-chief of the *Journal of Reformed Theology* and of *Studies in Reformed Theology*.

Susan K. Wood is a professor and chair of the Department of Theology at Marquette University. She serves on the U.S. Lutheran-Roman Catholic dialogue, the North American Roman Catholic-Orthodox Theological Consultation, and the International Lutheran-Catholic Dialogue. She has also participated in various consultations sponsored by Faith and Order of the World Council of Churches and the Joint Working Group. She is an associate editor of *Pro Ecclesia* and serves on the editorial board of the journal *Ecclesiology*. In addition to numerous articles, she has published *Spiritual Exegesis and the Church in the Theology of Henri de Lubac* (Wipf & Stock, 2010), *Sacramental Orders* (Liturgical Press, 2000), and *One Baptism: Ecumenical Dimensions of the Doctrine of Baptism* (Liturgical Press, 2009). She is the editor of *Ordering the Baptismal Priesthood* (Liturgical Press, 2003) and with Alberto Garcia, co-editor of *Critical Issues in Ecclesiology* (Eerdmans, 2011).

Phyllis Zagano is a senior research associate-in-residence and adjunct professor of religion at Hofstra University, Hempstead, New York. A founding cochair of the Roman Catholic Studies Group of the American Academy of Religion, Dr. Zagano has published nearly two hundred articles and review essays in a wide variety of journals, and among her thirteen books is the award-winning *Holy Saturday: An Argument for the Restoration of the Female Diaconate in the Catholic Church*. Her column "Just Catholic" appears regularly in the *National Catholic Reporter*.